Praise for *Sixty Degrees North*:

'It is a brave book in its honesty and self-exposure, I think, and a beautiful book in terms of the subtlety of its thinking and the quality of its descriptive prose, that at times possesses the lucidity of the northern light in which so much of it is set'
Robert MacFarlane

'a subtle, thoughtful study of life on the sixtieth parallel'
Financial Times

'It's a joy to read, its prose as clear as the light on the Greenland ice-cap. In the past year I've read three or four books combining travelogue and memoir in which a writer, unmoored by loss, seeks a resolution of some kind on a journey; this was the best'
Michael Kerr, *Daily Telegraph*

'Malachy Tallack is the real deal, a writer given over to pure curiosity, honest witness and that most precious of gifts, an unself-conscious sense of wonder. *Sixty Degrees North* reveals, not just a vibrant new voice, but a wise, questioning and highly sophisticated talent'
John Burnside

'The high point of the book is the acute and sensitive evocation of the natural world. Tallack's imagery is apposite without becoming self-consciously poetic . . . He does not suffer from naïve romanticism about the north'
Stuart Kelly, *Times Literary Supplement*

'Tallack is one of a burgeoning group of young travel writers who have reinvigorated their increasingly tired genre with elements of psychogeography: the study of how places make us feel . . . Tallack does travelogue well, acutely balancing fact and fancy'
Will Self, *Guardian*

D0367597

SIXTY DEGREES NORTH

Malachy Tallack has written for the *New Statesman*, the *Guardian*, the *Scottish Review of Books*, *Caught by the River* and many other publications, online and print. He won a New Writers Award from Scottish Book Trust in 2014, and a Robert Louis Stevenson Fellowship in 2015. As a singer-songwriter he has released four albums and an EP, and performed in venues across the UK. He is contributing editor of the online magazine *The Island Review*, and co-editor of *Fair Isle: Through the Seasons*. His next book, *Undiscovered Islands*, will be published by Polygon in 2016. He comes from Shetland and lives in Glasgow.

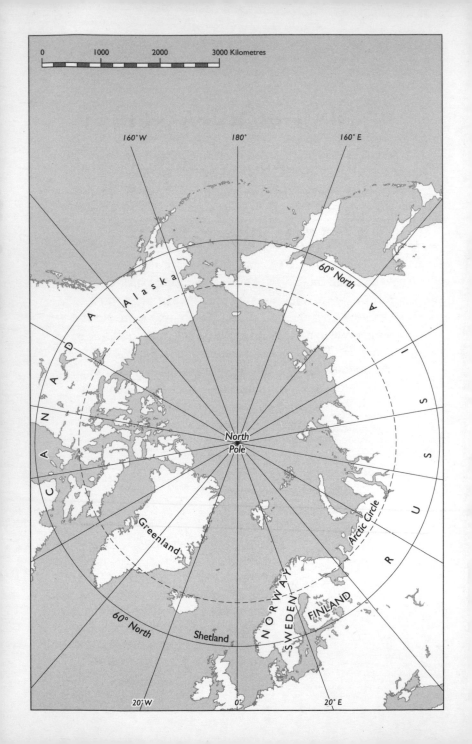

SIXTY DEGREES NORTH

around the world in search of home

Malachy Tallack

First published in 2015 by Polygon. This paperback edition
published in 2016 by Polygon, an imprint of
Birlinn Ltd
West Newington House
10 Newington Road
Edinburgh
EH9 1QS

www.polygonbooks.co.uk

Extracts from *Sixty Degrees North* have previously been published in
Irish Pages, *PN Review* and *Earthlines*

ISBN 978 1 84697 342 0

British Library Cataloguing in Publication Data
A catalogue record for this book is available from the British Library.

Typeset in Sabon at Birlinn

Printed and bound in Great Britain
by Clays Ltd, St Ives PLC

Contents

Illustrations

Maps

HOMEGOING

I can remember the day: silver-skied and heavy with rain. It was early winter and I had just turned seventeen. The morning had been spent in bed, sick and sleepless, but by lunchtime boredom made me move. I stood up and shuffled towards the window, pulling a dressing-gown around my shoulders. The house in which I spent my teenage years faced east over the harbour in Lerwick, Shetland's capital town. From my room on the second floor I could see out onto our little garden, with the green picnic bench and the wooden trellis set against a low stone wall. Beyond, I could see fishing boats at the pier, and the blue and white ferry that chugged back and forth to the island of Bressay, just across the water.

Shetland lies at sixty degrees north of the equator, and the world map on our kitchen wall had taught me that, if I could see far enough, I could look out from that window across the North Sea to Norway, and to Sweden, then over the Baltic to Finland, to St Petersburg, then Siberia, Alaska, Canada and Greenland. If I could see far enough, my eyes would eventually bring me back, across the Atlantic Ocean, to where I was standing. I thought about that journey as I looked out over the harbour, half-dressed and shivering. Though I'd never travelled anywhere at this latitude before, I imagined then that I could see those places from above. I felt myself carried around the parallel, lifted and dragged, as though connected to a wire. The world turned and I turned with it, circling from home towards home again until I reached, inevitably, the back of my own head. Dizziness rose through me like a gasp of bubbles, and I fainted, briefly, landing on my knees with a jolt on the bedroom floor. Exhausted, I hauled myself back up again and into bed, and there I fell asleep and dreamed my way once more around the parallel. That dream, that day, never left me.

A few months earlier, my father had died. He left me one morning beside a lake in Sussex, not far from where he lived, and I spent the hours that followed fishing beneath August sunshine. It was the kind of quiet, ordinary day on which nothing extraordinary ought to happen. But it did. By the time the afternoon rolled towards evening and I began to wonder why he had not returned, he was already dead – killed in a car crash on his way to visit my grandmother in hospital. Waiting there alone, I clung to hope for as long as I could, but I had already imagined the worst. And though eventually I walked away, in search of someone to tell me what had happened and somewhere I could spend the night, part of me was left there beside the lake. Part of me has never stopped waiting.

On that evening, all of the plans I had came to an end, and when I returned to Shetland the following week it was with nothing in front of me. My parents had separated years before, and while I lived with my mother and brother in the islands, my father was in the south of England, at the other end of the British Isles. That summer I had been offered a place to study music at a school of performing arts in South London, and so I went to live with my dad. I had found a direction and followed it. When he died, just before the first term began, that direction was lost forever. I had no choice but to go north again, and once there I had no idea what I would do. On the day I stood beside the window, dreaming of the parallel, I had been stranded for months, lost and half-hollowed by grief. I was looking for something certain. I was looking for a direction.

Over the years, Shetland has made much of its latitude. When I was at high school, our youth club was called 60

North. Later, there was a fishing industry newspaper with the same name. And a tourist radio station. And an online magazine. And a skip-hire company. And a beer, brewed in Lerwick.

Part of this ubiquity is down to a lack of imagination, and part of it to a kind of brand mentality: selling our northern exoticism, or something like that. But there is more to it, I think. Sixty degrees north is a story that we tell, both to ourselves and to others. It is a story about where – and perhaps also who – we are. 'Shetland is at the same latitude as St Petersburg,' tourists are informed, 'as Greenland, and Alaska'. And they are told this because it seems to mean something. It seems to mean more, for instance, than the fact that Shetland is at the same longitude as Middlesbrough, or as Ouagadougou. To be at sixty degrees north is to be connected to a world that is more interesting and more mysterious than the one to which the islands are usually bound. To highlight it is to assert that this is not just a forgotten corner of the British Isles; Shetland belongs also to something else, something bigger. Once it was at the geographical heart of a North Atlantic empire, enclosed within the Norse world in a way that provokes nostalgia even now, more than five hundred years after the islands were pawned by the king of Denmark and Norway to Scotland. Unlike political or cultural geographies, the sixtieth parallel is certain and resolute; it is impervious to the whims of history. Shetland belongs to the north, upon this line with no corners to which it may be consigned. At sixty degrees, Shetland is as central as anywhere and everywhere else.

But what of those other places on that list we recite to tourists? What do we share with them, beyond a latitude? What exactly is this club to which we so enthusiastically belong? Looking at a map, it is possible to claim that the sixtieth parallel is a kind of border, where the almost-north and the north come together. In Europe, it crosses the very top of the British Isles and the bottom of Finland, Sweden and Norway. The line skirts the lower tip of Greenland, and of South-central Alaska. It slices the great expanse of Russia in half, and in Canada it does the same, marking the official boundary between the northern territories and southern provinces. All along the parallel are regions whose inhabitants are challenged, to some extent, by the places in which they live. They are challenged by climate, by landscape, by remoteness. And yet those inhabitants choose to remain. They make their peace with the islands and the mountains, the tundra and the taiga, the ice and the storms, and they stay. The relationships between people and place – the tension and the love, and the shapes that tension and that love can take – are the main focus of this book.

It was more than a decade after that day beside the window, when I dreamed my way around the world, that I finally set out to do it for real. I had spent half of those years away from Shetland. I had been to university, in Scotland and in Copenhagen, then lived and worked in Prague. I had found new directions and pursued them. And then I had come back, through choice, finally, rather than necessity. During those intervening years I thought so often about the parallel, imagining and reimagining the line, that when eventually I decided to follow it, I hardly paused to ask myself why. Now, though, I think I know the reasons.

It was curiosity, first of all. I wanted to explore the parallel, and to see those places to which my own place was tied. I wanted to learn about where I was and what it meant to be there. I wanted to come back laden with that knowledge, and to write it down.

Then there was restlessness – that fizzing pressure within that makes me long for what is elsewhere, for what is far away. That restlessness, that joy and curse that I have known for most of my life, brings unease when I ought to be content; it brings contentment when I ought to be uneasy. It sends me out into the world, almost against my will.

But finally, and perhaps most potently, it was homesickness that made me go. It was a desire to return to somewhere I belonged. My relationship with Shetland had always been fraught and undermined by my own past, and somehow I imagined that by going – by following the parallel around the world – that could change. To make such a journey, in which the final, certain destination must be home, was an act of faithfulness. It was a commitment that, for the first time in my life, I felt ready to make.

And so I went, visiting in turn each country on the sixtieth parallel. I travelled westward, with the sun and with the seasons, to Greenland in spring, North America in summer, Russia in autumn and the Nordic countries in winter. But I began by finding the line.

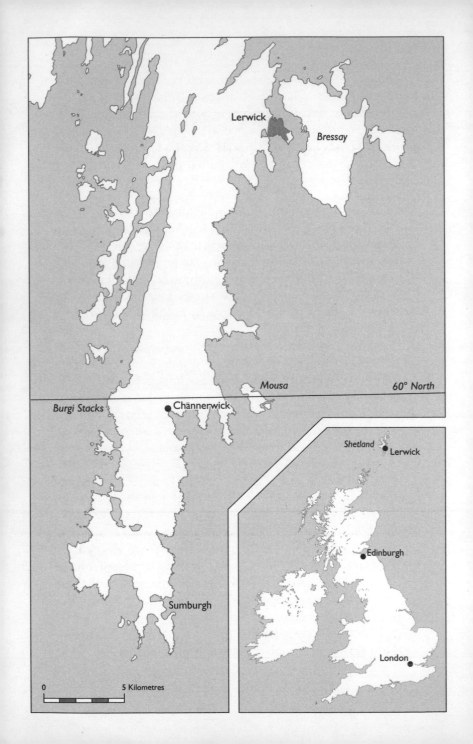

SHETLAND
between the hill and the sea

Driving through the hamlets of Bigton and Ireland at the south end of the Shetland Mainland, the sun was icy bright and the sky a polished blue, barely troubled by clouds. Half a mile away the Atlantic lay like a desert, and beyond, the horizon, a soft, blunt edge interrupting a view that might otherwise stretch all the way around the world. On days like this it is hard to think of leaving. Days like this extinguish all other days.

The narrow road I was on stooped towards the coast, then faded to an unsurfaced track. A mile or so beyond the last house I stopped, parked the car and got out. The air was still and quiet, and warm enough to leave my jacket behind. It felt good to be there, to inhabit the day. Somewhere along this stretch of coast, the sixtieth parallel tied the ocean to the island, passing unmarked between land and water. A few miles or so to the east, it would meet the sea again, connecting Shetland to Norway. As I reached the cliff top, I pulled the map from my bag and unfolded it, exploring the space between where I was and where I wanted to be. The lines on the map were solid and stark, dividing the blue water from the white land. Everything on the page was certain of itself, but the world in front of me was nothing like that. It took a moment to pull these two images together, to merge them, and imagine how they might be reconciled.

I was standing at the top of a steep-sided cove, a *geo*, perhaps thirty metres above the water. From there the land fell sharply towards a bouldered beach, and then the sea, where a thick mat of kelp was tousled by the ebbing tide. Half a dozen seals, alert to my silhouette, abandoned their positions on the rocks and heaved themselves back into the waves. Once safe, they turned to look more carefully at this figure above them, unable to restrain their curiosity. Just offshore, three skerries lay littered with cormorants, black wings outstretched, as the sea around them shivered and shook in the sunlight. Far beyond, to the northwest, the island of Foula lay like a great wave on the horizon. If my map-reading skills were to be trusted, these skerries were the Billia Cletts, which would place me just a few hundred metres south of where I wanted to be. As I walked carefully along the cliff edge the seals were still visible below, their thick bodies dark in the clear water. I stepped slowly, on grey rocks glorious with colour; each stone was splashed yellow-orange by lichen, every crack and crevice was speckled with sea pinks.

The cliffs along this part of the coast are heavily pitted with caves, hollows and geos. In winter, this side of Shetland meets the full weight of the Atlantic and the southwesterly gales that thunder their way across the ocean. Waves that began life thousands of miles away find their way to these shores, growing larger and more powerful as they go. Water carves itself into the land, and throws giant boulders up the cliffs like marbles. Pondering the many battered coastlines of the world, in her book *The Sea around Us*, Rachel Carson concluded: 'it seems unlikely that any coast is visited more wrathfully by the sea's waves than the Shetlands and the Orkneys'. Summer visitors may imagine these islands to be only a timid north, a place protected from the climatic severities of other northern lands. But bring that visitor back in the middle of a winter storm and they would feel differently. This is one of the windiest places in Europe, and recounting stories of storms past is a favourite occupation for islanders.

There is, for instance, the 'Hogmanay Hurricane' of New Year's Eve, 1991, in which gusts of over 173 miles per hour were recorded before the anemometer was torn from the ground. Then there is the month of January 1993, which brought a record twenty-five days of gales, and saw the oil tanker *Braer* wrecked on the coast, just south of the parallel. Wind is the dominant and most extreme element of Shetland's climate. It can, at times, seem so utterly unremitting that the air itself becomes a physical presence, as solid as a clenched fist. And on those rare calm days its absence can be shocking and wonderful.

It is this violence, of wind and sea, combined with its glacial past, that makes Shetland's coastline what it is: a ragged, fractal form. 'Hardly anything can be imagined,' wrote John Shirreff in 1814, 'more irregular than the shape of this island.' According to the Ordnance Survey, the coastline of Shetland amounts to almost 1,700 miles – sixteen per cent of Scotland's total – and a glance at the map shows why. The largest of the islands, known as 'the Mainland', is fifty miles long, north to south, and just twenty at its widest point. But nowhere is more than three miles from the sea. This southern end is a peninsula, almost thirty miles in length and rarely three wide, which extends like a finger from the fist of the central Mainland. Further north, the coast is a panoply of beaches, coves, steep sea cliffs and narrow inlets, known as *voes*. These voes, like mini-fjords, are deep valleys, flooded by the rising sea after the last ice age. They bite into the land, creating distance, and making the ocean always, everywhere, inescapable.

When Shetland emerged from beneath the ice, 12,000 years ago, it was an empty place. There was no vegetation, no birds, no mammals, no life at all. It was a blank space, waiting to be filled. And as the climate steadily improved, that process of filling began. Lichens, mosses and low shrubs were the first colonisers, followed by sea birds, exploiting the abundant food resources of the North Atlantic. As more birds arrived, they carried with them the seeds of other plants, on their feet and in their stomachs.

The first land mammals in Shetland were people, who arrived around 6,000 years ago. The islands that met these original immigrants would have looked very different from the islands of today. Low woodland dominated – birch, juniper, alder, oak, willow – as well as tall herbs and ferns, particularly around the coast. It was a lush, green and mild place, and the lack of land prey, of deer in particular, was more than compensated for by the lack of predators and of competition. There were none of the wolves and bears the settlers had left behind in Scotland. Here they found an abundance of birds, providing meat and eggs, as well as seals, walrus, whales and fish.

This early settlement of Shetland coincided with the latter stages of a major change in lifestyle in northern Europe. Agriculture, which began in the Fertile Crescent of the Middle East, had gradually spread west and north across the continent as the climate improved and stabilised. Land that had once been scoured and scarred by ice was being transformed by the hands of people. Forests were cut down and burned, and the space given over to domestic animals. The early Shetlanders were also early farmers, and it is hard not to be impressed by their achievements. That they managed to cross the dangerous waters between Britain and the islands in their fragile, skin-covered boats, and in sufficient numbers to build extensive communities, is astonishing enough. But that they also managed to take considerable quantities of livestock with them – pigs, sheep, goats and cattle – is doubly so. These animals, and the people that brought them, were to prove the greatest factor in altering and reshaping the landscape once the ice retreated.

Shetland was at the very far edge of the world for these settlers. Beyond the edge, in fact. It was as far north as it was possible to go through Britain, and the people that came took huge risks. So why did they bother? What pulled them northwards? Could it be that the spirit of adventure was enough – that the cliffs of Shetland, just visible on the horizon from Orkney, taunted people until they could resist no longer? Was it simply human beings exploring the limits of what was possible?

It is tempting to suspect this might be so. But there are other alternatives. There is, in particular, the possibility that the development of agriculture itself may have pushed the settlers onwards. Changes in land use in northern Britain were placing pressure on the available space, and creating tension and conflict between neighbouring peoples. A society without walls or borders was evolving into one in which they were essential. Perhaps it was precisely this tension that drove people north to Shetland.

There was a light breeze now, spilling up and over the cliff top, and fulmars were clinging to it, riding like fairground horses up and down on the shimmering air. One bird lifted higher, close to my head, and hung for a moment against the wind. He seemed almost to float there, and as I watched him I was sure he was looking straight back. For those few seconds we eyed each other, fascinated: me by his sublime disregard for gravity, and he by my clumsy bulk and strange attachment to the earth. Fulmars must be the most inquisitive of seabirds. They seem unable to ignore cliff walkers, pestering them with nosy flybys and showing off their aerobatic skills. They are graceful, but with an air of menace too. Something about them – their blazing, black eyes perhaps, shadowed in front, with a comma flick behind, or their bulbous, petrel beaks – gives them a sinister expression. It is an appearance that is only reinforced by the sharp, clattering cackles of those birds ensconced on their nests, and their habit of throwing up a vile, oily substance on those unfortunate enough to step too close.

Further along the cliff top I reached the Burn of Burgistacks, where wheatears scattered at my approach, each clacking like pebbles in a cloth bag. As I walked they kept their distance ahead of me, hopping a little further with every few steps I took. The burn here clambers hastily towards the sea, down a rocky slope and then a brief waterfall, lined with sopping green moss. Beyond the burn were the Burgi Stacks themselves. And then, according to the map, I was almost at the parallel.

I stopped, and looked carefully at the contours of the land. It was harder than I'd expected it to be to distinguish one point from another, and to be sure exactly where I was. The map showed a cave, over which my line appeared to cross, but from where I stood the cave was entirely hidden. I walked north until I was sure I had crossed the parallel, then retraced my steps. As I peered over the edge of a steep scree slope, the map's clean lines were shattered into stones and grass and waves. The angle of the cliff and the jutting rocks prevented any kind of certainty.

I was tempted then to climb down the slope towards the water, where things might be clearer. There was, it seemed, an almost navigable route down. But it would take me alongside two fat, fluffy fulmar chicks, who would no doubt relish the opportunity to practise their vomiting skills. It was a stupid idea, and I thought better of it. I sat instead on the cool grass, the map open in front of me, tracing the lines with my fingers.

I was hot and thirsty, and annoyed at myself for not bringing a GPS to make things clearer. For a moment it all seemed arbitrary and pointless; there could be no real certainty like this. But still I wanted a fixed point, a starting block from which to begin. So I looked again at the paper, read again every word of the surrounding area: to the south, the Burgi Stacks, the cave, then the Seat of Mandrup and Sheep Pund to the north. Just east was the Green of Mandrup, the field behind me.

And then I saw it. Almost completely hidden by those words – 'Green of Mandrup' – but just protruding from behind the letters on either side, was a solid, straight line: a fence. And as it reached the cliff, it corresponded with the parallel. I stood and faced east, following the posts that ran through the field and up the hill, and then looked back to where the fence ended in a muddle of wire and wood hanging over the cliff edge. So this was it: sixty degrees north of the equator. This was my starting line.

*

Geography begins at the only point of which we can be certain. It begins inside. And from there, from inside, rises a single question: where am I?

Imagine yourself stood upon a hill. Or better, imagine yourself stood on a tall hill on a small island, the horizon visible in every direction – a perfect, unbroken line. From early morning until late in the night you stand there. You watch the sun rise from one side of the island and arc its way above, moving slowly and predictably through the sky until it reaches the opposite horizon, where it gradually disappears. As the light fades, stars freckle against the mounting darkness. They too turn about you, on an axis rooted at the North Star, Polaris. This great arena of night and day seems to roll over the stationary world and surround you with its movement. And that question rises: where am I?

The universe that we can see is a place of mirrors and illusions, tricks of the eye and the mind, and it takes a great leap of scientific faith to come to terms with the facts as we now know them to be: that nothing is still; that both our universe and our planet are in ceaseless motion. To look upwards and to acknowledge this is to take a nauseating lurch of the imagination. It is to be overwhelmed not just by a feeling of insignificance, but of fear, vulnerability and exhilaration. Amid all this movement, this unfathomable distance, it seems somehow impossible that we could be anywhere at all.

But our understanding of where we are on the Earth has not been built with this celestial motion in mind. Since people first began to use the sun and stars as navigational aids, they have done so by being ignorant of, or by ignoring such disorientating facts. That the North Star is not a stable point within the universe does not matter so long as it seems to be a stable point. That the sun does not turn around the Earth makes no difference if it continues to appear to do so, and that its appearance is predictable. For the roots of that question – where am I? – are not so much philosophical, nor exactly scientific; they are practical. Where we are only truly makes sense in so far as it relates to where we have been and where we want to be. In order to move in a purposeful way, to avoid wasting our time and endangering our lives, we must build an image of our location, and where we stand in our surroundings. We must make maps.

I stared out at the calm ocean, at the tide lines laced like skeins of white hair. I looked towards the horizon – blue fastened to blue – and beyond, towards unseen places: to Greenland, to North America, to Russia, Finland, Scandinavia and back here again across the North Sea. I looked out for several minutes, then felt ready to go. I turned and walked up the hill, alongside the fence. From my starting line at the cliff I made my way back along the parallel, glad to be moving again.

Soon, the lavish green that had fringed the shore gave way to low heather and dark, peaty ground. The land flattened into a plateau of purple and olive, trenched and terraced where the turf had been cut. White tufts of bog cotton lay strewn about the hill. Shallow pools of black water crouched below the banks of peat and in the narrow channels that lolled between. I hopped from island to island of solid ground, trying to keep my feet dry, as a skylark hung frantically above, held aloft by the lightness of his song.

After only ten minutes or so I was walking downhill again, into the lush valley that folds around the loch of Vatsetter and the Burn of Maywick, flanked by bright yellow irises. The thick heather faded back into a lighter, leaner green, and on the opposite slope was a field, striped by cut silage. A gust of golden plovers sprang suddenly from the ground ahead, and curled its way over the valley. Two lapwings crossed their path above the loch, guttering towards the sea with a clumsy kind of grace. I watched the birds until they tumbled out of view, and then continued to the burn below.

The steep descent into the valley meant an equally steep climb out again, on a gravel track that, according to the map, crossed back and forth over the parallel several times before waning into nothing. I carried on, and was soon back amid the peat. The hill rose sharply to 200 metres, and I was hot from the walking, but it was worth it. As I reached the higher ground, the air opened up without warning, and I could see from one side of Shetland to the other: the Atlantic behind and the North Sea in front. Above, wisps of cirrus cloud were combed across a bold sky, as wide as any sky I had ever seen before.

Human beings have always moved from here to there, from one place to another, with a combination of memory, acquired knowledge and curiosity. We have made use, most commonly, of internal maps – remembered routes from one point of significance to another: a place of food, a place of shelter, a place of danger. Elements of these maps would have been passed from generation to generation, in songs and in stories. They were embellished, updated and, if necessary, discarded. These are living maps, where space and direction are sealed off and separated from the world outside. They can be as intricate and mysterious as the songlines of the

Australian Aborigines, or as straightforward as remembering how to reach the shop from your front door.

To build a more concrete image of where we are it has been necessary to externalise our maps: to make pictures of the world. The very first visual maps were of the stars, such as those on the walls of the Lascaux caves in France, drawn more than 16,000 years ago. But looking up at the sky is easy. To draw a picture that could encompass a particular space on the Earth, or encompass the whole planet even, is a far greater challenge. The mapmaker is forced to become other than himself, to imagine the view of the birds. The mapmaker must look down from above and become god-like, re-creating his own world.

Unlike internal or 'story' maps, early world maps were intended as scientific or philosophical exercises rather than navigational guides. Their practicality was limited by two significant factors. Firstly, the ancient Greeks who pioneered cartography had limited geographical knowledge. Centred on the Mediterranean, their maps extended eastward only as far as India, with their westward edge at the Strait of Gibraltar. Beyond these boundaries the world was more or less unknown, though speculation about the grotesque barbarians dwelling in northern Europe and Africa was widespread. The other major problem for the Greek mapmakers was their lack of a practical means of representing distance and shape accurately. What was required to do this was some kind of scale or grid, which could be applied both to the spherical surface of the Earth and, potentially, to a globe or a flat map. That grid was provided in the second century BC, when Hipparchus of Nicaea devised the system that we still use today: measuring the Earth in degrees of arc. Although similar methods had been proposed previously by the Babylonians, Hipparchus' achievement was to divide a circle into 360 degrees of arc, and so provide the foundation stone for trigonometry.

A degree was a measurement of the angle at the centre of a circle, between one radius and another, like the hands on a clock. If the time is three o'clock, the angle between the two hands is 90°: one quarter of a full circle. On the outside of the circle, the points where the two radii, or hands, touch the edge can also be said to be 90° apart. This measurement could further be applied to spheres, like the Earth, with the north-south angle denoted by one measurement – latitude – and the east-west angle by another – longitude. It was then possible, at least theoretically, to give co-ordinates for any place on the planet, and that information could further be used to represent geographical space accurately on a map. This was a revolutionary step for navigation and for cartography.

Whereas longitudinal lines, or meridians, are of equal length, running through both poles, and dividing the planet like the segments of an orange, circles of latitude are parallel lines, progressively decreasing in size, from the planet's full circumference at the equator to a single point at the Poles. They are represented as an angle up to 90° north or south of the equator. At 60° north, where I was standing, the parallel was half the length of the equator, and two thirds of the way to the Pole.

For the Greeks, the pinnacle of their cartographic tradition came in the mid-second century AD, in Roman Alexandria. It was here that Claudius Ptolemy created his *Geographia*, a work that gathered together the geographical knowledge of both the Greeks and the Romans. Ptolemy gave co-ordinates for around 8,000 places, stretching between his Prime Meridian at the Fortunate Isles (Cape Verde) in the west, China in the east, central Africa in the south and Shetland, which he called Thule, in the north. This was the known world, reaching 180 degrees in longitude and eighty in latitude, and Shetland then was at its very edge. Despite all but disappearing for more than 1,000 years, the influence of this book, eventually, was immense.

Today, we need only consult a map to learn of our location, or just press a button on our handheld GPS or phone, which can tell us our longitude and latitude in degrees, minutes and seconds of arc. But still somehow that question feels unanswered, still it gnaws at our certainty. Where am I?

*

This is a strange place up here, this landscape of peat and heather. Often called generically 'the hill', it forms the core of Shetland, covering more than fifty per cent of the land. From that spot I could have walked to the north of the Mainland, forty miles away, and hardly stepped off it at all. It is a place separate from the places of people, a semi-wild moorland, divided by fence and dyke from the croft land below. It has also been, and in many parts of Shetland remains, a shared place – a common ground – with grazing and peat-cutting rights held collectively by crofters in adjacent communities.

In descriptions of the hill by travellers, certain words recur frequently: barren, desolate, featureless. The land is considered to be missing something, lacking in both aesthetic appeal and agricultural worth. The *Encyclopaedia Britannica* of 1911 proclaimed Shetland's interior to be 'bleak and dreary, consisting of treeless and barren tracts of peat and boulders'. It is a heaving, undulating terrain, without the drama of a mountainscape or the quietude of a valley. It is a place neither tame enough nor wild enough to be considered valuable. It is, in many senses, an in-between land. On the map, there is little to see here but contour lines, and the serpentine scrawl of the burns, where black water chuckles seaward from the inertia of the bog. Looking around, the eye seeks places on which to settle, to focus, but nothing breaks the heavy swell of the land. The hill presents an expanse of sameness that draws the walker in and creates a sense of separation from the world below. There is a kind of space, a vastness, which is somehow surprising in such a limited land. The peatscape opens out and unfolds in what Robert Macfarlane calls 'active expansiveness'. The horizon, the cupola of the sky and the clarity of the air, all become part of the land's measure and its bulk. Together in this arena they uphold an illusion of distance, and make Shetland seem a larger place, a place in which it is possible to become lost. Here you can feel yourself entirely remote from other people, and sit alone, amid an unfamiliar quiet.

Like those who dwell in the shadow of mountains, Shetlanders live with the constant presence of the moor and the hill. It is a presence that is, I think, as central to the character of the islanders as it is to the islands. For just as we inhabit the landscape, the landscape inhabits us, in thought, in myth and in memory; and somehow the openness of the land invites us to become attached, or else attaches itself to us. Our understanding of space and our relationship to that space are affected, and so too is our understanding of time.

We are used to imagining time as a fixed dimension, through which we are moved, steadily and unfalteringly. But there are places where this image seems inadequate, where time itself seems to move at another pace altogether. There are places where we sense the moments rush by, unhindered, so close and so quick that we feel the breath of them as they pass. And then there are other places, such as here on the hill, where time seems to gather itself, to coil and unravel simultaneously. Here the past is closer. We find its memory embedded within the earth, like the eerily preserved bodies, centuries old, drawn out of peat bogs across Europe, with clothes, skin and hair intact. Or like the peat itself, a biological journal of the islands' history. Things move slowly here. Change is stubbornly, solemnly recorded. To examine the land closely, and to take into account its own life and the lives upon and within it, is to be faced with a multitude of other times and other worlds. Here on the hill, where land and sky open out, past and present do the opposite; they wrap themselves tightly together. There is, here, a native timelessness.

It is hardly surprising therefore that the hill has played such a significant role in the mythology of these islands. In particular, it has long been, and remains, the home of Shetland's resident 'hillfolk', the trows. Nocturnal, troll-like creatures, sometimes benign and sometimes taking the role of trickster, the best known trow stories tell of musicians, bribed or lured down into the earth beneath the heather. There they must perform in a world where the human measurement of time no longer applies. The fiddle player will entertain his hosts for the evening, and be offered food and drink, even a place to sleep; but he may emerge from his night's performance to find that his children are grown, his wife remarried or long dead. One unfortunate fiddler, Sigurd o' Gord, lost an entire century beneath the hill. He returned home with a tune he had learned, 'Da Trows' Spring', but discovered that everything had changed in his absence: his home belonged to someone else; his family were long gone.

The popularity of these tales refuses to fade. The stories are endlessly repeated, recorded and published, overshadowing virtually all other native folklore, and I'm sure there are still some Shetlanders who claim to have met one of these creatures while out wandering on the hill. The trow may appear suddenly out of the mist, or from behind a rock, or it may even emerge from the rock itself. They are integral, it seems, to the landscape in which they live, and their stubborn persistence, as a subject and as a species, must at least in part be down to the equally stubborn persistence of this, their habitat. It should also be seen, I think, as a manifestation of the ongoing ambivalence in our relationship with that habitat, an ambivalence expressed most clearly in the debates that have raged for years over the building of windfarms in the central Mainland.

The uneasiness that the peatscapes can invoke has deep cultural roots. Human society in Shetland developed together with, rather than simply alongside, the hill, and that development is reflected in the relationship between them. When people first arrived in the islands, peat had not yet begun to form over large areas. It existed in isolated, poorly-drained patches, but the blanket bog that now stretches across much of the land would simply not have been there. The arrival of humans in Shetland, though, coincided with a downturn in the climate. Temperatures dropped and rainfall increased, and in waterlogged, acidic ground, where vegetable matter cannot properly decompose, it instead begins to accumulate as peat. The process would have been a natural one, determined by both soil and climate, but sustained deforestation and agricultural development also played an important role. Further climatic deterioration speeded up the peat growth, and spread the bog across new areas. More and more, Shetlanders were forced to abandon previously useful land that had become saturated, acidic and infertile, and were squeezed into a thin, habitable wedge between the hill and the sea. By 2,000 years ago, the land would have looked much as it does today.

Paradoxically though, the development of peat was eventually to provide the means by which people could survive this climatic shift. For while the destruction of the native woodlands must have contributed to the growth of the bogs, the forest had never been very substantial anyway. The fuel that was available to people, both from indigenous trees and from driftwood, was most likely becoming scarce by the time that peat had grown to useful depths. And it is peat – cut, dried and burned – that has sustained people in these islands ever since. Those communities without access to it struggled, and sometimes failed to survive. It was, until very recently, an essential element of life in Shetland.

Today, electricity, gas, coal and oil have largely replaced peat in island homes. But it is still dug by some, out of habit or nostalgia, or because the smell of burning turf has a warmth and a redolence that cannot be replicated by any other fuel. Its thick, blue-grey smoke is inviting and evocative, wrapping a house in warmth and in memories of warmth. But its necessity has now passed, and there on the hilltop it seems the life of the peat itself may be passing too. On the slopes around me, much of it had eroded to the bedrock, drying out and degrading. And below, as I began descending again, towards Channerwick, I could see great swathes of black and grey all around, scars of soil and of stone. In the autumn of 2003, after two dry summers and one dry winter, a single night of heavy rain resulted in thousands of tonnes of peat slipping off the hill where I stood, covering the road, destroying a bridge and walls, killing sheep. Other landslides have occurred elsewhere in the islands since, and as the climate continues to change – with temperatures rising and both droughts and storms increasing – the illusion of stability and permanence that exists on the hill is likely to be shattered more and more often.

I paused just above the main road, where a small, yellow sign confirmed the latitude. Ahead of me were Hoswick and Sandwick, hidden behind the crest of the next hill; and beyond them lay the sea, and the island of Mousa. There is no cover here, no shelter or protection. Everything is exposed like the bare rock scars. A kind of melancholy had settled on me as I crossed the moor, but I was reluctant to move on and leave the hill behind. I sat on the heather gazing at the sky above, where a few, sluggish clouds drifted east towards the sea. Then I lay back and closed my eyes for a moment, and dreamed I was exactly where I was.

*

I first visited Shetland when I was about five years old, on a holiday with my parents. My mother's elder brother had moved to the islands from Belfast in the late 1960s for work, then married a Shetlander and had a family. My other uncle had followed and stayed, and we came to visit them several times. My mother and father had considered moving north before I was born. Both of them felt drawn here, away from the south of England where I spent my first few years, but it was not until after they separated that my mother eventually made the move. My memories of those early trips are vague, and have mingled with photographs from the family album, which fix them more solidly but less certainly in place. They are images more than they are true memories, snapshot moments that carry little weight. A boy on a beach, playing and swimming in the sunshine; games and tears in the Lerwick street where my uncle lived.

When we moved north permanently, my mother, brother and I, I was ten years old. My parents had separated some time before that, but family life in Sussex had otherwise continued much as I had always known it. I was too young to really understand the significance of their split, and was anyway surrounded, always, by love.

The idea of a relocation felt like an adventure, as such things always do to a child. From the moment it was first discussed, I was excited and eager to go. The reality though was different, like going away on holiday and discovering, while there, that you can never go back home. That half my family were with me did not detract from the sense that I had been lifted up and dropped in an alien place, a place that was not and could not be my home. The word for it, I suppose, is deracination – to be uprooted. That was how it seemed to me. My past was elsewhere, my childhood was elsewhere, my friends, my grandparents, my father were elsewhere.

That feeling of division and separation cut deep into me then. A sense that who I was and what I needed were not here but somewhere else grew inside me, and continued to grow. That sense evolved, over time, into the restlessness that dogs me even today and that triggered, in part, this journey. It evolved too into an unshakable feeling of exile and of homesickness, and a corresponding urge to extinguish that feeling: to be connected, to belong, to be a part of somewhere and no longer apart. It was what Scott Russell Sanders has called 'The longing to become an inhabitant', intensified and distorted by an unwillingness to inhabit the place in which I had to live.

My separation from Shetland was, I thought, as obvious to others as it was to me. And my antipathy, I believed, was reciprocated. According to the twin pillars of island identity – accent and ancestry – I was an outsider and would always be so. Growing up in Lerwick I imagined myself unable ever to truly fit in. I was often unhappy in school, sometimes bullied, and it was those differences, naturally, on which bullies would focus. For the first time I discovered that I was English, not because I had chosen to be so, but because that was the label that was tied around my neck. For a while I wore it proudly, like a badge of distinction, but in the end it didn't seem to fit. My unsettledness in those early years, my sense of exile and longing, did not find a positive direction until I was sixteen, when I decided to go and study music and to live with my father. To make that choice – to decide the place where I would be – was enormously important. And then came the accident, and choice, again, was gone.

*

Shetland, like other remote parts of Scotland, is scarred by the remnants of the past, by history made solid in the landscape. Rocks, reordered and rearranged, carry shadows of the people that moved them. They are the islands' memory. From the ancient field dykes and boundary lines, burnt mounds and forts, to the crumbling croft houses, abandoned by the thousands who emigrated at the end of the nineteenth century, the land is witness to every change, but it is loss that it remembers most clearly. For some, these rocks reek of mortality. Their forms are an oppressive reminder that we, too, will leave little behind us. In 'The Broch of Mousa', the poet Vagaland wrote of how 'in the islands darkness falls / On homes deserted, and on ruined walls; / The tide of life recedes.' People have come and gone from these islands, and with them have passed 'their ways, their thoughts, their songs; / To earth they have returned.' We are left only with the memory of stones.

The island of Mousa was once a place of people. It was once home to families, to fishermen and farmers, who lived and died there. But now the people are gone and their homes deserted. The island has been left to the sheep, the birds and the seals, and, in the summer at least, to the tourists. On the day I visited, there were fifteen of us – British, Scandinavian and North American – making the journey on the little ferry, *Solan IV*, which carries passengers between April and September. It is a short trip from the stone pier in Sandwick to the jetty on the island, and as we galloped across the grey sound I looked about at the other passengers. One, a man wearing beige combat trousers, checked shirt and red baseball cap, consulted a handheld GPS for the full five minutes of the crossing. He never looked up, never looked out at the water or the approaching island, just stared at the little screen in front of him. It was an odd way to experience the journey, but I was jealous of his gadget, and of the accuracy it promised. I wanted to see what he could see.

A remote island of just one and a half square miles might seem an unusual tourist attraction, but people come to Mousa for several reasons. First, there is the opportunity to explore an island once occupied, now uninhabited (what you might call the St Kilda factor). There is, too, the chance to see birds and seals, which take advantage of the

25

lack of people to breed here in large numbers. But most of all, people come here for the broch. While Mousa is just one of around one hundred known Iron Age broch sites in Shetland, and several hundred in the whole of Scotland, it is nevertheless unique, for only this one still looks much as it did when it was first built, over 2,000 years ago. For this fact alone Mousa would be impressive, having withstood two millennia of human and climatic violence; but no less remarkable than its longevity is the actual structure itself, standing at forty-four feet: the tallest prehistoric building in Britain. In shape, it is rather like a power station cooling tower, bulging slightly at the base, where its diameter is fifty feet, and slimming gently, then straightening to vertical towards the top. Constructed entirely of flat stones, the broch is held together by nothing more than the weight of the stones above and the skill of the original builders. It is an outstanding architectural achievement. Inside is a courtyard, separated from the world by double walls more than three metres thick. And between the two outer walls a stairway winds upwards, giving access to cells at various levels, and ultimately to the top of the tower, where visitors can look at the island spread out around them.

Will Self has called Mousa Broch 'one of my sacred sites. For me, comparable to the pyramids'. And that comparison is understandable. The broch is beautiful and mysterious, imposing and tantalisingly intact. Yet we know almost nothing of the people who – around the same time that Ptolemy was marking Shetland on the map – decided to build this structure. It is safe to assume that the architects of Scotland's brochs were a militarised people, for the towers' defensive capabilities are obvious. But there is something about this broch that implies more than simply defence. Its massive size seems beyond necessity, and the sheer extravagance of it suggests that, if security was the primary concern, it must have been built in a state of extreme paranoia. So perhaps a more likely possibility is that the brochs were built not for defence alone, but as acts of self-glorification by Iron Age chieftains. They were status symbols, born of a bravado much like that which created skyscrapers in the twentieth century: a combination of functionality and showing off.

That this particular example has survived so perfectly for so long is partly a result of its remoteness, and partly because nobody has ever had the need to take it to pieces. While other ancient buildings have been plundered for useful material over the millennia, Mousa's beaches are still crowded with perfect, flat stones, providing all the material the island's inhabitants ever required. The rocks which helped to create such an extraordinary structure have remained plentiful enough to help ensure its long life. And today, those rocks are protecting other lives too. Press your ear to the walls of the broch and you will hear the soft churring and grunting of storm petrels, the tiny seabirds that patter their way above the waves by day, returning to the safety of their nests at night. Seven thousand storm petrels – eight percent of Britain's population – nest on this island, on the beaches and in the broch itself. The building seems almost to breathe with the countless lives concealed within: past and present hidden, sheltered among the rocks.

The people who built this broch, who lived in and around it, seem far out of reach to us today, an enigma. Archaeologists and historians examine the available clues carefully and they make assessments, suppositions. But in our desire to eradicate mystery from the past, and to understand and know these people, we forget one crucial point. We miss the real mystery. Sitting on the grass beneath the broch, looking back towards the Mainland, I scratched my wrists and brushed the midges from my face. There was no wind, and the insects were taking advantage of the opportunity to feed. The clouds hung low over the sound, and draped softly onto the hills across the water. What struck me then, as I leaned back against the ancient stone wall, was not the great distance and difference that lay between now and then, nor was it the tragedy of all we do not know. What struck me was the sense of continuity, and the deep determination of people to live in this place.

Rebecca West once wrote that certain places 'imprint the same stamp on whatever inhabitants history brings them, even if conquest spills out one population and pours in another wholly different in race and philosophy'. This stamp is what Lawrence Durrell called 'the invisible constant'; it is the thread that holds the history of a place together, the sense of sameness that cuts through the past like a furrow through a field.

In Shetland, human society has evolved in both gradual and sudden movements. For a few hundred years people built brochs, and then they stopped. In the two millennia that followed many other changes took place. New people came, bringing a new language and a new religion, before they too disappeared when the Vikings arrived in the late eighth century. Yet despite these changes, despite all that came and went in that time, always it was the land that dictated the means of survival. The Norsemen arrived as Vikings, but they became Shetlanders. They became fishermen and farmers, just as the Picts had been, just as the broch-builders had been, and all those before them. Crops were sown and harvested; sheep and cattle were reared and killed. The land scarred the people, just as the people, in turn, scarred the land. If there is an 'invisible constant' or identity bestowed by a place upon its inhabitants, it could only be found there, in that relationship, that engagement with the land. It is not inherited, but earned.

As I walked slowly back towards the boat, a cloud of Arctic terns – called *tirricks* in Shetland – billowed like a smoke signal from a beach just ahead. Some of the birds drifted southwards, swooping then hovering above me, pinned like little crucifixes against the sky. Everything about the terns is sharp – beak, wings, tail – even their cries are serrated. And their tiny forms belie an aggression that can terrify the unwary walker. Like the Arctic and great skuas that share this island with them, tirricks attack without hesitation anyone who seems to threaten their nesting ground. There is no subtlety in their assault. They simply wheel and swarm above, then dive, each in turn, screaming as they drop. It is enough to discourage all but the most determined of trespassers.

It occurred to me, almost too late, that I had forgotten why I was here on the island. The departure time for the ferry was approaching, but I pulled the map out of my bag and tried to locate the parallel on the paper. I was only a hundred metres or so from the line, it seemed, so I hurried ahead to find it. But when I turned the next corner I stopped again, for standing just where I was heading was the man in the red baseball cap, staring down at his GPS. Clearly he too was looking for the parallel. The man took a few steps back, and consulted the gadget again, head down. By this time he was only ten metres or so away, and soon noticed that I was standing watching. He turned, as if to ask what I was doing. I smiled the best smile I could muster, which probably looked more half-witted than friendly. He didn't smile back. I wasn't sure what to do. I could have spoken to him, told him that we were both looking for the same thing, but somehow the seconds passed and we continued to stand there, each hoping the other would just go away. I had no particular desire to explain myself, and he, it seemed, felt the same way. It was an awkward moment, and in the end it was me who gave up and moved on. I nodded, then put my head down and walked towards the jetty, where the little boat was waiting.

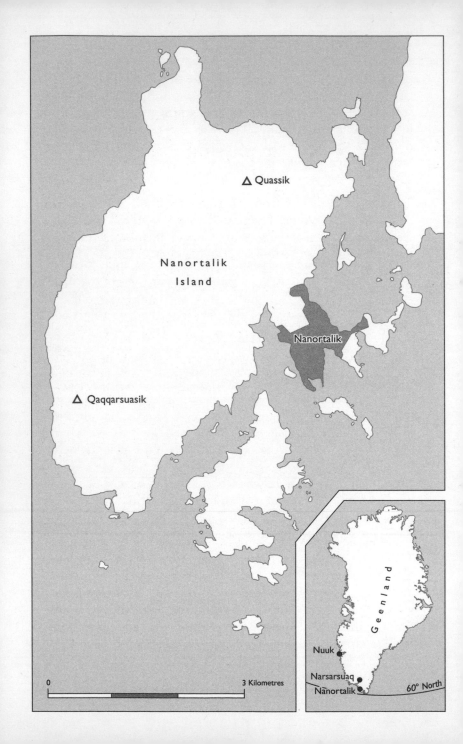

Quassik

Nanortalik
Island

Nanortalik

Qaqqarsuasik

0   3 Kilometres

Geenland

Nuuk

Narsarsuaq

Nanortalik

60° North

GREENLAND
in passing

To reach Greenland from Shetland required a detour in completely the wrong direction, through Scotland and then Denmark, via Amsterdam. From Copenhagen I took a flight back over the North Atlantic, crossing almost directly above Shetland again, and arrived in Narsarsuaq, a tiny airport that clings between Greenland's southwestern coast and its icecap. My final destination was Nanortalik, a village further south still, but I took my time in getting there, enjoying the chance to explore a place I expected never to see again.

Public transport in Greenland is by boat or by helicopter – there are no roads between communities – and in springtime it is largely the latter. On the last of my flights, from Qaqortoq to Nanortalik, we lifted calmly from the tarmac, then thundered up and over the fjord, flying low above bare valleys and hillsides, over tundra, lakes, rocks and snow. Below, the land stretched out in a patchwork of brown and green, studded with scraps of white and blue and grey. And then, suddenly, the sea.

In my travels south along the coast I had seen a lot of ice. In Narsaq, I had walked across beaches strewn with stranded bergs, decomposing in the warm spring sunshine. They were a thousand forms: some pointed, with sharp fingers and shards; others smooth, like the curves of muscle and flesh on an animal. Some were as large as cars or caravans, others I could lift and hold in the palm of my hand: tiny fragments, faded almost to nothing. I wandered among these shapes, watching their quiet disappearance, and I felt a peculiar kind of grief. Here was a difficult presence, almost alive and almost unreal, like shadows made solid, or crystalline astonishment. Out in the water beyond, the icebergs were much bigger, but still somehow precarious. They seemed out of place in the sunshine, beside the colour of the town and beneath the blackness of the mountains. Bright, blue-white against the vitreous shiver of the water, the ice like clouds took form in the imagination. Reclining bathers, ships, mushrooms, whales and kayakers. They seemed caught in constant imbalance, between two worlds.

But now, from the window of the Air Greenland helicopter, I saw something else entirely. Stretched out beneath us, reaching away to the horizon and beyond, was an immense carpet of sea ice, a dense mosaic of flat, white plates like crazy-paving on the dark water. I felt immersed. As far as I could see, the fractured ice lay tightly packed. Great slabs the size of tennis courts, and bigger, were crammed together, and between them smaller pieces in every possible shape. This was *storis* – pack ice formed in the Arctic Ocean, east of Greenland. Each winter, a dense band of this ice drifts southwards on the East Greenland current, rounding Cape Farewell in the first months of the year, then moving slowly up the southwest coast, disintegrating as it goes. The whole scene was unfathomable. There was nothing for the eye to hold on to; all sense of scale was lost. Here and there an iceberg protruded, but it was impossible to know how large they were. When we buzzed low over a cargo ship, slogging its way through the solid ocean, it looked far too small, like a toy, dwarfed by the cracked expanse of white and glacial blue all around it. I took the camera from my bag and held it up to the window.

That picture hangs above my desk as I write. A blanket of shattered ice leads out to the horizon, swollen by a blue-black bruise reflecting the clear water beyond. I return to the image over and over, as if searching for something that I know is there but cannot seem to focus upon. Framed within that photograph is the very thing I came to Greenland to see. It is an image of the north: bright and brittle, terrifying and intensely beautiful. Looking back on it now, the distance between myself and that ice-laden image stretches out and becomes an unimaginable gulf. I have tried to forge a connection, a bridge between, but the picture remains shocking, long after I hung it there.

The helicopter came to rest on the rough landing strip at Nanortalik, the southernmost of Greenland's main settlements. The village is decked out in northern Scandinavian uniform, its wooden houses red, yellow, purple, green, even pink – some pastel pale, others vivid as children's paint. The village is home to around 1,300 people, with a few smaller hamlets scattered through the surrounding fjords. It sits on one of the many islands that pepper this coast, but is no more isolated for that. The hostel where I was to stay was at the other side of town from the heliport, beyond the houses and the main street, at the old harbour with its white wooden church and timber cottages. Most of the buildings around the harbour were occupied by the town museum, but one little red bungalow served as a hostel, in which I was the only guest.

I threw my bag into the living room, where two bunk beds huddled around a gas fire, and went back outside to sit on the front step. The morning had cleared and warmed a little, though there was a bitter breeze lifting off the sea. The bay in front of the hostel was loosely cluttered with ice, just clear enough for boats to make their way in and out of the harbour. There was a slow shifting of everything, almost discernible as I sat watching, and now and then a booming crack and splash as an iceberg split and collapsed into the water. The view from the doorway was southwestward, out to sea, but took in the hunched bulk of Qaqqarsuasik, the island's highest point. From the step I could see ravens swoop and wheel around the dark slopes, silhouetted as they rose above the peak, then almost hidden against the blackness of the rock. Their caws, clicks and splutters echoed around the bay, puncturing the silence as they punctured the air with their flight. A flurry of sounds – manic gulps and underwater barks – rained down on me as I sat, listening, watching, until hunger persuaded me to move.

*

Shaped like a great arrowhead hurled southward from the Pole, Greenland is the largest island in the world, stretching from Cape Morris Jessup, 83° north of the equator, to Cape Farewell, just south of 60°. From its earliest, uncertain appearances on the map, it has largely been a blank space, an enormous emptiness into which centuries of European fears, myths and misconceptions have been poured. This is a land of concentrated northness, where childhood images of Eskimos and polar bears, ice and isolation, come together. It is a paradoxical place, both intensely alien and deeply familiar. Geographically and culturally it is a meeting point between Europe and the American Arctic, where north and south come awkwardly together. Here, certain tensions and certain conflicts between these two worlds are played out, day to day.

But this situation is far from new, for it is here that European people first encountered American people more than 1,000 years ago, and it is here that two visions of the Arctic and two very different understandings of place have been tried and savagely tested. The familiar story of Greenland is the European story: the westward advance of the Norsemen at the end of the first millennium AD. With their empire expanding, from Shetland and Orkney south to Britain, Ireland and beyond, and from Faroe north into Iceland, the Vikings were apparently unstoppable. They flourished in these northern lands – lands once considered beyond the habitable edge of the world – and it was not long before they ventured further still, into places that no European had ever gone before.

But in some ways this story is unlike other colonial histories. For one thing, there is the rather peculiar fact that, in Greenland, the colonisers arrived before the colonised; the Norse reached this island prior to the arrival of the Inuit. When Eirik the Red first landed in Greenland in 982AD, somewhere not far from present day Nanortalik, Greenland was populated by an entirely different people, the Dorset – part of a wider northern culture, known as the Tuniit, which is now extinct – but their small population was restricted to the far northwestern coast. This might have come as a surprise to Eirik, had he known, for although the Icelander met no-one as he explored the western fjords, he did find evidence of people. It was clear that he was not the first man to reach this place. Old settlements were still visible, the remains of hearths and homes still apparent. But no fires had been lit along this coast for more than 1,000 years. The people that had been here – the Saqqaq, from 2400 BC, and the early-Dorset, from 900 BC – had long since died out or retreated northwards.

By calling this place Greenland – 'for he said that people would be much more tempted to go there if it had an attractive name', as the *Grænlendinga Saga* has it – Eirik the Red succeeded in convincing enough of his fellow Icelanders to follow him to the new land to found two major settlements. The larger of these, known as the Eastern Settlement, was based on this southwestern coast; the other was further north, where Nuuk, Greenland's capital, now lies.

Initially, the Norse lived much as they had in Iceland and elsewhere, as farmers. Their options were limited somewhat by the shortage of suitable ground for crops, but the climate was good and the colony succeeded, with large numbers of goats, sheep and cattle reared at the wealthiest farms in the south. The Norse hunted too, making use of the plentiful seals to supplement their diet. Soon, a trade in northern goods – walrus ivory, furs, polar bears, and narwhal or 'unicorn' horns – opened up between Greenland and Bergen in Norway. This was a valuable trade. Ivory and furs were luxury items in the south, and narwhals' tusks could fetch more than their weight in gold. King Christian V of Denmark would later have an entire throne constructed from these horns, and Queen Elizabeth I of England could have had a new castle built for the price she paid for a single, decorated tooth. But the Norse probably saw very little of this money; coins would not have helped them much in Greenland. They exchanged their Arctic treasure for iron, timber and other necessary materials. And just as importantly, this market allowed them to keep open the contact between the colony and Europe, to remain part of the Scandinavian, Christian world. They had neither the knowledge nor the desire to survive without this ongoing connection.

As exploration of the area expanded, the settlers began to encounter other peoples, whom they called *skraelings*: wretches. Despite the all-encompassing word, there were at least three distinct groups that came into contact with the Norse. The first of these were late-Dorset Tuniit, whom the settlers would have met as they travelled north on hunting trips. The second were Algonquin Indians living on the east coast of North America, whose violent resistance, probably more than any other factor, put an end to the Vikings' western expansion. The final group encountered by the Norse were the Thule, ancestors of today's Inuit, who first arrived in the country between 1200 and 1300 AD, when the colonies were at their strongest. A highly adaptable and successful marine culture, the Thule emerged first in the Bering Strait region of what is now Alaska. In addition to hunting and fishing they had also learned to use dog sleds and to build boats and kayaks, from which they caught whales, using harpoons made of iron. During the Mediaeval Warm Period, when the Norse were pushing westward across the North Atlantic, the Thule made a similar push eastward through the Arctic. They understood how to live in this environment; they were deeply at home in the landscape. But they too were traders, and the supply of iron for making tools was critical to their success. In Alaska this iron was most likely acquired through exchange with peoples in East Asia, but there were rich sources of iron in the east too, at meteor crash sites in northern Greenland, and in the hands of the Norse settlers.

Recent archaeological evidence suggests that the migration of the Thule across the Arctic may not have come about merely through nomadic curiosity or as part of a natural expansion of their homeland, but because the existence of iron – and of the Norse themselves – had become known to them. Indeed, far from being an insular and isolated society, as they were long portrayed, the Inuit's development as a culture may effectively have been defined by their contact with other peoples, from both west and east.

When the Norse finally met the Thule, in the thirteenth or fourteenth century, an uneasy balance was struck between the two cultures. Most likely neither trusted the other very much, and for understandable reasons. Throughout their time in Greenland the Norse proved themselves to be exceedingly poor when it came to public relations. Their default approach on encountering unknown people was violence, and no doubt tensions simmered in all of their dealings with these new neighbours. Ultimately though, it was not hostility or mistrust that was to upset the balance between these two peoples. It was something far more mundane, and with unexpectedly dramatic consequences. It was the weather.

In the centuries of Viking exploration and Norse settlement, the north had been enjoying a mild climate and hospitable summers. Temperatures had peaked around the time Eirik first arrived in Greenland, when, according to *Njal's Saga*, corn was being grown on Icelandic farms. But this fruitfulness was not to last. From the late fourteenth century onwards, there was a significant cooling of the climate in Europe and the Arctic. Winters became longer and more severe, and summers less predictable. It was a trend that was to continue. Farming in Greenland was immediately made more difficult. Crops failed, meaning fewer animals could be kept, and the Norse soon found themselves in trouble. Seal hunting may have increased to cover some of the loss in reared meat, but it seems the farmers were slow to adapt. They held on to their way of life even as it became impossible, as though familiarity itself could offer them some kind of protection.

There were other consequences of this colder weather, too. Sea ice increased, so that trading ships from Norway, already intermittent after the arrival of the Black Death in Europe and the rise of the Hanseatic League, now ceased entirely. This was a serious blow, both materially and psychologically. The Norse found themselves isolated from Europe, and all trading relations with the Thule came suddenly, necessarily, to an end. This would not have gone down well. A good supply of iron was as important to the hunters as it was to the farmers, and it is likely that, unable to obtain it through trade, they began to take it by force.

Many theories have emerged over the years to account for the ultimate failure of the Norse colonies in Greenland. Plagues, inbreeding, attacks by pirates: all have been blamed. Jared Diamond has argued that overuse of the land and a taboo against eating fish could have been the deciding factors. But perhaps no final nail is required in this particular coffin, for the facts themselves are enough to lead to the conclusion. The climate changed; farming became increasingly difficult and certainly impossible in places; trade with Norway and with the Thule ceased; relations between the groups soured, and conflicts erupted over scarce resources. The threat of starvation would then have hung over the colonies like a vulture. Some people may have tried to flee eastwards to Iceland, others may even have fled west. Those who remained died. In 1350, the Western Settlement was found to be empty of people, their few remaining animals roaming free. And before the end of the fifteenth century, all of the Norse were gone. While the Inuit had continued to thrive, and had expanded their range across the American North, the Europeans had been entirely wiped out. For the proud, hardy Scandinavians, it was a terrible conclusion. The creeping cold, the suffocating fear, the inevitable end: this was a slow Arctic nightmare that would recur many times in years to come. For another century, or perhaps even less, the Inuit had the American Arctic to themselves. But European exploration was about to begin again in earnest, and before long the Scandinavians were back in Greenland to stay.

*

I was sitting drinking coffee at the kitchen table on the morning after my arrival when a face appeared at the window, hands cupped around eyes. The face didn't see me at first so I waved in front of it. David Kristoffersen grinned. 'Hello Maleeky,' he shouted, then walked round to the front door and let himself in. 'Home sweet home,' David laughed, looking around the tiny room. I made more coffee and we sat down together at the table, gazing out at the ice in the bay.

David is the curator of Nanortalik's museum. A small man, smiling and fidgety, with a baseball cap permanently attached to his head, he had introduced himself to me the day before, recognising me immediately as the only tourist in town. 'Kristoffersen,' he said. 'Like the American singer.'

Although David's English is certainly better than my Danish, when we met previously I had made the mistake of explaining that I had lived in Copenhagen for six months as a student, but that I had forgotten most of what I knew of the language. It is an explanation that I have practised in Danish so many times that my ineptitude is apparently no longer convincing. Each time I used it in Greenland, English was immediately abandoned, as though false modesty alone was preventing me from communicating. And so David began to talk. Hesitantly at first – the pained, puzzled looks on my face slowing him down just now and again – but with increasing pace and enthusiasm, he spoke. Despite my minimal comprehension, I was aided by the fact that he was the most exuberant speaker I have ever met. He would stand suddenly in the middle of a sentence, as though what he was saying could not properly be expressed from a seated position. His hands held out before him, he would point at his chest and then hurl his arms outwards with his words. It was exhausting to watch, but it did help. A little.

David explained that his great-grandparents had come to Nanortalik from remote southeast Greenland to have their children christened. They knew about the religion from Moravian missionaries, and had decided that they should convert. 'That is why I am David Samuel Joseph,' he said. 'We must have Christian names, not Greenlandic names.' Many people migrated from the east coast and the Cape Farewell region to settlements around Nanortalik during the nineteenth century. Previously they had visited trading stations in the area only occasionally, but eventually they began to settle on a permanent basis. By the beginning of the twentieth century, southeast Greenland was entirely depopulated.

During a prolonged pause in the conversation, David examined the map I had spread out on the table. He seemed at first not to recognise his own town, turning the paper this way and that with a slightly uncertain look, but soon he nodded as the shapes and names began to make sense.

He pressed his forefinger to the paper and began to speak the Greenlandic place-names aloud, inviting me to repeat them. I tried my best, but he was a strict teacher and every mistake was corrected. The sounds were not easy. There is an odd, almost lisping effect in Greenlandic – a sound produced, I think, by pushing air around the sides of the tongue rather than over the top. The glottal Qs are awkward too, half-swallowed into the gullet, almost gulped down. For an English speaker these are not comfortable noises to make, but David insisted, so we continued. He tried to explain the meanings of some of the names too, pronouncing them first, then offering definitions when he was able: 'Nanor: ice bear; talik: the place where it is'. Other words were acted out. One, described partly in Greenlandic, was accompanied by a physical demonstration that suggested nothing less than a chronic bout of diarrhoea. My bewildered expression prompted him to persist with the action, becoming increasingly graphic until I could no longer imagine anything else he might be referring to. When I laughed, he laughed too, and raised his thumb to indicate that I had got it right.

Later that morning I walked back and forth through the dusty streets of the village, among houses and apartment blocks that sit up, away from the water. Most of these houses are small, with perhaps only one bedroom. They are basic, rectangular boxes, raised slightly above the ground, with steep roofs and metal chimneys. There is little to distinguish them one from the other, except for the colour of the paint and the varying states of disrepair. There are few cars in Nanortalik – there is nowhere to drive beyond the confines of the town – and people were out walking, alone or in couples. Away from the supermarkets, which stand opposite each other on the main street, the place felt quiet. No hum of industry, no traffic. Later in the day, when school was finished, children appeared, playing along the shore and among the buildings, their toys and bicycles picked up and then abandoned wherever the afternoon carried them.

Travellers often complain of the untidiness of Greenlandic towns; they are described as squalid or chaotic. But the root of this impression is not simply the human detritus, it is the non-human disorder that is found there. It is the wild land that laps up against the buildings. Bare rock is not covered here as it would be in a European town; hills and slopes are not smoothed or flattened. In between the houses is empty, uncivilised space – rocks, earth, grass, growth. There are very few gardens, and these are almost never partitioned or fenced off. People walk between the buildings, creating dusty paths with the regularity of their footsteps. Elsewhere, this between-space would always be allocated to one person or another, but in Greenland there is no private land ownership. All land belongs collectively to the state, and therefore to all people. Public space, wild space, is both out there and here, in the village. The wild is part of the community, it dwells among the houses; but the community, too, dwells within the wild. In the industrialised world we imagine a division between nature and culture, country and town, wild and domestic. We may allow a park to smudge the lines a little, or permit a river to run feral through a city, but we still see that division and that fence between. Here, the line that separates nature and culture has been erased completely. The wild roams freely in the streets.

The crucial difference between these two attitudes has nothing to do with towns and streets though, it has to do with fields and furrows. For ours is, at its root, an agricultural society, and has been for thousands of years. The Inuit, in contrast, have a hunting society. Land ownership and land division are fundamental to agriculture. Our ground is claimed, marked out and used; it is changed and dominated. We impose ourselves upon it, and we alter it to suit our will. For a hunting culture, the ownership of land simply does not make sense. Land is part of the space they inhabit, like air and water and ice; its ownership, in the private sense, is meaningless. A hunter may have rights of use in a particular area, but he no more owns the land than he owns the animals that live upon it.

The relationship is better described as one of belonging. The Greenlandic politician, Aqqaluk Lynge, has explained that 'we live there, together, therefore the land belongs to us, all of us'. But this is a reciprocal belonging: the land belongs to us, and we to it. And there, I think, is the essential disparity between the agricultural and the hunting view. The hunter sees himself as part of a natural order; he adapts to his landscape, and he accepts his place within that landscape. His aim, in Barry Lopez's words, is 'to achieve congruence with a reality that is already given'. Whereas, in our own culture, 'We hold in higher regard the land's tractability, its alterability'. The farmer, for the most part, does not adapt to his landscape, he adapts the landscape to suit his own needs. Nature is tamed, fenced off and altered. This is the attitude of the coloniser. It is the attitude with which the Norse arrived 1,000 years ago, and it is the attitude with which they died 500 years later. The Inuit have always been at home in Greenland, in a way that Europeans have never quite learned to be. They moulded their way of life around the challenges and the opportunities that the place provided. They wedded themselves to the place.

The conflict between the Inuit attitude to the land and that of Europeans is instructive, and it has significant consequences in terms of land rights, and particularly mineral rights, which Greenland currently shares with Denmark. There are a growing number of foreign companies eager to dig things out of Greenlandic ground, and the social and economic future of the country may well depend on how it chooses to deal with this situation. The trade in northern treasure, which began with the furs and narwhal tusks of the Vikings, is now more important than ever. The south still wants what the north can provide. Today, though, that treasure comes from the earth; graphite, rare metals and gold are already being mined, and there is pressure on the country to relax its ban on the extraction of uranium. The oil industry too is coming.

Many see this as an ideal solution to Greenland's economic uncertainties; it is a guaranteed income, with employment opportunities into the bargain. Others, though, are not so sure. Sheila Watt-Cloutier, a Canadian former president of the Inuit Circumpolar Conference, has called mining 'the easy way out'. She has warned that 'It could run counter to everything we are trying to recover in our culture. We need to step back and ask ourselves what kind of society we are hoping to create here. Will we lose awareness of how sacred the land is, and our connection to it? . . . Do we want to lose the wise culture we have relied on for generations?'

Land use is far from the only arena in which fundamental cultural differences have been fought out here in Greenland. As I wandered down by the harbour, old men sat outside the little shack that served as meat and fish market, smoking, laughing and talking. Some held their walking sticks in front of them, palms clasped around the handles, quietly watching the afternoon pass by. Others leaned in close towards each other, their stories told in whispers. In Qaqortoq I had seen this too, a gathering of people near the water, as if this place, where seals and fish were brought to be cut up and sold, were the social hub of the town. I imagined the men had once been hunters themselves, and now the closest they could get was to come and watch the day's catch being brought in. But the stories they were telling would connect them to those who today were wielding knives. Those stories, and the memory they contained, would connect them too to their fathers and their grandfathers, whose own knives carved into the meat, the seals, taken from the ice. These men were witnesses to a silent inheritance, a deep flash of blade and blood.

Hunting in Greenland is an issue of identity and an issue of culture. It is also an issue of very serious controversy. In particular, the killing of sea mammals – seals and whales – has for decades attracted criticism from outside. In the 1970s, following the global backlash against the killing of seal pups in Canada, Greenland's seal fur industry collapsed. The livelihood of the country's hunters was severely threatened, and so Greenland's Home Rule government stepped in to offer a solution. It nationalised the fur company, Great Greenland, and began offering a guaranteed price to hunters for every skin. It was a bold decision which, ultimately, was nothing to do with economics and everything to do with tradition. Today, while hunting is not a particularly rewarding career choice from a financial perspective, it does still remain a choice.

There is a belief among many Greenlanders that their traditional way of life – a way of life that entirely underpins their sense of identity – is under constant threat from the ignorant views of people from outside their country. A kind of moral imperialism is suspected – the imposition of alien values onto a people for whom those values do not make sense. Individuals such as Finn Lynge, a politician who in 1985 negotiated Greenland's tactical exit from the European Community, have worked hard to convince the world that the traditional Inuit culture is entirely compatible with environmental sustainability. Others have argued that the increasing European and American focus on 'animal rights', is born not from an increased empathy and understanding for the natural world but entirely the opposite. The Canadian activist Alan Herscovici has written that 'the animal-rights philosophy [is] widening rather than healing the rift between man and nature . . . [it] may be more of a symptom of our disease than a cure.'

Lynge would agree. For him, the focus on individual animals' rights demonstrates a failure to understand nature, or to recognise our own place within it. What the Inuit see in the European and American attitudes to Arctic hunting is the gaping distance between our people and our environment. They see a hypocritical culture that frets and recoils over the deaths of individual animals elsewhere in the world, yet which engages in industrial farming, 'pest-control' on an immense scale, widespread polluting and the devastating destruction of natural habitats. As individuals, we consciously distance ourselves from killing, we close our eyes to it, yet our culture is, in general, 'characterized by its propensity for cruelty and death', as Lynge has it. And our distaste for hunting is a very recent development.

As a teenager I knew men who had been whalers. Shetland has always had a strong connection with that industry. As Herman Melville noted in *Moby Dick*, 'the Greenland whalers sailing out of Hull or London, put in at the Shetland Islands, to receive the full complement of their crew. Upon the passage homewards, they drop them there again. How it is, there is no telling, but Islanders seem to make the best whalemen.'

From the seventeenth to the nineteenth century, thousands of Shetland men sailed west to Greenland, leaving wives and mothers to look after the crofts in the islands. They would return months later with more money than could ever be earned at home. By the twentieth century, though, the industry had moved to the south Atlantic, based around the island of South Georgia. Again, many Shetlanders travelled the length of the ocean to work, to kill whales. I would listen to the stories these men told – men not much older than my father – and I could barely believe that they could have lived such a life, that these things could have taken place so recently. It seemed incredible, like another world, so quickly have we distanced ourselves from whale hunting.

It is easy to understand why the Inuit see hypocrisy in the European attitude to whaling. Britain and others led an intense industrial assault on the whale for centuries, an assault that ended only in the 1960s, when that industry ceased to be profitable. And today, the pollutants we pump into the air and sea are far more of a threat to Arctic wildlife than the hunters who live there. So the moral high-ground, from which we lecture on the evils of killing sea mammals, seems at least a little shaky. For if these animals are now endangered – and some species certainly are – the blame lies not with the Inuit but at our own door.

It would be a mistake, though, to dismiss concerns about hunting entirely. Wildlife in the Arctic is vulnerable, and the needless killing of animals and birds in Greenland has been well documented, both historically and in the present day. Today, some claim, hunting regulations are routinely flouted and rarely enforced, and populations of some bird species, such as Brünnich's guillemots and eider ducks, are well below sustainable levels. Lynge and others have been accused of misrepresenting the truth, and of propagating 'the myth of the sustainable Inuit'.

It is commonly agreed, however, even among groups such as Greenpeace, who led the anti-sealing campaigns of the 1970s, that Greenland's seal hunt is not damaging the animals' population. Numbers of the four main species – ringed, bearded, harp and hooded seals – are stable or rising, and there is little prospect of increased demand for fur threatening this balance. Watching the hunters arrive at the market each afternoon, seeing them carefully slice and distribute the meat, I was glad that this was so, glad it could continue.

One evening over dinner, a young Greenlandic couple who had invited me to their home, asked whether we had seals in Shetland. When I replied that we had many but that islanders had never really eaten them, they seemed confused.

'Why wouldn't you eat them?' the woman enquired.

I did not have a good answer. I thought, perhaps, that an abundance of fish might have made seal meat superfluous in the past, but that didn't seem very plausible. I wondered also whether superstition might have played a part. Stories of selkie folk – seal people – were widespread in Shetland as they were elsewhere in northern Scotland, and perhaps this notion that seals were somehow too human to be eaten, that they might have souls, was the real problem. I wasn't sure, and I am still not sure. The young woman seemed dissatisfied with my answer, and I was not surprised. The idea that a seal might have a soul did not seem, to her, a good reason for it not to be eaten.

A shaman once explained to the explorer and anthropologist Knud Rasmussen that 'the greatest peril lies in the fact that to kill and eat, all that we strike down and destroy . . . have souls as we have, souls that do not perish with the body, and therefore must be propitiated lest they revenge themselves.' For the traditional Inuit, souls are not the exclusive property of human beings, they are widespread and take many forms. Propitiation is achieved by following certain cultural traditions and, at all times, by showing respect towards the animal that is killed. It is both atonement and thanksgiving. In our own culture, meat has been increasingly divorced, for most of its consumers, from the death that makes it possible and the life that it once held. Because of this, there is a kind of thankfulness and humility that we no longer know how to feel, and a grace we have forgotten how to say.

*

Fat grey clouds tumbled heavily around the mountains, punctured and crushed between the peaks, rolling, blowing and inflating, from slate to black, turning over in the wind. There was rain there, on the slopes. It had not reached the town yet, but it was coming. I was stranded inside the cabin. Flu had struck me on my second day in Nanortalik, and had worsened until I felt unable to leave the warmth of the building. I was hot and shivering, my nose was blocked and sinuses throbbing; my throat was raw and my muscles ached. I felt dreadful, and sat on the sofa next to the fire looking out of the window. Hours passed slowly. I read, but found it difficult to concentrate for long. I turned on the television, but switched it off again when I saw what was there.

Outside, the ice shifted, clearing then clotting the dark water again, as the wind dragged from east to south to southwesterly. I watched its steady migration back and forth across the bay, and something inside me moved as it moved. My thoughts drifted from the island where I sat, to my own island 1,500 miles east along the parallel. I thought about the people in this town, and I thought about the great space that lay between their lives and my own. I thought, too, about my father, who seemed as close to me then as the ice outside, or the warmth within the room, but as distant and unreachable as the ravens across the bay, their black lives pinpricked against the sky.

Above the water, glaucous and Iceland gulls bustled their way between the bergs, camouflaged on the ice. As they lifted up to shift to another place now and then, they shone bright white in the grey air. Rain wrapped itself around the town then, and I opened the window a little to listen to it falling. Inland, a thick fog was slumped around the mountains, but out to sea, from where the breeze was blowing, the sky was bright. It was an illusion – the reflection of the sea ice on the clouds above – but it was welcome nonetheless, and added to the ever-present promise of change. Gretel Ehrlich has written that 'Arctic beauty resides in its gestures of transience. Up here, planes of light and darkness are swords that cut away illusions of permanence'. In Greenland, that transience is impossible to ignore; it permeates each moment of each day. It is there in the melting icebergs on the shore, and in the meat on the market counters; it is there in the rushing clouds and the changing climate. It is there in the air itself. There is the sense here that, at any moment, all certainty could be undermined – that the land could reach out in an instant and wipe people away, as the Norse were once wiped from this country. There is terror in that thought, but there is comfort, too.

When my father died I learned that loss is with us always. It is not a punctuating mark in our lives, it is not a momentary pause or ending. Loss is a constant force, a spirit that moves both within and without us. It is an unceasing process that we may choose, if we wish, to bear witness to. And if we do make that choice, then we are not committing ourselves to a lifetime of grief and melancholy. Instead, we offer ourselves the opportunity of a firmer sense of joy and of beauty. It is no surprise and certainly no coincidence that we experience our greatest appreciation of life in those things that are fragile and fleeting. We find it in the song of a bird, in the touch of a lover, or in the memory of a moment long passed. So it should be no surprise that by attuning ourselves better to the process of loss and transience, we may in turn be brought nearer to beauty and to joy. It is in loss – in the anticipation of loss – that we find our most profound pleasures, and it is there also that we may find a sense of true permanence.

In traditional Inuit society, permanence was to be found in the concept of *sila*, a kind of life force or spirit, which is sometimes translated as air, wind or weather, or, more widely still, as 'everything that is outside'. *Sila* was the essential ingredient of life – it was breath itself – and it held the inner and outer worlds together. When a person died, their life, their breath, returned to the world and became one with it again, or it found form in another person's body. But *sila* was not a predictable permanence; it was not certainty. *Sila* encompassed both weather and climate. It was changeable, surprising, and sometimes malign. Death was part of its process and part of its force, and the Inuit understanding of the world was shaped by this belief. Or perhaps it would be more true to say that the world in which the Inuit lived shaped this understanding. For natural philosophies do not spring from empty space, they are born from the land. And this seems to me a particularly northern view of life and death. Here, where the seasons turn heavily, emphatically, and where impermanence cannot be disguised, *sila*, somehow, makes sense.

Death is at once an ending and a continuation. A breath is given back to the wind, just as ice returns to the sea. It finds new shape. But a life, too, lives on through stories and through memories, joyful in their retelling and their fleeting recollection. Loss shapes us like a sculptor, carving out our form, and we feel each nick of its blade. But without it we cannot be. Of the many absences that I carry with me – for we all, I think, are filled with holes – the absence of my father is the one that has taught me most. It is the space through which I have come to see myself most clearly. I thought of him then, as an ice-laden wind pawed at the cabin window, and I thought of myself in those first few months without him. His was the loss that had led me to this place.

*

It was another two days before I felt well enough to venture out beyond the shelter of the hostel again. My strength had drained in the stifling heat inside, and I needed to walk. The morning was dry and calm, and so I aimed for Quaqssuk – Ravens' Mountain – which rose just beyond the north end of the village. Nanortalik's main street was filled with teenagers that morning, just finished their final term at junior high school. They were dressed in white T-shirts, all painted with slogans and pictures, or printed with photographs of their friends and classmates. Spray cream was everywhere, and treacle too, on their hands and faces. They were chanting a song like a football anthem, and smiling as they went. Cars beeped and people cheered in congratulation.

Much earlier in the day, at five or six a.m., the rabble would have been prowling the streets, dragging tin cans on strings behind them, banging metal trays and yelling loudly outside the homes of their teachers. In Narsaq, further up the coast, I had seen (or at least heard) the same ritual, and wondered at first if some kind of early morning riot was unfolding. But this was an annual event, I was told. It was a ceremony, marking the end of one part of the children's lives and their imminent entry into another. Most of them now would have to leave home, to complete high school in another town.

As I walked out on the dirt track towards Quassik, the sounds of the street faded and the sounds of the mountain grew. Lapland buntings flung themselves into the air around me, then glided back to earth again, wings outstretched, singing as they fell. Among the low bushes, redpolls danced and darted, some stopping close by to watch me pass. The air shimmered with song. Beneath my feet, the lower slopes were thick with life: crowberry, dwarf willows, tiny white flowers among the rocks, plump beds of mosses and lichens. There was, everywhere, an anticipation of summer.

It was warm as I began to climb the trail, and I soon took off my jacket, then my jumper. The walking wasn't difficult, but after three days lying down I wasn't feeling fit. It took an hour to gain the steep 300 metres to the top of the hill, and just a few more minutes from the first cairned summit to the highest point, topped by a pyramid of stones. The view was astonishing. To the north and east, snow-studded mountains rose abruptly from the fjords, all cluttered with ice. Peak after ragged peak stood whisped in haze and shadows. Behind me was the town, looking tiny and worn out, its colour drained by distance. Beyond it, to the south and west, was the straight line where the sea ice began, a carpet of white and blue and light, with only a few huge bergs protruding above the flat surface.

I sat down on a rock just north of the peak and ate my lunch. There was only a hint of a breeze, and everything was close to silence. The far-off hum of a helicopter; the drone of a bluebottle nearby; an outboard motor, somewhere among the fjords. Besides these, the only sound was the whispering of air among the mountains, a kind of live white noise.

I lay back with my head on the lichen crust of the rocks. The sun was only just breaking through now as the cloud slowly thickened, but it was still warm on my skin. I listened to the quiet and closed my eyes. There is great pleasure to be had in lying down outside. On a sun-drenched beach or a cold Shetland hillside, wrapped up warm or in shorts and a T-shirt, a doze in the open air is rarely a bad idea. Wild sleeping is as rejuvenating an activity as wild swimming, and it has the major benefit of being a lot less wet. I think my fondness for the activity – if you can call it an activity – in part explains why I am such a poor mountaineer. The lure of the summit is rarely strong enough to lead me further than a good view and a comfortable napping spot, and unless I can combine the two goals, such as here on Quassik, recumbency usually wins out. On this occasion, though, I didn't sleep long. Almost as soon as I had closed my eyes, something changed. I felt a breeze on my face – a sudden gust from the north that failed to fall away – and the temperature dropped. Even with my eyes shut I could sense a darkening of the sky. So I decided to move.

The walk back down the slope was easy and enjoyable, and the threatened downpour failed to materialise. I made my way into the village again, through the ramshackle streets of its eastern edge, but I was stopped by a loud voice calling. A man was beckoning me from his open window,

Danish rock music pouring out from behind him. I couldn't understand what the man was shouting, nor could I see the expression on his face, friendly or angry. But he stretched his arm in my direction and called me over, so I moved, somewhat reluctantly, towards him.

'Dansk?' he asked, when I was close enough to comprehend.

'Nej, Engelsk,' I responded, for simplicity's sake.

'Where are you from?' he said slowly, in English.

'From Scotland,' I answered, a little more accurately this time.

'Scotland, yes,' he smiled. This was clearly a welcome answer, for the man immediately invited me in to his house, and sat me down opposite him by the window. An open can of beer stood between us on the table. 'I am Thomas,' he said, then elaborated. 'Thomas Jefferson – you know? – the United States' president. That was not me!'

He laughed, then lapsed back into Danish, where he remained for the rest of the conversation. I tried my best to follow.

He told me he was a pensioner, though he was only 57 years old. He used to be a sailor, working on the ferry between Esbjerg in Denmark and Harwich in England, but now he was retired. This was his house, he said, but he didn't really live here; he lived with his mother. There was a photo of her on the wall, which he pointed out to me with pride. He lived with his mother, but he came to this house during the day to listen to music and to get drunk. In the summertime he went hunting and fishing in his boat, and sometimes he took tourists up the fjord. But for now, it seemed, the next can was as far as he was going.

A big man, with a slight limp, and a face that smiled even when his mouth did not, Thomas was, I thought, somewhat shy, though alcohol had brought him confidence. His exuberance was not really talkativeness either, just enthusiasm for sharing a moment; and like many of the Greenlanders I met, his conversation was punctuated by long, silent gazes out of the window.

Thomas was not the only person in town who spent his days with a beer in front of him. I was visited at the cabin on more than one occasion by men some considerable distance from sobriety. They were always polite and quiet, but still I was disconcerted by these uninvited guests. Alcoholism in Greenland, as in many Arctic communities, is a major problem among the native population. More recently, drug and solvent abuse have also become serious issues, along with a rise in teenage pregnancy and in health problems such as obesity. The reason, in part, is poverty, and a lack of education. But it goes deeper than that.

In Narsaq, two weeks earlier, I had spoken to Bolethe Stenskov, a social worker and counsellor, who told me that the country was suffering from the problems of rapid social change. 'We have moved from being hunters to modern life very quickly,' she said. In just a few decades a massive cultural transition has been made, and it has not been an easy one. Low self-esteem is a particularly significant problem, she explained, especially among men, who find themselves without their traditional community status. Once they were hunters, providing for their family. Now it is much harder for them to find a role. Capitalism has introduced a new set of values to Inuit culture – a framework of indulgence – and while Western materialism has yet to be fully embraced, our compulsive consumption has been adopted in an altogether damaging way. Alcohol, drugs, tobacco, junk food: this is non-accumulative consumption. It is our own excess, translated into Greenlandic.

Bolethe offers support, advice and information to those who need it, and despite her familiarity with the problems, she maintains a remarkably positive outlook. She sees her job as, unfortunately, a necessary one within this society.

The damaging cycles of addiction, of abuse and ill-health, passed down between generations, cannot be broken without intervention. And key to that intervention, Bolethe believes, must be education, for both children and adults. Currently, many youngsters struggle in school. They struggle because their parents may be unable to help them, or unwilling to encourage them. They may have a Danish teacher, but may not have the necessary skills in that language to carry them along. There is, too, a shortage of positive role models among the adult population. These factors can easily lead to a lack of interest in education, and a failure to connect with the learning process. But if they are to find a meaningful place for themselves within society, as it exists today, they must make that connection.

There is a paradox here, though, as there is in many traditional societies. For Greenlandic culture is deeply woven together with the idea of place, and the community is central within people's lives. Yet with each step in the education process, and with each successful progression, children are likely to find themselves drawn further and further away from their place and their community. At fifteen, they must leave home to complete high school elsewhere. Then, if they wish to go further, to college or university, they must go to Nuuk or to Copenhagen. These students must travel far from home, and that distance will not just be geographical. Almost as soon as they enter the education system, children are already leaving behind the traditional knowledge of their grandparents, and the higher they climb the greater that distance will become. Education promises choice and opportunities, but in return it asks for aspirations and ambition. These aspirations are rarely compatible with a small Greenlandic community; they are rarely compatible with a life that maintains a real connection to culture and tradition. There is much to be lost here – much that has already been lost elsewhere – and while education represents an opportunity, it also potentially poses a threat.

When I put this to Bolethe, though, she disagreed. There is no contradiction, she told me. 'We need to improve education and quality of life, but also retain our culture as hunting people.' So how is that possible, I asked. How do you retain a culture that is, at its heart, at odds with the education system and with the economic system that education underpins? Bolethe smiled and looked out of the window. She lifted her hand and gestured out towards the harbour, the ice and the mountains across the fjord. The answer was simple, she said. 'We have the nature; we have the landscape and the sea. There is our culture. It is with us.'

I looked out and tried to muster the same confidence. I tried to persuade myself that Bolethe was correct. Here in Greenland, as elsewhere on the parallel, the landscape and climate continue to bring the same challenges they always have. The place continues to make demands upon the people. And while individuals might struggle to reshape themselves as society changed, perhaps the culture would still yield to those demands. I hoped it was so. I hoped that she was right.

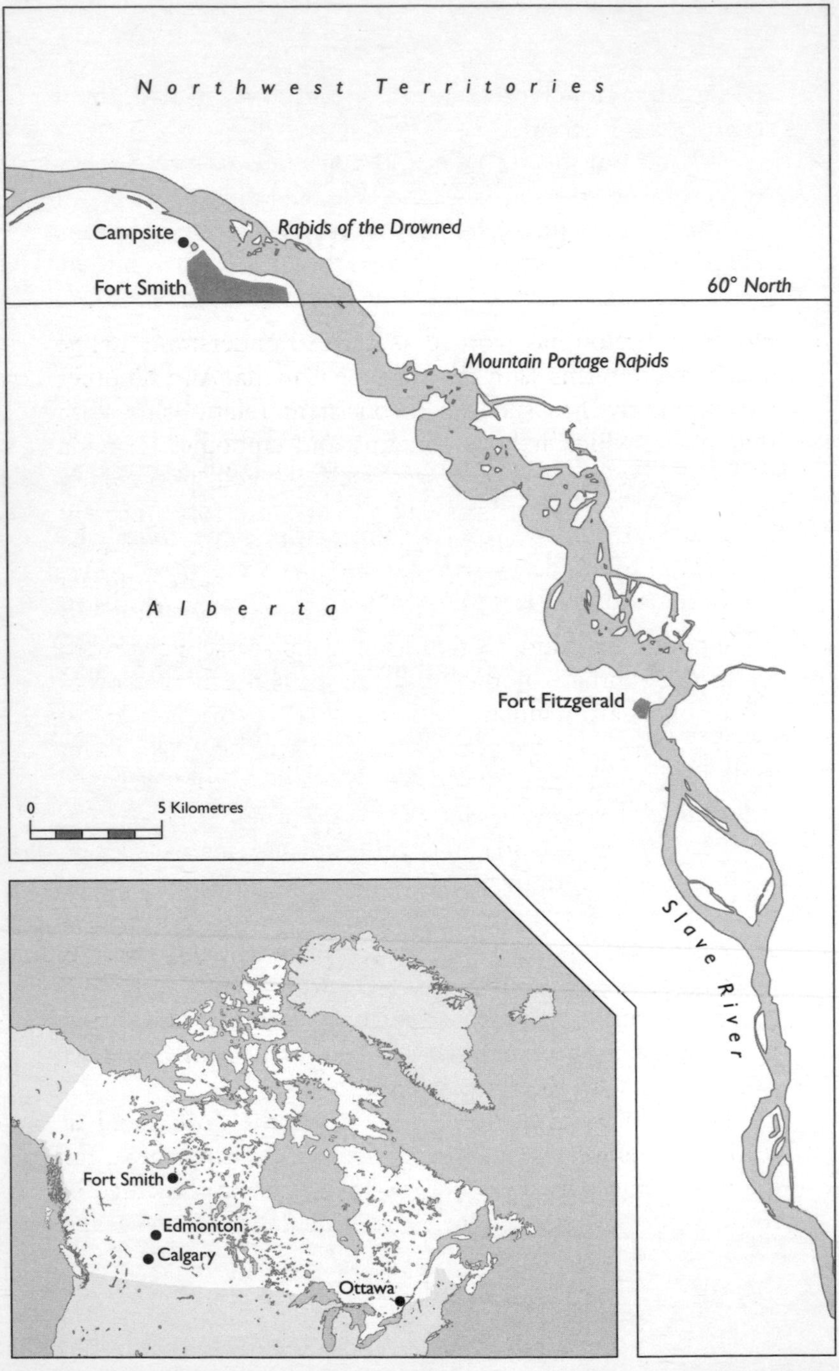

Northwest Territories

Campsite

Rapids of the Drowned

Fort Smith

60° North

Mountain Portage Rapids

Alberta

Fort Fitzgerald

0   5 Kilometres

Slave River

Fort Smith

Edmonton

Calgary

Ottawa

CANADA
beside the rapids

No other nation has worked as hard to understand, define and come to terms with the north as Canada. And no other nation, surely, has such an inconsistent relationship with that place, which it both contains and embodies. Canada is a northern country and sees itself as such, particularly in relation to the United States. Around forty percent of its landmass lies north of sixty degrees – a vast area, comparable in size to the entire European Union. And yet the country's centre of balance is firmly in the south. The population – around 33 million in total – is concentrated along the southern border, and the most northerly city of more than half a million people is Edmonton, just above fifty-three degrees, the same latitude as Dublin. Only about 100,000 Canadians actually live above the sixtieth parallel – considerably fewer, in fact, than Americans.

For most in Canada, then, the north remains alien, a neighbour but a stranger. Many dream of it, but few ever wake up there. It is a place read about in books, seen in films and on television, but rarely visited. Viewed from afar, the region is tangled in contradictions. North means danger and adventure, but it also means refuge. It offers possibility and fear, beauty and horror. It is almost empty of people and yet overflowing with their imaginings.

But for those who do wish to know the north, and to see it for themselves, the first difficulty is getting there, for the north is nearly always beyond the horizon. I arrived in the country in Calgary, Alberta, and my destination was the town of Fort Smith, just inside the Northwest Territories. It was a twenty-four hour coach ride away.

A cluster of tall buildings raised like an exclamation in the flat prairie, Calgary was bathed in summer heat that afternoon. As always, my fear of flying had left me unable to sleep while in the air, and the time change had made things worse. By eight p.m., when the Greyhound bus pulled out of the depot into the clean sunlight of the streets, it had been a very long time since I had last been asleep. We drove north from the city and into the broad plains beyond. In the west, clouds were piled like rubble above the Rocky Mountains, haze-drawn on the horizon. The bus was filled with chatter, but outside the soft light of the evening lay like a blanket of quiet upon the fields.

Our first stop was Red Deer, shortly before ten p.m., just as the sun was setting. My head was cluttered with half-formed, exhausted thoughts, but I held myself awake, staring dazedly through the window. As we continued towards Edmonton an hour passed, but the memory of the sun lingered. Colours washed out, leaving behind a muted light; and as the sky softened to golden grey in the northwest, farmhouses dissolved into silhouettes – fat, black stains on the disappearing land.

At Edmonton we changed buses. It was midnight, but the depot was still full of people. Many of the passengers had brought pillows and blankets with them, and as we drove on into the darkness, voices settled into silence. I bundled up my jacket, then wedged it between the seatback and the window. Closing my eyes, I tried to sleep.

By the time we reached the town of Slave Lake at three a.m., a smear of white was in the northeast sky. Soon after, darkness began to lift again. Trees emerged from the night, close against the road, blocking the view beyond. An hour or so later the prairie returned, with fields stretched out in every direction. The farms were tidy – all straight lines and well-kept gardens, quaint wooden houses and giant grain silos. Even the old cars had been abandoned in neat rows, lined up, perhaps, in the order in which they stopped working. A few white-tailed deer grazed here and there, and once the driver blew his horn at a pair that strayed into the road. The deer were forced into a quick decision, the right decision.

The journey north – in history, in literature, in the imagination – is a journey away from the centres of civilisation and culture, towards the unknown and the other. Margaret Atwood has written that, 'Turning to . . . face the north, we enter our own unconscious. Always, in retrospect, the journey north has the quality of a dream'. Looking out through the tinted windows of the coach, my own journey felt dreamlike. But it was not my own dream. Rather, it was as though someone else's unconscious were being projected against the glass. The honeyed light of the early morning, the procession of fields, farms, trees and towns, all seemed remote and unreal somehow. I felt disorientated and disconnected from the place outside. I observed but couldn't engage. I let the morning wash over me, hour after hour.

In 1964, the pianist Glenn Gould travelled on the Muskeg Express, a thousand-mile train journey lasting a day and two nights, from Winnipeg to Churchill, on the shores of Hudson Bay. It was his first northern journey, and on his return Gould made a radio programme about the trip. *The Idea of North* is not a documentary in any conventional sense; it is a collage of voices. Using interviews with a civil servant, a geographer, a nurse and a sociologist, all with experience of northern Canada, as well as a narrator of sorts called Wally Maclean, Gould created, to use his word, a 'contrapuntal' picture of the north. Like a choir of competing melodies, these voices rise, tumble and are lost. Ideas emerge then vanish again, as though glimpsed from a moving train. Sometimes they come through clearly, with only the gentle clunk and clatter of the tracks in the background; other times the sounds overlap, with voices jostling for the listener's attention. Towards the programme's end the last movement of Sibelius's Fifth Symphony begins, and soon it rears up above Maclean's closing monologue, threatening to overwhelm his words, until at last there is only silence.

Going north to me means going home, and every journey I take in this direction brings with it the feeling of return. Once that feeling was an unwelcome one, reminding me always of the times I made it when I didn't wish to do so. But that has changed. It was two years after I was brought back to Shetland, aged sixteen and fatherless, that I found another way out, and another way forward. In that time, I suppose, I'd come to understand that, wherever I went from then on, Shetland would be the place to which I returned. I no longer had close family or friends elsewhere; I no longer had much to connect me with anywhere except the islands. My centre of gravity had shifted north, and though I didn't yet feel its pull, I knew that change had taken place.

It was without a great deal of enthusiasm that I decided, eventually, to go to university. Others were going, and it made sense for me to go too. It was a logical escape route. But a handful of mediocre exam results from my last year at school were not enough to get me anywhere, and so I enrolled in night-classes and took more exams. Further mediocre results followed. In the end I managed to persuade one university to take me, based on the quantity rather than the quality of my grades, I suppose. And it was my good fortune that they did, because I enjoyed almost every moment of those four years, from arrival until graduation, and I thrived there in a way that I'd failed to do at school. It was during those years in Scotland that I began to look north when I thought of home, and even to feel relief at holiday times as the train took me back up the country, towards the ferry, and a night on the North Sea.

*

It was a little after six a.m. when we descended into the Peace Valley. No one had spoken for three hours, though a few, like me, had sat awake throughout the night. In Peace River, dazed and dazzled, we had a break. Given ninety minutes in which to fill our stomachs and stretch our legs, I took a short walk through the centre of town, then went for coffee and breakfast in Rusty's Diner. It was just me and the waitress. A pile of steaming pancakes arrived, doused with maple syrup, and I ate them greedily, enjoying every mouthful. I felt almost refreshed.

When the time came to continue, only seven of us got back on the bus. It was raining heavily then, and we trundled into a changing landscape. Though we were still among the prairies, the agriculture was less intensive, the farms smaller, the roads less straight. Land space was shared about evenly between fields of cattle or fodder, and light, mostly deciduous woodland. In places, cows grazed among the trees.

In this country there are a multitude of lines and frontiers behind which lies the north. These frontiers have cultural and political, as well as geographical, significance, and much effort has been expended locating them. On a map it's possible to draw a series of boundaries and borders between north and south, or between 'near' and 'far north'. There is the tree line, above which the boreal forest gives way to tundra; the southern limit of permafrost; the Arctic Circle; the sixtieth parallel. Other measurements are also made. Temperature, precipitation, accessibility, population density: all are calculated, and a level of 'nordicity' can be assigned, according to a scale developed in the 1970s by the geographer Louis-Edmond Hamelin.

For scientists, politicians and civil servants, such measurements are useful. They allow direct, accurate comparisons of environmental and social situations across the country.

But there is a problem. Nordicity is a southern concept – an attempt to contain what cannot truly be held – and the criteria by which it is assessed are not really measurements of northernness (other than latitude, of course); they are measurements of cold, isolation, inaccessibility and foreignness. In other words, they are calculations of how places correspond to a preconceived notion of what the north ought to be, epitomised by that most foreign of all earthly places, the North Pole. So Hamelin could write of 'a 25% denordification across the North [over the past century]', as though by changing, by developing, by warming, the north can actually become less like itself.

The view from inside, though, is different. The north is all that it contains. It is a place capable of change and diversity, a place immeasurable. It holds the preconceived, yes, but also the unimagined and the unimaginable. Above all else, for those who live there, the north is home. It is neither remote nor isolated nor far away; it is the centre of the world. For me, the very arbitrariness of the sixtieth parallel, its total lack of what Hamelin called 'natural relevance', is its great advantage, making it an ideal place along which to explore the north. For the parallel is not a line by which to measure anything quantitatively, nor is it a clear border between one place and another. Instead, the parallel is entirely undefining. It allows for a plurality of norths to exist.

By mid-morning there were only trees – birch, spruce, trembling aspen, tamarack, balsam poplar – and a narrow space on either side of the road. Here and there a stretch of swampy ground emerged from the forest, or a lake, often with a beaver's lodge or two tucked up against the bank. The rain had stopped and the sky cleared by then, and the day was swollen with sunshine. I watched the trees, half-hypnotised, and thought about what lay beyond this parting of the forest. Out there, away from the road's slender imposition, lay the whole country, and more. This immense boreal forest, of taiga and muskeg, stretches across northern Canada and Alaska, then on through Siberia, the Urals and into Scandinavia, tying the top of the planet together. It is easy to imagine stepping out among the trees here and walking within their shadow, until you emerge somewhere else entirely, some other part of the north. Except of course that you wouldn't. More likely, the person who stepped into the forest, unless they truly knew this place, would become disorientated immediately, then they would be lost, and sooner or later they would die. Nature here is a contradictory presence. It is abundant and overflowing with life, and yet threatening and hostile to our intrusions. The forest is the road's antithesis. We no longer know how to live with it, and so we pass quickly through, on our way to another clearing.

The highway carried few vehicles. Every ten minutes or so a pickup went by, or sometimes a truck, and once a yellow school bus appeared like a daydream, then was gone. The hours passed, and morning became afternoon. We stopped for lunch at High Level, with its ugly strip of motels, bars and fast food restaurants, then the insect-choked gas station at Indian Cabins. At half past two we crossed the sixtieth parallel and the border into the Northwest Territories. Only three of us remained. For mile after mile nothing changed, the view appeared identical. We turned a corner and we might as well not have moved. It was as though there were nowhere else left but the forest.

The Greyhound reached Hay River, the end of its line, at four p.m. The tiny, dusty depot seemed intensely hot, and a shock after the air-conditioned coach. When the time came for the minibus to depart fifteen minutes later, I was the only passenger taking the 170-mile trip southeast to Fort Smith. (In the north, distances between towns are often so great that it makes more sense to measure them in hours than in miles. This would be a three-hour journey, with no stops between here and there.) My driver, Andrew, insisted that I come and sit up in the front with him so that he could 'give me the tour'. As we set off, Andrew explained that he was partially deaf, so I would have to speak clearly and face in his direction. This partial deafness also required him to talk just a little too insistently throughout, as though he suspected I might be doubting every word he said.

We began the drive with the kind of tales I had been hoping not to hear. For my entertainment, Andrew recounted in detail the stories of two fatal bear attacks in the region. The first of these was a driver who had crashed his vehicle on this very road, then attracted the bear's attention by lying at the roadside bleeding. He was found too late, halfway through being consumed. The second attack involved a couple from Hay River who were camping beside Great Slave Lake. Needless to say, they never came home. It seemed there were a lot of bears around here. In fact, the last time Andrew made this trip he'd seen six of them between the two towns. I tried to look impressed, or at least unafraid, but it was hard. I was thinking about the little tent in my bag, in which I'd intended to sleep.

'I'm a bit nervous about bears, actually,' I admitted. Andrew turned to me, unsure whether I was joking or not. 'Oh, you don't need to be nervous,' he said, when he saw that I was serious. 'You'll be fine.' While this reassurance was not entirely adequate, I was relieved to learn that the animals in this area were black rather than brown bears. Smaller, less aggressive, more easily deterred, they were a safer kind of bear all round. And though they did kill people once in a while, it was rather more unusual an occurrence than Andrew's stories might have led me to believe. As he said, I would probably be fine.

When Andrew pressed his foot to the brake, he was mid-sentence and mid-sandwich. 'Buffalo,' he spat, pointing up ahead. The animals were impossible to miss. A group of six, some standing, some rolling in the dust at the roadside, the creatures were enormous, and unconcerned as we slowed almost to a stop just a few metres away. They were strange beasts – their back-ends like cattle, but their front halves and heads like something else entirely: broad, dark, woolly, bearded and horned, they looked like relics of another age. The adults stood well over six feet tall at their humped shoulders, with the large males weighing in at up to a ton. The youngsters were lighter in colour, and not dissimilar to the calves of domestic cattle. These wood buffalo are the largest land mammals in North America, one of two subspecies of the American bison that once roamed the Great Plains in their tens of millions, and which were slaughtered almost to extinction.

For most of this journey from Hay River to Fort Smith we were driving through Wood Buffalo National Park, a UNESCO World Heritage Site and, at 17,300 square miles, the second largest protected area in the world, after Northeast Greenland. The park was established in 1922 to help protect one of the last existing herds of free-roaming wood bison, and today there are around 5,000 of them in the area. Like many large animals, the bison appeared weighed down by their own bulk, and seemed to live at a slower pace than other creatures. They lumbered unhurriedly across and alongside the road, apparently oblivious to the vehicle in their midst. Flies clouded around their backs and heads in thick, sickening swarms, but even their short tails swished and swatted the insects at half speed. Over the next hour we saw another thirty or forty bison, some in groups, others alone, and each time they were somehow unbelievable. And then there was something different.

A black mark beside the road, a hundred yards ahead. A boulder-sized shape that came to life as we approached. A shape that lifted its head, unfurled itself, and became a bear. This time it was me who alerted Andrew. The bear stood and watched the vehicle as we slowed down. It was not a large animal – perhaps only a year or two old – but it seemed confident, and held still for a long time, not moving until we'd drawn up almost alongside it. The eyes peered at us, perhaps assessing the threat, and we stared back, safe within our box of glass and metal. But at the precise moment we came to a stop, the bear turned, moving without much haste back into the forest. We drove on in silence.

Andrew dropped me at the campsite just outside Fort Smith. There was no one else around. I wandered among the lanky jack pines looking for a flat, sheltered spot on which to put up my tent, then struggled, in bursts of rage and frustration, to put the pieces together and press the pegs into the ground. A difficult job was made harder by mosquitoes and exhaustion, and I scratched at my face and neck, half-hallucinating in the warm, evening air. I was weak and dizzy, and my eyes hurt when I tried to concentrate. It had been almost forty-eight hours since I last slept. Fatigue flooded over me as I crawled inside the tent and lay down with my head upon my jacket. A slight nausea rose too, as though to engulf my whole body, then it slipped away like a sigh and was gone. I felt entirely alone, then, yet too tired to be lonely. I felt exhilarated, briefly, to be there in the forest. And then I was asleep.

*

Moving through this country has always been difficult. Dense forest, boggy ground, extreme temperatures and hostile insect life: the early European travellers found their way slowed by innumerable dangers. The most convenient means of travel, historically, has been to step off the land altogether and to get on the water, and lakes and rivers have long been the highways of the north, reliable for paddling in summer and for sledging and walking in winter. In 1789, the Scottish-born explorer Alexander Mackenzie was searching for a northern route to the Pacific Ocean, but found something else instead. Making his way from Lake Athabasca, in what is now northern Alberta and Saskatchewan, north along the Slave River to the Great Slave Lake, then onwards along a second, much longer river to the Arctic Ocean, he opened up what was to become one of the great Canadian trading routes. That second river, which he named 'Disappointment' upon reaching its end, is now called the Mackenzie, and is the longest river lying entirely within Canada.

That route to the Arctic was to become immensely important over the next two centuries, providing a reliable means of reaching northern communities for the missionaries and traders who travelled the region. The great advantage of this particular route was its simplicity. Over the entire 1,500 miles between Lake Athabasca and the Arctic, there was only one major obstacle to transport. Halfway along the Slave River, just as it crosses the sixtieth parallel, four huge sets of rapids churn the water into a riotous wash of foaming white and brown. High waves, deep holes and hidden rocks combine to make much of this seventeen-mile stretch entirely impassable by boat.

Today, sections of these rapids provide some of the most challenging and exciting water in the world for kayakers and canoeists, but in the past travellers had to do their best to avoid the danger. That meant getting out of the river. Since before the first Europeans ever reached this place, a series of portage routes existed, and these were gradually developed as people made the journey more regularly. By the early nineteenth century, larger vessels had come into use, and they too had to be hauled out, requiring incredible effort. This was particularly true at Mountain Rapids, where the portage involved a precipitous climb of 75 feet, then an equally steep descent back to the river. A winch system made it possible, but certainly not easy. The travellers, however, had no choice; the river was simply too treacherous to follow. And for any voyager who might have been tempted to risk the water, there was a constant reminder of the potential dangers. For below the first three sets of rapids – today known as Cassette, Pelican and Mountain – lies the last, called then, as now, the Rapids of the Drowned. The name, coined after an accident in 1786 in which five men lost their lives, served as both a memorial and as a warning to others.

During the late nineteenth century, the Hudson's Bay Company established two small settlements on the west bank of the river, one at either end of the portage system. At Cassette Rapids was Smith's Landing (now called Fort Fitzgerald), and on a high bluff overlooking the Rapids of the Drowned was Fort Smith. When the shorter portages were eventually succeeded in the 1880s by a single, seventeen-mile trail, and steamboats began to operate on either side of the rapids, a new simplified era of transportation began. The country opened up, and changed forever. The north became accessible to anyone who wished to go there, and Fort Smith, in effect, was its gateway. The town grew rapidly. Freight companies appeared and prospered; labouring work and other employment was in plentiful supply. By 1921, it had become the administrative centre for the entire Northwest Territories.

*

It was a short walk along the highway from my campsite to the town. The air was hot and humming with insects, and I clung close to the shadows at the forest's edge, keeping out of the sun. A single vehicle passed as I walked – an old grey pickup heading west towards the airport. Other than that, the road was empty.

The first houses were large and set some way back from the road, behind wire or wooden fences. The street was wide and edged with dust and gravel, with deep ditches on either side, and a yellow-stained pavement. Some of the gardens looked unkempt, but not uncared-for, and the air smelt of pine, flowers and early summer soil. From behind one house, two small dogs came bounding, yapping fiercely as I passed, but neither would venture further than the open gate.

I had no map, and no idea where I was going. I had no plans, other than the one my stomach had made for breakfast. I followed McDougal Street, vaguely expecting a town centre to emerge, which it vaguely did: a crossroads – McDougal and Breynat Street – with Wally's drugstore on one corner, Saint Joseph Cathedral on another, and a few wooden benches on which to sit and watch the traffic. Crowded close around this junction were a library, two supermarkets, the fire station, town hall, hotel and red-brick post office, and a shop selling flowers, chocolates and coffee. Trees were lined up neatly on the lawn outside the cathedral, and extravagant hanging baskets dangled like cherries from the street lamps. On impulse I turned right onto Portage Avenue, then stopped at Kelly's gas station for something to eat and drink. I sat down in the sun with my juice and sandwich, and was joined by a gang of hungry wasps.

Virtually all of this town is squeezed into a slim stretch of land between the river and Highway 5. 'Smith', as it's referred to by residents, is home to around two and a half thousand people, but feels larger because of its isolation. It has the amenities of a much bigger place. There is a college here, a primary and a secondary school, a leisure centre and a golf club, a local paper, a few places to eat, a few bars, some churches and a museum, though very few tourists this early in the summer. The town also has a beguiling openness. People smiled and said hello to me as they passed. If I saw them a second time I was offered another smile and a nod of recognition.

The air was heavy and humid as I wandered about the streets, and a hint of thunder trembled through a black cloud in the west. A few spots of rain fell, but the pavements dried as soon as each drop touched the ground. Early in the afternoon I picked up a map from the National Park office and continued to walk, circling the town centre and exploring its edges. At some time in the mid-twentieth century, in a moment of cack-handed inspiration, many of Fort Smith's streets had been given names that not only strained towards geographical and cultural 'appropriateness' but were also, quite inexplicably, alliterative. Prior to that almost all roads had been anonymous, and in the minds of many residents most remain so. But now, officially at least, at one end of McDougal Street are Woodbison Avenue, Wilderness Road, Whipoorwill Crescent and Weasel Street, while at the other are Park Drive, Paddle Street, Portage Avenue and Pickerel, Poppy, Pine and Polar Crescents. Some of the names are sickeningly twee, such as Teepee Trail, while others are reminiscent of another place entirely – Primrose Lane could have wound its way through a tale by Beatrix Potter, but here it is a rough gravel road leading out into the forest, where a carved monument hides amid the trees to Edward Martin, 'the best woodcutter of the north'.

I returned in the late afternoon to the corner of Breynat and McDougal and sat down on one of the benches there, watching the cars and pickups go past. It was not long after five and the brief homeward rush had begun. Ignoring the traffic, ravens strutted at the street's edges with a nervous arrogance, calling to one another from pavement to telegraph pole to cathedral roof. A breeze brought dust and cool air up the road, dragging the evening behind it. I stopped and listened a while longer, focusing my ears on the dull white noise that hung like a mist in the air. Beneath the urgent cawing of the ravens, and beneath the sounds of the street, was a thin whispering on which all the other noise was built. That whisper was the river.

At the beginning of the twentieth century, Fort Smith was still a very long way from civilisation. In western Canada, the Klondike gold rush had led to a massive influx of people. The Yukon Territory had been connected to the outside world by railway, by telegraph and by economics, but change had not come so quickly elsewhere, and trappers, traders and missionaries were still virtually the only non-native people living above sixty. Things were beginning to change, though, and the pace of development would quicken over the coming decades. Increasing quantities of food, trading goods and machinery were carried through the Fitzgerald-Smith corridor, particularly after the discovery of oil at Norman Wells in 1920, uranium at Port Radium in 1930 and gold at Yellowknife in 1934. The fortunes of Fort Smith were inextricably linked to those of the Territory itself, and when the American army arrived in town in the early 1940s, major changes were under way across the north.

During the Second World War, the United States took on two major building projects in Canada. The first was the Alaska Highway, passing through British Columbia and the Yukon, which the army completed with immense effort in just eight months in 1942. The road cut a 1,700 mile slice through a part of the country few had ever visited, and it made regular land access to the north a reality for the very first time. The second project was the Canol (Canadian Oil) road and pipeline, between Norman Wells and Whitehorse. Equipment and supplies for that project had to be carried through Fort Smith, and the increase in traffic required an upgrade of the portage road from Fort Fitzgerald, which the army undertook. The work also necessitated a winter road to Hay River, on the south shore of the Great Slave Lake. These projects, along with the air bases the army constructed at Smith and elsewhere, changed the north forever. The region would never again be so isolated from the rest of the country. When the Second World War came to an end, the population quickly began to rise.

Canada's north is woven together with the stories of people who've chosen to leave the south behind. A considerable percentage of the non-indigenous population were born elsewhere, and they bring with them a profusion of histories. Some come here to escape the frantic pace of the south; others come to find work, or quiet. Some stay only a short time; others never leave. But these people bring to the north an instinct towards change. They help to create a sense of a place not yet complete, a place still in the making.

One such immigrant is Ib Kristensen, who has spent more than forty years in Fort Smith. On a warm afternoon I sat with him outside North of 60 Books on Portage Avenue, the shop and café that he and his wife Lillian opened together in 1975. We sipped our coffees and watched as his sheepdog ran to greet each visitor to the store. A few ragged clouds moved overhead, throwing thin shadows onto the grass around us. Ib leaned back in his seat, his white hair and beard neatly trimmed, his glasses perched comfortably upon his face. He smiled as he spoke of the half-lifetime he'd spent in this town. 'I'm very fortunate to have found this place,' he told me.

In the winter of 1959, after a stormy Atlantic crossing, Ib and Lillian arrived in Halifax, Nova Scotia. They had $400 in their pockets and not a word of English in their mouths. Remembering how he felt on that cold day, more than fifty years ago, Ib shook his head. 'How on earth did we get here?' he laughed. Just a few months before, the couple had walked into a Canadian government travel bureau in Copenhagen and sat down to watch a film about Vancouver. They'd made up their minds to leave Europe, but hadn't yet decided where they would go. 'I didn't feel there was enough room for me in Denmark,' Ib explained. In that film they saw a place with more room than a person could ever need, more room than a person could even imagine. The pair signed their emigration papers that same afternoon.

From Halifax, the Kristensens travelled west by train through the vast belly of the country. They crossed from the Atlantic to the Pacific coast, arriving in Vancouver, which would be their home for the next eight years. Ib was a bookbinder and typographer, and Lillian a weaver, and both found employment in the city. But Ib's work would later take him back east, to McGill University in Montreal. There, the Kristensens and their two sons spent the end of the 1960s. But the stay was not an entirely happy one. Quebec nationalism was on the rise, and with it came an increasing military presence in the city. 'I grew up in the war,' said Ib. 'I didn't want to see a uniform ever again.' And so the couple looked north. They wanted a place where they could live together as a family and as part of a community, and in 1971 they chose Fort Smith. They purchased an old log house for $500 and the land it sat on for $1,000. Ib took a carpentry course at the college, and they made themselves a home.

By the time the Kristensens arrived here, Fort Smith had either become a victim of northern development or its beneficiary, depending on your view. Its former roles, as entryway and de facto capital of the Northwest Territories, had both come to an abrupt end during the 1960s. In the early years of the decade a road and railway had been built all the way from Edmonton to Hay River, bypassing Fort Smith and effectively making its portage route redundant. Then, in 1967, the Canadian government decided upon an official capital for the Territory, and 'luckily', as Ib puts it, 'Yellowknife got that'. While a few government jobs did and do remain, the focus shifted elsewhere, and the town's responsibilities disappeared. Almost overnight it changed from a bustling gateway to a place without purpose at the end of a long dirt road. Things could easily have ended, but they didn't.

Ib Kristensen is an old man now. He talks slowly, with the composure of someone who's considered his words long before he's spoken them. He smiles broadly and often, with a warmth that is both generous and genuine, and he talks of this town as though there were nowhere else he could be. There is a place for everyone, he told me, and this is his place.

When Lillian Kristensen died in 2004, Ib decided to retire and sell North of 60 Books. He joined me there as a fellow customer (albeit one who was welcomed with a hug by the current owner). As we sat speaking on the lawn, Ib recalled the freedom and potential he found here in the early '70s, when Fort Smith's future was uncertain. Those who shared this town felt a responsibility to create the kind of place they wanted to live in, the community was a thing to be moulded and improved. And that sense, of somewhere unfinished and bristling with possibility, has not yet faded away. 'There's an immense opportunity to do things in a place like this,' Ib said. 'If there's something you want to do and there isn't anyone else doing it here, you just start. If you want that kind of freedom, it's still here.'

When the portage route along the Slave River became redundant, everything changed. No longer was this town a key staging post on the road to the north; no longer was it held aloft on the tide of northern development. Instead, the country's eyes looked elsewhere: to Hay River and Yellowknife and Whitehorse. And the town turned too – away from the river, and away from the flow of people and money that had given it life. Fort Smith turned towards itself, and became, to borrow Wendell Berry's phrase, 'the centre of its own attention'. This was once a transient-hearted gathering of service providers on a portage route to the north. Like a commuter town, its focus was always on the elsewhere. But today this is not the case. Today Fort Smith is that most precious of things: a community that recognises and values itself as such. It has an inward gaze and a preoccupation with the local that both requires and reinforces a genuine acknowledgement of interdependence. That acknowledgement is crucial to the nature of the place.

We live in a time of great division and alienation, in which 'social networking', a parody of community, is passed off as a viable alternative or replacement for it. To recognise the interdependence of people upon each other – of people who share a place – is the fundamental act of community. And it is, today, a radical act, a willing and deliberate entanglement that ignores the siren cry of solitary freedom. The places where this is still the dominant way of living are, for me, places that foster hope. Not the hope that we may go backwards, and try to live as our grandparents lived. But rather, the hope that what has been diminished in this past century – the wisdom and intimacy of community life – may not be entirely lost. Fort Smith is such a place, and the reasons it remains so are primarily geographical.

Where economic factors allow, communities are strengthened by remoteness. In Shetland, small islands such as Fetlar, Out Skerries and Fair Isle have maintained a kind of togetherness even as they have battled depopulation, job losses and other threats. In part this is due to the inherent centeredness of islands, but it's also an issue of simple practicality. In places such as these, recognition of the community is not really optional. Any other way of living would be destructive. Remoteness exposes the vulnerability of a place, and it makes clear the absolute dependence of people upon each other.

Fort Smith too is an island, surrounded not by water but by an ocean of trees. And it is certainly remote. Hay River is the closest settlement of any size, and a 350-mile round trip is, happily, too far for commuting or for regular shopping excursions. With the exception of those few who fly back and forth to Yellowknife for well-paid jobs in the diamond mines, Fort Smith's citizens are largely contained in Fort Smith and in the neighbouring hamlets of Fort Fitzgerald and Salt River. The community that's developed here, for that reason, seems very much like that of a small island. People recognise that they are indebted to each other, and that such indebtedness is not a burden. There is, too, a kind of levelling that leaves few observable social divisions within the town, and the relationship between 'European' and indigenous Canadians is generally good. (The population here is mixed quite evenly. Around one third are Dene, a group of northern First Nations with languages in the Athabascan family; one third are Métis, aboriginal people of mixed European and First Nations descent; and one third are 'white'.) For those who choose to accept the constraints of geographical remoteness and to stay put, a connection necessarily develops with the *here*, and that connection can grow into a deeper, broader engagement. Such communities are never perfect, but they strive in the right direction.

*

It was early afternoon. The hot, sticky day thickened and grew heavy. A dark warning grumbled above the forest, and everything hung silent for a moment. There was a pause like a breath inhaled, then held, and the pressure rose as though from the ground itself. The air seemed to stiffen around us like a tourniquet. And then the storm opened. The first fat raindrops fell in a clatter, then a roar, punching the dust up from the street's edge. Then came the thunder, raging into the town. Rain descended in great, gasping sheets, punctured by lightning. The ditches, which earlier seemed needlessly deep, were full and overflowing in minutes. Everywhere was water.

I escaped into the Church of St Isodore, part of the Mission Historic Park, where buildings from the town's Catholic mission are being rebuilt or restored. The hammering rain increased, and soon it was coming through the roof and in the door. Hail stones erupted from a bulging black sky. The noise was enormous. I wandered around the room, taking my time with the interpretive signs, loitering, until the girl behind the desk invited me to play pool on the old table in the centre of the church. We shouted to each other across game after game, struggling to hear above the noise outside. It was more than two hours before the rain eased enough for me to venture back out to the street.

Later, when the storm had cleared, I walked out to the bluff overlooking the river. From the bench there I could see the Rapids of the Drowned, and the white specks of pelicans on the water. I let my eyes relax into the view, enjoying the distance. For most of my life I've lived in houses that looked out over the sea. In Fort Smith, hemmed in by trees, I felt half-blinded, and that spot offered the nearest I could find to a horizon. I imagined that water rushing on to the Arctic. Ahead of it whole oceans had gone, while Fort Smith stood watching. The Dene name for this area is Thebacha: 'beside the rapids'. The story of this place has been defined by the river.

That night I struggled back into my tent. My arms were red and lumpy, sunburnt and bitten; I looked like a victim of some hideous disease. But the insects had vanished, and the evening was chilly and quiet. The jack pines around the campsite whispered and scritched, as though they didn't want to be heard, and the sharp, sweet smell of them filled the air. The more nights I stayed in the tent, the more I was conscious of the ground beneath me. I had no sleeping mat, and though I'd not noticed for the first few nights, I was now aware of tree roots, twigs and pine cones spread out underneath my body. I could feel their shapes pressing into me.

The storm broke again around 11.30 p.m., just as the fading light forced me to give up reading. A few distant rumbles had become closer and more frequent, and all at once the tent was lit up. I counted the seconds. One, two, three, four . . . it was twelve seconds before another crack and long burst of thunder filled the air. A few spots of rain turned at once into a deluge, clawing wildly at the sides of the tent. I sat up and checked that everything was tight and able to keep me dry, then lay on my back and waited. Another flash. Eight seconds. And another. Five seconds.

Wood Buffalo National Park was on high alert because of the long period of dry weather. Lightning strikes could easily set off a forest fire. The previous morning the sky had been blue-grey with smoke from a blaze somewhere in the park. The helicopters were out and the watchtowers would be manned. The rain was a constant howl on the canvas, and I closed my eyes, trying to let the sound wash over me. Somehow, I slept.

I was woken at six a.m. by the light and the cold. It was close to freezing, and I was shivering hard. I dragged more clothes on and curled up, trying to find some warmth. Sleep arrived again then, stealing quietly into the tent, and a clear, bright morning followed close behind, without a hint of the night's violence.

*

'White people have lost their relationship with the land', François Paulette told me. 'They must have had it or they could not have survived for thousands of years. But now all people think about is money. All they have in their heads is money.'

He looked at me, unsmiling, then returned to his lunch. Paulette is a former chief of the Smith's Landing First Nation. He is an influential and respected Dene Suline elder, who today spends much of his time campaigning on land rights and the environment. When we met, he had just returned from Norway, where he'd been invited to speak to shareholders of Statoil, one of the companies exploiting the Athabasca tar sands in northern Alberta. His speech that day in Stavanger began: 'What you do with your money is your business. But when you begin to spend your money in my territory [in a way] that disrupts and destroys our way of life, our civilisation, then that becomes my business.'

Paulette is an imposing and intimidating figure – well over six feet tall, with long grey hair pulled back into a pony tail, and a thin moustache on his broad, rough-sculpted face. As he enters a room, attention instantly surrounds him. Everybody turns to greet him. He shakes hands, asks questions and remembers names, like a perfect statesman.

As we sat together in a near-empty restaurant one afternoon, François spoke slowly and with a heavy accent. He paused between sentences, sometimes for long periods. During these pauses, he was not waiting for me to respond or to fill the silence. Rather, he was talking at the appropriate pace. He was gathering, carefully, his thoughts.

'The Dene culture is entirely about our relationship with the land,' he told me. 'It is a spiritual relationship. It is emotional, mental and physical. The land is sacred, and there are protocols for everything. When I take a plant from the forest I must leave tobacco in thanks. When I am out on the river I must thank the river.'

This insistence on gratitude and propitiation is not unlike that of the Inuit in Greenland. It is a focus on reciprocity, and on the bond between people and place. For the Dene, the land is not a resource, it is a presence; it is not something separate from their community, it is integral to it. When François told me about a hydroelectric dam that developers hoped to build on the Slave River – an idea first raised in the late 1970s but still no closer to reality at the time of my visit – he was adamant. By restricting the flow of the Slave and flooding the land above (some of which is owned by the Dene) the dam would not only 'desecrate the river', it would 'desecrate our history'. 'It will not happen in my lifetime,' he told me.

It would be fair to say that Canada's indigenous people suffered less direct violence, historically, at the hands of European settlers than those of the United States. But that would not be saying much. Over the centuries, native people here were exploited, discriminated against and abused. Battles over land rights continue to this day, and the active suppression of native traditions and culture went on until the late twentieth century. From the 1870s, thousands of young indigenous people were forced to attend 'residential schools' – such as Breynat Hall in Fort Smith – whose principal aims were the Christianisation and assimilation of 'Indians' into mainstream society. Often, children were banned from speaking their own languages, and some had little or no contact with their families for months or even years. Many suffered physical and sexual abuse in these institutions, and sanitation levels were often appallingly low; at least 4,000 children died, mostly from diseases such as tuberculosis.

In 2008, twelve years after the closure of the last of the residential schools, the leaders of all of Canada's main political parties issued a public apology, as did representatives of the churches who had run them. A 'truth and reconciliation' commission was established to assess the enormous psychological and cultural damage done, and millions of pounds in compensation has been paid to those who attended. The legacy of the residential system is an appalling one. In their aim of separating native children from their communities, the schools were very successful; but they were far less so when it came to 'assimilation'. Graduates often found themselves unable to fit in, either back at home or elsewhere, and a wide range of social and psychological problems became commonplace: post-traumatic stress disorder, criminality, alcohol and drug abuse, depression.

Although what happened to young native Canadians has been described as 'cultural genocide', the residential schools did not succeed in eradicating the traditions of indigenous people. Those traditions survived. And they did so, in part, thanks to the tenacity and articulacy of campaigners like François Paulette, who have helped to bring the concerns of Canada's First Nations to the fore. But François's words troubled me. His verdict on 'white people' sounded like a judgement that could not be overturned; it was a sweeping, cultural indictment. And that was hardly surprising. The Dene's relationship with the land has evolved over countless generations, and is passed down through stories and protocols. But these are culturally exclusive, and the ways of thinking they engender cannot be recreated from the outside. The understanding of the Dene is, for the rest of us, largely inaccessible. So if François Paulette is right – if European cultures have entirely lost the traditions by which a relationship with the land is maintained, are we then destined to be estranged from our places? Can we never truly be at home?

An answer to these questions was offered to me by Jacques Van Pelt, whom I met, so I thought, to talk about pelicans. This stretch of the Slave River is the northernmost breeding ground of the American white pelican. Their nesting sites are concentrated on the rocky islands of Mountain Portage Rapids, but I had seen them in the air, soaring like ghosts above the town. There are few people who have spent as much time observing, recording and studying these birds as Jacques Van Pelt. But on the day I met him, Jacques wasn't much interested in talking about pelicans, at least not in the way I had expected. Instead, he wanted to talk about connections.

Jacques came to the north in 1959 and moved to Fort Smith the following year. He was employed to work across the northern territories on community development projects for the government. Later, he and his wife ran a tourism company, taking visitors on excursions down the river and out on the land. When we met for the first time, Jacques greeted me with a hug and called me 'Brother Malachy'. He moved laboriously, but his mind was quick. He talked with enthusiasm and excitement, though with no clear train of thought. Some of his words made me wince, reminiscent as they were of New Age platitudes. He referred to 'the communion of people and nature', and advised that '"I" must become "we"'.

Jacques spoke often of circles, of how indigenous people had built circular homes rather than straight-sided ones. They'd understood the significance of the shape, he said, and recognised its physical and metaphorical strengths. The sixtieth parallel excited him for the same reason; it connected people and places. My conversation with Jacques also seemed to turn in circles. During the hours I spent with him we returned again and again to his vision of nature's 'connectedness' and 'togetherness'. When he did speak about pelicans it was to try and explain to me what these birds had taught him. Over the past few decades, Jacques had spent innumerable hours observing the Slave River pelicans, counting them, getting to know them and warning others about the fragility of their population. He had walked and kayaked throughout the region, often for weeks at a time. He had brought visitors to see this place that he loved, and to share it with them. And though he could no longer do these things, though his back was bent and his joints stiff and sore, he still coursed with a kind of static energy and a relentless positivity. And the time he'd spent with the birds, his time on the river and in the forest, were somehow at the core of the person he'd become.

I was drawn to Jacques, to his openness and generosity, and to the joy that seemed to brim up inside of him as he spoke. But the cynic in me recoiled. As I listened, I found it

hard to hold on to his vision of the world. I felt I was grasping at water, clutching at something that was vivid and alive,
but which slipped through my hands as I tried to close them
around it. And yet I couldn't brush off his words. I couldn't
ignore the feeling that I had missed some fundamental point,
something truly important that I'd not been able, or perhaps
willing, to comprehend.

It was not until later that it struck me: behind the
spiritualised language, behind the platitudes and the positivity, Jacques' lesson was simple. What mattered was not
understanding, exactly. One could never, just by looking or
thinking harder, fully comprehend the connections between
your own body and the pelicans on the river, or the river
itself. The extent of those connections was beyond understanding. What was important, rather, was recognition.

In *A Sand County Almanac*, Aldo Leopold wrote of a
'land community', encompassing the entire biosphere of a
given place. This land community is not separate from, nor
exactly additional to the human community; both are part
of each other. What he described does not require any kind
of spiritual insight or enlightenment to see, merely a certain
awareness of reality. The food we eat is born of the earth
and is fed by the lives of other organisms, by the sun that
warms us and by the water that quenches our thirst. We are
joined in a myriad of ways to the world around us. These
relationships are matters of fact, and they exist at every level
from the atomic to the macroecological.

Jacques' vision of connectedness was an active recognition of the interdependence of things. It was, in a sense,
the most banal and commonplace of understandings, a
conscious acceptance of what ought to be obvious. And yet
today, like the very idea of community, that act of knowing
feels radical. What Jacques was advocating was a kind of
placefulness: an engagement with place that is united with
and strengthened by our engagement with people. No one

can disconnect themselves entirely from the world; we are all dependent, always. But if we fail to recognise and to consciously reassert these connections and this dependence, if we fail to build placefulness and community, then we risk being homeless. And that is no kind of freedom at all.

*

After the storm, Sam Stokell and Shawn Bell, housemates and journalists at the town's paper, took pity on me and invited me to camp in their basement, which was drier than my spot beneath the pines. They looked after me, and supplied me with good food and good company. Then, on my last day in Fort Smith, and with the clouds departed, they took me to see the river.

Inside the car, the radio demanded our attention. A story about North America's growing Prozac addiction rolled into a feature on cocaine and its impact on the short-term memory of slugs. Inside the car, Sam, Shawn and I listened, and were finally unable to suppress our laughter.

Outside, a trail of dust followed us along the gravel road out of town. We turned left on the track that leads east towards the river, drove a little further, then stopped and cut the engine. Quietness fell upon us and we emerged into a sharp heat, held immobile by the trees. A steep trail descended from the road, and together we clambered down through the forest, led onward by the sound of the water. At the bottom of the slope the track opened out at the riverbank, a sand and mud beach littered with dead trees and scattered wood of all sizes. Here the river was perhaps a quarter of a mile across, and a thick, soupy brown.

Together we walked upstream towards Mountain Portage Rapids, the clamour increasing with every step. At the lower end of the rapids we gathered wood – lifting and turning the smaller pieces, collecting those that were dry – and arranged them in a sheltered spot on the pink granite

bank. Beside us was the constant rush of the water, bound for the north. Surging white, the river twisted in upon itself in eddies and whirlpools, piling up in unbreaking waves. It was a ceaseless, tumultuous motion that was both hypnotic and unnerving. I found it hard to look away.

Crouching over the wood pile we tried to light our fire. Sam and I held the matches close in among the bark and twigs, hoping they would catch. A flame. Some smoke. Then nothing. Again. After several attempts, the flakes of bark began to crackle and a gasp of light leapt among the sticks. We stood back and watched as it spread, and smoke lifted from the pile of wood, palling skyward. The fire raged into itself and we retreated, lying out in the sunshine, waiting for it to settle.

Once the flames had sunk a little, the three of us gathered around the blaze. We skewered hotdogs with flimsy green sticks twisted from the forest's edge and laid them out on an improvised grill, the smoke swirling up from the fire and into our eyes and lungs. As we coughed and choked, the meat cooked with varying degrees of failure, until eventually each of us had eaten enough to feel satisfied, and we abandoned our barbecue for the rocks up above.

Two young pelicans paddled close to shore, and out in the river, amid the rocks and rushing water, were many others. Most were settled on the granite islands where they breed; some were fishing, holding themselves steady in the tumbling river, dipping their heads beneath the surface. Above us were more, heavy-bellied like seaplanes, with great yellow bills thrust out in front. The wings, pure white at rest, showed a dark edge as they lifted themselves skyward. Enormous and unwieldy on land, in flight they become graceful, gliding in the warm air with the black of their wings blinking as they fly. In a few months these birds would travel south to rivers and lakes around the Gulf of Mexico, returning again the next spring. Always they know when to move and when to stop moving.

I thought of Ib then, and of Jacques, who had come to Fort Smith and stayed, and of Sam and Shawn, who were here temporarily, to work, and then to move on to somewhere else. How can we know, I wondered, when we have found our place in the world? How can we know when we ought to cease our wandering?

The sky was a cavernous blue, without clouds, and the breeze rising from the river was just enough to keep the mosquitoes at bay. A raven explored the fire's edge looking for scraps of sausage, its silent mouth gaping wide in the heat of the day. On the baking pink rocks beside the river, the three of us sprawled happily out and closed our eyes. The smell of the fire was in our nostrils and our heads were filled with the roar and hush of the rapids.

ALASKA
back to nature

The rain was not falling, exactly, but clinging to the air, as though in expectation of a fall. A haze of grey evening mizzle softened the street, washing all memory of warmth away. I sat alone, looking out through the window of a café, my fingers cradling a heavy caribou burger. I was the only customer. Outside, crowds of elderly men and women trudged up and down Fourth Avenue, wrapped in dark waterproofs, their hoods raised like congregations of monks all bowed against the unholy elements.

Seward's small-boat harbour was filling up with cruise ships and charter vessels, from which these sodden swarms were emerging. All along this part of the avenue were restaurants, souvenir shops and businesses flogging fishing and wildlife trips. Most of the buildings strove towards a kind of small town quaintness, but did not succeed. They seemed too desperate, too insistent, to be anything other than what they were: tourist bait.

The door opened and cold air poured through, shrinking the room. A gaggle of damp children and parents followed the draught in towards the counter, chattering to each other. I hauled my coat up around my shoulders and continued to chew at the thick slab of bread and meat in front of me.

All around Resurrection Bay, the mountains were swaddled in cloud, almost hidden and yet as present and as dominating as if they'd been standing among the shops and cafés. The mountains were the backdrop to everything here,

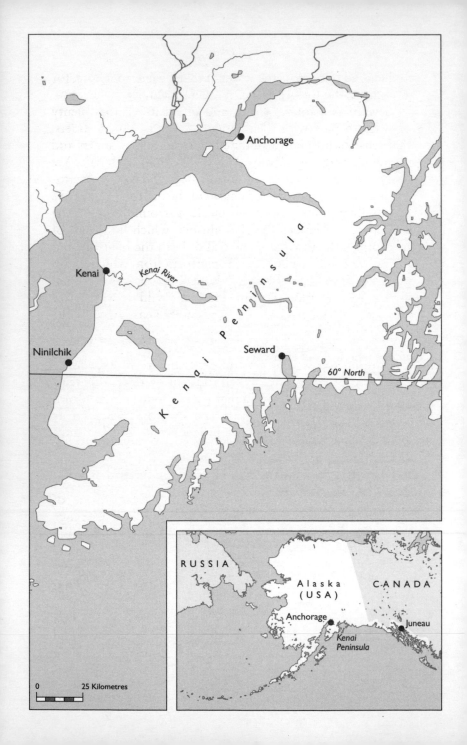

Anchorage

Kenai

Kenai River

Ninilchik

Seward

K e n a i   P e n i n s u l a

60° North

0   25 Kilometres

RUSSIA

A l a s k a
(USA)

CANADA

Anchorage

*Kenai
Peninsula*

Juneau

and I gazed out across the water at them, eager to ignore, for a moment, the foreground of noise and activity.

Seward is a tourist town, and offers its visitors plenty of ways to part with their money. There is, on its streets, that sense of hospitality polluted by retail, where smiles and warm greetings feel always like the foreplay to a sale. Yet despite the proliferation of souvenir stalls and nice-places-to-eat, and despite the affected charm of the old town, Seward's main selling point is not itself but its surroundings. On the east coast of Alaska's Kenai Peninsula, which lies south of Anchorage, the town is at the end of both the highway and the railway, and is a convenient platform from which to dip one's toes into 'the wilderness'. Both Kenai Fjords National Park and the Alaska Maritime National Wildlife Refuge are close by; forests, glaciers and fjords are all easily accessible. Like many other such towns, Seward has become what it is because of its proximity to what it is not.

Without doubt, the most effort-free way to experience these wild places is to be taken to them by boat. Day-trips and mini-cruises in the national park abound, each promising views of wildlife – sea otters, sea lions, whales – as well as lunch stops on remote beaches and empty islands, and a chance to see the Alaska that lies beyond the tarmac. Each morning, beneath heavy clouds, I watched the flotilla of tour boats pushing southwards through the bay, their onboard guides audible even from shore, the crackle of loudspeakers drifting over the still water. It was a strange sight, this armada, with its cargo of expectant tourists, eager to glimpse something that perhaps even they could not quite specify. For what was this thing that drew them out there? What was it that took them north in the first place? What exactly did they hope to find?

It is said that Vitus Bering, who was not quite the first European to reach Alaska, but who thought that he was and is widely remembered as such, was not impressed by what he saw. Suffering, perhaps, from the stifling melancholy of one who does not expect to see his home again, and from the unknown malaise that soon would kill him and prove his fears well-founded, the Dane looked upon this place 'indifferently and without particular pleasure'. This was his second voyage to the Russian far east, in the service of the imperial powers in St Petersburg, and in the summer of 1741 his ship, the *St Peter*, finally reached the North American continent. According to Georg Steller, the German naturalist on board, their captain did not rejoice at his discovery, but instead 'in our very midst shrugged his shoulders while gazing at the land'. The crew were fools, Bering declared, 'full of expectations like pregnant windbags!' They 'do not consider . . . how far we are from home, and what accidents may yet happen.'

The *St Peter* anchored on 20 July, near what is now called Kayak Island, in the Gulf of Alaska, five degrees east of Seward and only a couple of miles from the sixtieth parallel. Steller spent the few hours he was granted ashore breathlessly exploring the island, gathering new plant species and making notes on the native human inhabitants, half intoxicated by the delight of discovery.

Bering, in contrast, did not even bother to disembark. In this place that so thrilled and enthralled the scientist, the captain had little interest. Instead, he seemed haunted by the fear of what lay ahead, and anxious to escape before a possible change in the weather. On the morning after their arrival, before his crew had even had time to fully replenish the ship's fresh water supplies, Bering announced that they were to sail westward again for Kamchatka. Those who protested the decision were ignored, and the *St Peter* that day began its journey back to Russia. The captain, along with thirty of his seventy-six-strong crew, did not survive the crossing.

The land Bering found that summer was a place thus far untroubled by the careless hands of colonists, traders and professional adventurers. It was a place of immense forests and towering mountains; of fish-filled rivers and wing-beaten skies; of coastal waters crowded with sea otters, fur seals and whales; of plenitude and abundance; of a natural wealth that seemed, at first, boundless. And though like others after him Bering was unable to see it, Alaska was a place of dazzling, exhilarating potential.

The men and women who crowded onto these tour boats every morning, and who chugged out of the bay and then back again at night, were looking for what Steller saw. They were hunting for that place of abundance and boundlessness which greeted the very first arrivals in Alaska. They were trying, in some curious way, to go back in time. I found myself torn. I wanted to join one of these tours, to sail away from the town and see for myself the wildlife and the wilderness, and then to return to Seward in the evening, to a café meal and the relative comfort of my sleeping bag and tent. But something held me back, and for some days I struggled to reconcile my feelings. What troubled me most, I think, was the idea – advertised incessantly – that out there somewhere was the real Alaska, and what was here was something else, quite different. Those well-waterproofed tourists had been promised a journey into another world, and yet it seemed to me that that world was made impossible by their very presence within it. For what those passengers were being promised was their own absence, and that is something we can only imagine. Perhaps I was wrong, but I thought I could see disappointment in those faces as they disembarked and spread out among the town's restaurants and hotels in the evening.

On my final night in Seward I sat beside the shore, looking southwards across the bay, a cheese sandwich clutched in my hand. That afternoon, the sky had been a wide palette of greys, but the clouds were dispersing as the light diminished. I was close to moving on when I saw it, and when I did I almost laughed. Down in the water, just a few metres away, was a sea otter – pale-faced and as sleek as polished walnut. I watched it, amazed. I saw it dive, then resurface, oblivious to or unconcerned by my presence. It lay there, sprawled on its back, one foot then the other breaking the surface, then sinking again. The otter had caught what looked like a crab, and I could hear the crunch of its teeth against the shell. It clung on, sometimes knocked off balance by the swell, but each time rolling back into position, like a kayaker.

I sat for ten minutes or more and I could see, or thought I could see, the pleasure it found in its meal, the catlike satisfaction on its face. And when, moments later, a sea lion porpoised its way past the otter, I did laugh. I hadn't needed to leave town. The other world had found me.

*

'This is about as far from pristine Alaskan fishing as you can get', said Jeff, from the other side of the boat. I smiled back. 'That's okay,' I said, and nodded. And it was okay. Like many anglers, I had dreamed about coming to this place for so long that I wasn't going to let my enjoyment be dimmed by the fact that I wasn't there alone. I felt lucky, and perhaps even a little smug. I certainly did not feel disappointed.

The Kenai River runs from Kenai Lake in the centre of the peninsula to Cook Inlet, eighty miles to the west. It is a beautiful river – milky blue and sun splashed – and extremely popular with fishermen and seekers of white water. We had launched our boat (a 'cataraft', in fact: a metal frame held between two inflatable tubes, with a pair of seats on either side and another perched in the centre for the oarsman) at Cooper Landing, just below Kenai Lake, and were drifting downstream in search of fish. We shared the river with other anglers, in boats and on the shore, as well as with tour groups chasing rapids. In addition to these mostly quiet companions was the Sterling Highway, which ran alongside the upper stretch of the river. And though it may not be the busiest of roads, the hum of traffic was nevertheless a continuous accompaniment to the sighing of the water.

But fishing has a way of blocking out those things you wish to ignore; it has a way of disguising what needs to be hidden. The water around us swelled in our eyes and ears until it filled us, like a daydream or a vision. We were not alone, but we could just as well have been. Around us was forest, and beyond, snow-smeared slopes. Above the water, swallows danced like butterflies; and higher, a bald eagle cruised, as though following the same unquenchable current as the boat. All about us was the white noise of air and water, while beneath, the river flexed and writhed like a muscle.

We floated onward, our eyes wandering from the rod tips to the mountains around us. Slow drifts gave way to faster, shallower water, then deep, swirling pools. Mike, who held the oars, kept us as close to the 'good water' as he could, letting us know whenever he felt optimistic, or whenever we approached a likely spot. We cast, letting the heavy flies sink, then working them along the bottom, each retrieve imbued with hope and a renewed vision of the phantom trout below. Time and again we would approach those spots, those places of expectation. The water would move in the right way around the rocks; our eyes and fingers would focus on what could not be seen; every part of us would be ready for that moment when, as Ted Hughes wrote, 'the whole river hauls'. And then we were past. The boat would slip onwards and carry us away, and we would breathe comfortably again.

I have often thought that fishing brings a changed relationship with time. That mix of concentration and expectation, that sharpened gaze at float or fly, expands the present in every direction. Unlike the hill, in Shetland, where time contracts, out on the water it balloons. It admits more detail and swells, towards a prodigious breadth. Connected to an unseen world, the angler watches and waits with something more than patience. Lightheaded, both utterly present and absent at once, all attention is there, where air meets water. Vision and touch become entwined. Time extends, as it does in the moment of an accident, and eventually, as Norman Maclean wrote, 'all things merge into one'.

To fish is to be held in the heart of a stillness in which nothing is still. It is to wait patiently for a time that has already been imagined, yet which may never come. It is to live between tenses, in the anticipation of a perfect present. It is to be tangled in three time zones at once. As I fish – as I wait for the future to grab hold – I cannot help but be carried back to other days and other places. I am brought home, to cool, summer evenings in Shetland, where bright trout dash and tremor in black, peaty lochs. And further, to my first encounters with the water, in streams and ponds in Sussex, where I threw my cork floats and safety-pin hooks, hopeless but filled with hope. And then, again, to that warm, August day, when my father left me at the lakeside and never came back, when I lost so many things at once that I had never even dreamed of losing. All of this is held in the act of cast and retrieve, cast and retrieve.

Jeff and I first met in the early weeks of 2002. We were exchange students then, living for half a year in Copenhagen, studying at the city's university. We were taking Danish language lessons weekly, and one evening found ourselves sitting side by side in class. We did not immediately get along. Both of us were quiet, with a youthful inflexibility. We thought we understood things that neither of us truly did, and we had drawn our understandings from quite different directions. Our views, on politics in particular, were very far apart. On our first meeting I offended Jeff with an offhand comment about his country's president, and that could easily have been the end of it. We need never have spoken again. But we did – first out of politeness, and then from a mutual respect. Finally, we spoke for pleasure. Of all the people I met in that city, he is the only one with whom I am still in contact. We became friends, hesitantly, and we remained friends.

After university, Jeff moved to Alaska with his wife, who is from the state, and later they started a family. He had long dreamed of living in the north, and she wanted to come home. Since then, we had met only once, very briefly, in Shetland. So our friendship, by the time I visited, was concentrated in a time that had passed. The months we had spent together seemed a long distance away, and our communication in the intervening years had been brief and occasional, and in writing only. It had left an awkwardness, of which we both were aware, though neither mentioned it. But in the boat, connected to the water, that awkwardness drifted away. The space between past and present dissolved and faded into nothing. The river held us together.

There are many times in my life that I remember with longing. Some of them are clear to me now – I can see them, hear them, smell them – but they are never clear enough. I can hear the swishing of my father's corduroy trousers as we walked together; I can feel the pace and weight of his step. But I can no longer remember the sound of his voice. It is lost, and I cannot bring it back. Some nights I lie awake, gripped by a hollow, crushing nostalgia. Some days the desire to go backwards, to another time or place, is so strong that I am almost dazzled by tears. There are people whom I miss. There are places I have not seen in many months or years, but which are as plain to me now as if I left them only yesterday. They are as much a part of my present as the trees and the water, and the fish that I cannot see.

We look back, I think, towards times when we were not looking back. We are nostalgic for the absence of nostalgia. We long for those moments when we were not longing for what we could not have. We are restless to find rest. At home, beneath skies that I have known for most of my life, I still think of other places where I have lived – of Fair Isle and Prague and Copenhagen and Sussex – and I feel an aching, unquenchable homesickness. That feeling is related but not identical to the one that accompanied me through my teenage years. It is less hopeless, more inevitable. I think of all that cannot be brought back – a storm of pleasures, gone – and I curse my memories, just as I curse the lack of them.

Nostalgia was first recognised by Swiss doctors in the late seventeenth century. An illness primarily affecting soldiers at war, it was, literally, home-sickness, from the Greek *nósto*: to return home. For almost 200 years the disease – which was characterised not just by intense longing but also anxiety, lack of appetite, fainting, stomach pains and in the worst cases even death – was considered a serious physical ailment. The only cure for the most severely afflicted was to go back to that longed-for place. Yet this sickness is not exclusive to humans. Nostalgia is not our longing alone. It would be fair, indeed, to see homesickness as the crucial force that brings life to the Kenai, to Alaska, and to this whole corner of the continent. For what else, in truth, could you call that instinct – that desperate, anadromous urge – that pulls salmon back into this river, and to thousands of other rivers like it? What else could it be that brings those fish home, but an awesome and ultimately fatal nostalgia?

Around the 10th of June each year, the first sockeye or red salmon enter the Kenai from the sea. This particular run of fish are heading for a tributary called the Russian River. They are predictable both in their timing and their destination. Earlier, from the middle of May, the first king salmon, or chinook, climbed the river. Another run of kings will come in early July, and another of reds a few days later. In addition to these there will be two runs of coho or silver salmon – one in August, one in September – and finally, every second year, there will be pink salmon from late July through August. These fish are the lifeblood of the river. They are, indeed, the lifeblood of the whole Pacific Northwest. In extraordinary, incomprehensible numbers the salmon return to those places where they were born. In the same shallows and gravel beds from which they first emerged, thousands, then millions of fish come together to spawn. Then they will die. Great writhing masses of these creatures, increasingly grotesque as the end approaches – their skin discoloured and peeling, their flesh already rotting on the bone – will reach a place and then stop. This is their home, from where they can neither go on or go back. And by stopping there, by dying, they become in turn a part of the place itself. The flood of protein from their decaying bodies feeds everything, directly or indirectly, from the bears and eagles to the soil and the trees, and the next generation of salmon. It will feed, too, a great many people.

I had heard about the crowds that congregated on this river in summer and autumn. I had seen photographs too. But still I wasn't prepared for the sight that met us as we drifted down beneath the highway bridge and past the confluence of the Kenai and the Russian, where the sockeye fishermen were congregated. It was surreal and unsettling; like a carnival, at once horrifying and hilarious. A line of anglers filled the southern bank of the river, opposite the road. They stood perhaps two or three metres apart, like a picket fence, stretched as far as we could see. Along the bank only the occasional splash of a hooked salmon disturbed the remarkable, rhythmic order of it all.

Such is the quantity of fish moving through the river during these runs that even this extraordinary pressure from anglers is not sufficient to affect population levels. Enough salmon will pass through this barrier of people to maintain present numbers and ensure healthy runs in future years. And despite the United States' reputation for relaxed attitudes towards conservation and sustainability, populations here are well monitored and restrictions strongly enforced. Any notable fall in fish numbers would be followed by reduced catch limits. In this state at least, the notion of salmon as a shared resource, worthy of protection, is a powerful one.

The three of us floated through the middle of this strange gathering, then hauled the raft up on the north bank a little further downstream, where the crowds were not so dense. We found our own spots on a narrow branch of the river and began to cast, the water flowing in one direction, the fish in the other. Time resumed its little games. Everything moved. Nothing was still.

*

Two days later, and a few miles north of Seward, I stopped in a car park at the trailhead for Grayling Lake. There were no other vehicles there, but the highway was close behind and the town not far away. The sky was overcast and a light smirr thickened the air. Scanning the last few entries in the visitors' book I was disheartened. 'No fish.' 'No fish.' 'No fish.' I considered moving on and trying somewhere else, but the afternoon was already half complete and my enthusiasm was beginning to wane. Plus, it was grayling I was after, and if I was going to catch one anywhere it would be here. I signed my name, wrote down the date and time of my arrival (so that potential rescuers would have my details, should I go missing) and unpacked my things from the truck.

Stepping off the gravel and on to the trail, it seemed a line was crossed. Or perhaps it would be more accurate to say that some kind of balance was overturned. A car park in Alaska is not everyone's idea of civilisation, and a signposted trail might not qualify as wilderness. But there was a change – a shift from one side of that scale to the other – and I felt the change inside me as fear.

One of the marks of civilisation, perhaps, is the uncontested place of human beings at the top of the food chain. Where competitors have not been entirely wiped out, as in Britain, they have at least been heavily suppressed, or banished to reserves and shrinking pockets of wild land. But in Alaska it is people who live in pockets, towns and villages connected by thin ribbons of road. Despite the steady encroachment of industry, particularly oil and tourism, the vast bulk of the state is completely undeveloped. Even the Kenai Peninsula, which attracts large numbers of visitors, is dominated by a national park, a national forest, a 'state wilderness park', 'wilderness areas' and the Kenai National Wildlife Refuge, a two million acre protected region, established by Franklin Roosevelt in 1941. Step outside the town in Alaska – step off the road or away from the car park – and the rules of civilisation no longer apply.

As I took those first steps on the trail and into the forest, the fear rose quickly in my throat. Moving between thick, new-growth trees, with visibility down almost to zero, I could feel my heart beat harder. My fear was complicated and confusing, but as I walked the thump in my chest found its focus in one simple word: bear.

With fishing rod, tackle bag and waders in my hand, I felt clumsy and vulnerable, and I stopped almost immediately to rearrange my luggage. The pair of waders was flung over my shoulder together with the bag. In one hand I held the fishing rod, and in the other I gripped my fingers around a canister of bear spray just inside my jacket pocket. I checked that I could remove it easily and quickly; I set my index finger inside the looped safety catch; I focused my eyes and ears on the forest.

Pepper spray is pretty much the last resort when faced with a brown bear. Ineffective at a distance of more than a few metres, it is useful only when you are being charged. And if you are being charged by an animal that can be more than eight feet tall when standing, 600kg in weight, and which can run as fast as a horse, it is important that the spray is successful. If it's not, your only possible chance of escape is to play dead and hope the bear loses interest. If you're lucky it might paw you for a moment, perhaps breaking your limbs in the process. If you're not lucky, you won't have to pretend to be dead very long. In the few weeks I spent in Alaska, two people were mauled by brown bears. Neither attack was fatal, fortunately, but both left the victims – in one case a workman up north, in the other a cyclist in Anchorage – in hospital.

The best way to avoid such an attack, I was told – other than to remain indoors at all times – is to be noisy. Bears become angry when they're surprised or threatened, and as a rule they will stay away from people, given the opportunity. Many hikers wear a bell to alert animals to their approach; others simply shout or sing as they go. Somehow it feels odd to confront your fears in this way, to let the danger know you are coming. I wanted to sneak through the trees unnoticed as well as unscathed, but I followed the advice I had been given, and I tried to sing.

As the trail rose into old-growth forest, and the sound of the highway was lost behind me, I could feel the presence of the bear, like a ghost among the trees. The space was haunted by it, as was I. Beneath the canopy of leaves, a whole array of spirits seemed to dwell. Invisible insects clouded my face and birds moved unseen above; even the trees themselves were somehow not unmoved by my steps. The whole forest seemed aware, and held me with an attention that was mirrored in my own vigilance.

The singing didn't last for long. Somehow no words felt right, and the sound of my voice was alien and intrusive. My mouth became dry and useless, and I took instead to humming, both random tunes and familiar melodies – some of them ludicrously out of place, yet still strangely comforting.

I imagined myself from the outside: a man alone, walking fearfully through an Alaskan forest, laden with fishing tackle, humming 'Mr Tambourine Man' as loudly as he could manage. Surely a bear would be more likely to laugh than to attack.

After ten minutes or so of hiking, something made me pause and turn my head. I stood still and listened. My breath was loud and my heart thumping. But another sound, too, broke the forest's silence. A rhythmic pounding like feet or paws, running in my direction. I turned to where the noise came from, and looked out among the trees. It can have been a few seconds only between hearing the animal and seeing it coming towards me, but in that brief time I had imagined, in detail, what was to come. The beat of my pulse had fallen in time with the thud of the four approaching feet. The spray had been lifted from my pocket and gripped tightly around the top. I had steadied myself in anticipation and in regret. And then, there it was.

Had I been given a chance to identify this animal before it came into sight, I would have needed a great many tries before guessing correctly. A charging bear might well have been unlikely, but a big, bounding Labrador with its tongue hanging out seemed equally so. At that particular moment I was not capable of laughter, but if I had been I would have doubled up and fallen to my knees.

The dog had a name tag but no name, only a phone number scratched into one side of the metal label. I waited for it to leave, giving vague commands and gesturing back to where it had come from. But there was no one around and the dog stood looking at me, apparently urging me to go on. Having longed for a walking companion, I had accidentally found one, and so the pair of us turned and continued on the trail, he following, then running ahead, stopping every few metres to sniff at something – a tree or invisible marker at the trailside. Watching him run, then turn, then sniff, then listen, then run again, I realised just how illiterate I was in that place. The forest is filled with signs, but I couldn't read them. There was a language there, a complex vocabulary of which I was barely even conscious, and which I couldn't hope to understand or translate. Clutching the spray can in my hand and humming like a fool, I was helpless: as stupid as a bear in a bookshop.

People who encounter animals in the wild often talk about glimpsing a kind of intelligence, an innate wisdom, in the eyes that return their stare. But that story can be turned around; those eyes can be mirrors. For what we recognise in that strange gaze, I think, is our own stupidity. Faced with a creature that knows itself and its place so completely, that understands its own purpose and needs without the burden of doubt, we see in an instant just how ignorant we are. Both animal and human will be filled with questions during such an encounter, but only the animal will find satisfactory answers.

This is the root of my fear: this educated ignorance, this absence of understanding. Bombarded with information that I couldn't interpret, I felt anxious and overwhelmed. My eyes were of limited help in the shadows of the forest; my hearing is undeveloped and my nose almost useless. With such inadequate senses I was at risk, always, of being surprised. And as my new-found friend had proved, even a creature that wanted to get noticed could catch me unawares. What I had to rely on were my thoughts – which in a place such as that were more crippling than comforting – and my instincts.

Carl Jung believed that, in our contact with the natural world, it is our reliance on language that puts us most at a disadvantage. 'Man's advance towards the Logos was a great achievement,' he wrote, 'but he must pay for it with a loss of instinct and loss of reality.' The result of 'our submission to the tyranny of words' is that 'the conscious mind becomes more and more the victim of its own discriminating activity'. Faced with the unfamiliar, we struggle to understand. Our map through the world – language – can no longer guide us. Instead it creates a distance between ourselves and that which we observe, as well as that which observes us. Like the bright, sweet apple upon the Tree of Knowledge, word divides us from world. It is not Paradise that is lost, it is us. I felt fear, then, and I hated it. I hated it for everything it said about me. There in the forest a deep conflict emerged, between my desire to flee from human places and my desire – increasingly acute – to flee from that place. I was drawn in and repelled at once; I was fascinated and afraid. The wilderness was as much within me as I was within it.

Eventually the nameless dog and I reached the lake, which emerged from the forest like an afterthought, or a clarification of something previously said. It had taken much longer than I'd expected to reach the end of the trail – perhaps 35 minutes or more, though it was hard to keep track of time – but I was relieved to see the water, and relieved to be able to stop. There was a good breeze coming down the lake and rain was falling steadily, dimpling the surface. Trees crowded almost to the water's edge, and through the fog bruised clouds bumbled down from the mountains above. The air was like gauze, greyed by rain.

I set up the rod and tied on a small, dark fly, rubbing grease into its feathers to make it float. I had no particular idea what a grayling might like, but that one seemed worth a shot. I waded in up to my middle and began to cast, watching the fly as it perched on the water. I put to the back of my mind the list of dispiriting comments I'd read in the visitors' book. I persevered. After fifteen minutes or so, when the fly had begun to sink, there was a twitch on the line, then another twitch on the next cast. Then nothing. I stepped out and walked a few metres further up the bank, then cast again, moving back over the same water. The rain was steady, but I no longer noticed it. A cast. Another cast. Then a hesitation. The line tripped as I tried to retrieve. A stop. I pulled again. Once. Twice. On the second pull the line pulled back. I lifted the rod and there was the fish. It splashed against the surface, the silver back and tall dorsal fin appeared. My first ever grayling.

Twenty minutes later there was another stop. A tug. I retrieved again and the fish was on, bigger this time. It put up a stronger fight. The line shook, jerked and wrenched in staccato shivers. A jagging in the water, a burst to one side and a deeper pull. Then a splash that tore through the silence like a gunshot, and that beautiful, perfect dorsal fin in the air. I killed this one, then gutted it. I held the fish in my right hand and the knife in my left, slicing first across the neck, then drawing the blade up through the belly, pulling the insides out and letting them slip back into the water. I cut the head and tail off and dropped them, watched them sink, then wrapped the fish up and put it away. I washed my hands in the lake.

With that smell on my fingers and the fish in my bag I felt nervous again, and decided to go. I'd done what I came to do and was happy to leave the place behind. I packed my things away and arranged the waders over my shoulder so I could walk comfortably with the spray in my right hand, and I set off. Then I stopped. Just a few metres from where I'd been standing was something I'd not noticed before, something I didn't see when I first arrived. On the ground, almost hidden among thick bushes, was a kind of hollow, a space where the plants had all been flattened and crushed. Twigs were broken, and tufts of brown fur lay all around. There was an odd smell, too: thick and oily, like lanolin. Something had been lying here very recently.

In hindsight I wish I'd bent down to pick up a tuft of fur and bring it back with me, to be sure: was it a bear or was it a moose? But I didn't even think of it. Panic surged through me and I straightened, grabbed my things and went, without looking back. The dog with no name had long since abandoned me, and I walked to the car alone, wanting but not wanting to run, wishing for the trail to be over. It seemed to take hours, and that fear, that stupid, ignorant fear, never left me until I'd reached the car park and signed out. And there, in the visitor's book, I saw something else I had not noticed before. Three days earlier, someone had written the following words: 'Saw a large brown bear by the lake'. Had I seen those words when I first arrived I would never have set off. I am glad that I didn't see them.

That night, I took the fish from my bag, sliced the flesh, and rubbed salt and pepper into it. I fried it in butter, the skin crackling and tightening against the heat. Then I tasted the lake again.

*

I spent much of my time in Alaska driving. In an old red pickup I'd borrowed from Jeff, I roamed the Kenai Peninsula, following the highway from Anchorage to Seward to Homer and back again. With my rucksack, tent and sleeping bag piled up on the back seat, I felt a kind of freedom that pulled me onward down those winding roads. I followed mobile homes or 'recreational vehicles' (RVs) the size of coaches, overtaking no one. Once, on my brother's birthday, I drove nearly two hours out of my way in search of a payphone to call him, then drove back again, enjoying each of those extra miles. Mountains gathered around me like spectators, looming over the road. Here was a place where it was easy to feel small.

On a still evening, just outside the village of Moose Pass, I drove beside a roadside pool where, unconcerned by the traffic, a buck moose stood knee-deep in the water. He was enormous – two metres tall at the shoulders – and almost comical, like a cow on stilts. His strange, broad antlers seemed not majestic, like a stag, but fabulous nonetheless. Seated in that sealed-off little world, I rumbled around the peninsula, stopping when I felt like stopping. I would camp at night, though I never slept well. In those midsummer days, darkness didn't come, and I would doze on and off in the bright tent. Sometimes I would open my eyes, disorientated, unable to tell what time it might be, and only the silence from the road nearby would suggest that morning was still hours away.

The landscape was always astonishing. Sometimes it was hard to concentrate on the road, so beautiful was the world beyond the bitumen. Blue glacial rivers spilled through stony valleys, with white-capped peaks all around. Silvery lakes appeared, then were gone – rumours among the trees. Cottonwood seeds wisped through the air like flurries of summer snow. The sky folded and unfolded. The land invited both eye and mind. But all over the peninsula, among the pink and purple flowers at the roadside, among the trees and tall bushes, among the rivers, streams and lakes, there were signs: 'Private property', 'Keep out', 'No trespassing'. There were chains slung over driveways and roads; there were padlocks and high fences; there were lines that couldn't be crossed.

It's difficult to explain precisely why these signs offended me. Perhaps because I live in a country that does not have trespassing laws. Or perhaps because there is something about this place in particular, something about its vastness, its wildness and its wonder that makes the idea of property and of exclusion seem foreign. I thought back to Greenland, where land cannot be privately owned, and where the relationship between people and place is founded on the idea of use and of community. I thought of how appropriate that seemed, and of how inappropriate these signs felt. 'Keep out', they said. To which I responded, from inside the truck, with two equally offensive words.

THE NEW YORKER

- [ ] 23 issues for just $3.49 an issue
- [ ] I prefer 47 issues for $2.99 per issue

Subscribe and save up to 66% off the cover price.

Plus get a free notebook with your paid subscription.

Name _____ PLEASE PRINT

Address _____ Apt. _____

City _____ State _____ Zip _____

E-mail _____

Bonus: *To get 5 additional issues FREE, order at newyorker.com/go/fiveissues3*

- [ ] Payment enclosed   - [ ] Please bill me

Order now at:
newyorker.com/go/fiveissues3

NYRJ9DS5L

BUSINESS REPLY MAIL

FIRST-CLASS MAIL   PERMIT NO. 107   BOONE IA

POSTAGE WILL BE PAID BY ADDRESSEE

THE
NEW YORKER

PO BOX 37617
BOONE, IA 50037-2617

In Alaska, as in the United States as a whole, the relationship between people and the land, particularly people and 'wilderness', is fraught with historical and cultural baggage. The land is a place to be exploited and to be preserved; it represents both the country's past and its future; it is fragile and it is dominating. Here too, the notion of a frontier, with all of that word's emotive implications, remains strong, and brings its own tight bundle of conflicts and contradictions. Not least over the issue of ownership.

Offensive though these signs appeared to me, private land ownership is in fact not the norm here, as it is elsewhere in the US. The vast majority of Alaskan land is owned, in one way or another, by the state or federal government, and the extent to which they allow development – whether it be large-scale mining or the building of cabins and homesteads – is understandably controversial. Less than one per cent of the state is in private hands, with an exception that, for outsiders, is surprising.

Native Alaskans did not own Alaska before Europeans arrived. They did not, in fact, know what land ownership meant (nor, for that matter, would they have understood the concept of 'wilderness'). They didn't need to. Like the Inuit of Greenland, the indigenous people of northern North America were users of the land and its resources. They dwelled and were at home upon it. Possession was not only meaningless, it would have been entirely counterproductive to a sustainable relationship with the place.

But that changed, as it did for native people across the continent, when the land they had never thought to own was usurped by colonisers. And, here at least, it changed again in 1971 with the passing of the Alaska Native Claims Settlement Act (ANCSA), under which the state's 60,000 indigenous people received one billion dollars compensation between them, as well as 44 million acres of land, split between regional and local 'corporations'. According to

John McPhee, 'This was perhaps the great, final, and retributive payment for all of American history's native claims – an attempt to extinguish something more than title . . . The natives of Alaska were suddenly, collectively rich.' This was in some senses a real victory, and it was certainly better than anything that native people had been offered elsewhere in the country. But the price of this deal was the acceptance of a system of ownership and of value that was not their own. It was, in other words, complicity.

Susan Kollin has written that 'the corporate model introduced by ANCSA has brought with it new forms of "institutionalized competition" between native peoples that had not existed before and that violate a standard belief in forging reciprocal relations with the natural world.' The effects of this change are social and psychological as much as they are financial. Writing about the enclosure of common land into private holdings in England in the late nineteenth century, Deborah Tall observed that, 'After enclosure, the communal sense of place and identity was divided into numerous fenced and hedged private loyalties.' Those private loyalties were imposed on native Alaskans under the terms of ANCSA.

Jeff recently bought a piece of land from the government. The state continues to sell off a few small parcels to individuals who wish to homestead or build cabins, and that is precisely what Jeff wants to do: to build a cabin where he and his family can spend time together, on the land. Doing so has been a dream of his since he was a child. Though he grew up in the south, in Washington State, he has always looked forward to this place, longed for it. When he finished university, this is where he came. And now, settled here with his wife and children, he makes sense to me in a way that I don't think he ever quite did before.

One afternoon, the two of us set out from Anchorage to visit his 'property'. It was a two and a half hour drive from the city, then a short way on a dirt track into the forest. When it became impassable, we got out and hiked, first along the track, then out into the bush. The going was slow, over fallen trees and brush, up a steep ridge to where the land levelled out, then began to fall again. A fire several years before had left some of the trees brittle and dead. Some still stood, leaning at peculiar angles, while others cracked underfoot. The ground was alive with plants – bluebells and Labrador tea. Snowshoe hares scampered behind bushes as we approached. Every few minutes, Jeff would call out, calmly: 'Hey bear, just passing through. No surprises here.' And each time he spoke I felt relief.

It was easy to lose direction among the trees, and we walked half an hour or so before seeing a lake out to our left. As we stopped to look over the water, I noticed the silence. No human noise whatsoever, just the air fussing among the branches. An eagle cried from somewhere not far away. Mosquitoes hummed around our faces. A stillness rose, as though from the ground itself. We found the corner post of the property and followed the ribbon markers around its edges, first towards a small pond, then out to another lake. Neither of these pieces of water is yet named, and Jeff is considering the possibilities before making his mark on the map. We had reached a place away from people, where things had no name. It felt a very long way indeed from the road, from the city, and from home.

I asked Jeff again about his motivation for building a cabin here, about whether he was trying to escape from other people. I could sense him becoming defensive. It is not about escape, he said, or about living some kind of outlaw lifestyle. 'I just want a bit of peace and quiet.' He knew I was uneasy about the idea of owning this place, and that uneasiness was tainting our conversation. But in truth, despite my reservations, I was deeply jealous. I was jealous of the comfort that he seemed to find here – a comfort that, in my fear, was not available to me. But if I am honest with myself, I was jealous too of the very ownership that caused me to flinch. It was a quiet, wonderful place, and I had no difficulty in seeing why he wants not just to spend time there, but to call it his own.

I felt guilty then for the suspicion with which I had treated his purchase of the land, and for allowing my dislike of that word – property – to become a judgement. Jeff does not view this place as a commodity. It belongs to him, legally, but his desire I think is for that belonging to become deeper, beyond law and title. What he hopes to find here, over time, is a kind of belonging that is complex and reciprocal: a relationship based on affection, devotion and love. I can understand that hope.

The two of us stood together beside the lake, looking out through a haze of mosquitoes. Three ducks cruised the opposite shore in silence. 'I like it,' Jeff said.

'I like it too,' I agreed.

Driving back to the city together that evening, we spoke with more ease and frankness, it seemed, than we ever had done before.

*

On the west coast of the Kenai Peninsula, the sixtieth parallel skirts the edge of a small town. Ninilchik is centred on the Sterling Highway but reaches out in both directions – down towards the beach, where the old village lies, and up into the river valley. Most businesses are huddled around the highway, seeking passing trade: the gas station; the wooden general store, stocked with knives, fishing gear and food; a Chinese restaurant; a diner.

Down at the long, stony beach, I sat beneath a warm sun. Streaks of high cloud were skeined over Cook Inlet, and on the horizon the hazy blue peaks of volcanoes loomed. Mount Redoubt, fifty miles away, towered above its neighbours, a scarf of cloud wrapped around its middle. A high wooded bluff hangs over the beach here, with cabins and campsites at its top. A crow patrolled the seaweed line, requesting, repeatedly, that I vacate his scavenging ground. Out in the water, salmon jumped close to the shore. Fish followed fish as the thick silver bodies leapt skyward, their tails flapping in the afternoon air, then returning to the ocean. At the river mouth, by the old Ninilchik village, I watched a juvenile bald eagle wade out into the shallow water, bathing. He dipped one wing, then another, then bowed his head into the stream, then lowered his tail. He splashed, stretched out both wings and shook, then repeated the process.

Down in the village, rotting boats and dilapidated shacks shared space with new homes and restored cabins. This is one of the oldest settlements on the peninsula, first inhabited in the early nineteenth century by employees of the Russian-American Company. When Russia sold Alaska to the USA in 1867, many of these workers remained, and overlooking the village sits a wooden church topped by five tiny onion domes. This is the Orthodox church, built in 1901 and still doing business, though services are in English these days. Inside, a three-part iconostasis is covered with gilt portraits, including one of St Herman, who came to Alaska from western Russia, then ended his days as a hermit on Spruce Island, in 1836. Outside, the cemetery was overgrown and blooming with life. An old man knelt among the white wooden crosses, mending the little fences around the graves and cutting dandelions away from their edges. Magpies hopped from the church roof onto the grass, then croaked back up into the trees. Eagles winged slowly through the blue above. Birds scattered their songs onto the ground.

People come to Alaska for many different reasons. In Ninilchik, they come to catch big fish. I met some of these visitors at the hostel where I stayed, overlooking the river. There was Bill, an octogenarian from Chicago, who twice a year comes north to fish or to hunt, and who sometimes brings his grandchildren. Bill likes to tell stories about his previous trips to whoever will listen. Then there was Frank and Elaine, from San Francisco. They were staying for two weeks, and every day he would pay for a charter fishing trip: halibut one day, king salmon the next. Elaine stayed behind, and when Frank returned she cut up his catch and put it in freezer bags, ready to take home. 'This fish costs us about $800 a pound,' she laughed. Frank looked at her and smiled, proudly.

Other people travel here to see 'wilderness', that vague, indefinable thing they feel is missing from their own lives. They come to experience nature, to gaze at it or move through it, and then to go home. There is a kind of nostalgia in this: a desire to return and to connect to something that is lost, or in the process of being lost. It's a longing for the country's past, for an imagined American Eden, pre-Columbus and pre-Bering. To visit the wilderness is to cross 'out of history and into a perpetual present', in Gary Snyder's words, 'a way of life attuned to the slower and steadier processes of nature'. That crossing, for some who come to live here, represents freedom. It is a chance to escape from rules and bureaucracy, and from the noise and muddle of the modern world. 'The last frontier', as this state is often called, is a kind of refuge or a spiritual haven, just as America itself was to the first pioneers, and it offers an opportunity for people to feel more like themselves.

Some people come to Alaska – and Jeff, I think, is one – because they dream of the place and that dream will not let them go.

*

On the shortest night of the year, I sat on Ninilchik beach, looking west. At midsummer, at every point on the parallel, the sun is above the horizon for just less than nineteen hours. And though it sets, it does so at such a shallow angle that the light never entirely fades. At worst, in poor weather, these nights could be called gloomy; but if the sky is clear it will remain light enough outside to read a book (or to play golf, as Shetland tourist literature is fond of pointing out). It is a strange kind of light, this midnight glow. At home it is called the 'simmer dim': a washed out blush, where colours fade and edges soften. Day melts seamlessly into day, and a connection is made.

At nine p.m., the sun was still high and a sword of light lay across Cook Inlet, resting its point upon the peak of Mount Redoubt. The mountains were paling into silhouettes then, with snow barely distinguishable from rock. They seemed to sit up, as though suspended just above the horizon, held aloft by a thin white line. Feather streaks of yellow cloud were ribboned through the blue sky. Just offshore, boats were still fishing, and through my binoculars I could see an otter floating on his back. A bald eagle was tormenting a raft of ducks, each one diving in panic as the raptor flew low above them, over and over. On the beach, four quad bikes hurtled noisily about, while a pair of eagles sat still at the wave-edge, attended by a squad of restless gulls.

By ten o'clock the sun was just over Mount Redoubt. The few clouds were backlit, glowing at their edges. A group of people further down the beach had built a campfire, and like me were waiting it out for midnight. I settled back and closed my eyes, with the wind against my face. I thought about where I was, where I'd been and where I was going. At that moment, I was halfway through my journey; I was halfway home.

By 11.30, the sun had slipped behind the mountains, and thick cloud was gathering over the land. The last dregs of the day washed over Cook Inlet, leaving only the sweet aftertaste of light. As midnight came, I picked up my bag and walked back towards the truck, leaving the night and the beach behind.

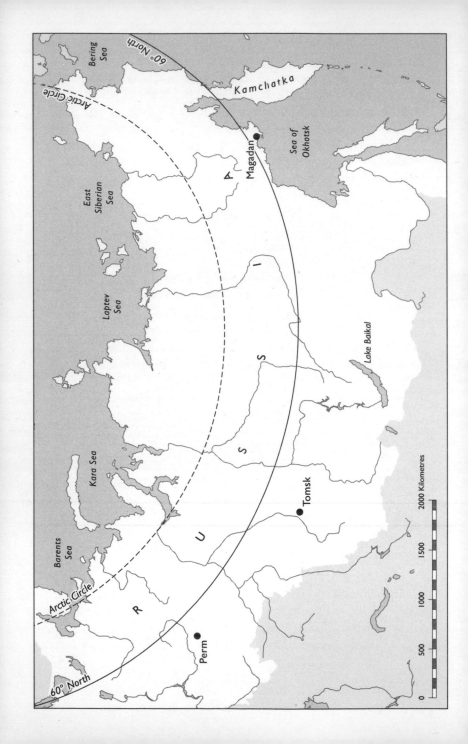

SIBERIA
exiled land

On a map of the world, there are few names that carry such a heavy burden as Siberia. Those four short syllables have come to signify more than just a place. They cast a shadow, and conjure a host of ugly images: of impenetrable forests and lawless towns, of poverty and alcoholism, of intense cold and intense cruelty. This is a region that lives in the mind, in daydream and in nightmare; it is more imagined than seen. And those imaginings, like a cloud of mirrors, reflect, disguise and distract from the land itself. This is a place almost lost behind its own myth.

To say anything at all about Siberia it is necessary to begin with size, for the enormity of the region is central to its story. Covering more than five million square miles – close to ten per cent of the world's landmass – Siberia has a population of less than forty million. It stretches from the Ural Mountains in the west to the Pacific Ocean in the east, and from the Mongolian steppes in the south to the frozen Arctic in the north. This is an area larger than the United States of America and Western Europe put together.

When I was twenty-one I went to Kamchatka, in the far east of Russia. I had found that wonderful name – Kamchatka – and a description in a travel brochure, and made up my mind to go. It was somewhere that nobody I knew had ever been before. It sounded exotic, and seemed, on the map at least, like a very long way away. Travelling there, from Shetland to London, from London to Moscow, from Moscow to Petropavlosk, it seemed even farther. That last

117

part of the journey, between Russia's capital and its most remote region, left me struggling to comprehend the vastness of the country. The flight lasted nine hours and crossed eight time zones. The country passed beneath us, hour after hour, emerging from the clouds now and then but revealing nothing. Land, water, space, nothing. What lay below seemed almost blank, in the way that a desert or an ocean does. From that height, that distance, it felt empty.

Kamchatka, like many parts of Russia, was effectively closed to outsiders during the Cold War, even to most of the country's own citizens. There was, and still is, a nuclear submarine base on the peninsula, close to Petropavlosk, the region's capital, which was founded in 1740 by Vitus Bering, and named after his two ships, *St Peter* and *St Paul*. Kamchatka was also a base for international surveillance, being, as it is, one of the closest points to the west coast of America, and on hillsides amid the trees that past was still in evidence. But in the decade or so that had passed between the end of the Soviet Union and my own visit, doors had begun to open to the outside. Individual travellers were still discouraged, but organised visits were possible, so I joined a small-group tour company – half a dozen strangers in a strange land – and went east.

We spent just two weeks on the peninsula, but in that time I fell desperately in love. Together with my fellow travellers, I clambered into the stinking maw of Mutnovsky volcano and camped for two days beneath it, as the tail end of a typhoon stranded us inside our battered tents. I bathed in hot pools that sprang like blessings from the earth. I stood beside the Kamchatka River as Steller's sea eagles cruised overhead and a young brown bear patrolled the opposite bank. Dumbstruck, I looked out over land so vast and so beautiful that I could hardly believe it was allowed to exist. I left Russia infatuated. Something in that extraordinary place grabbed me by the heart and refused to let go.

For most of my life I have felt myself somewhat distanced from love – within sight, but just out of reach. It is a feeling that mirrors the sense of separation that was with me from my youth. And though it may partly be of my own creation – an avoidance of that which it would hurt to lose – it is difficult to be sure. These knots in which we tangle ourselves are not tied consciously or by design, we simply wake one day and find ourselves bound. But because of this distance, those moments in which love, or something like love, have taken hold in me have been memorable and important. And this was one.

*

The sixtieth parallel runs through the north of the Kamchatka peninsula, then across the Sea of Okhotsk to the 'mainland', passing close to the city of Magadan. That city, as much as any place in Siberia, has come to signify the horror for which, in the twentieth century, the region became known. For Magadan was the port and administrative centre of the Dalstroy organisation, which ran the gulags of the Russian northeast. These were the camps known collectively and infamously as Kolyma. The gulag system of forced labour camps, which reached its zenith under the watchful eye of Joseph Stalin, has come to be considered one of the most appalling acts of barbarism of the twentieth century. Many millions were incarcerated in these camps, and many millions died. The scale of what happened is almost as unimaginable as the scale of Siberia itself.

But the region's history as a place of exile and imprisonment did not begin with Stalin or Lenin, it goes back much further. Indeed, almost as soon as Russia started to explore the lands east of the Ural Mountains in the seventeenth century, Siberia's value as a dumping-ground for undesirables was recognised. In a twisted reflection of America's westward development, the movement of explorers, trappers and traders in Russia was accompanied by another movement: of people forced into exile. It is an extraordinary fact that, while the first European Russian did not reach the Pacific coast until 1639, by the end of that century ten per cent of Siberia's population was already made up of convicts.

In the United States, the West became a symbol of hope and progress for the nation; in Russia, the East was always a darker and more ambiguous vision. It offered wealth, in the form of furs and later gold, but it always remained a place apart, far from the heart of the country. While America expanded to fill its natural boundaries, Russian power and wealth remained where it had always been, on the other side of the Urals. Siberia was conquered but never fully absorbed into the nation. Such was the extent to which the region was viewed as distant and distinct, indeed, that when the Decembrist revolutionaries were sent into exile in 1826 for plotting to overthrow Tsar Nicholas I, one of their number, Nikolay Basargin, wrote that he no longer considered himself to be 'an inhabitant of this world'.

Those who were sent to Siberia were being punished for a wide range of crimes. From genuine revolutionary activities such as those of the Decembrists, to apparently harmless ones like snuff-taking and fortune-telling: all could result in relocation. And the precise form of that punishment also varied considerably. For some, exile meant little more than a forced change of address, but many others were sent to labour camps, the precursors of the gulags. These camps, like the gulags, had a dual purpose. They not only removed unwanted elements from society and placed them where they could cause no further trouble, they also provided a large, cheap workforce for the exploitation of Siberia's natural resources. These were not concentration camps in quite the same sense as those operated by the Nazis. Their purpose was to make money, and convicts essentially took the role of slaves. Death was not the intended outcome for prisoners. At least not at first. It was simply an occupational hazard.

While the tsars certainly made use of forced labour prior to the revolution, the scale and brutality of the system that developed through the early decades of the twentieth century was entirely unprecedented. In 1917 when the Bolsheviks took power, around 30,000 people were imprisoned in camps across Siberia. But by 1953, the year that Stalin died and the network began to be dismantled, there were close to 2.5 million prisoners in the gulags. This was a system of exile and slavery that riddled the country like a pox, and was fed in large part by one man's paranoia and thirst for vengeance.

Among the thousands of camps spread throughout the USSR, those in Kolyma gained a reputation as the worst. The region was, in Alexander Solzhenitsyn's words, 'the pole of cold and cruelty'. The isolation, the extreme temperatures, the difficult, dangerous work and the consequent high death rates became legendary. Prisoners were underfed and kept in unsanitary conditions, cramped together in freezing barracks that crawled with lice and other insects. In the years after 1937, when Dalstroy's first boss – considered too lenient by Stalin – was removed and executed, Kolyma was a hell from which death was the most likely escape.

To prisoners, Kolyma was known as 'the Planet'. Like Basargin a century earlier, those transported to Magadan felt themselves to be travelling towards another world entirely, and the sheer difficulty of reaching the place only underlined this feeling. To get there, convicts had to travel across the country by train, in overcrowded, filthy cattle trucks, with neither enough food nor water. In summer many died en route of thirst and disease; in winter they froze. The trip by train took a month or more to reach the Pacific coast from Moscow, and once there prisoners were kept in holding camps until being taken by ship to Magadan.

These ships, by all accounts, were worse than the over-land transport. For much of the week-long journey, which took them through the Sea of Okhotsk, close to Japan, the convicts were locked in cargo areas that were never intended to hold passengers. So many were crowded below deck, some said, that it was impossible to lie down. Food was thrown into the hold from above, and the prisoners, often seasick and diseased, lived in their own filth. Common criminals ruled these 'floating dungeons', as the historian Robert Conquest called them, stealing food and clothing from the political prisoners and maiming or murdering anyone who got in their way. Women and young men were gang-raped, without consequence for the perpetrators, and those who died on the way were simply thrown by guards into the sea.

Such was the utter misery the journey entailed that the camps themselves may temporarily have seemed like a relief. Here at least was a ration of food for each person, and a little warmth, though not nearly enough of either. Here too was some modicum of order. Any relief would not have lasted long, however, as the reality of life in Kolyma sank in. The main job of the prisoners once they arrived at their designated camp was mining, principally for gold but also for other precious metals and, later, uranium. Prisoners were set work quotas that, even in twelve to sixteen hour shifts, were unachievable. If their productivity dropped too far, so too did their food ration. And if, as was almost inevitable, it continued to fall as starvation set in, they were likely to be shot as 'saboteurs'. The fact that there was not enough to go round ensured that everyone was always out for themselves. Gradually, reduced to little more than skeletons, ruled by hunger, thirst and exhaustion, the prisoners ceased to be themselves any longer; they became hollow people, with only the barest and basest of feelings. Varlam Shalamov, who spent fourteen years in Kolyma, wrote that: 'All human emotions – love, friendship, envy, concern for one's fellow man, compassion, longing for fame, honesty – had left us with the flesh that had melted from our bodies.'

Of those who survived the camps, many were broken forever. They were freed, but never free. In *The House of The Dead*, a fictionalised account of the four years he spent in Siberian exile in the 1850s, Fyodor Dostoyevsky wrote of how some convicts, once released, could not find the freedom they had longed for in the towns and villages to which they returned. Sometimes, 'a sedate precise man, who was promising to become a capable farmer and a good settled inhabitant [would] run away to the forest.' These former prisoners would become 'inveterate tramps', leaving behind their families to wander forever, living a life that was 'poor and terrible, but free and adventurous'.

Dostoyevsky's experience was mirrored in the twentieth century too, when some former gulags inmates found themselves unable to readjust to the settled life, to the towns or cities in which they had previously lived. Home, for these ex-prisoners, could no longer be located in a single place. Family, work, responsibility: all became chains that had, in the end, to be escaped. The taiga became home; the land itself was freedom.

Of course, Siberia already had its population of wanderers: native Russians – Evenki, Sakha, Nenet, Chuckchi, Koryak, Yukaghir and others – who, up until Soviet times, lived nomadic lives, herding reindeer and hunting wild animals. Their movement was governed by the natural migrations of the animals on which they relied. The idea of settlement – of tying oneself to a single place and staying put – was entirely alien; it made no sense at all in the context of their lives. To remain in one place in the taiga was to die.

In the region around Magadan, the predominant native culture was the Even, who lived in small family groups, herding reindeer. For 2,000 years or more, since these animals were first domesticated, the relationship between people and reindeer has been central to Even life, providing almost everything that was needed to survive. Their meat was eaten and their milk was drunk; their fur was used for clothing and for shelter; their antlers could be fashioned into tools. Fish, herbs, berries, wild mammals and birds all offered variety in people's diet, but reindeer gave stability. Without them, life in Siberia would have been virtually impossible.

Native Siberians' relationship with the land was one of absolute intimacy. In order to stay alive it was essential to know the places through which one moved, to know them psychically and geographically, but also to know their character. That character was the essence of the place, it was its soul or spirit. And for the Even, as for other Siberian peoples, spirits were a genuine, conscious presence in the land, to be respected, heeded, and appeased if necessary. Everything in this place had a spirit – every animal, every river, every mountain and valley – and according to Piers Vitebsky, 'Because such creatures, places, and objects have some kind of consciousness, they also have intention.' To live safely and successfully, therefore, one must 'strive to be aware of the moods of your surroundings and adjust your behaviour accordingly, in order to achieve your aims and avoid disaster.'

This understanding of the world, as a sentient place, would once have been almost universal. But it seems difficult to comprehend now when viewed from a distance, from the more or less soulless comfort of our own time and place. There are shadows of it still lurking, though, in our ways of thinking and in our language, and they lie not far beneath the surface. Siberia's climate, we might say, is *harsh*, and the land itself *cruel* or *unforgiving*. These adjectives are intended metaphorically, but it is not an enormous psychological leap, once we ascribe such characteristics to a place, to allow for the possibility that they might not be metaphors. To say that Siberia is an unforgiving place is to identify one element of its character, its spirit. And in difficult times, when faced by the reality of that lack of forgiveness, recognition of this spirit inevitably grows. In the *Kolyma Tales*, one gulag prisoner sees this with terrifying clarity. 'Nature in the north is not impersonal or indifferent,' he says, 'it is in conspiracy with those who sent us here.'

In central Kamchatka, my travelling companions and I visited a group of Even people. In the village of Esso, we boarded a decrepit orange helicopter that took us, noisily, nervously, to a treeless plateau that felt as far from our own lives, perhaps, as it was possible to go. As we stepped out and the engine was cut, the thundering of the blades was replaced by a thundering of hooves, as hundreds of reindeer – some white, some piebald, most a dark, chocolate brown – turned anticlockwise as one, in a tight defensive group. On the edge of the circle, men in khaki clothing stood watching the animals, one of them gripping a lasso in his fingers. Then, without warning, the loop was thrown and a reindeer was hauled out from the crowd. It emerged thrashing and dancing on the end of the rope – whole, vivid and vital. We watched in silence as the men dragged the deer away from the others, then pinned it hard against the ground. A blade was inserted in the back of its neck, just at the base of the skull, killing it instantly. What had been living and thrilling became dead.

It took only moments for the animal to be cut into useful pieces. First, slices were made up the length of the legs and the skin pulled back. The head was removed and placed upside down, facing away from the camp. Then, with breathtaking ease, the skin was stripped away from the body, and the innards removed from the carcass. More people appeared, wielding knives, with jobs to do. Six men and one woman worked together, cutting the animal into its constituent parts, disassembling it into food and fur. Cigarettes hung from their mouths as they bent over the body, cutting and dividing. A small, smoky fire was lit on the ground beside the meat to keep insects away.

When the work was done we were invited into the communal tent, a large, wood-framed structure, with an open fire in the centre and a blackened pot hanging over the flames. Into this pot, the deer's heart and other chunks of meat were dropped, and for an hour or two we sat together with the Even, speaking, drinking tea, and eating the animal we had just watched die.

More than any other event in the time I spent in Kamchatka, I have thought back to that day with the Even. There among the mountains and the reindeer was something that struck me and stayed with me, but which I have never fully understood. I knew, of course, that there is a falseness to any such interaction between native people and tourists, and that a deep economic perversity had made our encounter possible in the first place. But beyond that, beyond all of that, there was something else, something that moved me and which moves me even now. It was something in the thundering of those hooves, and in the parting of skin from flesh. It was something in the sharing of food. On that day I witnessed a familiarity between people and place that was far beyond what words could express. It was a bond that was more than a bond; it was a love that was more than a love. There in Kamchatka, those people were not really separable from that place. They and it were part of each other. It was a kind of union that once was normal and now is extraordinary, and though I knew that such concordance is no longer truly possible in the world in which I live, in seeing it I felt for the first time its absence. And from there, from that recognition, my own longing took shape.

That visit to the Even camp was in some ways misleading. While the life we saw out on the land looked much as we imagined it could have looked for centuries, in fact a very great deal has changed for all native Siberians over the past hundred years or so. Indeed, over that time, their culture and their way of life has been degraded, threatened and deliberately perverted, with consequences that are still being played out across the country. For the Soviets who took power in the early twentieth century, nomads were a problem. The native people's lifestyle, the authorities believed, was socially backward and incompatible with the new economy. Their solution to this problem was utterly destructive. From the 1920s onward, reindeer herding began to be treated in much the same way as any other form of agriculture, and was eventually brought under the control of enormous state farms. Herders became labourers, no longer working for themselves but instead for a wage from the farm managers. Animals became the property of the state. In addition, the authorities created 'native villages', in which herders were expected to live when not on 'shift' on the land. The number of men directly involved in working with the reindeer was limited – wages would be paid only to essential employees – and the number of women was limited much further, usually to just one for each herd. In this way, families began to be broken up, with fathers absent for long periods. The situation was made much worse by the removal of many children, who were sent to schools elsewhere in order to educate them out of their parents' way of life.

As well as these physical changes, the spiritual world of the people was threatened too. Shamans in particular, who had been crucial in perpetuating the native understanding of the land and its spirits, were persecuted, murdered and ultimately wiped out (the word 'shaman' is Even in origin, but similar figures existed across Siberia and northern Scandinavia, and still do in other hunting and nomadic cultures worldwide). The Soviets went to great lengths to try and replace native ways of thinking with their own brutal logic. In one example, shamans, who in their traditional rituals would embark on 'soul journeys' in which they would 'fly', sometimes held aloft on the back of a reindeer, were thrown out of helicopters to prove they could do no such thing.

The Soviets' plan, to a great extent, was successful, achieving much of what it was supposed to achieve. Though spiritual beliefs are still widespread among native people, the shamans have gone, and nomadism as a way of life was minimised as far as was realistically possible. But a high price for this success was paid by those who had to live with the impact.

When the Soviet Union collapsed, the people of Siberia were vulnerable in a way they had never been before. During seventy years of social upheaval, enforced from the outside, the communities of the region had lost the self-sufficiency that was once necessary for their survival. Reindeer herders who for millennia had been reliant only upon their own skills and knowledge of the land and its animals had become dependent upon supplies and services brought from elsewhere: upon vets, upon air transport, upon endless bureaucracy, upon vodka. And when communism disappeared, the economic safety net of the state disappeared, too.

In native villages today, the results of that change are all too apparent. Alcoholism, substance abuse, violence and suicide: it is a familiar list. Young people feel alienated from their culture and from their place. Women particularly, for decades urged to take up occupations rather than involve themselves in herding, now feel themselves entirely separate from that lifestyle. They are lost in a land to which they no longer feel connected.

What took place in Siberia – the enforced ending of shamanism, the restructuring and settling of native life – was an imposition of alien values upon a landscape and a way of living that was tied to that landscape. The Even's entire system of knowledge, their culture and identity, was centred around the taiga and around their reindeer. But during the

Soviet era, the centre became elsewhere. It moved to the villages and to the cities. The herders found that their lives had become peripheral. The taiga was now to be seen as a workplace; the reindeer, a product. At the same time that Soviet authorities were physically exiling prisoners in the gulag, they were psychologically exiling native Siberians from their own home, dividing them from the ways of living and thinking that had evolved in this place, naturally, necessarily, over thousands of years.

*

The longing for home and the longing for love are so alike as to be almost inseparable. The desire to be held by a person, or by a place, and to be needed; the urge to belong to something, and for one's longing to be reciprocated; the need for intimacy. These needs, these urges, these desires were within me when I travelled to Kamchatka, as they had been for years previously. But they had not yet found a way to express themselves. When I fell in love I had found something, somewhere, onto which I could project my longing from a safe distance. Kamchatka was beautiful and mysterious, and there was a stillness at its heart that seemed to calm, temporarily, the restlessness in my own. But Kamchatka was also, quite literally, at the other side of the world. By this time I had come to accept Shetland as my home, but I had not yet come to love it as that. The infatuation that I developed was a sign, first of all, that these feelings were building within me. And it was a sign, too, that place and landscape could be the foundation upon which love grew.

In the months that followed my visit to Kamchatka, I thought about it often. I kept in touch with people I had met there. I read everything I could find to read about it. I looked over my photographs obsessively. I even learned the Cyrillic alphabet and began to grapple with the Russian language. I made plans to go back, to spend more time there and, if possible, to come to know it properly. But I never did go back. Like all infatuations, this one began to fade. It ceased to occupy my thoughts to such an overwhelming degree, and it ceased, in the end, to lure me away. It was too expensive to go, I concluded, too complicated, too far away, and the reality of return was too liable to disappoint. Slowly, my dreams of Kamchatka were set aside.

*

As a place of exile, Siberia was extraordinarily effective. It is huge, cold and utterly strange: a natural repository for our fears and an ideal place in which to dump unwanted people. But the reason it has remained a land apart – unlike America's West, which was absorbed into the country – is, I think, as much about us as it is about the place itself. For in Siberia, the land and the climate resist the European understanding of home; they resist our desire to be settled. Pioneers in America did not move for the sake of moving. They migrated westward to find new places to live and to find land that could feed families and communities. They went to make better lives and to settle down. In most of Siberia, however, settling is an entirely unnatural thing to do. Much of the land cannot support meaningful agriculture, so towns and cities are reliant, always, on food and supplies imported from elsewhere. To try and settle therefore, means accepting peripherality. It is a literal and a psychological dependence on other places. Today, that is how the vast majority of the region's inhabitants live, but it remains a precarious kind of existence, vulnerable always to the impact of decisions made far away.

The appalling history of Siberia cannot be shaken off. It clings to the land, distorting and concealing it beneath the horror of what happened here. But the dark spirits that seem to haunt this region do not belong to it; they are not the spirits of the place itself but, rather, our own demons.

Western civilisation demands settlement. That is the relationship that our culture desires. But in Siberia, we are faced with somewhere in which such a relationship does not make sense. The native people of this region were nomadic because that is what the place and the climate demand. Their home was not a single location, it was the land itself, and their connection to that land – forged through hunting and herding – was entirely unlike our own. Siberia is an ideal place in which to exile Europeans because it is a place that rejects the European idea of what a home actually is. In Siberia, settlement itself is a kind of exile.

When I look back now upon the time I spent in Kamchatka, I can still recall those pangs I felt, and the deep longing I had to return. That longing was an urge to connect and to immerse myself in a place. I look back now upon Kamchatka with fondness and with nostalgia, as one might a teenage sweetheart, many years estranged. Sometimes my dreams of it return, and I wonder if I will ever see that place again.

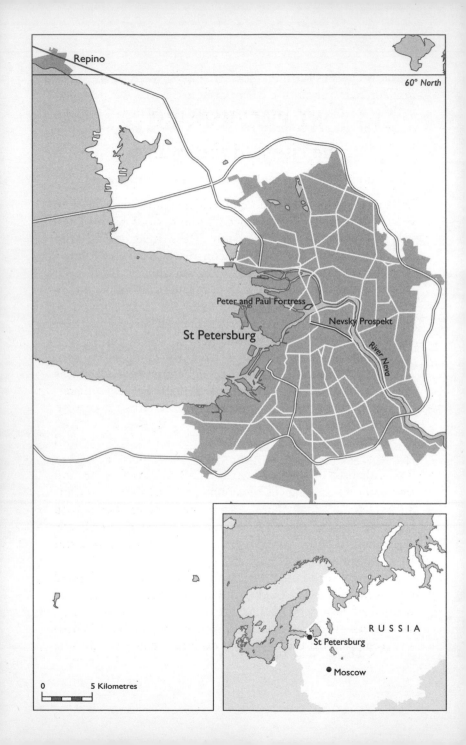

ST PETERSBURG
the city and the swamp

St Petersburg is a miracle city, which really ought not to exist. For three centuries, since its foundations were laid in swampy soil close to the mouth of the River Neva, both natural and human forces have conspired to try and destroy it, and several times they have almost succeeded. To many, it was a city that was doomed from the start. Its construction was an act of imperial folly that was bound to be repaid by failure. It was a place that did not belong where it was built, an affront to the natural order and to the nation itself.

Peter the Great conceived it while travelling in Western Europe at the end of the seventeenth century. There, he was impressed with London and most particularly with Amsterdam, and he imagined for himself a new Russian capital. When the long-disputed Neva estuary was won back from Sweden in 1703, Peter understood its importance. Up until that time the area had been thinly populated marshland, but it was also the only access that Russia had to the Baltic, and that made it essential for the country's development: culturally, militarily and economically. In the summer of that year, the new city began to take shape with remarkable haste. According to Peter, this was to be a Paradise on Earth, and Russia's 'window on the West'.

From its very beginning, though, the city was plagued by forecasts of its destruction. In its early years one prophet warned of how God would 'drown the Anti-Christ's city', and Peter's own first wife Eudoxia, whom he banished to a convent, cursed the place and declared that it would one day stand empty. Those predictions have sometimes seemed close to coming true. Great floods have swept through its streets, and fires have raged through its buildings. Devastation has always felt possible. In the Second World War, Adolf Hitler declared that he would be the one to finally destroy this city and empty it entirely of people, and during the 900-day siege of 1941 to 1944 he almost succeeded. More than a million died in those years, killed by starvation and by disease in one of the war's most appalling acts, a prolonged and deliberate mass murder.

And though he granted Leningrad – as it was then called – the country's highest award of honour in the last year of the war, Joseph Stalin was no more a friend of the city than his German adversary. According to the composer Shostakovich, Hitler merely 'finished off' the work that Stalin began. The Soviets had moved the country's capital back to Moscow after taking power in 1917, two hundred years after Peter the Great had done the opposite. They then set about emptying the city of the power and wealth it had hitherto accumulated. In the Great Purge of the 1930s, Leningrad suffered enormously. From ordinary families right up to Sergei Kirov, the Communist Party's leader in the city, tens of thousands of residents were exiled or executed. For Stalin, the city was a reminder of the old, tsarist Petersburg, and a symbol of the openness and cosmopolitanism that he so despised. It was, in Nikolai Gogol's words, 'a foreigner in [its] own fatherland', and after the war Stalin set about crushing it all over again. Those who had led Leningrad through the siege were murdered; writers, artists and intellectuals were disposed of in the gulags. The city's suffering continued.

*

It was a week into September when I arrived in St Petersburg, but autumn had not yet caught hold in this corner

Shetland: Mousa Broch.

Greenland: drift ice near Nanortalik.

Canada: American white pelicans on the Slave River.

Alaska: salmon fishermen on the Kenai River.
(John Tobin Photography, www.tobinphoto.com)

St Petersburg: the Bronze Horseman.

Finland: the Old Town of Ekenäs.

Sweden: Gamla Uppsala.
(Erwin Spil, www.erwinspil.com)

Norway: Stolmen.
(Fihu, www.flickr.com/photos/fihu, licensed under CC BY-SA 2.0)

of the north. A warm wind bustled down Nevsky Prospekt as I pushed my way through the crowds towards the river. And though it had passed six in the evening the sun was still bright, lingering like a blush against the pink walls of the Stroganov Palace. From edge to edge, the wide pavements were filled with people: tourists in raincoats and baseball caps, striding businessmen in suits and shades, girls in short skirts locked arm in arm, old women whose headscarves could barely contain their peroxide perms. The street overflowed with beeping horns and screeching tyres, over-revved engines, sirens and shouts; the smell of drains and exhaust fumes thickened the air. It was loud and chaotic, a heaving pandemonium, and I kept close to the buildings, nervous of the hustle and din that seethed between them.

Crossing the sluggish grey Neva to Vasilevsky Island, I lingered beside the red Rostral Columns that tower there, with their four marble figures representing the great rivers of Russia. Once, these columns served as oil-blazing lighthouses, aiding vessels, but today their only role is to lift your eyes up and away from the filthy water below. From there I continued to Petrogradskaya and across the walkway to Hare Island, and the fortress where this city was founded. The Cathedral of Saint Peter and Paul shone butter gold in the evening sun, its gilded needle spire reaching 400 feet upward, to where hooded crows blinked like black stars against the sky. A syrupy light lay dappled among the trees around the fortress, and yellow leaves were just beginning to fall, a step ahead of the weather. In drains and on paths they were piled, dry and crackling underfoot. I kicked them as I wandered through Aleksandrovskiy Park, feeling a childish pleasure in that most irresistible of acts.

There is nowhere else like this in the north. By a wide margin St Petersburg is the most highly populated place on or above the sixtieth parallel, with five million people now living in the city itself and many more in the surrounding area. In that sense, as in others, it is an anomaly: a strange city in a strange place, a new city designed to look like an old one, a former national capital that was intended, from the start, to appear foreign. I had arrived on the twentieth anniversary of the city's most recent name change, when Leningrad became St Petersburg for the second time in its life. For nearly seventy years it had held the name of the former leader, a tribute bestowed in January 1924, just five days after his death. Prior to that, though for only a decade, this had been Petrograd – a Russification of its original, Dutch name, pushed through in the patriotic fervour of the First World War. For the two centuries before 1914, it was St Petersburg. But by most of its inhabitants it is known simply as 'Piter'.

It has been said often that St Petersburg looks like nowhere else in Europe because it looks like everywhere else, and there is certainly truth in that. Peter and later leaders employed architects from across the continent to bring their own styles to the new Russian capital. The only place that its founder was adamant it should not emulate was Moscow. Over the following centuries, as the whims of tsars and tsaritsas were made solid across the city, Petersburg took on a schizophrenic, pieced-together feel. It was beautiful, yes, but also haphazard. Neo-Classical palaces stand alongside Baroque churches, flanked by apartment blocks and mansions in what Russians call Style Moderne, or Art Nouveau. The effect is intoxicating and confusing at once. The only consistent feature is grandeur. This does not feel like a city that grew and evolved here naturally, over time. It feels like an imposition, like a city commanded into being – which is precisely what it is.

The next day, autumn awoke with a start. Dark clouds smeared the sky and rain shimmered along Nevsky Prospekt. Looking down from my room, high above the street, a parade of umbrellas scurried back and forth like swarms of multicoloured beetles, and I gazed half-hypnotised at the city below. The whole world was in a hurry, and everyone, it seemed, needed to be elsewhere.

A little later, sitting in a café downstairs with my breakfast, I watched them go by, hunched and huddled against the rain. I had no umbrella myself and no particular desire to get wet, and so I waited, sipping my coffee, then washing it down with apple cake. From the rooftops outside, enormous metal drainpipes were slung like elephants' trunks, water gushing onto the pavement below. In the street, trams and trolleybuses rattled past on their wires and rails. Cars fizzed over the wet tarmac. Everything on Nevsky Prospekt was moving.

This street is the most famous thoroughfare in the country. It was also one of the city's first, begun in 1712. It runs more or less west to east, beginning at the Admiralty building on the banks of the Neva and running three miles towards Uprising Square. Some of Petersburg's most distinctive buildings lie along this street: the Cathedral of Our Lady of Kazan, with its sweeping arc of Corinthian columns; the sprawling arcade of Gostiny Dvor; the Stroganov Palace, built in 1753. Here, as elsewhere in the city, an extraordinary array of colours can be found, some earthy, some rich, some garish. The stone buildings are painted lime sorbet green, pastel blue, sweet salmon pink, the yellow of fallen birch leaves. There are colours here that I have seen nowhere else before or since.

Over the past two decades, the commercial accoutrements of every other large street in northern Europe have arrived on Nevsky Prospekt and made it home. Designer shops, identikit cafés, sushi bars and expensive restaurants all jostle for attention. Window displays compete to draw customers in from outside. It is hard to imagine now, amid all this human noise and commotion, that for a long time the city's rulers struggled to wrestle this place from the wilderness out of which it had grown. Right through to the mid-eighteenth century, deer and wild boar were hunted around Nevsky Prospekt (then known as the Great Perspective Road) and the last reported wolf attack on a person was as late as 1819.

When the rain subsided later that morning, I set off to wander the city's streets. And for days on end I did the same thing: breakfasted and then walked, usually without route or destination in mind. When it was damp I went inside, to museums or galleries, or I travelled the metro from station to station. I took a boat trip though the canals to see things from another angle, and several times I stood inside churches and cathedrals – places of incense and gold and genuflection – where bowls brimmed with donated coins, and where, on one occasion, the glorious sound of a choir hung above the congregation's bowed heads like the proof of a better world to come.

On a day when the drizzle would not lift, I wandered until evening through the Hermitage Museum, overwhelmed by the rooms themselves as much as by the artworks they contained. The high ceilings were adorned with frescoes, gilded cornicing and enormous chandeliers of crystal and gold. There were walls of deep forest green and crimson, pillars of marble and of malachite, shining parquet floors. It seemed almost obscene, this concentration of wealth and splendour. There was something surreal about it all, something too perfect and controlled to be true. I felt awed and uneasy as I passed, room by room, through the Winter Palace. Such beauty, such luxury, such order. This city is truly the opposite of the swamp on which it stands. Which of course was Peter's intention all along.

On other days, without a watch or a phone with which to tell the time, I walked for hours, until my legs and back were sore, enjoying the absence of a schedule. I stopped to eat when I was hungry, or to rest my feet in a café, and sometimes I learned the hour by checking my receipt. But mostly I didn't even look. Joseph Brodsky wrote of St Petersburg that, 'There is something in the granular texture of the granite pavement next to the constantly flowing, departing water that instils in one's soles an almost sensual desire for walking.' I felt that desire and I kept going, returning to my little room only when it was dark. And as I lay down and tried to sleep at night, the city went on living and breathing, shouting itself hoarse outside my window.

As the days passed, I began to find new routes through the city. Ducking off the main streets, through gates and under archways, I found myself in what felt like other worlds – spaces quite apart from the commotion outside. Many of the residential buildings here were created with courtyards in the centre, where stables and servants' quarters would once have been. Some of these spaces are small and claustrophobic, others are light and open. Virtually all are accessible from both sides, offering an endlessly diverse means of crossing from street to street. On stepping in to these courtyards, the sound of traffic is immediately softened, and sometimes, when one yard leads through narrow passageways into second and third yards, something close to silence can be found.

At first I explored cautiously, like a trespasser. But as the days passed I found myself seeking out these places. This was a secret world, to which visitors were not invited. Here, cats padded through the shadows, and old men stood chatting with their neighbours. Sometimes there would be columns of ivy covering the walls, or a solitary tree reaching up towards a square of grey sky. Here and there were cafés and guest houses, sometimes shops and small businesses. In one cramped yard I found an umbrella-repair workshop housed in a ground-floor flat, with a tiny window for customers to knock. Once these areas would have been rundown and dirty, and a few still are. They were the secret, squalid heart of the city. But today the seclusion and quiet they offer is, to many, as attractive as the coloured facades behind which they hide.

From high above, on the colonnade of St Isaac's Cathedral, you can see the true extent of these courtyards. They stretch across the city like a vast labyrinth of calm, secreted among the buildings. A huge swathe of St Petersburg is concealed like this, off the streets and off the map.

Above ground, there are the courtyards; below, the tunnels and stations of the metro. Down there, in rattling carriages, I saw lovers kissing, old women laughing, and young boys in military uniform, accompanied by their mothers. The stations, built deep beneath the surface, were called 'people's palaces' in Soviet times, and their opulence is striking. Intricate designs, mosaics, statues: they ape and mirror the grandeur above ground. Exploring these hidden places, I began to see the city expanding and revealing itself, like a set of Russian dolls, one within the other.

So much of this place has been hidden. Though it was conceived as a perfect city, it seems today like a kind of Oz, where curtain covers curtain and mask hides mask. This St Petersburg once was Leningrad, once was Petrograd, once more was Petersburg. But that most recent name change was not so much a return or unveiling as the latest in a long series of cover-ups.

Over the centuries, it is not just the city that has changed its name, but streets and squares and buildings and bridges. Time and again they have been retitled and reinvented. Petersburg has been viewed by the country's leaders as an unfixed thing, a place that can be shaped and altered to the needs of the day. The most aggressive of these leaders, of course, were the Soviets, who tried to alter not just names but history too. They tore down churches or put them to new use. With sledgehammer irony, St Isaac's Cathedral was converted into a museum of atheism, while the Old

Believers Church of St Nicholas was turned into a museum of Arctic and Antarctic exploration. Inside, paintings and photographs of frozen landscapes now adorn the walls and ceiling. Religious icons have been replaced by dioramas and the clergy swapped for stuffed penguins and polar bears.

The communists built statues, then took them down again. They created monuments to selective memory, and to the terrible absence of doubt. And yet today, Stalin, who did so much to mould the history of this place, has in turn been hidden. The many tributes to him that once stood around the city now are gone. His face, so perfectly familiar, is now hard to find. Yet he is still there, walking the streets unseen. Concealed beneath shirts, on the chests of many older men, are tattoos of that face, tattoos which once would have demonstrated loyalty or perhaps offered protection against the firing squad, and which now exist only in mirrors and in the eyes of wives and loved ones.

Within the people of this city are millions of lifetimes of memories, and within those memories are the secrets that might once have led to exile or death, and which now are kept only out of habit. Those secrets are the dreams and nightmares of the city, what it was, what it is now and what it might have been. Millions of Petersburgs, of Leningrads, of Petrograds: fragments of the place, each no greater or lesser than the other. And beneath it all is the swampy ground and the broad, brown river.

*

In the city centre, looking out over the Neva, is a statue that is more than a statue. Unveiled in 1782 and dedicated from Catherine the Great to Peter the Great, the figure known as the Bronze Horseman has come to symbolise the city itself, the fate of one entangled forever with the fate of the other. As grand and imposing as one would expect from a monument such as this, the statue shows Peter atop a rearing steed, towering over all onlookers. He wears a toga and a laurel wreath, and beneath the hooves of his horse is a snake, symbolising evil and the nation's enemies. Designed by the French sculptor Etienne Maurice Falconet, the statue took sixteen years to complete, and the single piece of rippled granite it stands upon, weighing more than 1,500 tonnes, was dragged much of the way here by thousands of soldiers, a few agonising metres a day.

The story of the cursed city, and the natural and human disasters that have repeatedly threatened to make that curse come true, have echoed through Petersburg's three centuries. And for much of that time, this figure has been part of that story. Most famously, in one of Russia's best-known poems, Alexander Pushkin cemented the connection between statue and city, and cemented too the ambiguous place that both Peter and Petersburg have occupied in the national imagination. 'The Bronze Horseman' was written in 1833 and is largely set in the great flood that took place nine years earlier. It opens with a standard, mythologised account of the city's beginnings, admiring how this 'lovely wonder of the North' rose 'From darkest woods and swampy earth'. The poem then turns to the eve of the flood itself, when the river 'stormed and seethed' and, 'like a savage beast, leapt at / The city'. Here we meet the central character, a poor clerk named Yevgeny, who seeks out his fiancée's house only to find it destroyed by the rising water. The girl and her family have disappeared. Distraught, he wanders the city for months, never again returning home. In part two, set a year or more after the flood, we find Yevgeny stood before Peter's statue, with 'a tightness in his chest' and a 'boiling in his blood'. Enraged, he shouts at the tsar and then runs away in terror, while behind him, 'One arm flung out on high, full speed, / Comes the Bronze Horseman in his flight'. Yevgeny is pursued through the night by the living statue.

This is a poem riddled with tensions, ironies and contradictions. On the one hand it glorifies Peter and his creation, while on the other it paints him as a tyrant, trampling the ordinary man. Yevgeny, we are told, is the 'hero' of the story, but Yevgeny is mad, pathetic and, by the end of the poem, lies dead. Is the real hero not Peter, the great emperor, who made this city and saved the nation with his strength and guile?

For his contemporaries, Pushkin's choice of setting would have made these tensions clearer still, since this square was the location of the failed Decembrist uprising of 1825 (the year in which the poem's dramatic conclusion is also set). On that occasion, three thousand soldiers and officers assembled in an effort to stop Nicholas I from taking the throne after the death of his brother Tsar Alexander. These rebels sought a more liberal, freer Russia, with improved conditions for their ordinary countrymen. It was a cause with which the poet sympathised, and his closest friends were among the insurgents. Pushkin himself would have been there, as he later told the tsar, had he not already been in exile at the time. But the coup was a disaster. More than a thousand of those who gathered in the square were shot by troops loyal to Nicholas. Of those who survived, many were sent to Siberia, and five of the ringleaders were hanged. Political repression in the country worsened under the new tsar as a direct result, and Yevgeny's shout of anger in 'The Bronze Horseman' echoed, if not directly paralleled, the Decembrists' own ultimately futile protest. And so statue and city were entwined, and in literature as in life Petersburg took on a dual character: both Paradise and Hell, both doomed and fated for glory. This duality, as Pushkin and others recognised, came straight from the character of its founder. They were the embodiment of Peter's own contradictions: hero and villain, wise ruler and merciless despot.

Peter the Great was a giant of a man, literally and metaphorically. At over six foot seven, with legendary strength and stamina, he was physically imposing. He was intelligent and brave – fearless, even – and he laid the foundations not just for this city but for the modern Russian state. Through his wisdom, skill and acuity, Russia was turned from a backward country into a significant and influential European empire. But Peter was also a profoundly strange person, cruel and sadistic. He took pleasure in tormenting prisoners – among them his own son Aleksey, whom he personally tortured for the young man's alleged patricidal intentions. The tsar was highly skilled in many trades, including carpentry and shipbuilding, but his hobbies also included dentistry, and Peter would regularly remove teeth from courtiers for his own amusement, then store these tiny trophies for posterity. He was cultured, and a bringer of Enlightenment values – he built the world's first public museum and founded the Academy of Sciences, as well as Russia's first library and school for non-nobles – but he was also an old-fashioned autocrat, utterly convinced of his own infallibility.

Most famous among his idiosyncrasies however, was the tsar's passion for what he called 'monsters'. For as well as collecting books, historical objects and art, Peter also gathered 'natural curiosities', alive and dead. These included dwarves, a hermaphrodite, Siamese twins, a multitude of deformed human and animal foetuses, a two-headed lamb and many other gruesome artefacts, which he pickled and put on public display. As his fascination with this collection grew, Peter declared that, by law, his subjects were required to donate to him any such 'monsters' they encountered. Many of these specimens can still be seen in the Kunstkammer on Vasilevsky Island.

It is difficult to think of another, comparable figure to Peter in recent Western history. A man who achieved so much at so great a price; a man whose myth – great as it is – is more than matched by his reality; a man who founded one of the world's great cities, but who did so in the most unlikely of locations. But here he is, Peter, in what is now called Decembrists' Square, facing out towards the river. Rearing up, his horse stands upon that symbol of evil, the snake, trampling the creature beneath its hooves. And yet, in a quirk of the sculptor's ingenious design, which has ultimately become part of its ambiguity, the horse is also supported by it – held in place, literally, by the serpent's coils. The statue celebrates a glorious emperor, but also a horseman of the apocalypse.

In Russia the question of who is the hero of Pushkin's poem is perhaps more complicated than it is for Western readers, who would tend, particularly today, to side with the trampled underdog. For here, the conflict is not just a narrative one, it is the central tension of Russian politics. Individual versus state, freedom versus power: these conflicts were unresolved for the poet, and they remain unresolved now. After centuries of repressive feudalism and more than seven decades of communism, it seems surprising, to Western minds at least, that Russians would be so quick to return to an autocratic style of government, repeatedly re-electing a leader who is in many ways akin to the leaders they left behind in the early 1990s. But the popularity of Vladimir Putin is undeniable. Despite protests from some quarters, and despite some suspicious election results, there seems little doubt that Putin and his style of democratic authoritarianism is supported by the majority of the Russian people.

As we sat on plastic chairs outside the Kazan Cathedral one afternoon, nursing bitter espressos procured from a coffee van, Mikhail Volkov told me something that, at first, I found shocking. 'Sometimes dictatorship works,' he said. 'Sometimes you need that kind of order.' I looked at him, unsure if he truly meant it, or if he was just trying to provoke me. I didn't respond, but waited for him to go on. 'Russia is a huge country,' he explained, 'and dictatorship might be the best thing for now. Putin created order out of chaos.'

Mikhail is an English teacher and occasional tour guide, in his late thirties. He is tall and handsome, and wears a baseball cap over his close-cropped hair. Intelligent, well-travelled and socially liberal, he doesn't conform to any stereotype I might have held of a typical Putin supporter. Speaking slowly, in almost perfect English, he seems to enjoy my surprise, and pauses dramatically before saying anything I might consider controversial. 'In the '90s we had chaos,' Mikhail told me. 'Everyone was just out for themselves. The big oil companies were privatised by individuals who made a lot of money – they were the oligarchs, like Roman Abramovich. People were just trying to get a house and a car of their own by whatever means they could. Then Putin came in and he said, "I know what you've been doing and how you made your money, but now you're going to have to play by the rules. And they're my rules".'

The transition from communism to capitalism in Russia was certainly a chaotic period. Many people saw their standard of living fall dramatically during the 1990s, as inflation and unemployment spiralled, while others made enormous fortunes from assets that had previously belonged to the state. Corruption was rife, and the safety net of the old system was replaced by an overwhelming sense of alienation and vulnerability. People could no longer rely on the certainties they'd once known. For more than seventy years, the country had – in theory, at least – shared a common goal, and a common set of values. Each citizen was – again, in theory – equal in worth to all others. When the Soviet era came to an end, though, all that changed. For those who did not experience that change first hand, it's hard to imagine the sense of disorientation that must have been felt by so many. It's therefore hard to imagine the relief with which Putin's arrival in politics at the end of the '90s was met.

Here was a man who offered an antidote to that disorder and disorientation; who seemed to promise a return to common ends and common means; who claimed that strong state power was the only guarantee of freedom.

And yet still it surprised me, the extent to which Mikhail was, if not exactly enthusiastic about what was happening, at the very least willing to overlook its flaws. He praised Putin, his achievements and style of governance, and dismissed his critics as irrelevant. He bemoaned the lack of political engagement across the country, but did little more than shrug his shoulders at the abuses of power of which he was in no doubt the government was guilty. He was angry about the re-emergence of the church as a political force in Russia, but refused to condemn Putin for exploiting religion for political gain. For Mikhail, as for many other Russians, the preservation of order and stability trumps all other concerns.

To the outside observer, this country can feel like a chaotic and unruly place. But that sense is not exclusive to those looking from elsewhere. Russians too are deeply aware of it. Perhaps, as Mikhail suggested, the country's size is partly to blame. It feels too vast and too disparate to be managed. But what's notable, regardless of the reason, is the extent to which, despite the upheavals the country went through at the beginning and end of the twentieth century, the nature of politics and power in Russia has remained the same, concentrated to a very great extent in the hands of one person. This is a country in which democracy is viewed by many as too unstable a system, the constant flip-flopping of power inconsistent with the desire and demand for order. It is a country that seems, constantly, to be battling with itself.

Nowhere else is this conflict between order and chaos so apparent as here in St Petersburg (of which both Putin and his right hand man Dmitry Medvedev are natives). This city was, from its very beginning, an imposition of order upon the chaotic land, a manifestation of human will and imperial power. Peter the Great imposed straight lines upon the islands and swamps of the Neva delta. He imagined canals where streams had run, he drew streets through the mud. The magnificence of this city was a direct response to the difficulty of its location. It was an act of defiance, not just against Russia's neighbours but against the country's own terrain. St Petersburg was conceived as an ideal city, but for a long time it remained a battleground, where flood and fire threatened to destroy what humans had created. And frequently, as Pushkin's poem describes, it was people who were on the losing side. Today, that battle feels less like one of man against nature than of man's desire for order against the chaos he creates: the chaos of poverty and corruption, of squalor and discontent, versus the order of authoritarianism and political power, of clean streets and brightly painted buildings.

On a drizzly afternoon I visited a museum dedicated to the short life of Alexander Pushkin, housed in the last building in which the poet lived, close to Palace Square. There were paintings, letters and furniture, as well as glass-fronted displays that recreated and retold episodes from his childhood in Moscow to the duel he fought in St Petersburg in 1837, in which he was shot and fatally wounded, dying two days later. The museum was cold and dusty, and when a stray column of light pierced the windows, I could see the motes glitter like a shoal of tiny raindrops, suspended. The place was virtually empty, apart from its staff – an army of elderly women, dressed in greys, browns and beige. By each doorway in the many rooms was a stool, and on each stool sat one of these women. As I walked through the museum, I felt their eyes follow me, observing everything. I noticed too that in every room, as I replaced the laminated information sheets provided in English, one of these attendants would swoop in to check the paper and to straighten it. I sensed a tut of disapproval following me as I walked, and I began to feel that, by being there, by lifting those sheets and then returning them, I was creating havoc.

I took to straightening the pages myself on the display cases, leaving them just as I had found them. I took care to ensure that each page was perfectly aligned, so that no fault could be found. Lingering close to the doorways I noted that the staff were still unable to resist their impulses. As I moved on, an attendant would invariably appear, approach the paper, only to find it just as it ought to be. Silently she would return to her seat, looking even more dissatisfied. Watching this strange ritual, I realised that the care I was taking was not what they had been hoping for at all. Their desire was not for straightness, it was for straightening. They did not wish to find order, but to impose it. I left them to it, then, and headed back out into the rain.

*

I decided to take a train to the north. I wanted to cross the parallel, which lies towards the edge of the city, but also to escape the noise and commotion for a few hours. I chose as my destination the village of Repino, almost, but not quite, at random. A resort on the Gulf of Finland, about twenty miles from the centre of St Petersburg, it seemed, I suppose, as good as anywhere. It had a museum dedicated to the artist Ilya Repin, after whom the village is named, and it would also have a view over the sea, which seemed like a good antidote to my urban weariness.

I found my way to Finland Station, the place where Lenin had returned to Russia in 1917 after his years in European exile, and where his statue still stands, draped in garlands of pigeon shit. After a discussion with the ticket vendor that was longer and more arduous than either of us would have liked, I found myself a space in a busy carriage. Squeezed in together on yellow plastic benches, my fellow travellers were *babushkas* doing crossword puzzles and young families shouting at each other, most seemingly on their way to weekend cottages in the country.

As the train pulled out from the station, an odd procession of people began to enter the carriage, all with goods to sell. First there was a selection of ice creams, then magazines and puzzle books, fake amber bracelets, torches, waterproof overalls, Russian and pirate flags, and jumping plastic spiders. As each seller arrived, they would stand at one end of the carriage and shout a sales pitch, like an air steward doing a safety demonstration. Then they would walk down the aisle in search of customers, though few appeared to sell anything at all. Some were good at their job, managing to be both loud and charming, but others seemed nervous – too quiet, or jittery, even. Perhaps they were new at the job, or perhaps it was just the latest in a line of failed careers. The worst of these vendors seemed pathetic and humiliated, as though worn down by the effort of the task.

Rumbling north, the train passed a succession of bleak industrial estates, some of which looked long abandoned. Crumbling factories, warehouses and chimneys; acres of rust and decay. Three inspectors arrived in the carriage then, with the smart uniform and menace of soldiers. Everyone hurried at once to find their tickets.

I showed mine and then closed my eyes for a moment to rest. When I opened them again we were among pines and grey-skinned birches. Here and there amid the forest a few houses could be seen, and sometimes a gathering of *dachas*. Some of these looked ramshackle and close to collapse, many years since their last encounter with paint. But others were smart and well-tended, with roses blooming all about. These dachas have long been a part of Russian life. In the eighteenth century they were gifts bestowed by the tsar upon loyal allies, country houses and estates to which ordinary people could never aspire. But after the revolution, when properties were nationalised, the Soviet authorities began to distribute them to community organisations. Restrictions were imposed on the size of dachas and their gardens in order to maintain the appearance of equality, and by the 1990s, when they were privatised once again, a great many families had one, usually on the outskirts of the city in which they lived. These dachas were used not just as retreats, where people could escape from the city at weekends and during holidays, but equally importantly, their gardens allowed people to provide themselves with vegetables and fruit, commodities that were often hard to come by during the food shortages that afflicted the country.

From the station at Repino I crossed the tracks to where a car park and a large modern building – half restaurant, half supermarket – stood. I looked around, in search of a direction. I was intending, somewhat vaguely, to find Penaty, the former home and studio of Ilya Repin. This is where he lived from the late nineteenth century until his death in 1930. When the area was ceded to Russia in the 1940s (it had previously been part of the Duchy of Finland, in the Russian Empire) it was named after its former resident.

Repin had been the most important and influential of the Wanderers, a group of artists dedicated to portraying the social problems and realities of their country. His most famous painting, *Barge Haulers on the Volga*, hangs now in the Russian Museum in St Petersburg. It portrays a group of peasants dragging a boat up the river, ropes tied over their shoulders. The faces of the men tell the story: of oppression, suffering and deprivation. The image is both beautiful and horrifying at once, a vision of social injustice that is, also, an explicit demand for change.

Repino seemed like a small place, but I had no map and there were no obvious signs that might point me in the right direction. Having walked back and forth around the building for a few moments, I returned to the car park, where elderly women were selling fruit and vegetables from pots and buckets on the street. In one corner of the car park was a noticeboard, and I scoured it for something helpful. Among a plethora of signs, I found one that was in English. It said, simply, 'This Way', with an arrow that pointed towards a lane in the forest. Other than these two words there was nothing I could understand. Nor was there anything to indicate what might be found in that direction. But since I had plenty of time and nowhere in particular to go, I followed it, enjoying the absence of logic in my choice. 'This Way' could lead anywhere at all, but anywhere was better than nowhere, and so I continued. I followed the path down the hill between the trees, noting the myriad little trails that branched off into the forest, to places unseen and unknown. A light rain shivered among the pines and dribbled down my neck and shoulders.

When I reached the end of the path another road lay in front of me. Beyond, I could see the sun glittering on the Gulf of Finland. I turned right and walked along the shore path. A wide golden beach stretches along this part of the coast, and offers somewhere to stroll for the spa visitors and rich dacha or apartment owners. Above the beach, expensive restaurants and hotels mingled with brand new apartments, some unfinished and advertising for owners. There was plenty of money in this town, it seemed. From the beach I looked out over the water, then turned to see the outline of the city to the south east, with the glittering dome of St Isaac's Cathedral clearly visible at its centre.

When the spas and restaurants thinned out I stopped and turned round, then tried the other direction. My feet and legs were getting wet and coated with sand from the path, and I was beginning to feel disheartened. Once or twice I walked down from the road to the beach to see if I could locate the museum from the sea side, but I couldn't, and so I just continued walking. Again, when the buildings thinned out I returned to where I'd first emerged from the forest. Without much thought I took another road that led away from the water, but again, in the end, I turned back without success. Twice I stopped to ask fellow walkers where I might find the museum, but each time I was met with a shake of the head and a 'Nyet!' It was impossible to know whether they'd failed to understand or whether they didn't know the answer. Or whether, even, they just didn't want to tell me.

By then I'd been walking for more than two hours and I still had no idea where I was going. I was searching for a building that I'd never seen before, in a place I didn't know, without a map, without directions, without a single clue. I realised then that I wasn't going to get there. I wasn't going to find what I was looking for.

Deflated, I walked back through the trees to the place where I had begun, at the restaurant and supermarket. My feet were damp and muddy and sandy. I felt hungry and irritated. I looked again at the noticeboard and its little arrow saying 'This way', and I made a mental note: the only sign you are able to read is not necessarily the right one.

Crossing the road back to the station, I stood on the platform waiting for the next train. Beside me, an elderly couple talked quietly to each other. In his hands, the man held a wicker basket, brimming with fat, golden mushrooms, plucked from the forest. Together we made our way back towards the city.

＊

On a Sunday afternoon, in dappled sunshine, I stopped for a coffee on Yelagin Island, to the north of the city centre. The island is a popular weekend destination, a wooded park, with young people rollerblading and families out walking. Half-tame squirrels roamed the pathways, pursued by screeching children. The deciduous trees were turning bronze and yellow, smouldering among the evergreens, and a chilly wind brought leaves and acorns tumbling to the ground.

I sat in the café courtyard looking out at a large metal cage, just across the path. The cage held three ravens, for the amusement of customers, most of whom ignored them. The birds stood apart from one another, each staring out in a different direction. They watched as people passed by, and sometimes they cawed pathetically out towards the trees. But there was nothing that could respond. There were no other ravens around. Everywhere I had travelled on the sixtieth parallel I had seen ravens. They are the great circumpolar bird, the avian natives of the north. At times they had felt rather like companions on this journey, and until that moment I had always found pleasure in the sight of them. Playful and intelligent, graceful and violent, they are creatures of both dreams and nightmares; they are scavengers and acrobats, murderers and artists, tricksters and prophets. I could not help but feel depressed by the sight of those three individuals, calling out to their imagined kindred. For them, home would always be in clear sight, but forever unreachable.

Like many people, I find myself both attracted and repelled by cities. I am drawn in by the choices they offer and by the freedom they promise, but I am left sometimes feeling lonely, particularly on short visits such as this one. In cities I can be struck, without warning, by a sense of alienation and by a feeling that, while there, I am separated from something important, or essential, even. When I finished university I moved, almost by accident, to Prague. I went for a month to train as a teacher of English as a foreign language, but at the end of my course I was offered a job and decided to stay. And so with little more than a shrug of my shoulders I found myself a resident of one of the most beautiful cities in Europe. It is a city that, over the year that followed, I came to know and to think of with intense fondness.

That year was one of the happiest of my life, but it was also one of the most surprising. Surprising because, in the midst of that happiness, caught up in the novelty of being where I was, something began to niggle at me. It was at first only a minor distraction, an encroachment on my least occupied moments, when my thoughts would turn north without warning. But it grew. Steadily, certainly, those thoughts grew. Until, in the end, I was almost obsessed. And this was not some vague, undirected nostalgia. This was not the ache I had known since I was ten years old. This was homesickness. It was a longing for one specific place: Shetland.

Though I had called the islands home for a long time by then, I don't think I had ever really imagined them as such. For years Shetland was just the place in which my family lived, and in which I stayed not really by choice but by necessity. It was not until I was in Prague that I really began to think about home, about what that word meant and why. 'Where are you from?' people would ask. 'I am from Shetland,' I said. But what did I mean by that? What did that 'from' imply, beyond the bare fact of my former residence in an archipelago of that name?

In Prague it occurred to me, I think for the first time, that it really did mean something. Previously my nostalgia had always been for things I couldn't bring back: for a childhood that was gone, in a place that would never be home again, with a father who was dead. But suddenly I understood that there was more to it: a bond I had not recognised before, or had refused to see. It was a thread or a leash, even, with me at one end and the islands at the other. Mad as it may seem, the thought that my homesickness could be pinned to a real place – to the place, indeed, that had been home for most of my life – was revelatory. I felt much as those ravens might feel if, after years of calling out hopelessly into the forest, they found that their cage door had been open all along. And so, after my year in Prague was up, I went home. And that, I suppose, was all I had ever wanted to do.

FINLAND and ÅLAND
neither one thing nor the other

Through a narrow crack in the curtains, I could see the morning coming to life. It was after eight but the sky was still dim, and paled by a haze of snow. From outside I could hear the squeal of metal on tarmac as ploughs roamed the streets, carving smooth trails through the night's fall. I drew the covers close around me and lay there in bed, listening, until I felt ready for the day.

I rose and showered, then reached into my bag for clothes. I pulled on two T-shirts, two pairs of socks, a pair of thermal long-johns, jeans and a thick, woollen jumper, then my jacket, scarf, hat and gloves. It was a ritual I undertook with anticipatory pleasure, because I like the cold. Not the blustery, biting chill of Shetland, but the calm, still degrees just below zero; the cold that fully fills the air, and necessitates the wearing of 'sensible clothes'. There is a cleanness to it, and a satisfaction that comes with the knowledge that it can be held at bay. The slap of frozen air against the face; the sharp gasp, deep in the lungs; the sting of pleasure that puckers the skin. It is as sensual and reviving as the thickest of tropical heats, and though I felt well-padded and well-prepared, I was looking forward to that first gulp of frost.

The town of Ekenäs lies at the very tip of Finland, southwest of Helsinki, where the body of the country peters out in a splutter of islets and skerries. In summer it is a tourist resort, offering access to the national park that sprawls across 5,000 hectares of the region's archipelago. Campers, kayakers, walkers and anglers can all find their fun around

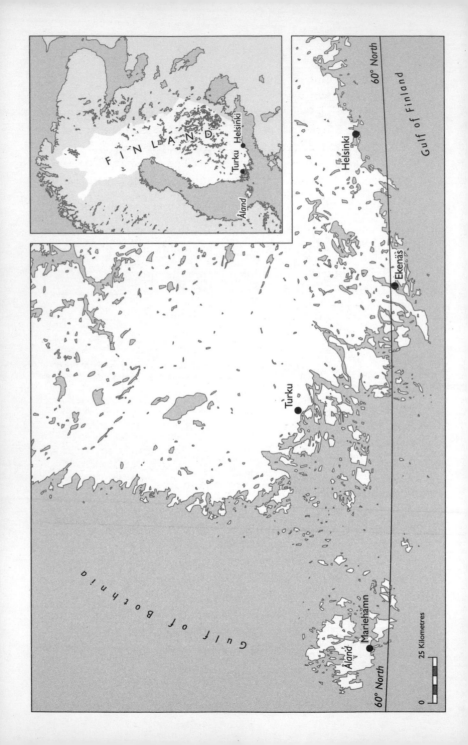

these shores. But in winter things are different. In winter it feels like a town waiting for something to happen. At half past nine, as I left the hotel, the light was still tentative, and though the flurries of early morning had ceased, an iron sky was glowering above. After the frantic rush of St Petersburg, Ekenäs was a haven of quiet. The snow muffled and dampened all noise. It gathered and enclosed, covered and concealed. It swaddled the town like the scarves and jackets that swaddled its red-faced pedestrians. Such weather insists on movement, on the necessity of keeping warm by activity, but thick clothing and icy pavements insist otherwise, and make moving difficult. So with heads bowed, the town's walkers hurried, slowly, in their various directions, breath billowing in the morning air.

As I trudged through the town, there were white piles of clean snow on the verges and brown piles of dirty snow along the kerbs. Winter turns orderly Nordic streets into messy thoroughfares. The pavements were slippery and uneven. Trees, in parks and in gardens, looked ghostly in their white coats. Conifers slouched beneath the frozen burden of their branches.

From somewhere nearby I could hear the ploughs still working their way through the town, mounding up the snow, as they did day after day. It is a Sisyphean task, this constant clearing of the streets. The snow falls and is shifted out of the way. More falls and that is shifted, too. Time and money are swallowed just pushing snow around, from one place to another. The Finns talk of *sisu*, a kind of stoic perseverance in the face of adversity. It is a stubbornness and a refusal to give in that is considered a personal quality as well as something of a national trait. And perhaps this might be an example of sisu right here: the men in their ploughs each morning and the families clearing drives and pathways with broad-mouthed shovels, then doing it all over again tomorrow. Over and over again tomorrow. Despite its practical necessity, this heroic repetition still feels faintly absurd and overwhelming. But perhaps, as Albert Camus concluded, 'One must imagine Sisyphus happy'.

Although there has most likely been a settlement in this area since at least the thirteenth century, the town of Ekenäs was officially born in the winter of 1546, by royal decree. At that time, as for much of its history, Finland was under the control of its neighbour to the west, and when the Swedish king, Gustav Vasa, decided to create a new town to compete for trade with Tallinn (then called Reval), Ekenäs was chosen to be that town. Money, materials and men were sent to the region to make the development as swift and effective as possible. And so it grew. But Gustav was not a patient man, and when Ekenäs failed after five years to live up to his expectations, he founded Helsinki a little further north, and concentrated his efforts there instead. Many of this town's early residents were ordered to relocate to the new settlement, and were not allowed to return until after Gustav's death.

For centuries, fishing was the main industry here, alongside the export of cattle, timber and animal hides. Craftsmen too began to congregate in the area – tailors, weavers, tanners, cobblers – and in the higgledy-piggledy lanes of the old town, streets still carry the names of the professions they once housed. There is Hattmakaregatan (hat-makers' street), Smedsgatan (smiths' street), Linvävaregatan (linen-weavers' street), Handskmakaregatan (glove-makers' street). The buildings too are named after the fish and animals that once would have driven the local economy: the eel house, the goat house, the bream, the roach and the herring.

Some mornings, Ekenäs felt stripped out, almost absent from itself, as though in winter the town didn't fully exist at all. I enjoyed exploring at those times, walking back and forth through the hushed streets, past the same shop windows and the same houses. Sometimes I walked out to the edge of town, where the trees took over, then turned back. I crossed the bridge to the little island of Kråkholmen, then turned again and headed to the Town Hall Square, where the sweet tang of antifreeze rose like cheap perfume from the parked cars.

At night things were quieter still. Parents and grandparents dragged young children on sleds through the town centre, the snow lit like lemon ice beneath the streetlamps' glow. A few walkers, dog walkers, youths, couples and me: it was peaceful, and pleasant to be out. Only later on was the stillness broken, when boy racers practised handbrake turns at the icy junction outside my hotel, their cars spinning and sliding from one side of the road to the other.

Quietest of all, though, were the narrow streets and lanes of the old town, where footsteps creaked like leather on the trampled snow. Along Linvävaregatan, the oldest section, many of the houses were painted that earthy, Swedish red, with white window panels and features, while on nearby streets the boards were pastel blue, peach, olive and butterscotch. In the garden of one of these houses, a male bullfinch, bright ochre-breasted, seemed almost aware of how perfectly he fitted in this colourful corner. The brightness of the town was completed by strings of Christmas lights slung over windows and trees. Though it was already mid-January, Yule wreaths were displayed on front doors, and electric candle bridges were arched behind glass. In Britain we rush to remove our seasonal decorations, to maintain an arbitrary tradition. Here, though, lights and candles are kept in place. They feel like a natural response to the cold and darkness, not just for Christmas but for the whole winter.

In a narrow lane in the old town, I stood one evening outside the small, square windows of a house. On the vertical weatherboards, the red paint was flaking away, leaving scars of age on the warped wood. Inside, there was no light, but I thought that I could make out two pictures hanging on the far wall: one a painting of a sailing ship, the other of a snowbound landscape. I could see only a few details of the room, but not the room itself. It looked abandoned, as though no one had been in there for years. It was an empty house that held a piece of the past intact. I am not sure what prompted me to want to take a photograph of this window. Perhaps it was the incompleteness of it, and the suggestion that, somehow, what lay beyond the glass was not entirely of the present. I wondered, maybe, if the lens might capture what I could not see, if it might illuminate the fragments and make them whole. But as I lifted the camera from my bag there was a movement inside, a shadow that crossed the space between me and those paintings. It looked like a person shuffling past in the darkness. I jumped back, as though I'd been caught doing something terrible, then turned and walked on, feeling guilty and unsettled. As the moments passed I found myself uncertain about what exactly I'd seen. Had there been a person there or had I only imagined it? I still can't say for certain.

*

Until the twentieth century, Finland had never existed as a nation, only as a culturally distinct region under the control of one or other of its powerful neighbours. Sweden occupied the territory from the mid-twelfth century up until the beginning of the nineteenth, but after the Napoleonic wars it was ceded to Russia, and became a semi-autonomous 'grand duchy'. In the century that followed, a cultural and political nationalism began to grow in the population. Although the Finnish parliament opened its doors in 1905 (and was the first in Europe to offer universal suffrage), it was not until more than a decade later that the country truly became a country. In the wake of the Russian revolution, Finland declared independence in December 1917, and despite the violence it had suffered at Russian hands in the past, it did not, in the end, have to fight for that independence. Lenin, who had spent time in hiding here from the tsarist authorities back in St Petersburg, was a supporter of Finnish nationalism, and one of his earliest acts as leader was to let the grand duchy go. Had his own history been a little different, the history of this country might also have been so. Though a short, bloody civil war ensued, between those who wished to emulate the new Russian socialism and those in favour of a monarchy, the country ultimately settled on neither, becoming instead an independent democratic republic.

Finland is often described as a strange place, one of the most culturally alien of European states, and in a sense that fact is remarkable. For despite being dominated from outside until just a century ago, this country always maintained an identity that was very much its own. That identity, and that very real sense of difference, was founded first of all upon linguistics. Contrary to a common misrepresentation, Finland is not a Scandinavian country, and its language is entirely unrelated either to those of its Nordic neighbours or to Russian. In fact, Finnish is not an Indo-European language at all. It is Uralic, and related therefore to Estonian and, more distantly, to Hungarian and Sami. However, this cultural odd-one-outness is complicated by the fact that, in parts of Finland, Swedish still predominates, with around five per cent of the population using it as their first language. This southwest region is one of those parts. Ekenäs is a Swedish town, and its Finnish name – Tammisaari – is far less commonly used by its residents. In cafés here, both languages rise from the tables, and nearly every sign, label and menu is printed both in Finnish and Swedish. This biculturalism is different from that of Greenland. For though they once would have been, these are no longer the dual languages of coloniser and colonised. These are two cultures existing side by side, complementary rather than competing. And the difference between the two is not one of national allegiance, either. Swedish speakers in Ekenäs do not consider themselves to be Swedes living in Finland but, rather, Swedish-speaking Finns. To me this seems a refreshing contrast to the simplistic vision of a national identity that is ethnically and culturally defined. It is an acknowledgement that identity – even linguistic identity – is always complicated. But of course, not everyone agrees.

In the centre of town, a row of boards displayed campaign posters for each of the eight presidential candidates in the forthcoming elections. These candidates included a representative of the Swedish People's Party, which fights to protect the interests of Swedish speakers, and also a candidate from the True Finns, a nationalist group hostile both to immigrants and to the Swedish minority. Supporters of the True Finns resent the continuing use of Swedish as an official second language, and its compulsory teaching in schools. They thrive on a lingering bitterness over the country's historical mistreatment by its neighbour. On a Friday night during my stay, in an act of quiet political sabotage, one of the True Finns' posters was removed from its board, and the face of their leader, Timo Soini, was torn from the other, leaving a blank hole that drew laughs of approval from shoppers the following morning. Though replacement posters had been put up by Saturday evening, those did not make it through the night unscathed either. Once again Soini's face was removed from one, while on the other a neat Hitler moustache was added. In a place as clean and graffiti-free as this, such vandalism was notable. Ekenäs clearly was not natural territory for the party.

In most nations, urban, literate culture has traditionally been valued more highly than rural or peasant culture, and Finland was once no different. But here, up until the nineteenth century, the culture of the town was Swedish, while the culture of the countryside was not. Finns were largely excluded from urban, economic life, and theirs for the most part was an oral culture, a culture of the home, the fields and the forest. After the annexation by Russia in 1809, however, things began to change. For the first time there was a sense that this rural culture could become a national one, and since they were keen to minimise Swedish influence in the territory, the Russians did nothing to discourage this new nationalism. And so, gradually, it grew.

Key to the rise of a rural, national, Finnish culture was the publication in the middle of the nineteenth century of a work of epic poetry called *The Kalevala*. This huge book, consisting of almost 23,000 lines, was based on the oral verse of the Karelia region, and was collected, collated and expanded by Elias Lönnrot, a doctor, who began his schooling in Ekenäs in 1814. Lönnrot brought together creation myths and heroic tales in a work of folklore and of literature. It was a deliberate attempt to set down a national narrative, comparable to the Icelandic sagas and Homeric epics. And though *The Kalevala* is less famous internationally than those predecessors, there is no doubt that within his own country Lönnrot succeeded. The book had an extraordinary influence, politically and culturally, and continues to do so even now. A national day of celebration, Kalevala Day, is held each 28th of February.

The oral poetry of Finland persisted into the nineteenth century not *despite* the fact that it was a suppressed language but *because* of it. The verses Lönnrot gathered were a kind of treasure that had been kept safe from harm in homes and villages across the region. And likewise, the survival of Finnish as a language and as a culture was possible precisely because its rural heartland was separate from the urban heartland of Swedish. The result of this geographical divergence was that, as a national culture came to be imagined and created, it was the countryside that was at its core. It was the landscape of Finland – the forests, lakes and islands – that shaped the nation's art, its music and its literature.

Though his first language was Swedish, Jean Sibelius was a fervent Finnish nationalist, and throughout his career he produced work directly inspired by *The Kalevala*. But it was nature that provided the energy and imagery that moved him most of all. It was that 'coming to life', he wrote, 'whose essence shall pervade everything I compose'. While working on his Fifth Symphony – the last movement of which was the only music to be heard in Glenn Gould's *The Idea of North* – Sibelius wrote that its adagio would be that of 'earth, worms and heartache'. And seeing swans fly overhead one day he found the key to that symphony's finale: 'Their call the same woodwind type as that of cranes, but without tremolo,' he wrote. 'The swan-call closer to trumpet . . . A low refrain reminiscent of a small child crying. Nature's Mysticism and Life's Angst! . . . Legato in the trumpets!' Gould, hearing this music in his native Canada, recognised something distinctively northern about it, something that chimed with the themes he wished to explore. It was, he said, 'the ideal backdrop for the transcendental regularity of isolation'.

*

On the broad pier down at the north harbour, summer restaurants stood abandoned, their outside tables, chairs and umbrellas deformed beneath six inches of snow. On one side of the pier, behind a tall metal gate, was a jetty that housed two public saunas, one for men and one for women. To the right of the jetty were the saunas themselves, and to the left was a square of sea enclosed between three platforms. Half of this square was covered by ice, like the rest of the harbour (the Baltic's low salinity means that it freezes more easily than most seas). But a patch beside the boardwalk was kept clear by a strong pump bubbling from below. Those few metres of ice-free water were the swimming pool.

I have swum in the sea in Shetland on many occasions, though mostly when I was young and stupid. That was cold. It was always cold, even on the warmest day. The Gulf Stream may keep the North Atlantic milder than it might otherwise be, but knee-deep in the waves, goose-pimpled and shivering, you would be hard-pressed to notice. But the difference between that cold and the cold of Ekenäs harbour was probably several degrees. And though I'd come to experience the sauna for myself, the idea of plunging into that ice-edged water, either before or after the heat, did not fill me with excitement. It was an experience that could surely be pleasurable only in hindsight: as something I *had* done, not as something I was *about* to do. And certainly not something I was in the process of doing.

The swimming, I'd been told, was optional, which was a relief. But beyond that, I really didn't know what I was supposed to do. There must be rules and protocols for a sauna, I thought. There are always rules and protocols for such culturally significant activities. I had assumed there would be other people whose lead I could follow, to avoid any serious lapses in social etiquette. But the only other guest was just leaving the changing room as I arrived, and so I was on my own. I'd read somewhere that most saunas do not permit the wearing of trunks, and so I'd not brought any. In fact, trunks had been pretty low on my list of things to pack for Finland in January, so I had none to wear even if I'd wanted to. Public nakedness is not something I have engaged in often, but in this case I was willing to do as is done, and so I stripped, opened the door to the shower room, and then went in to the sauna.

The room itself was just two metres deep and about the same wide, with wood panelling all over, and three slatted steps rising up from the entranceway. There were two windows on one side, and a metal heater was in the corner beside the door. On the top step, where I gingerly sat down, was a pail with an inch or two of water and a wooden ladle inside. I scooped a spoonful out and flung it onto the hot rocks. The stove screamed in protest. The temperature rose quickly in response, and steam curdled the air. An unfamiliar smell, sweet and tangy, filled the room: the smell of hot wood oils.

I sat back against the wall and looked out of the windows at the ice-covered sea. I was sweating from every pore, and my breath felt laboured on account of the steam. It was relaxing, but not entirely. One could rest, but not sleep. Again I wished for guidance: how long was I supposed to stay in the sauna? Was there something else I ought to be doing, other than just sitting? Was now the moment I should be throwing myself into the sea? I could hear people next door, in the women's sauna – there was laughter, and even the occasional shriek – but I could hardly pop in to ask for their advice. So instead I compromised and took a cold shower. It seemed suitable and not too cowardly an option. Open-mouthed and shaking hard, I stood beneath the flow of water for a moment that felt like an hour, my whole body trying to resist the ache of it. Then I rushed back into the sauna again, sweat bristling on my wet skin.

This ritual of intense heat and intense cold is considered a bringer of health, good for both mind and body. It has been part of the culture of this region for over a thousand years, and its importance is perhaps reflected in the fact that *sauna* is the only Finnish word to have found its way into common English usage. Today most Finns have one in their home, and many enjoy them at their workplace too. People socialise here; they have business meetings; and sometimes they just come to sit alone.

A sauna is an ideal place in which to be *omissa oloissaan*, or undisturbed in one's thoughts. Quiet contemplation is something of a national pastime here, instilled from childhood. 'One has to discover everything for oneself,' says Too-ticky, in Tove Jansson's *Moominland Midwinter*, 'and get over it all alone.' Silence and introspection are not just socially acceptable in Finland, they are considered positive and healthy. They are traits often misinterpreted by those from more talkative cultures as shyness or even bad manners.

Saunas mimic the Nordic climate – the heat of summer contrasted with the cold of winter – and when enjoyed at this time of year they hint at a kind of defiance or protest. To step into a little wooden room at eighty degrees celsius is to declare that even now, in darkest winter, we can be not just warm but roasting hot. We can make the sweat drip from our brows, then leap like maniacs into icy water. It is both an embrace of the season and a fist shaken in its face. It is a celebration of the north and an escape from its realities. The actress and writer Lady Constance Malleson went further. For her the sauna was 'an apotheosis of all experience: Purgatory and paradise; earth and fire; fire and water; sin and forgiveness.' It is also a great leveller, and appeals therefore to the spirit of Nordic egalitarianism. 'All men are created equal,' goes an old saying. 'But nowhere more so than in the sauna.'

After repeating this dash from cold shower to hot room twice more, I decided that I'd had enough. It was strangely exhausting, and I felt the need, then, to lie down. As I stood drying and dressing in the changing room, two men came in. They were in their sixties – one perhaps a little older. Both stripped down to trunks quickly, opened the door without a hesitation and went outside. I heard them splash into the sea, and a moment later they returned, dripping but not shivering, took their trunks off and went past me into the steam and heat next door. For a moment I considered turning round and joining them, as though I could shed my awkwardness by sharing others' ease. But I decided not to intrude on the silence of friends, and so I headed back out into the cold.

*

From the centre of town I trudged ankle-deep down the tree-lined streets until, at the end of Östra Strandgatan, the trees took over. A woman and her little dog went ahead of me into the forest and I followed, treading carefully down the path. When she stopped to allow a procession of school-children to pet the dog I overtook and continued beneath the branches, their giggles and chatter rippling into silence behind me. This was the first of the town's nature parks – Hagen – with the islands of Ramsholmen and Högholmen, accessible by footbridge, lying beyond. The forest was mostly deciduous, so bare of leaves, but a map in my pocket identified some of the species: oak, wych elm, common hazel, horse chestnut, small-leaved lime, black alder, common ash, rowan, bird cherry. Away from the old town, with its colourful buildings, this place seemed altogether monochrome. Dark trunks against the white ground, beneath a bruised, grey sky. Even the birds – magpies, hooded crows and a flock of noisy jackdaws – added no colour.

I walked along the trail, through Hagen, then Ramsholmen, without purpose or hurry. The path was well maintained and trodden, though I could neither see nor hear anyone else around me. As I moved further from the town, the only sounds remaining were the patter and thud of snow clumps falling from branches to the ground, and the occasional bluster of birds somewhere above. Despite the absence of leaves, the canopy was dense enough to make it hard to see much at all, just now and then a flash of frozen sea emerging to my right. When I crossed the second footbridge, to Högholmen, the path faded, but still the snow was compacted by the footprints of previous walkers, and I continued to the island's end, where I could look out across the grey ice to the archipelago beyond.

In Finland, familiarity with nature is not just approved of, it is positively encouraged, and the state itself takes an active role in this encouragement. The path on which I had walked was well tended, despite the season, and street-lights had continued for much of the way, so even darkness couldn't interfere with a stroll in the forest. There were bird boxes everywhere, and benches, too, where one could stop and think and rest. The right to roam is enshrined in law in this country, as it is in the other Nordic nations. It is called, here, 'Everyman's right', and gives permission for any person to walk, ski, cycle, swim or camp on private land, no matter who owns it. Food such as berries and mushrooms can be gathered on that land, and boating and fishing are also allowed. The restriction of these rights by landowners is strictly prohibited. Indeed, the legal emphasis is not on the public to respect the sanctity of ownership, but on those with land to respect other people's right to use it. This means that, while land can still be bought and sold, it is a limited and non-exclusive kind of possession. The public, always, maintains a sense of ownership and of connection to places around them.

The emphasis on access and on the importance of the countryside in Finnish culture harks back to the rural nationalism of the nineteenth century. But it has become, in the twentieth and twenty-first centuries, a deep attachment to nature that finds its most notable expression in the profusion of summer-houses dotted around this country. Around a quarter of Finnish families own a second home or a cottage outside the town, and most have regular access to one. Often these are located on an island or beside a lake, and while many have no electricity or running water, nearly all are equipped with a sauna. This region alone has about five thousand of these cottages.

There is an old stereotype that says Finnish people, given the choice, will live as far apart from one another as possible, and perhaps there is a grain of truth in that. Perhaps the desire to remain close to nature necessitates a certain geographical distance from one's neighbours. But there seems to me something extraordinarily healthy in the attachment to place that is so prevalent here. There seems, moreover, something quite remarkable in this longing not for what is elsewhere but for what is nearby. It is an uncommon kind of placefulness that is surely the opposite of isolation.

On my way back towards town I stopped on the bridge between Högholmen and Ramsholmen. I took ham and rolls out of my bag and put together some crude sandwiches. I stamped my feet on the wooden planks to try and compensate for my gloveless state. As I stood eating, an old man in a bright green coat appeared from behind me. He must have been close by during my walk around Högholmen, though I never saw nor heard him once.

The man stopped beside me and gazed out over the frozen water. His face was soft and wrinkled, and a little sad, topped by grey, sagging eyebrows. His dark-rimmed spectacles seemed to hang precariously at the end of his nose, and yet, at the same time, they pinched his nostrils so tightly that his breathing must have been restricted.

'I've been looking for an eagle,' he said.

'A sea eagle?' I asked.

'Yes, a big one.' He extended his arms and flapped slowly, in demonstration of what a big sea eagle might look like in flight.

'I didn't see it today,' he explained, solemnly. 'But some days it is here.'

We stood together in silence for a moment, both looking in the same direction.

'Well,' he said, glancing up at the sky, 'it is fine now. But for how long?'

I smiled and nodded, recognising both subject and sentiment.

'What is coming tomorrow?' he added, turning away to go, then paused a second longer and shook his head, sadly. 'I don't know.'

*

Returning to Shetland from Prague in my mid-twenties was not the joyous homecoming I might quietly have hoped that it would be. It was difficult and tentative, and for a short time I questioned whether my decision had been sound at all. By then, my mother had moved away from Lerwick and away from the house in which I'd spent my teenage years, the house overlooking the harbour. Much had changed since then, and much was new to me. I had returned to Shetland because, finally, it had come to feel like home, but in those first few months a great deal again was unfamiliar.

Not long after coming back I got a job as a reporter for *The Shetland Times*, and a little flat in Lerwick, a few lanes away from where I'd been brought up. I settled in to a life that I felt I had chosen, and, as I walked through the town again, those buildings and those streets, those lines and those spaces, seemed as though they were etched inside of me.

In the months that followed I began to write every day, more than I had ever written before. I started work on what I thought was a novel: the story of a man's return to the islands after many years away. In that story, the man – I never chose a name for the character, he was simply 'the man' – reconnected himself with his home by walking, obsessively, the places he once knew. The steps he took not only rejoined him to the place, physically, they also drew him back, through his own history and into the history of the islands themselves. Or perhaps it would be more accurate to say that, through his physical connection, he drew the past upwards into the present. To fuel this work, I read books about Shetland history. I read novels and poetry. I visited the archives and the museum, and I learned much that I had never before been interested in learning. Through that anonymous character, I strove to relate myself to a place from which, previously, I had always maintained a distance.

It was then, in that time of research and writing, that I realised something which now seems obvious: that this history in which I was immersing myself was not separate from me. These islands' history could be my own. Though I had no connection by blood to Shetland, though my ancestors so far as I know had nothing whatsoever to do with the place, none of that truly mattered. The ancestors of whom I am aware lived in Norfolk and Cornwall and Ireland, places I know hardly at all. My connection to those places, carried in fragments of DNA, has little real meaning. Certainly it means nothing when compared to the connections I have made in my own lifetime. For culture and history are not carried in the blood. Nor is identity. These things are not inherited, they exist only through acquaintance and familiarity. They exist in attachment.

As I came to understand that fact, a sense of relief washed over me like a slow sigh, and I began to imagine that a matter had been settled and that something broken was on its way towards repair. By day, as a reporter, I wrote about Shetland's present; by night I read and wrote about its past. As familiarity and acquaintance grew, attachment brimmed within me.

*

In Turku, the country's second city, I boarded one of the enormous ferries that ply back and forth between Finland, Sweden and the Åland Islands. In the terminal, crowds had gathered in advance of departure time, laughing, talking cheerfully to each other, and once on board they filed into cafés, restaurants and – most popular of all – the duty-free shop. Soon, the ship was full of people, most of them weighed down by bags of alcohol and cigarettes.

Åland is separated from mainland Finland by a stretch of the Baltic that never fully unleashes itself from the land. From Turku we passed densely forested islands with bright summer houses at the shore. And though, as the morning progressed, the islands thinned out and decreased in size until an almost open sea stretched out around us, here still were holms and islets, some as smooth and subtle as whales' backs, just breaking the surface. From the boat, these islands looked as though they had just risen up from beneath the water – which in fact many have. The land here is rising at fifty centimetres per century, so new islands are emerging all the time. And when they do so, it doesn't take long before they are occupied by trees. Even the smallest of skerries, it seemed, had at least one rising from it. Coming from a place where such extravagant vegetation needs to be coaxed and coddled from the ground, it was amazing to see this profusion. In the Baltic, trees won't take no for an answer.

The sixtieth parallel runs through the south of the Åland archipelago, not far from the capital, Mariehamn, where we docked around lunchtime. Disembarking, with rucksack slung over my shoulder, I was surprised to see most of my fellow passengers walk out from the ferry and then straight back on to another one heading in the opposite direction. For the majority, it turns out, the journey is simply the first half of a full day's cruise to Åland and back, with good food and tax-free shopping more important than the destination. I stepped out into the town's grey winter light and headed for my hotel.

If there is ambiguity in the relationship between Swedish Finns and the state in which they live, in Åland the situation is rather different. Here, there is less ambiguity and more complexity. These islands belong, officially, to Finland, but they are culturally Swedish and politically autonomous. The residents are highly independent-minded. The archipelago has its own parliament, its own bank, its own flag and its own unique system of government. Despite a population of fewer than 30,000, spread over 65 inhabited islands, Åland has the power to legislate on areas such as education, health care, the environment, policing, transport and communications. It is, to all extents and purposes, a tiny state operating within a larger one, and its separation from that larger state is fiercely maintained. Finnish is not an official language in these islands, and the army of Finland is not welcome on its shores.

This strange situation did not come about because of a long-held sense of nationhood here (unlike, say, in the Faroe Islands). Instead, it was the result of a peculiar and, in hindsight, rather enlightened decision by the League of Nations. For centuries these islands had been a de facto part of Sweden, but in 1809 they were annexed together with Finland. Åland became, then, part of the grand duchy that survived until the revolution of 1917. At that time, as Finland prepared to announce its own independence, Ålanders demanded that the islands should be returned to Sweden, both for reasons of cultural continuity and to be brought under the protection of an established and stable state. But given the history of this region, the request was not a simple one to grant, and when the three sides failed to agree, the matter was referred instead to the League of Nations. In attempting to come up with a solution that would please everyone, the League settled on a compromise. Rather than staying with one state or joining another, Åland would instead become autonomous and demilitarised. It would function within the state of Finland, but its Swedishness would be enshrined in law. It would be, in other words, neither one thing nor the other. Such a precarious compromise could easily have been a disaster, but in this case it was not. In fact, it turned out remarkably well. Today islanders are proud of their autonomy and what they have done with it. They maintain strong links with both neighbours, but have fostered and cultivated a sense of distinctiveness and independence that is now, almost a century later, firmly embedded.

Mariehamn sits on a long peninsula, with a deep harbour on one side where the ferries come in and a shallow one on the other, for pleasure craft. In the smaller harbour, expensive boats were hidden beneath plastic wrappers, while the wharf was chock-a-block with empty spaces, to be filled by summer visitors.

I strolled across the bridge to Lilla Holmen, a snowy, wooded park that was more or less empty of people. An aviary stood among the trees there, teeming with zebra finches, budgerigars, parrots and love birds, and there was even a tortoise, lying still in the corner. Outside in the park were giant rabbits in hutches, and three peacocks that approached me, then raised and shook their fans as though in protest.

There is an unmistakable air of self-confidence to Mariehamn. The town feels like what it almost is: the capital of a tiny Nordic nation. The wide linden-lined boulevards; the grand clapboard villas; the lively, pedestrianised streets: Mariehamn pulses with a kind of energy that belies its scale. Just 11,000 people live in this town, and yet it seems many times bigger. It feels creative and vibrant and prosperous. In the summer this place would be full of visitors – Finns and Scandinavians, mostly – but in January there were few of us around. Yet unlike in Ekenäs, that didn't feel like a loss. There was no sense of limbo, or of absence. Tourists bring money to the islands, but they don't bring purpose. Åland's focus is upon itself and its own concerns. After all, how many other communities of 28,000 can boast two daily newspapers, two commercial radio stations and one public service broadcaster?

I couldn't help comparing this place with home, and with Shetland's own capital, Lerwick. As I wandered Mariehamn's rather grand streets I thought of the streets in which I grew up. In the time I've known it, my home town has changed significantly, and despite the islands' wealth it has begun to look a little run down. An enormous supermarket on the edge of town has sucked much of the life from its centre. Once home to a host of independent businesses, the town's main shopping street is now a place of hairdressers and charity shops, and Lerwick's museum and its recently-built arts centre are outstanding in part because of what they are set against.

I wondered then, as I have often wondered, whether more autonomy could have brought some of the benefits to Shetland that Åland has seen, and I think perhaps it could. But Åland's success has been bolstered by two factors that are not on Shetland's side: geography and climate. These islands are not just beautiful, they are also sunny and warm in summer, and therefore very popular with tourists. Åland is also fortunate to lie halfway between two wealthy countries, and a tax agreement means that Finns and Swedes can take day cruises here and come home with bags full of cheap booze. Åland is politically autonomous, but it is still financially reliant on its neighbours. In the 1930s, the largest fleet of sailing ships in the world was owned by the Åland businessman Gustaf Erikson, and the economy is still very much dependent on the sea. The ferries which today carry around a million passengers each year back and forth across the Gulf of Bothnia are, by a considerable margin, these islands' biggest industry.

*

Wandering on a half-faded afternoon, I stepped on impulse in to the Åland Emigrants Institute, which occupies an unassuming building set back from Norre Esplanadgaten, one of the main streets in the centre of town. I'd read somewhere that there was an exhibition inside, but the institute is not a promising looking place and it wasn't clear if visitors were actually welcome. Inside there was little to indicate whether I was in the right place at all, just a narrow hallway and corridor with an office at the far end, its door open. I turned to go again, disappointed, but was stopped as I did so by a woman beckoning me back. 'It's not really an exhibition,' she said, in answer to my question. 'It's just a few things. But do come in anyway.'

The office was cramped. Inside were two large desks facing each other, with books and files and folders stacked everywhere around the room. The exhibition, as warned, consisted of a few odds and ends – some old photographs, crockery and medals – but I wasn't really shown any of it. Instead I was sat down, offered a cup of tea, then bombarded with questions.

The woman who had shown me in was Eva Meyer, the director of the institute, and her colleague at the other desk was Maria Jarlsdotter Enckell, a researcher. Eva was middle-aged, quiet and attentive; Maria was in her seventies, with well-tended white hair, and a pair of glasses clutched in her hands. As I sipped at my tea, the two women asked about my travels. Where was I from? Where had I been? Where was I going next? Why was I doing it? We spoke about the sixtieth parallel, and about the countries through which it passed. They liked the idea of my journey, they told me; they liked the connections that it made. Eva took a globe from the corner of the room and returned to her desk, turning it slowly as we spoke, her finger following the line. Both women had been to Alaska recently, they said, to attend a conference about Russian America. I told them about my own time there, and about the village of Ninilchik, with its little Orthodox church. Eva and Maria looked at each other, their eyes widening. 'Ninilchik? Really?' they asked. I nodded and waited for an explanation.

I had arrived at the institute at 3.30 p.m., half an hour before it was supposed to close. But at four o'clock Maria and Eva were only just beginning their story. The place of Finns in Russian history, they told me, had been vastly underestimated, particularly in terms of its colonial expansion. After all, at the beginning of the nineteenth century, Russia was still struggling to man its overseas developments.

St Petersburg was only a hundred years old, and the country simply didn't have enough trained and experienced seamen. Residents of the grand duchy, with its longer maritime history, were extremely useful and often were willing recruits. The Russian American Company offered Finns the security of a seven-year contract in Alaska, with as much salmon as they could eat, as well as an annual salary and accommodation. By signing on as mariners, or with other trades and skills, the men would have a chance to climb in society, working their way up from cabin boy to skipper.

Maria told me the story of one such recruit, Jacob Johan Knagg, who was born at Fagervik, close to Ekenäs, in 1796. By the time he came of age, Finland was under Russian control, and with his mother dead and his father remarried, Knagg decided to go abroad. He left Finland first for Estonia, on a trading ship owned by the local ironworks, but at some stage – probably around the end of the 1820s – he must have joined the Russian American Company.

In 1842, Knagg was working on a cattle farm on Kodiak Island along with his wife, whom he probably met in Alaska. Six years later he applied for colonial citizenship – an application that was ultimately successful. By that time, he was reaching retirement age, and as was customary he was discharged with enough food to last for a year, plus the equipment and supplies he would need to build a home. The Knagg family were then sent to the newest Russian settlement in Alaska. Which is where, in the summer of 1851, Jacob Johan Knagg died, leaving behind his wife and seven children. That settlement was Ninilchik.

Every so often, Eva or Maria would search for something to help illustrate the story. They brought out files, lists of names and family trees. According to Maria, as many as a third of 'Russians' in Alaska were not Russian at all; they were Finns, Estonians, Latvians, Danes and Poles. There was a deliberate attempt, she said, to minimise and even deny this fact, because it didn't fit with Russia's official, patriotic story. Historians in North America too were reluctant to accept her research, Maria explained. They had, she told me, been 'blinded by politics'. Much of her work now was an attempt to prove what she already believed: that a significant number of Finnish migrants arrived in Alaska decades before the great waves of European migration swept westward across the Atlantic. Together with their descendants still living in the state, she was tracing the stories of men and women such as the Knaggs, and drawing new lines in the process, between here and there, between now and then.

At half-past six, when the talk had come to a natural pause, the pair insisted we should eat. 'We will be having . . . stuff,' Eva said. 'Picnic style.' She put her coat on and headed for the door. 'We have lots of things to eat, but I will just go out and get some dessert.'

Half an hour later, we sat down together at a little table in the hallway, strewn with food. We ate chicken legs, salad, fruit and bread rolls, and drank cranberry juice to wash it down. Then we returned to the office and to the conversation.

In that room, filled with fragments of the past, time seemed to tighten and turn back on itself. The space was crammed with stories of those who had left their homes, reluctantly or by choice, for a life elsewhere. It was crammed, too, with the stories of those, here and around the world, who were trying to learn something of their family's past. Eva and Maria took great pleasure in bringing those pasts back to people, telling them who their ancestors had been, where they had gone and how they had lived.

At half past nine, six hours after I had arrived, Eva and Maria sent me back out into the evening, wishing me well on my travels. In my hands I clutched the twin tokens of their generosity: a bag of files and papers in one, a bag of bananas in the other.

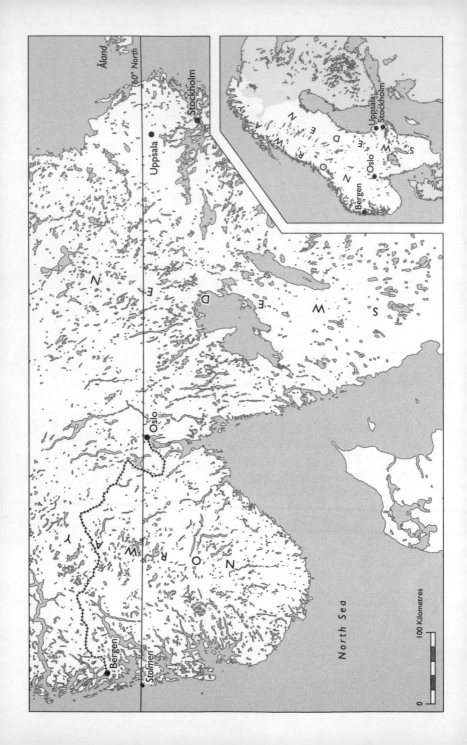

SWEDEN and NORWAY
last lands

Like many university towns, Uppsala has the feel of somewhere both ancient and youthful at once. A centre of learning since the fifteenth century, and of religion for at least a thousand years before that, this has long been the intellectual and spiritual heart of Sweden. The city's skyline is dominated by two historic landmarks: the Gothic, red-brick cathedral – the tallest in all the Nordic countries – and the rosy pink castle that sits on higher ground, just a few hundred yards away. In the centre, a third building stands out: the Gustavianum, whose unmistakable cupola of oxidised green, topped by a globe, was built by Olof Rudbeck in the 1660s. Inside that space, high above the streets, the illustrious professor – who began his career by discovering the lymphatic system and ended it by claiming that Swedish was the language of Eden and Uppsala the site of Atlantis – pioneered dissection techniques under the gaze of his students. The bodies of hanged criminals would be brought in to the steep-sided anatomical theatre and laid upon a table. There they would be taken apart, to better understand the pieces that, together, make up a life.

In the shadow of these and the city's many other grand buildings are 24,000 students, who make up a significant proportion of the population. And on the cobbled streets that shatter outward from the River Fyris, there is no escaping them. Young, beautiful people gather in the bars and cafés that punctuate the city; they shiver arm-in-arm along the pavements, and pose for photographs in their black and white 'Uppsala caps'. Everywhere, their bikes carve runnels through the slush, and sputter filthy arcs into the air behind. Like Oxford, like Prague, like Copenhagen, this is a very youthful old city.

On my first morning in Sweden, I stopped beside the river, where a narrow fish ladder – built for migratory asp – bypasses the weir. There, a dipper was perched upon one of the ladder boards, ducking and bobbing like a tiny boxer. Again and again the bird would bow its head under the flowing water, then submerge itself completely. Up it would come, with a flicker and fluster, then down again, its white throat and breast winking in the grey air. Around me, the snow was falling in fat lumps, all puffy and swollen, yet with crystals as clear as if they were caught beneath a magnifying glass. I stood watching the bird as the flakes settled on my shoulders, cheeks and eyelashes, until I could ignore the cold no longer.

Inside the cathedral, a few moments' walk away, I closed the door and a kind of stillness descended. The place was almost silent and almost empty. The only other person I could see was a hunched cleaner, mopping and polishing the flagstone floor. As she moved back and forth with her eyes to the ground, I stood looking the other way, the great pillars dragging my eyes upwards, towards a sky that was just beyond seeing.

Inside this cathedral are buried some of the city's most famous former inhabitants. In the Lady Chapel at the far end lies King Gustav Vasa. The walls of that chapel are adorned with murals depicting scenes from the king's life; the star-studded ceiling, a glorious eggshell blue, hangs like a pardon over the extravagant sarcophagus. Elsewhere in the cathedral are the relics of Saint Erik, an earlier king, as well as those of Bridget, the country's patron saint. The scientist and philosopher Emmanuel Swedenborg lies in the Salsta Chapel, and Olof Rudbeck is buried beside the central altar.

Close to the entranceway, a plain, unadorned stone marks the grave of Carl von Linne, or Linneaus, who died in 1778. Physician, botanist and biologist, he was the creator of modern taxonomy. Under his system, each species of animal and plant was part of a kingdom, class, order, family and genus. It was Linneaus who finally separated the whales from the fish, and it was Linneaus who brought human beings together with the apes. His system, like Rudbeck's dissections, both divided and connected the world.

*

In those first few months after my return from Prague to Shetland, as I worked and walked and wrote, reacquainting myself with the home that finally felt like home, I thought I had reached a point at which I could stop. For years I had felt like a moth, drawn in by lights that were no use to me, and held back by panes of glass I could neither see nor comprehend. I had blustered this way and that, confused and lost. But now I was back – back where I had been, years earlier, only this time by choice. This time the direction had been my own. In those first few months I didn't imagine that this return would be temporary, that within a year I would have moved again. In those first few months, I didn't account for love.

I fell in love with Fair Isle the moment I arrived there. Or perhaps it was earlier still, on the ferry, as we approached the island and it grew from an indistinct shape on the horizon into something both complete and completing, something that felt as though it was already a part of me, and had always been so. It was as intense and surprising a feeling as that which had struck me in Kamchatka – more so, in fact. Only this time the feeling was directed somewhere closer, more attainable.

That first trip to Fair Isle lasted only two days, but its impact on me was enormous, and in the year that I came back to Shetland I began to visit every fortnight. My brother was working at the bird observatory there that summer, which gave me both opportunity and excuse. And then I met a girl. She had grown up on the island, and through her I came to know it better. Each time I made that journey, by boat or by plane, I felt a kind of relief, as though I were going back to a place in which I felt more fully myself. And when the opportunity arose for that girl and I to move to the island, I didn't hesitate. There seemed nothing more natural and more logical to me at that moment than to go. And so Fair Isle, three miles long by one and a half miles wide, and separated from Shetland by twenty-five miles of water, became my home.

It is impossible to untangle attraction. We are drawn in our various directions for reasons both inexplicable and inexpressible. We desire what others find repellent; we cling on to what others do not want; we are magnets with unpredictable poles. What I found in Fair Isle was a place that was both new and familiar at once, both nearby and far away. Like Fort Smith, it was a place, too, that was utterly central to itself. Though it is in theory the most remote inhabited island in Britain, and though on many days of the year one can look out and see no other land at all, it never felt remote to me. In Fair Isle, it was other places that were far away. The island itself was exactly where it ought to be. That feeling of deep centredness and settledness suited me. Here was somewhere I did not feel torn or pulled in opposing directions. Here was somewhere I could just be.

Most of all, though, it was Fair Isle's community that drew me in. It was the connections that people had with each other and with their place – connections that were obvious to even the briefest of visitors. To live in Fair Isle was unlike living anywhere that I had known before. It was to become a member of something bigger and more important than any individual. It was to belong to a community that was greater than the sum of its parts, independent from and yet dependent upon each member. On that island, among those people, I came to understand and to experience a sense of attachment that was stronger, more intricate and yet somehow simpler than any I had felt before. Fair Isle was the first place in which my desire to be at home felt welcomed and reciprocated. It was the first place in which that desire that had dogged me for most of my life truly identified itself. An unanswerable longing took shape, then, and that shape became its own answer.

I moved to Fair Isle with no particular idea of how I might survive financially. With a population of less than seventy, there are just two or three full-time jobs on the island; everyone else has several part-time roles that, together, constitute a living. Every service that elsewhere is taken for granted, there must be carried out by the same few people. Every role must be filled, or the whole cannot work. I began my time on the island by joining the knitwear co-operative and learning how to operate a knitting machine. It was a process for which I had no particular aptitude. In my first winter, I made hats and scarves, a couple of jumpers and a cardigan, which were sold to visitors the following summer, and are probably still in use somewhere in the world. But I didn't stick to the knitting for long once other opportunities arose. I became a road worker next – digging ditches, filling potholes, pouring tar, shovelling grit in the winter – and I worked a few hours each week as a classroom assistant in the primary school. At the end of my first year, I began editing a magazine in Shetland, which I could do from home and fit in around my other roles. I kept a couple of dozen sheep among the communal herd on the hill; I joined the coastguard cliff rescue team; and towards the end of my three years on the island I worked as an occasional deckhand on the ferry, *Good Shepherd IV*. Almost every day I could wake up and do something different from the day before. It suited me better than I ever could have imagined.

When I lived in Fair Isle, I felt proud to be part of something that I believed in completely; and I still believe in it, though I am no longer there. That island came to mean more than any other place to me; that community left me changed forever. When I think of Fair Isle, as I do almost every day, each thought is bound by gratitude and by love, and each thought is sharpened by the memory of leaving. When I moved away, after three years on the island, it was with intense sadness. But I did so because, to put it simply, I was no longer fully there. For the last of those years I was living alone, and that was a long way from ideal. I began to miss my family and friends in Shetland, and I began to spend more time visiting them. Were Fair Isle more accessible, that would not have been a problem. But Fair Isle is not accessible. Travelling back and forth is difficult and expensive, and the weather makes it unreliable. The island can be cut off for days at any time of year, and in the winter it can be weeks. In the end I took what seemed like the most sensible option, and I moved back to Shetland. It was one of the hardest things I have ever had to do.

*

Beneath dim orange lights in a corner of the University of Uppsala's library building, the Carolina Rediviva, hangs a glass-fronted case, and inside that case is a map. At 1.7 metres wide and 1.25 metres tall, the map is impressive in its scale, but it's even more so in its content. Though slightly faded and honeyed by age, the image itself is clear. It shows the northernmost parts of Europe – the Nordic countries, the Baltic region, Scotland and Iceland – and it shows them all in their right places. Known as the *Carta Marina*, and printed in Italy in 1539, this was in fact the earliest map to show the north with such a degree of accuracy. A masterpiece of cartography, it was created by Olaus Magnus, a Swede living in exile in Rome.

Olaus Magnus was born in Linköping, southern Sweden, in 1490. He was educated in the church and became a Catholic priest, employed by Gustav Vasa for diplomatic work in Scandinavia and on the continent. When the Protestant Reformation began in Sweden in the late 1520s, however, Olaus and his brother Johannes, then archbishop of Uppsala, were forced to flee, and their possessions were confiscated. The pair finally settled together in Rome, and when Johannes died in 1544 Olaus was given the title – by then entirely symbolic – of archbishop. He was unable to ever visit this city or his home country again.

Despite this, Olaus remained obsessed with Sweden and the north. He produced the *Carta Marina* in the early years of his Italian exile, and then in 1555 he published his *History of the Northern Peoples*, a work in twenty-two books that brought together much of the information and misinformation about the region that was then in existence. It covered politics, geography, history, natural history and folklore, alongside observations based on his own extensive travels. It was for a long time the most significant and widely-read work available on the north, and together with this map comprised something like an extended love letter to his homeland. According to Barbara Sjoholm, both 'are products of an exile's recollection and imagination, produced in part to make a case for his country, and also as an act of memory and longing.'

The *Carta Marina* almost disappeared forever, after all of the known originals were lost before the end of the sixteenth century. But in 1886, one was located in Munich, where it remains today. And in 1961, another was found in Switzerland. That copy – this copy – was purchased immediately by the University of Uppsala and brought back to where, in a sense, it belonged.

The map is illustrated with an extraordinary degree of detail. Each country is adorned not just with place names and geographical features, but also with buildings, animals and people. Uppsala is there, with its cathedral clearly visible; so too is the castle at Raseborg in Finland, close to where Ekenäs would be built shortly after the map was produced. At the southern tip of Greenland, a Norseman and Inuit are fighting; and in the eastern Baltic, Swedish and Russian troops face each other across the water. But the map, like the books, blends together the familiar with the mythical. In the far north and in the ocean, geography and fantasy become entwined. More than a dozen marine monsters populate the North Atlantic – some of them attacking ships, some attacking each other. Several of these creatures are presumably whales, drawn by someone who had never seen a whale. Others have less obvious origins. According to the map's Latin key, these include 'Rosmarus, a sea elephant' and 'The terrible sea-monster Ziphius', which boasts a tall fin, stripes, a spiny mane and webbed feet. At its side is 'Another grisly monster, name unknown'. The ocean, according to the *Carta Marina*, is a terrifying place to be.

Somewhat to the left of the map's centre is my home. Unlike the outline of Scandinavia, Shetland is not drawn with much accuracy. It looks rather like a boiled egg, sliced into six pieces. 'The Hetlandic islands and bishopric [are] a fertile country,' the key declares, and they boast 'the most beautiful women'. But Olaus clearly did have access to reliable information about the islands because, of the few place names he includes, most are still recognisable. The island of Mui on the east coast is likely to be Mousa, and Brystsund is surely Bressay Sound, on the shores of which Lerwick would later be built. Skalvogh is Scalloway, which would have been capital of the islands at that time, and Svinborhovit in the far south is Sumburgh Head. The little island just below – Feedero – is Fair Isle.

What is striking about the *Carta Marina* is that it shows the north not as an empty, desolate region, as many in

Mediterranean Europe would still have imagined it, but as a place bursting with activity and life: animal life, marine life, human life. This is a map that seems to pulse rather than lie still; it is a restless, dynamic image, infused with the energy of the world it depicts. No one else was in the room with me that morning, and for a long time I stood gazing at it, exploring those shapes and spaces that were at once so familiar and yet so unlike the cartography of today. The purpose of this map was to do more than educate; it was to inspire a reimagining of place, and to turn southern heads towards the north. Despite its many distractions – the beautiful and the monstrous – my own head kept turning towards home.

*

On a bright, Sunday afternoon I walked from the cathedral down to the river bank, then northwards on the pilgrims' trail towards Gamla ('Old') Uppsala. This is the path along which the remains of King Erik Jedvardsson – later, St Erik – are supposed to have been carried in 1167, towards their final resting-place in the city. The trail follows the river Fyris, where mallards skulked among the frosted bulrushes, then it turns away into the fringes of the city, past a bowling alley, sports centre and car park. Neat rows of tiny cottages and allotments, all closed up for the winter, lead on through tree-lined lanes and smart housing schemes, their windows glittering in the icy sunlight. The trail was busy, despite the cold. Children in down jackets dragged plastic sledges behind them, while parents pushed prams in front; lovers strolled hand in hand, joggers panted past, and elderly couples took careful steps, their walking poles clacking like magpies against the pavement. All of us were headed in the same direction, away from the city, to where the day would open out. Across a busy road, then down a lane, past sleepy bungalows and gardens, the landscape began to change.

Trees replaced buildings, and a series of low hillocks rose up on one side of the path. Out ahead, flat white fields stretched towards the horizon.

I left the main trail there and walked up towards the edge of the trees, where several boulders stood, each with coloured pebbles glued on top. According to a leaflet I found nearby this was a 'place of meditation', and the pebbles were 'pearls of life'. They were, it said, 'an aid for modern pilgrims. For the greatest and most significant of all journeys – the journey inwards'. I thought about that label – 'modern pilgrim' – and wondered if it could apply to me. I hoped not, for the mawkishness of it made me wince. But still, the question lingered. There I was, treading a long road towards where, exactly? Looking for what? I'd often on these journeys felt uneasy about my motives and my desires. I'd often questioned what I was doing, and what I was trying to do. But I'd never once thought of myself as a pilgrim. So if that's what I was, I was either an accidental or a dishonest one, a pilgrim guarding himself against disappointment. For a few moments I stood there, unmoving, as a woodpecker thrummed nearby and a pair of nuthatches scraped at the corrugated bark of a pine.

Returning to the path below, I continued northward through thinning light. The sky was a broad, watery blue, broken only by vapour trails crisscrossing above. The sun slouched over the western horizon, with a pale yellow glow that dragged gangly shadows across the landscape. Everything was more clearly defined in this light; everything seemed more certain of itself. The fields were striped by ski trails and by the memory of ploughs. The stalks of last year's crop protruded through the snow like the stubborn bristle of a day-old shave. From there I could see what I had come to see: three gently-sloping lumps, with a stone church beyond. These were the 'Mounds of the Kings' or 'Royal Mounds', one of the most important archaeological sites in all of Scandinavia, and looking out towards them I was struck by two conflicting feelings. The first stemmed from the knowledge that this is an important place – a sacred place, even. Such knowledge brings with it a kind of wonder and mystery, and Gamla Uppsala certainly has both. Yet at the same time that feeling was contradicted by the utterly unexceptional appearance of the place, by the tameness and the tediousness of it. The 'Mounds of the Kings' are precisely that – mounds – and are neither dramatic nor particularly engaging, in and of themselves. Were it not for the flatness of the surrounding land, these tumuli would be barely noticeable at all. As it is, they stand out like ripples in a millpond.

It takes a fair leap of the imagination to conjure up, in this place, the scene described by Adam of Bremen in the late eleventh century. Furnished, he claims, with eyewitness accounts, Adam described a temple then standing on this site that was 'entirely decked out in gold'. Here, 'the people worship the statues of three gods', called Thor, Wotan (Odin) and Frikko (Freyr), the last of which was built 'with an immense phallus'. But as if a giant penis were not bad enough, Adam also reported that during midwinter feasts at this temple, human and animal sacrifices were made. '[Of] every living thing that is male,' he wrote, 'they offer nine heads, with the blood of which it is customary to placate gods of this sort. The bodies they hang in the sacred grove that adjoins the temple . . . Even dogs and horses hang there with men.' This festival would go on for nine days, and by the end of it, scores of human and animal remains would be strung up among the branches.

Gamla Uppsala, then, was once a place of power and worship. It was also, most likely, one of the last real strongholds of paganism in Europe. Here, a distinctly northern mythology held out against the steady expansion of Christianity. According to the medieval Icelandic scholar Snorri Sturluson, the reason the temple on this site had such significance was that it had been built by Freyr himself. And the god – a king, perhaps, deified after death – was buried here beneath one of these mounds.

The archaeological evidence for a temple at Gamla Uppsala is inconclusive, though there were certainly buildings here before the current church was begun, back in the thirteenth century. There is no doubt, however, that the three central mounds were used for burial purposes, as indeed were hundreds, perhaps thousands, of other, smaller mounds in the area, most of which have since been destroyed by agricultural and quarrying activity. Excavations at this site have confirmed that people were cremated here around 1,500 years ago, within large cairns of stone, wood and mud. Because of the intense heat of these cremations, what remains is largely ash and burnt bones, together with a few trinkets, so little can be conclusively determined about the occupants of these tumuli. But it's been suggested that the mounds may indeed be the final resting places of kings – perhaps Ane, Egil and Adils, of the Yngling dynasty – while those graves in the surrounding area contained people of lower status.

H. A. Guerber has contrasted the 'graceful and idyllic' mythology of the 'sunny south' with the 'grand and tragical' ones of the north. 'The principal theme of the northern myths,' she explained, 'is the perpetual struggle of the beneficent forces of Nature against the injurious.' The gods themselves came to represent these various forces, and to personify the motivations, the joys, the troubles and the unfairness of the natural and human world. Like the Inuit concept of sila, this was a religion that directly reflected the place in which it developed. The three gods linked to Gamla Uppsala – Thor, Odin and Freyr – are the best known of the Norse deities. Thor, according to Hilda Ellis Davidson, is 'the characteristic hero of the stormy world of the Vikings'. Son of Odin and of Mother Earth herself, Thor is violent, defiant and extremely strong. His hammer could kill giants, but it could also bring life, and he was considered 'both destroyer and protector'.

Freyr, the supposed founder of the Uppsala temple, was a less contradictory figure than Thor. A bringer of fertility and peace, some version of the god may have been recognised for thousands of years, since the very early days of agriculture. Rites and rituals developed as crops were sown and harvested, and these rituals must certainly have included sacrifice. Life grew from death just as summer grew from winter, and here in the north, where the cycle of the seasons is extreme, the propitiation of a fertility god or goddess would have been of great importance. No matter how warm the summer or how good the harvest, still the cold and darkness and fear will return. It's not surprising that Freyr was worshipped at this time of year; northern religion was surely born in winter.

The third of the Uppsala deities, like Thor, was a complex one. Principally associated with war, Odin was seen as the father of Asgard, the realm of the gods. But that prominence did not make him, necessarily, a 'good' figure, as we might understand that word today. In the sagas and Norse poetry, Odin is sometimes portrayed as untrustworthy and treacherous. He is powerful and wise, certainly, but is more than capable of misusing those qualities. At times, Odin displays older, perhaps pre-agricultural, attributes. Like a shaman, he communicates with the dead and can change his shape, sometimes sending forth his soul in the form of an animal. He employs two ravens – Huginn and Muninn (Thought and Memory) – to keep him informed of events in the world, and his great wisdom is not, like the Christian god's, inherent, but was gained through an act of self-sacrifice. That ordeal, in which Odin hung himself for nine days and nights on the World Tree, Yggdrassil, provides the template for the mass hangings that took place at Gamla Uppsala. Out of suffering would come wisdom, out of death would come life, out of winter would come the spring.

By the time Adam of Bremen was writing, this was already a long-established seat of political and religious power, but it was also a place of tremendous conflict and change. Sweden in the eleventh century was in the middle of a long, difficult conversion from the old religion to the new, a conversion that was not complete until at least one hundred years later, and perhaps more recently still. What we find in Adam's description, therefore, is not just a scene of heathen worship; we see a moment in which two entirely different understandings of the world are painfully coexisting, and in which both are vying for supremacy. Though the man-god Jesus must have seemed familiar to the Norsemen, with his story of sacrifice and rebirth, much else in Christian teaching would have been alien. And in response to the threat of this new faith, it's not difficult to imagine that the rituals of the pagans were becoming stricter, more inflexible and, as Adam's account suggests, more violent. Yet at the same time, both religions were also interacting with and even borrowing from each other. Just as Christianity absorbed some of the old rites, such as the midwinter festival of Yule, so too did the pagans adopt some of the habits of their spiritual opponents. By the tenth century, amulets of Thor's hammer had become quite commonplace across Scandinavia. Wearing such an item would have been an act of open defiance, mimicking the crucifixes worn by Christian converts. It was a battle of symbols as well as ideas.

By the time I'd walked around the three mounds, and down towards the trees, where magpies and jackdaws scrummed among the branches, I was very cold indeed. My cheeks and forehead stung with the chill, and my fingers were numb inside my gloves. Though the sun glowed a fierce orange, it seemed a pathetic effort, and no match for the bitter blows of winter. I stepped inside the church to rest, and to find some warmth, and sat down on a green-painted pew at the back. Upstairs someone was playing the organ, and the sound roared through the building like thunder. Perhaps the organist thought no one was around to listen, for the music was loud and disjointed and unlike anything I'd ever heard in a church before. There were deep blasts of brooding chords, interspersed with what sounded like circus tunes, that together leapt uneasily around the room.

Without warning, the music stopped, and I heard the thud-thud-thud of the organist descending the wooden stairs from the loft. As he emerged at the back of the church I saw he was a man of about forty in a neat, black suit. He moved towards the altar, and was joined by an older woman with dark hair and glasses. Together they began to prepare the church for a service. She set a short crucifix in the centre of the altar, then returned with two candles, placing one on either side of the cross. The lights overhead were dimmed, and those above the altar made brighter. The woman then returned from the vestry, this time with a microphone and cable, and at the back of the church, close to where I sat, she flicked a switch. An electronic clunk said the PA system was now turned on. The woman lit the candles and then shook the match in her hand until it guttered into smoke. She used a wick on a long pole to light the twelve candles sitting high above the altar. The young man hanging on the cross looked down on all of us from his place on the wall, at the front of the church.

One day, perhaps, all of this will be as distant and unfamiliar as whatever it was that happened out there among those trees, one thousand years ago, or within those mounds, five hundred years earlier. One day, the ruins of this building may be as blank and mysterious as the broch on Mousa, which would still have been in use at the time of Christ's death. All of this ceremony, these rituals of allusion and metaphor, will no longer be understood; its meaning will have withered into nothing. How easily we unlearn our codes; how easily a sacred tomb becomes a pile of earth, or a crucifix two planks of wood. Like trying to resurrect the dead from memory alone, our interactions with places like Gamla Uppsala or Mousa will always be thwarted. For the whole is not present in the scraps that remain. It is not present in the stones or the ash or the trinkets or the words. Though we may excavate and examine, take things to pieces and put them together again, so much always will be unrevealed.

Looking back now, my father seems increasingly mysterious to me. I knew him only as a child knows a parent, which is barely at all. And sometimes, when my mother speaks of him, I feel she could be describing a stranger. That awful distance, between the fragments that I still carry and the man that he once was, grows greater each day. The erosion of memory eases grief in time, but is also its own kind of loss. 'I fear for Thought, lest he not come back,' declared Odin, in the poem 'Grímnismál', as he fretted over his two ravens. 'But I fear yet more for Memory.'

The ability to remember and to think, to imagine, are tied tightly together. They are the root of both our salvation and our fear, and the one must be balanced by the other. In the coldest moments of winter we can close our eyes and think back to sunshine. But such memories would be intolerable were it not for the vision of summer to come, and the belief – whether religious or scientific – that it *will* come. Similarly, the pain of loss can be endured only because we can remember the absence of that pain, and so can foresee the day we might awaken whole once more. Rituals are conceived in the darkest hours of winter and of grief, when certainty is hardest to hold on to, and when we imagine not the return of summer or the passing of pain, but the opposite. Through repeated acts of metaphor, fear can be translated into hope, much as memory and imagination can be translated, through acts of metaphor, into writing. Each is a kind of ordering – an effort to forge calm from chaos and meaning from its absence. Each, too, is a kind of faith. My own writing, born in grief, is no exception.

From behind me, three women entered the church, talking in hushed voices. One of them dropped coins into a little box, picked up a candle and lit it, then placed it carefully into a holder nearby. As the congregation began to arrive for the afternoon service, I stood up to leave, pausing for a moment beside four tall clocks near the entrance. Each of these clocks was handsomely made, but none was working. The only explanation for their presence was a notice on the wall, in English, that read: 'One thing is for sure, we are all going to the death in a speed of 60 minutes per hour. This watches (and time) stands still – do the same and give your own time a thought.'

As I stepped back outside, the snow on the Royal Mounds sparkled blue in the bitter light. Every contour had its shadow; every dip and curve in the land was emphasised. Turning back towards the city, I could see the cathedral spires and the pink of the castle in the distance. And as I walked away, on the path through the fields, the church bells behind me began to ring.

*

In their dealings with the outside world, the Nordic countries have all taken slightly different approaches. Of the three that sit upon the parallel, Sweden and Finland have both been members of the EU since 1995, though neither ever joined the European Community prior to that. Between them, Finland has perhaps been most enthusiastic about its place in Europe, embracing the euro right from its launch, while Sweden has chosen to retain its own currency. Norway, on the other hand, has kept out of the EU altogether, yet was a founding member of NATO in 1949, which its eastern neighbours have never joined. Buoyed since the 1970s by its extraordinary oil wealth, Norway has, on the surface, appeared the most aloof of these nations, but this is deceptive. The Norwegian oil fund, worth well over half a trillion dollars, is believed to be the largest stock market investor in Europe. The country may sit outside the EU, but its fingers reach across the continent, and all around the world.

Despite these differences, there's been a great deal of collaboration and integration between the states since the Second World War, and indeed their development through the twentieth century was remarkable in part for the degree to which each chose very similar political roads. Social democratic parties began forming governments and coalitions across the Nordic countries in the Great Depression of the 1930s. Their response to that crisis shaped the region socially as well as economically, and it continues to do so even today. A comprehensive system of welfare, pensions, social housing and healthcare provision, paid for through high taxation and pursued alongside growth and full employment, gradually transformed these nations from economic backwaters into some of the wealthiest in the world. Each of them today boasts an excellent standard of living, combined with low levels of poverty and high levels of income and gender equality. Recent decades have seen liberalisation in their economies, but the Nordic Model, as it's become known, is still looked upon enviously by social democrats the world over. It is still the goal to which others aspire.

But just as many are eager always to laud the social achievements of these countries, others are equally quick to point to a 'dark heart' within the Scandinavian system – a rot that threatens to consume and destroy the positive image projected onto the world. Right-wing extremism is one part of that rot, and its growth in the region has been noted with dismay by liberals across the continent. Ethnic nationalism seems somehow out of place in countries such as these, particularly in Sweden, which until recently had been perhaps the most enthusiastically multicultural and pro-immigration of all European states. There has, undoubtedly, been a change here – a turn towards the right, and a worrying embrace of xenophobic politics among a minority of the population. But ethnic nationalism has been on the rise right across Europe over the past two decades: France, the Netherlands, Austria, Italy, and increasingly the UK, have all seen support for far-right parties increase. The difference in Scandinavia is the sense that such parties ought not to exist there. Such is the degree to which tolerance and social cohesion are portrayed as defining Scandinavian characteristics that current trends have begun to undermine what people outside the region understand it to be. Paradoxically, many Nordic nationalists justify their hostility to immigration by highlighting the threat that multiculturalism poses to the society they have worked so hard to create. By allowing those whose culture is illiberal to come in, they argue – and Muslims are most often the target of this troubling logic – liberalism itself is endangered.

Another development, this time more imagined than real, is crime. In the world of fiction, a parallel Scandinavia, where murder is commonplace, has been growing for decades. It has become a literary and small-screen sensation. Writers such as Stieg Larsson, Henning Mankell, Karin Fossum and others have held up a distorting mirror to their society. Engagement with social and political realities is a distinguishing characteristic of much 'Nordic noir', but the place depicted in these stories is not one that would be familiar to any visitor to the countries in which they're set. Both Norway and Sweden have among the lowest murder rates in Europe, and part of the success of the genre is that very contradiction. Scandinavian crime writing sits at odds with what its readers think they know about Scandinavia; it disfigures and exaggerates the raw material of its location, and is all the more unsettling for that.

It has been said that one single event stands behind the eruption in Nordic crime fiction in recent decades: the assassination of the Swedish prime minister Olof Palme in February 1986. That event was shocking enough at the time, but the fact the murder remains unsolved so many years later has left a wound in the country's politics, and a mystery that refuses to go away. The more time that passes, the more the mystery deepens. In 2011, Norway had its own catastrophic event, which, though very different in character and scale, may yet prove as culturally significant. That the bombings in Oslo and the shootings on the island of Utøya, which together killed 77 people, were carried out by a Norwegian nationalist, who called his actions an attack on Islam, multiculturalism and Marxism, made it somehow all the more shocking. Few could ever have believed that something like this could happen in open, tolerant Norway.

Outside the country, there was a tendency to frame the actions of Anders Behring Breivik within the wider changes in Scandinavian politics and society. Some pointed again to that growing Nordic extremism, and to the region's shift away from its previously-held values, while others argued the opposite: that those very values were at fault, and were somehow responsible for creating the cultural tensions that led to these attacks. Within Norway, however, there was considerable resistance to the idea that these events should be allowed any kind of context. For the crime writer Jo Nesbø, Breivik's self-justification did not deserve to be taken seriously. 'He represents himself and not many others,' the writer argued. 'From a social or political point of view, this is not a very interesting event.'

If crimes such as the massacre in Norway or the murder of Olof Palme are more likely in Scandinavia it may be only because security measures in these countries are less intrusive than elsewhere. And that, many feel, is a risk worth preserving. In the Nordic nations, the possibility of tragedy is considered preferable to the security measures that might be required to prevent it; and that, in the Western world, is a refreshing view. When Oslo's mayor, Fabian Stang, was asked whether this attitude would need to change in the wake of Breivik's attacks, he responded: 'I don't think security can solve problems. We need to teach greater respect.' The country's prime minister Jens Stoltenber echoed that sentiment. 'The Norwegian response to violence,' he said, 'is more democracy, more openness and greater political participation.'

*

The last time I was in Oslo, I was with Jeff and a small group of other friends. All of us were students in Copenhagen at the time, and were spending our Easter break travelling through Scandinavia. One of these friends was Norwegian, and her parents had graciously agreed to house and feed us all for a night. Sitting down that evening to eat, her father asked each of us in turn where we were from. Alongside Jeff and me, there was a Canadian, an Australian, a Dutchman and a Scot. Her father listened and nodded, occasionally asking questions. When it came to my turn and I answered, 'Shetland', he looked at me and smiled. 'So,' he said, 'you are one of us.' Many Norwegians still cherish the links between the islands and themselves. As a Shetlander, one feels welcomed in this country, like a distant relative come to visit, or an emigrant returned.

On that occasion, as on this one, I felt close to home here. But this time I also felt ready to go back. Wandering the grand streets of Oslo, frozen half to the bone, I found it hard to keep my mind where it was supposed to be. The stinging cold made it difficult to concentrate; it clawed at my face and crackled inside my nostrils. And everywhere I stopped, it seemed, were reminders of other places. In Oslo, the parallel kept turning in on itself. It was no longer a straight line at all, but a tangled, knotted thread that looped this way and that around the world.

Inside the National Gallery, an exhibition of work by Tom Thomson and the Group of Seven brought me back, inevitably, to northern Canada. Those magnificent paintings – of lakes and rivers; of dark forests, empty of people – cried out for reverence. They demanded quiet. For the Group of Seven the landscape was something close to sacred, and they, as artists, were its faithful congregation.

In the University of Oslo's historical museum I was carried back further still. Displayed there were clothing and other artefacts from Roald Amundsen's Arctic expedition of 1903, on which he traversed the Northwest Passage for the first time. On a globe in the exhibition room was marked the route he had taken, following the sixtieth parallel west from Norway, past Shetland, past Cape Farewell, before turning north through the Davis Strait. Amundsen returned from this successful trip in 1906, shortly after his country's independence from Sweden. On future expeditions he was the first to reach the South Pole, thirty-four days ahead of Captain Scott, and he made the first undisputed visit to the North Pole too, by airship, in 1926. Like Tom Thomson, Roald Amundsen would later disappear in the north, but unlike Thomson, his body was never found.

Visiting the Viking Ship Museum on the western edge of the city, I was brought home. It occurred to me there that, while I was in Oslo, Shetland's Viking festival, Up Helly Aa, was taking place. That event – a piece of revivalist pageantry invented by nostalgic Victorians – is one of the big moments in the islands' calendar. Each year, hundreds of men (and only men) march through the streets of Lerwick, with flaming torches held aloft. Some are dressed as Vikings, all Hollywood helmets and gleaming chain mail, while others sport costumes that range from Disney characters to local celebrities. At the end of this procession, a replica longship is burned in a park in the centre of town. And then the men get very drunk, which is perhaps the most authentically Viking thing about Up Helly Aa. Many Shetlanders take the festival extremely seriously; others roll their eyes each time it comes around.

I couldn't remain in Oslo long. I was restless and impatient, and increasingly eager to be moving. Sitting in a café one afternoon, I decided to cut short my trip and go west towards the coast. There I would be closer to the end of the line. In front of me was a mediocre cup of coffee and a few slices of bread and jam that together had cost almost £10. From the speakers, a twenty-second snatch of an Elvis Presley song was playing, stopping, then repeating, over and over. The woman behind the counter didn't seem to notice, and I didn't feel like mentioning it. Each time I looked up she seemed to be staring at me, with a gaze that could have been friendly or suspicious, it was hard to tell. There was something disorientating about the woman: her white hair was too large for her head and her glasses too small for her eyes. I threw back the last mouthful of coffee, stood up and nodded a thank you, then I walked to the train station and booked my seat to Bergen for the following day.

The morning was still gloomy and grey as we headed west from the station, just after eight, through the suburbs and out towards wooded hills and snowy valleys. I fought the urge to close my eyes, and watched instead as we moved through the brightening pre-dawn. At the town of Drammen, the sun was just rising over the water, glowing orange as an ember, though still soft and uncertain around its edges. For a moment it seemed to droop or melt, no longer a circle but an oblong, wilting beneath its own distant heat. In the harbour, steam curled upwards from the sea into the frozen day. I tried to remember a less than flattering Norwegian joke I'd heard once about this town: It's better to have a dram an hour than an hour in Drammen. Or something like that.

Pushing along steep mountainsides, blinking in and out of tunnels, the train threw puffs of ice into the air around us, like smoke belching from an engine. As we climbed higher, the clouds seemed to stoop to meet us. The peaks were all obscured, and everything faded upwards into grey. Even close by, the green of the pines seemed no longer a real colour at all, but instead a new shade of darkness. On either side of the track, each tree bore its burden of snow differently. The conifers were heavy with it – needles and branches arched towards the ground – while silver birches stood delicate as feathers, their leafless twigs a perfect web of white. Up here, the land lay as though in suspended animation. We passed a river, not quite frozen but congealed, as thick and lumpy as custard. In the mountain hamlets, little houses sat with a foot of snow upon their roofs and an exclamation mark of smoke above their chimneys. Flags hung listless from poles. Everything was still except for the train rushing past. From each of these things we were separated by glass and metal, and then by time. In seconds they were gone, a glancing memory, as though perhaps they never quite existed at all. There is much that time takes away and doesn't give back. There is much we wish to keep but lose, just as there is much we wish to lose but can't.

In Geilo, the carriage began to empty as people gathered bags and ski equipment and stepped outside. There, at eight hundred metres above sea level and fifteen degrees below freezing, the sun was just beginning to break through. And further still, at Finse – the highest train station in northern Europe, at more than twelve hundred metres – the sky finally cleared. Snow covered everything there. The buildings were swamped by it. The fences had disappeared. There were no trees and no cars, only quads and snowmobiles, skis and paraskis. From my seat at the window, I squinted out into the dazzling day, where the whole world was winter-lit, and sparkled with anticipation.

*

Bergen must be one of the most picturesque cities in Europe, with its wonky, multicoloured waterfront and precipitous backdrop of mountains. But it is also, certainly, one of the wettest cities. It seems to rain almost constantly from the heavy clouds cradled above the fjords. On this occasion, a steady drizzle covered everything, and the streets were ankle-deep with slush. Everyone stepped slowly and carefully through it, trying to avoid slipping or being splashed by the traffic. But neither was entirely avoidable. Every so often a head would drop down and a pair of legs would come up, accompanied by a yelp. The unfortunate pedestrian would be assisted back to their feet, and everything would continue as before. I spent two damp days exploring the city, then made my preparations to go on.

There are few places in the world where a return journey requiring four buses and three ferries could be planned with confidence for a single day. But in Scandinavia, where public transport is about as reliable as the over-pricing of beer, I didn't doubt for a moment that such a journey would be possible. My destination was the island of Stolmen, a little further south along the coast. It was the last point of land on the sixtieth parallel before it dropped back into the North Sea and then returned to Shetland, and it seemed the most appropriate place to complete my journey before going home. Flicking through the timetables in my hotel room in Bergen, I could see that buses were scheduled to coincide with ferries, and that each connection could be made to fit. The route to Stolmen was rather convoluted, with several changes required, but the return journey was much simpler. A single bus could bring me all the way, including on to the ferry. I could get there and back in a day without any trouble at all, it seemed. I could even have a few hours to wander and explore the island if the weather was good.

The bus drove southwards, past villages and half frozen fjords, in a misty brightness like an English autumn dawn. The sun was uncertain, haze-hidden then bright – a game of celestial hide-and-seek. It seemed a good day to be moving. The route was southwards first, from Bergen to Haljem, where the bus boarded a ferry to Sandvikvåg. From there I took another ferry, northwest to Husavik, on the island of Huftarøy. It was all so easy and effortless, and after only a couple of hours I was most of the way there. At that point, though, the plans I'd made dissolved. There was no drama and no panic, they just dissolved. The connecting bus was due five minutes after the ferry arrived in Husavik, and so I stood and waited at the stop beside the terminal, enjoying the pace of the day. From that stop I had an excellent view of the bus as it appeared, right on schedule, along the road just adjacent to the terminal. I watched it drive along that road, carefully follow each curve, then continue on its way without taking the turn down to where I was standing. It was one of those static moments, like when you shut the door and immediately remember that your keys are on the other side. For a few seconds it seems that, if you regret it hard enough, you might just be able to turn back time. Only the click of that lock separates you from your keys; only a few steps separated me from the correct bus stop on the road above. I stood there doing nothing for several minutes, as though some unimagined solution might just fall from the sky in front of me. The next bus was not for hours – too late to get me to Stolmen and back by the end of the day. I had only two choices: return to Bergen or go on.

I hate hitchhiking. I truly hate it. Perhaps because I only ever do it when absolutely necessary, there is a deep sense of humiliation in me every time I am forced into that position.

And what increases that humiliation, what marks it like a scar upon me, is that I am terrible at it. In the half dozen or so times I've tried to hitchhike in Europe, I've been successful only twice. I have come to believe that somehow my face is unsuitable for the task. It must be a face that people just don't want in their cars, because nobody ever stops for me. They don't stop for me in Shetland and they certainly didn't stop for me in Norway. Following the road west towards where the bus had gone, I stuck out my thumb and smiled at every approaching car. And every car sailed on by, without so much as glance. After an hour or so of this repeated rejection I understood that my choices had been reduced to one. The least humiliating option was to ignore the cars and just keep walking.

I had no idea how far that walk would be, or whether it would get me where I wanted to go in time; and to begin with that absence of certainty only increased my fury. I took every passing vehicle as an insult and every magpie's cackle as a slight. I cursed my journey, and the sheer futility of what I was doing. I cursed myself for my own stupidity. I was looking for a line that didn't really exist, on an island about which I knew nothing. I was striding through a winter afternoon, cold, cross and dejected.

But as the walk wore on, an invigorating acceptance descended on me. I put one foot in front of the other and moved forward. I didn't know when I would get to Stolmen, that was true; but I knew that I would get there. And I didn't know if I could get back to Bergen that day, but I would get back sometime. Walking like that, blocking out the worries and the doubts, I barely noticed the places through which I passed. My thoughts were elsewhere entirely, and yet nowhere in particular. When I arrived in Bekkjarvik after two hours of walking, I was almost as surprised as I was relieved, and when I consulted a timetable at the bus stop by the harbour, I found that a school bus was scheduled to leave the village for Stolmen twenty minutes later. It would give me just over an hour on the island before I had to make my way back to Bergen.

We drove from Bekkjarvik out over the bridge to Selbjorn and onward, over the next bridge, to Stolmen. Red-faced children in snow-suits filled the space with chatter and joy, and every so often a bundle of them would be released into the arms of waiting parents at the roadside. Stolmen was stern and beautiful. Boulders and low trees along the verges stretched out towards rough moorland and crags beyond, and small lakes, distorted by ice. I got off at Våge, at the far south of the island, the end of the road. There was a turning circle at the top of a slope, with a bus shelter on one side and several huts and houses on the other. I stepped out into a thin light and a familiar, salt-ridden breeze.

Once the bus had departed, I could hear no cars, no voices and no machines of any kind – only the intimate whisper of the sea, just a few hundred yards away. It looked like a ghost village, yet at the same time I felt I was being watched from behind a curtain. Some of the buildings, I guessed, might be summer houses, so were probably empty. But others must be occupied. The island has a population of 200, which is not much, but enough.

I had read that Våge was the 'commercial centre' of Stolmen, and I walked back down the road a little way in search of the evidence. So far as I could see, it consisted of a small shop with a petrol pump outside. I went in and browsed the shelves, not wishing to buy anything but just to be there. The shop was well stocked, as stores in out-of-the-way villages usually are, and it gave the impression of a place in which the exchange of words was as important as the exchange of goods and money. Besides me, there were two staff members and two customers. One of them, a woman of about forty with long, curly hair and a thick jacket, was talking quietly and fondly to an elderly man in a fur hat. He seemed to be struggling, as though confused about what he needed, and the woman touched his arm lightly. She was offering suggestions, I thought, and guiding him back towards certainty.

The two women behind the counter then joined the conversation, and each of them spoke in an affectionate, familiar way, oblivious to the roles that elsewhere would define them. Though the words were unknown to me, the tone was not. These were neighbours and members of a community: a connection far deeper than the tenuous bond between buyers and sellers. 'Commercial centre' was a rather inappropriate title for a shop like this, but it was, certainly, a centre.

Wandering those few short aisles, I felt a deep longing to be spoken to in the way those people spoke to each other. By then it was several days since I'd had any kind of conversation with anyone, and I was lonely. But it was more than that. My desire was not really to talk, it was to be known. I wanted to be enclosed and included within that thing of which these people were a part. I wanted to belong, as they belonged, to something bigger than themselves. I missed Fair Isle then, and I longed to go back.

Once outside, I walked briskly towards the sea, over rough ground that crunched with ice at every step. Just above the shoreline I found a rock that looked almost comfortable and I sat down. There was little wind, and the waves unfolded onto the stones with an uncommon tenderness. Towards the west, the tell-tale streaks of a rain shower stained the orange horizon with blue. Everything here was as I knew it should be: the smell of it, the sound of it, the sight. Everything was familiar.

Sitting there beside the sea, two hundred miles from home, I thought back to the traffic that had ventured west from this coast towards my own shores. To the Vikings who had sailed in the eighth and ninth century, and who had made their way ultimately to Greenland and beyond. To the refugees of the Second World War, who were carried in fishing boats and other vessels, in what became known as the 'Shetland Bus'. And then to the oil tanker *Braer*, which left the refinery just north of Bergen in January 1993, carrying 85,000 tonnes of crude oil. She was bound for Quebec in Canada, but made it only as far as Quendale on the south east coast of Shetland, where she hit the rocks and spilled her cargo. It was a few years after my family moved to the islands, and a few miles from the spot where, later, I would find the parallel.

I'd come to Stolmen by following that line around the world. Once there, I had nowhere else to go but home. I'd known all along, of course, that this was a journey with only one possible destination. But faced with that last stretch of water that separated beginning from end, I felt nervous and uncertain. Would the place I was going back to be the same place that I had left? And did I even want it to be? Perhaps I'd expected answers, but I hadn't found any. I'd been left with only questions. Ahead, the sky was like a welt, blue and purple ringed with pink. A crack in the clouds brought sharp fingers of light down onto the blackening waves, and the cold chafed against my face. I sat for ten minutes more, perhaps fifteen, and then it was time to go. I stood and flung a stone into the water, towards Mousa, as though to reach as far as I could towards home, and then I walked away.

HOMECOMING

You can take a ferry north to Shetland almost every night of the year, leaving Aberdeen in the early evening and arriving at breakfast time the following day. It's a convenient, if not always pleasant, way to travel. But on the day I headed home, having flown from Bergen to Scotland, there was no ferry. One vessel was in dry dock undergoing repairs, and the other was leaving Lerwick in the opposite direction. Instead, I booked myself onto the freight boat, which meant a longer and less comfortable journey across the North Sea. But at least it would get me there. And so at three in the afternoon I boarded the *Hellier* together with four other passengers, climbing stairwells and following corridors, each of which reeked of diesel, salt and cold metal.

As the boat shuddered away from the dock an hour later, the five of us were served food: soup, roast beef, chips, cake. A few polite words were shared, but no one was very interested in talking, and as we cleared our plates one after another of us stood up and retired to our separate cabins. The sailing would take eighteen hours, with just a brief stop in Orkney after midnight, and almost as soon as we reached the mouth of Aberdeen harbour the ship began to rock heavily, to an inconsistent beat. The crash of metal on water seemed to shake time loose from its rhythm and drive it forward, confidently, into the night.

Unlike flying, when the moment of arrival is clearly defined – that solid thud as the wheels hit the tarmac – arrivals and departures by sea feel less distinct, more negotiable. To be afloat is to be neither fully detached nor connected, neither here nor entirely there, but suspended, like the boat itself, between elements. I like it. There is something about the pace of the journey that puts me at ease: the sheer slog of it, and the boredom that unravels, wave by wave and roll by roll. Once at sea, I feel almost back where I'm going.

The American writer Harry W. Paige said that 'home is not a place only, but a condition of the heart'. That is to say not that home can be anywhere at all, but that the relationship between person and place is an emotional one. Like being married, being at home is not a passive state. It is a process, in which the heart must be engaged. That is as true for the reindeer herders of Siberia, whose home may be hundreds of square miles, as it is for the inhabitants of a tiny village on a tiny island.

For many people this is not so. Home for them is nowhere in particular. It is the house in which their belongings are kept and in which they go to sleep at night. It extends no further than that. This is the condition of our time. It is a marriage without love, a relationship without commitment. And it is, surely, a kind of homelessness.

But there is another kind of homelessness, too, one which has the opposite effect on its sufferers; and that is the ailment with which, from an early age, I was afflicted. For much of my life I felt myself to be exiled from a home that no longer existed, and which in some sense never really had. In her book, *The Future of Nostalgia*, Svetlana Boym described this feeling as 'akin to unrequited love, only we are not sure about the identity of our lost beloved'. For me that feeling arrived with our move to Shetland, and was compounded by the loss of my father. It became a hole within which I tried, desperately, to find form. Like the north, home is defined in its absence, in the distance between longing and belonging. But, like the north, it is only through intimacy, through love, that it can come to be known.

The landscape that truly shaped me was that of Shetland. This is where I became the person I became. This is where the conflicts that would form me were fought out. That I came to love this place, having once hated it, is strange and yet entirely coherent. It was a process of understanding, familiarity and, I suppose, of forgiveness that brought me back here. In the end, I accepted the centre around which my world was spinning, and I turned towards it.

＊

When I woke in the early morning, the *Hellier* was pitching hard, swaying like a drunk heading for bed. We were somewhere around Fair Isle, I guessed, most likely in that stretch of water called the Roost, between the isle and the Shetland Mainland, where tides and currents and winds collide. The water here can be as wild as water ever can be. Something in the cabin was banging each time the ship lurched, a solid clatter against the wall. Hazy headed, I got up to find the cause, groping in the darkness at the end of the bunk. A ladder hung there by its top rail, the bottom half a pendulum swinging in time with the waves. I lifted it from the wall and wedged it at an angle, where it could neither fall nor slide, and I lay back down and closed my eyes.

The lurching became more pronounced then, more violent and uncomfortable. Things that had previously been static were on the move, and each time we rolled to port the curtains remained vertical, inviting a wedge of grey light in to the room. I stood up again and rearranged the cabin, trying to prevent noise and damage. Anything that could move was put somewhere that would stop it; anything that could make sound was silenced. I knew that I wouldn't sleep again, but at least I could lie in peace, rocking almost comfortably through the final miles, until we docked in Lerwick on a dull, wet morning. It was a day much like any other day, except my journey around the world was complete.

It was while living in Fair Isle that I began to write this book. My fixation on the parallel and the idea of a journey around it had never gone away, and there on the island I realised that I might finally be able to achieve it. I abandoned the novel I'd started months earlier, but the ideas that had grown within that book spilled over into this one. What was most important in making this journey seem possible, though, was that I recognised and welcomed, for the first time, my destination. To travel around the sixtieth parallel was ultimately to return to Shetland. Going away was possible, then, because coming back was desirable.

When I set out, I had no idea what I hoped to find, I just wanted to go. Curiosity, restlessness and homesickness: those were the things that had set me on my way, and those were the things that kept me going. Perhaps, somehow, I hoped to satiate those urges, as though by following the parallel to its end I could return settled and content. But things are never quite that simple.

During my travels, I met people who *were* settled and who *were* content. Some had only ever lived in the place where they were born; they were shaped and defined by those places. Others had left one home and found another, in which they felt a deeper sense of belonging. Jeff in Alaska, Ib and Jacques in Fort Smith: I admired their certainty, and their commitment to the places they'd chosen. It was a commitment that, in each case, was renewed and reinforced by engagement, in thought and in action.

But along the parallel there were also those – past and present – who'd been estranged: political and religious exiles; indigenous people whose cultures had been undermined. And perhaps in the north estrangement is more pronounced than elsewhere. For in the north, landscape and climate are uncompromising. They demand, of those who stay there, ways of living that are native to the place. And though it's increasingly easy to ignore such demands, wherever you choose to be, estrangement is never without cost.

*

A few months after I completed the journeys described in this book, something happened to me. It would not be helpful, perhaps, to put a name to it here, for such afflictions always feel distant from the labels we give them. It was, anyhow, a crumbling of certainties and a steady erosion of things I had expected to stay whole. An overwhelming sense of disorientation struck me then, and I felt myself sinking, much as I'd sunk to my knees on that day beside the window, sixteen years earlier. I don't know whether the ending of my travels was the trigger for what happened next, though I can't fully untangle the two things in my mind. Somehow my return seemed to bring me back to the very point at which I'd begun: to grief and to loss and to an absence of direction. Whatever the immediate cause, the result was a year in which I could barely write, and several months when I couldn't work at all. It was a year in which I left yet another house, and a partner who cared for me very much. Turned inward as I was, I lost friendships I didn't want to lose. I felt plagued, in that time, by a darkness I'd not known since my teenage years, and by a hopelessness I thought I'd long left behind.

The most surprising result of this period of sadness and confusion was still to come, however. Since returning from Prague ten years before, I'd been certain I would remain in Shetland. I was stubborn in that certainty, and critical of those friends who, as I saw it, gave in to the appeal of elsewhere. The urge to move comes and goes, I'd told them. You just ride it out and commit to home. Yet at the end of that year, as I began to emerge from beneath my own shadow, I left Shetland and moved south. I left Shetland and I began, once again, to write. In *The Idea of North*, Wally Maclean declared that 'You can't talk about the north until you've got out of it.' And perhaps he was correct, for in those months after leaving I found myself able to complete this book. I understood, finally, what I had to say.

There are moments in life that are remembered quite differently from all other moments. They are replayed and replayed and replayed, as though in doing so the story might turn out differently. But it never does. The story always ends the same. The car always rumbles out of the car park, and it never comes back. I was sixteen when my father died, and I've lived just over half my life without him. In another sixteen years I'll be older than he ever came to be. I couldn't decide the ending on that day; nor could I change it later. But this story is different. Sixty degrees north is a story whose ending I chose.

When I look back to the beginning, to that little boy beside the window in Lerwick, dreaming his way around the sixtieth parallel, I feel sorry for him. He is lost, grief-stricken and alone; or at least he thinks he's alone, which is almost the same thing. If I could, I would reach out to him and take him by the shoulders. I would tell him that one day he will feel whole again. I would tell him that, impossible as it may seem in that moment, he will find his way home.

Index

223

Acknowledgements

Peter Davidson offered me encouragement when all I had was an idea. He read the earliest chapters and patiently guided me in the right direction. Without his kindness this book would probably never have been written.

During my travels the following people were particularly helpful and hospitable: Rie Oldenburg in Narsaq; Hilary LeRoy-Gauthier, Shawn Bell and Sam Stokell in Fort Smith; Eva Meyer and Maria Jarlsdotter Enckell in Mariehamn; and especially Jeff and Cassandra Raun in Anchorage.

Numerous friends assisted me in one way or another, but Jordan Ogg, Amy Liptrot, Martin MacInnes, Rob Duncan, Ruth Cockshott and Charlene Storey all deserve particular mention. So too do my friends at Nice 'n' Sleazy's acoustic night in Glasgow, who helped me through the last months of writing with their fine company and songs.

Thanks to my agent, Jenny Brown; to Esther Woolfson for her invaluable input; to Gavin Francis; to my editor, Tom Johnstone; and to everyone at Polygon/Birlinn. Thanks also to Creative Scotland, the Scottish Book Trust, Emergents, Shetland Arts and the Arts Trust of Scotland.

I began writing this book while living in Fair Isle. My love for that place and that community will last a lifetime, as will my gratitude towards people there. I felt truly at home on the isle, and still do, in a way that I have never done anywhere else; and my understanding of that crucial word – home – which is at the heart of this book, was shaped by my time there.

Thanks, finally, to my family, for putting up with me.

Author's Note

Three people quoted in this book were unaware that our conversations might be published. I have therefore changed their names.

SWORD ART ONLINE ALTERNATIVE: GUN GALE ONLINE 1

ART: TADADI TAMORI
STORY: KEIICHI SIGSAWA
ORIGINAL STORY: REKI KAWAHARA

Translation: Stephen Paul   Lettering: Brndn Blakeslee

This book is a work of fiction. Names, characters, places, and incidents are the product of the author's imagination or are used fictitiously. Any resemblance to actual events, locales, or persons, living or dead, is coincidental.

SWORD ART ONLINE ALTERNATIVE GUN GALE ONLINE
© KEIICHI SIGSAWA © REKI KAWAHARA 2016
© TADADI TAMORI 2016
All rights reserved.
Edited by ASCII MEDIA WORKS
First published in Japan in 2016 by KADOKAWA CORPORATION, Tokyo.
English translation rights arranged with KADOKAWA CORPORATION, Tokyo, through Tuttle-Mori Agency, Inc., Tokyo.

English translation © 2017 by Yen Press, LLC

Yen Press
1290 Avenue of the Americas
New York, NY 10104

Visit us at yenpress.com
facebook.com/yenpress
twitter.com/yenpress
yenpress.tumblr.com
instagram.com/yenpress

First Yen Press Edition: November 2017

Yen Press is an imprint of Yen Press, LLC.
The Yen Press name and logo are trademarks of Yen Press, LLC.

The publisher is not responsible for websites (or their content) that are not owned by the publisher.

Library of Congress Control Number: 2017954143

ISBNs: 978-0-316-44241-1 (paperback)
       978-0-316-44242-8 (ebook)

10 9 8 7 6 5 4 3 2 1

BVG

Printed in the United States of America

POSTSCRIPT

I'm pretty sure that I'm new to just about every reader of this book. My name is Tadadi Tamori.

Through a number of very fortunate circumstances, I got the job of drawing this manga. There's a lot of pressure working on such a big-name title, but knowing I get Sigsawa-san's thrilling writing and Kuroboshi-san's cute characters to work with is a big help. I'll admit that I'm still figuring out how to draw the gun battles though... (LOL)

If there's one thing I'm unsatisfied with, perhaps it's the current lack of a more voluptuous presence in the story. I'm eager to see someone like that join the cast!

Hoping I'll see you all again in the next volume.

Tadadi Tamori

CONGRATULATORY COMMENTS FROM

AUTHOR KEIICHI SIGSAWA -SENSEI & **CHARACTER DESIGNER** KOUHAKU KUROBOSHI -SENSEI

Congrats on putting out the first volume of the *GGO* spin-off manga!
As the writer, it brings me no end of joy to be able to witness Llenn bounding across the pages of this book.
The battles are only getting started, and I'm sure they'll get much tougher to draw... so good luck!

Keiichi Sigsawa

CONGRATULATIONS ON
THE RELEASE OF VOLUME 1
OF *SWORD ART ONLINE
ALTERNATIVE: GUN GALE
ONLINE.*

I'M BLOWN AWAY BY THE SHEER
PRESENCE AND TENSION OF
TADADI TAMORI-SAN'S WORLD
OF WAFTING GUNPOWDER!

I CAN'T TELL YOU HOW FUN IT
IS TO SEE THE *GGO* CHARACTERS
IN ACTION. I LOOK FORWARD
TO EACH INSTALLMENT!
THANKS SO MUCH!

I CAN'T TAKE MY EYES OFF
LLENN-CHAN'S SPEED!
KOUHAKU KUROBOSHI

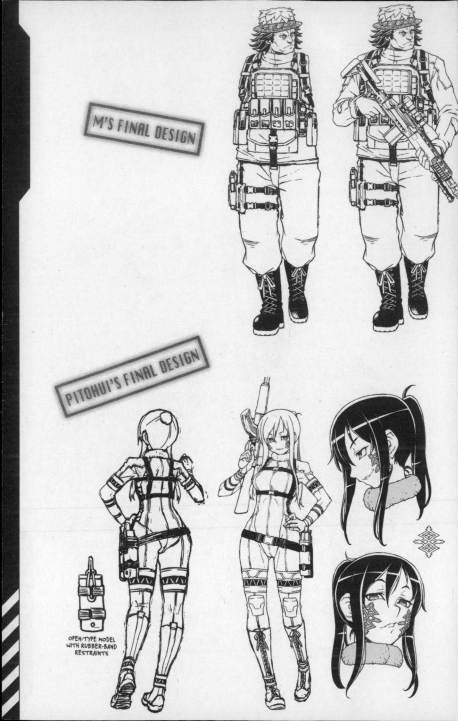

M'S FINAL DESIGN

PITOHUI'S FINAL DESIGN

OPEN-TYPE MODEL
WITH RUBBER-BAND
RESTRAINTS

M

M'S INITIAL DESIGN

LLENN'S INITIAL DESIGN

LLENN'S ACTIONS

SWORD ART ONLINE ALTERNATIVE
GUN GALE ONLINE
TADADI TAMORI'S DESIGN SKETCHES

LLENN'S FINAL DESIGN

Translation Notes

PAGE 10
Llenn: The avatar's title is actually a creative nickname derived from her IRL name, Karen. In Japanese, "Llenn" is pronounced the same as "Ren," as there is no distinction between the "R" and "L" sounds.

PAGE 132
Team ZEMAL: The acronym comes from ZEn-nippon MAchine gun Lovers. "Zen-Nippon" means "All-Japan."

PAGE 156
Self-Defense Forces: The Japan Self-Defense Forces (JSDF) is the de facto military force of Japan, which is prohibited from having a standing army by the post-WWII constitution instated by the Allies.

TO BE CONTINUED...
in Volume 2!

I MEAN, THEY LITERALLY GET PAID TO DO BATTLE.

THOSE SIX ARE EITHER POLICE, MARITIME SAFETY, SPECIAL FORCES...

...OR SELF-DEFENSE FORCES.

I DIDN'T KNOW YOU COULD LEARN THAT SKILL...

I WANNA GET IT TOO!

HOWAAA (DROOL)

WOW, WHAT WAS THAT? AMAZING! IT'S WAY FASTER THAN TAKING THE STAIRS!

IT'S RAPPELLING—VERTICALLY DROPPING DOWN A ROPE.

SO HOW'D THEY DO IT, THEN?

ACTUALLY... YOU CAN'T DESCEND THAT FAST JUST BY UTILIZING THE IN-GAME SKILL.

I CAN TELL BECAUSE I'VE DONE IT.

.... PITO-SAN DID SAY SOMETHING LIKE THAT ONCE...

VLP...

IN OTHER WORDS, THEY KNOW HOW TO DO THAT IN REAL LIFE.

IT'S THE ACTUAL PLAYER'S PERSONAL ABILITY—

153

OH! I SEE THEM!

HM?

THEY PROBABLY EXPECT WE'VE GONE BACK INTO HIDING IN THE WOODS.

ROGER THAT.

LET'S WAIT THIS OUT AND OBSERVE A BIT LONGER.

OH? WHERE?

FOUND THE OTHER TWO.

WAIT... THEY'RE GONE ALREADY?

● DEAD

● DEAD

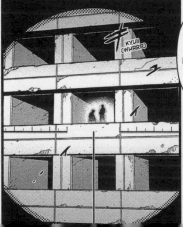

KYUII CWHRRR

MID-LEVEL.

PAST THE RUINS

LOOK AT THE BUILDING WITH THE CURVED DESIGN.

AAAND
······

···
THERE
THEY
GO.
THAT
WAS
QUICK
···

First time 14:10 → Second time 14:20

HMM?
THAT MEANS WE
HAVE SIX MINUTES
UNTIL THE NEXT
SCAN. WE CAN SEE
THE ENEMY, AND
THEY DON'T KNOW
WHERE WE ARE.

IN JUST
FOUR
MINUTES
FROM THE
SCAN···

HRMPH.

NOPE.
I COULD
GET ONE, BUT
THE REST
WOULD TAKE
COVER.

M-
SAN,
GET
'EM!

THEN
WE'D HAVE
TO DUCK
INTO THE
FOREST
AGAIN.

IN THE GREEK TYCOON'S BED

They're dangerously handsome and impossibly wealthy….

They're used to having it all….

The secluded beaches of their private islands make the perfect setting for red-hot seduction….

These Greek billionaires will stop at nothing to bed their chosen mistresses— women who find themselves powerless to resist being pleasured….

IN THE GREEK TYCOON'S BED

At the mercy of a ruthless Mediterranean billionaire…

CHANTELLE SHAW lives on the Kent coast, five minutes from the sea, and does much of her thinking about the characters in her books while walking on the beach. An avid reader from an early age, she found that school friends used to hide their books when she visited. But Chantelle would retreat into her own world, and she still writes stories in her head all the time.

Chantelle has been blissfully married to her own tall, dark and very patient hero for over twenty years, and has six children. She began to read Harlequin novels as a teenager, and throughout the years of being a stay-at-home mom to her brood, found romance fiction helped her to stay sane! Her aim is to write books that provide an element of escapism, fun and of course romance for the countless women who juggle work and a home life and who need their precious moments of "me" time.

She enjoys reading and writing about strong-willed, feisty women and even stronger-willed, sexy heroes. Chantelle is at her happiest when writing. She is particularly inspired while cooking dinner, which unfortunately results in a lot of culinary disasters! She also loves gardening, taking her very badly behaved terrier for walks and eating chocolate (followed by more walking—at least the dog is slim!).

THE GREEK TYCOON'S VIRGIN MISTRESS

CHANTELLE SHAW

~ IN THE GREEK TYCOON'S BED ~

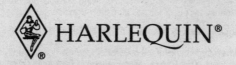

TORONTO • NEW YORK • LONDON
AMSTERDAM • PARIS • SYDNEY • HAMBURG
STOCKHOLM • ATHENS • TOKYO • MILAN • MADRID
PRAGUE • WARSAW • BUDAPEST • AUCKLAND

ISBN-13: 978-0-373-82081-8
ISBN-10:   0-373-82081-X

THE GREEK TYCOON'S VIRGIN MISTRESS

First North American Publication 2008.

www.eHarlequin.com

Printed in U.S.A.

THE GREEK TYCOON'S
VIRGIN MISTRESS

In memory of my mum, Gabrielle

CHAPTER ONE

THE dying rays of the sun glanced across the sandstone walls of Otterbourne House so that it appeared to glow like burnished gold. As Anna scrunched across the gravel drive she reached into her handbag for her compact, flipped open the lid and scrutinised her appearance in the mirror. Her career as a model and the 'face' of an international cosmetics company necessitated spending hours being made up, but in private she usually opted for a more natural look.

Tonight she'd gone for the full works. Her reflection revealed an exquisite mask of porcelain skin stretched taut over sharp cheekbones, the deep blue of her eyes emphasised by the careful application of a taupe-coloured shadow and her lips coated in chic, scarlet gloss.

On any other occasion, dinner with her closest friend Kezia Niarchou and her husband Nik at their home in the Hertfordshire countryside would have called for casual attire suitable for crawling around on the floor with her little godson Theo. But tonight was different and she looked the epitome of glamour in her black designer cocktail dress.

Goodbye, Anna—hello, Anneliese Christiansen, sophisticated supermodel, she thought derisively as she snapped the compact shut and took a deep breath. Ever since Kezia had dropped the bombshell that Nik's cousin Damon would

be present at the dinner party, Anna's nerves had been on edge. Damon Kouvaris was something else and right now she wished he were somewhere else, preferably on the other side of the world.

'Fashionably late is one thing, but you're pushing it,' Kezia greeted good-naturedly when she opened the door and ushered Anna inside. 'Luckily it's a cold first course, but I've been detecting rumblings from the kitchen that Mrs Jessop's fretting about her *boeuf en croûte.*'

'I'm sorry, didn't you get my text? I had a flat tyre,' Anna murmured apologetically. 'Fortunately that young guy from the ground-floor flat fitted the spare for me.'

'I should hope so; you could hardly have jacked up the car in that dress. You look gorgeous but I'm curious to know who you're hoping to impress,' Kezia murmured softly, her eyes widening when Anna blushed. 'It couldn't be Damon by any chance, could it?'

'No, it could not,' Anna drawled, managing to affect just the right amount of lazy amusement in her voice. They had been as close as sisters since their first day at boarding-school and their friendship had weathered her parents' bitter divorce and Kezia's battle with leukaemia. The bond between them was unbreakable but some things were too personal to share, certainly her inexplicable fascination with Damon Kouvaris.

Nik's cousin's reputation as a ruthless businessman was almost as legendary as the rumours of his prowess in the bedroom. He was said to be a dynamic lover with an insatiable interest in sophisticated blondes and Anna had no intention of joining his list of conquests. Yet, to her extreme irritation, she had been unable to forget him these past two months.

The guests were assembled in the drawing room. She followed Kezia through the doorway and smiled warmly at the group of her most trusted friends.

'Anna, what can I get you to drink?' Nikos Niarchou strode across the room to greet her. Tall, dark and impossibly handsome, Nik had exchanged roles from jet-setting playboy to devoted husband and father without a backward glance. He dropped a light kiss on Anna's cheek but his gaze returned immediately to Kezia.

This was how marriage should be, Anna acknowledged hollowly, noting how Nik's dark eyes glowed with love for his wife. No man had ever looked at her with such tender adoration and she was aware of a faint pang of envy that she quickly suppressed. Kezia, more than anyone, deserved to be happy and Anna was genuinely delighted for her. It wasn't as if she had any great desire to sample the joys of matrimony anyway, she reminded herself. Her parents were both on their third attempts and she had no intention of following their rocky path down the aisle of nuptial bliss.

'I hear you had trouble with your car. You should have let us know earlier—I would have sent my driver to collect you,' Nik admonished lightly. 'You're almost as stubborn as my wife,' he added with a grin. 'Come and say hello to the others.'

There was no sign of Nik's cousin but Anna felt as tense as an overstrung bow when she greeted the other couples. It was instantly apparent that she was the only person present who did not have a partner. It wasn't an unusual occurrence—she had no one special in her life and at social engagements she usually relied on a select group of male models and actor friends to play the role of her escort.

Tonight, knowing she was among friends, she had come alone but now she wished she had brought one of her faithful band of chaperons. She could only pray that Damon was accompanied by one of his numerous lovers because the idea of sitting next to him throughout dinner caused a peculiar feeling in the pit of her stomach.

For a second she seriously considered asking for a large gin and tonic to settle her nerves. She was being ridiculous, she told herself sternly as she followed Nik to the bar and requested her usual choice of iced water. Since Kezia's marriage, Otterbourne had become a second home to her and she had been looking forward to spending a pleasant evening. No way would she allow Nik's spine-tinglingly sexy cousin to unsettle her.

Forcing herself to relax, she was drawn into conversation with the other guests and her tension eased. Perhaps Damon wasn't here after all? she brooded, dismayed by the sharp pang of disappointment the thought evoked. As the head of Kouvaris Construction, he took a personal interest in every element of his business and she knew he led a hectic life-style travelling between the company's various projects. Maybe he had been called away to deal with some crisis, as he had when she had first met him on Nik's private Aegean island, Zathos, two months earlier.

The conversation was light and entertaining and she gave a peal of laughter when one of her friends recounted an amusing anecdote, but a sudden prickling sensation on her skin set the fine hairs on the back of her neck on end. Some innate sixth sense warned her she was being watched and she turned her head sharply as a figure appeared in the doorway leading to the terrace.

Damon!

Instantly she was overwhelmed by his exceptional height and the formidable width of shoulders. Silhouetted against the evening sunshine he appeared so muscular and powerful that for a moment she could almost believe he were a figure from Greek mythology. Angrily she gave herself a mental shake and sought to tear her eyes from him, but he trapped her gaze and she swallowed at the brooding sexuality reflected in his midnight dark depths.

'Ah, Damon, there you are,' Nik said with a smile. 'You met Anna on Zathos, at Theo's christening, if you remember.'

'I haven't forgotten,' came the dry response. 'It's good to see you, Anna.'

His voice was low-pitched and melodious, reminding Anna of the sound of a bow being drawn lovingly across the strings of a cello. His Greek accent was heavily pronounced. Her name had never before sounded so sensual and her reaction was instant. A quiver ran the length of her spine and she affected a brief, impersonal smile.

'Mr Kouvaris! How nice to meet you again.' She extended her hand in formal greeting and gasped when he entwined his fingers through hers to draw her close. Before she had time to react he lowered his head and brushed his lips first on one cheek and then the other, the touch of his mouth on her skin causing goose bumps to cover every inch of her body.

Her career as a model meant that she frequently travelled abroad and was accustomed to the continental greeting, but her instant and overwhelming awareness of Damon caused hectic colour to stain her cheeks. Abruptly she stepped back, her heart racing as warmth coursed through her veins. Her head was spinning as if she had drunk a whole bottle of champagne and she inhaled sharply, desperate to compose herself.

'I hope you are well, Mr Kouvaris?' She managed the polite enquiry through gritted teeth and felt a flash of irritation when his mouth curved into a slow smile that told her he was well aware of her reaction to him.

'Very well, thank you,' he assured her gravely. 'My name is Damon—in case you've forgotten,' he added in a tone that spoke plainly of his confidence that she had not. 'I think we can dispense with formality, don't you, Anna? After all, we're practically family.'

Anna's brows lifted fractionally. 'I'm not sure how you've reached that conclusion,' she drawled, grateful that the years of practice at masking her emotions ensured she sounded cool and aloof, despite the erratic thud of her heart.

'I'm Nik's cousin and you are his wife's closest friend. According to Kezia, the two of you are practically sisters.' Damon had moved without her being aware of it and Anna discovered that she had been manoeuvred into a corner, slightly apart from the other guests. He was much too close for comfort. Her eyes were drawn to his face, noting the contrast between his dark olive skin and his brilliant white teeth revealed when he smiled at her.

He wasn't handsome in the conventional sense and certainly did not share the perfect features of the male models she worked with. With his strong, slightly hooked nose, heavy black brows and square jaw, Damon reminded her of a boxer who had gone several rounds with a forceful opponent. The formidable width of his shoulders and his powerful physique added to his air of raw, earthy masculinity but it was his mouth, full lipped and innately sensual, that captured Anna's attention.

His kiss would be no gentle seduction, she acknowledged faintly, moistening her suddenly dry lips with the tip of her tongue. Damon exuded a degree of sexual magnetism that warned her he would demand total submission. He would be an uninhibited, possessive lover and would use his mouth as an instrument of sensual torture that would be impossible to resist.

Where on earth had that thought come from? she wondered frantically, dragging her gaze from his face to focus on his crisp white shirt. She was tall but he dwarfed her and she felt intimidated by his sheer size, the latent strength of his broad, muscular chest.

'So, Anna—' his voice caressed every syllable of her name

'—you look stunning. You've been abroad.' His eyes skimmed over her, noting her soft golden tan. 'South Africa, I understand.'

'Yes, but how did you—?' She broke off with an impatient shrug. Kezia must have told him—it was hardly a state secret after all—but the knowledge that he must have asked about her was unsettling. No wonder Kezia had teased her about him when she'd first arrived. She just hoped her friend wasn't harbouring any hopes about matchmaking.

'I discovered your whereabouts from your agency,' he admitted without a hint of contrition, amusement glimmering in his dark eyes when she rounded on him indignantly.

'Why?' she demanded crossly, unable to disguise her confusion at his apparent interest. He hadn't bothered to hide his faint disdain of her chosen profession when Nik had first introduced them on Zathos. Indeed, she'd gained the distinct impression that he believed her to be a brainless bimbo, and the knowledge still stung. 'The agency wouldn't have given out information like that to just anyone,' she snapped.

'They gave it to me. But I am not "just anyone",' he stated with breathtaking arrogance, 'I am Damon Kouvaris, and once I'd convinced them that I was a personal friend of yours they were most helpful.'

'But you're not. We barely know each other. We've only met once, and the fact that we danced together at our godson's christening does not make us bosom buddies.'

The moment she'd uttered the word bosom, Anna could have cut her tongue out. Her chest was heaving with the force of her emotions. She felt Damon's gaze slide over her and was mortified to feel her breasts swell and tighten beneath the sheer black silk of her dress.

'There you are, you see. Already you've mentioned the unbreakable link between us. Theo, our godson,' Damon

elucidated when she stared at him in confusion. 'He's one very good reason why we should take the opportunity to get to know one another better. You could even say it is our duty, *ne?*'

He was laughing at her, damn him, she realised furiously. She'd been thrilled when Kezia had asked her to be god-mother to her little adopted son. It was an honour she had vowed to undertake to the best of her ability and she had travelled to Zathos, eager to meet her fellow godparent.

Unfortunately Nik's disturbingly sexy cousin was nothing like the sort of guardian she had imagined Kezia would have chosen for her son. Damon was Nik's choice, her friend had explained. She didn't know him that well but Nik thought a lot of him and, as far as Kezia was concerned, that settled the matter. Anna had been forced to swallow her doubts but she couldn't imagine that Damon, with his rugged good looks and magnetic charm, had any interest whatsoever in children.

His interest in women, however, was not in doubt. He possessed a blatant, simmering sexuality that was an almost primitive force. One glance from his dark, flashing eyes was enough to render any woman weak at the knees. Anna knew this from experience; hers had practically given way when Nik had first introduced them and now she was aware of the same trembling in her limbs as she faced the full on-slaught of Damon's potent charm.

'Sorry to interrupt, but if we don't go in to dinner Mrs Jessop is likely to spontaneously-combust.' Kezia's light tone was a welcome release from the tension that gripped Anna and she expelled her breath sharply.

Damon stood aside and smiled at their hostess. 'Then we must come at once,' he said in the deep, gravelly voice that sent a delicious shiver down Anna's spine. 'I note that you don't have a partner this evening, Anna,' he murmured

silkily. 'I, too, am alone and it would give me great pleasure to escort you to dinner.'

It was a perfectly reasonable request, Anna acknowledged, giving him a tight smile and allowing him to draw her arm through his. But she didn't feel reasonable. Damon unsettled her so that she felt edgy and irritable and yet at the same time wildly alive, her senses heightened to an unbearable degree.

When they followed the other guests into the dining room she was conscious of the brush of his thigh against hers and her body clenched. What was happening to her? She was Anneliese Christiansen. Her nickname of Ice Princess by certain elements of the press was well-deserved. Nobody got under her guard—ever—and it was infuriating to find that this arrogant, presumptuous Greek had the ability to shake her equilibrium.

No more, she vowed when Damon drew out a chair for her to sit down, before taking his place next to her at the table. She caught the tang of his aftershave, a spicy, exotic concoction that set her senses racing and it took considerable will-power to unfold her napkin and smile at him with an air of self-assurance she did not feel.

He was too pushy, too confident—she would take great delight in countering his outrageous flirting with the cool indifference that she had perfected to an art form, she decided firmly.

The first course was a delicious seafood salad. Plump, pink prawns nestled on a bed of crisp lettuce, dressed with a delicate sauce that stirred Anna's taste buds. She'd eaten nothing since her usual breakfast of yoghurt and fruit and had spent the day in a state of pent up tension at the thought of meeting Damon again. Now she forced herself to relax and speared a prawn with her fork.

'Did you enjoy your trip to South Africa? It boasts some spectacular scenery.'

The sensual resonance of his voice curled around her so that she found it suddenly hard to swallow. 'It was a working trip and there was no time for sightseeing,' she replied politely. As usual, the trip had been a whirl of airport lounges and hotel vestibules with a few days on the beach where she had been too busy modelling a range of swimwear to take more than a cursory interest in her surroundings.

'That's a pity. The wild flowers on the veldt are stunning at this time of the year. Do you often work to such a tight schedule?' Damon enquired lightly, his tone plainly implying that he did not consider standing around in a selection of designer frocks hard work. He'd made other, faintly disparaging, comments about her job the first time they'd met and his attitude fanned Anna's irritation.

'Surprising though it may seem, modelling can be a demanding profession and I take my work seriously. I was paid to do a job in South Africa, not enjoy a freebie holiday,' she informed him coolly.

'Your attitude is commendable,' Damon assured her gravely, although she detected the glimmering amusement in his dark eyes. Nothing infuriated her more than the belief that pretty women were, by definition, airheads. For a second she was tempted to tell him that she had recently completed a four-year home study course and been awarded a business degree, but then thought better of it. Why did it matter what Damon Kouvaris thought of her? she thought defensively. It wasn't as if she cared about his opinion of her.

She returned her attention to her starter and found that her appetite had deserted her. He, on the other hand, was eating with evident enjoyment. She was aware of every movement he made and when he reached for his drink she stared, transfixed, as his strong, tanned fingers curled around the stem of the glass.

From her brief conversation with him on Zathos, she

knew that his father had once insisted he should learn every aspect of the building trade. His family might own the multimillion-pound Kouvaris Construction company but Damon had started his working life as a labourer.

Twenty years on, he had an expert knowledge of his trade and, although he now spent most of his time in the boardroom rather than on site, he still retained the superb physique he'd gained through hard physical labour. His hands were strong and darkly tanned. She watched him lift his glass and could not repress a tremor at the thought of those lean fingers caressing her body.

His touch would be slightly abrasive against her skin. She wondered if the black hairs she glimpsed on his wrist covered the whole of his body. Certainly his chest, she decided. She doubted that he shaved his body hair, as was common with many of her male friends in the modelling industry. And his golden tan was from the hot, Greek sun, not hours stretched out on a sunbed.

In the superficial world she inhabited, Damon's overwhelming masculinity was alien and unnerving, but undeniably sexy. He evoked thoughts and feelings within her that were as unexpected as they were shocking. Her tension returned with a vengeance and as her throat closed up she choked on a prawn.

'Easy…try to drink a little water.' His quiet concern made her eyes sting with stupid tears and she forced herself to take a sip of ice-cold water from the glass he held to her lips. 'Better?' His eyes were not black, as she had first thought, but a deep, dark mahogany, velvet soft as he focused intently on her.

'Yes, thank you,' she mumbled, groping for her self-possession to disguise the fact that she felt a fool. Get a grip, she ordered herself impatiently. She spent a good part of her life attending social functions in the company of some of the

world's most eligible men. Surely it wasn't beyond her to cope with Damon Kouvaris for a couple of hours without making a complete idiot of herself?

The main course was served but Anna could not do justice to Mrs Jessop's excellent cooking and toyed with her food, hoping to give the appearance that she was eating.

'Are you simply not hungry, or are you one of those women who religiously count every calorie?' Damon murmured in her ear. 'You have a spectacular figure, Anna, but I wouldn't like to see you any thinner,' he added, plainly unperturbed by her fierce glare.

His words were the last straw. How *dared* he make personal comments? She wouldn't be affording him the opportunity to *see* her at all, whatever her shape, Anna vowed furiously, unaware that he could read the murderous thoughts that darkened her eyes to the colour of cobalt.

Anna Christiansen was as exquisite as a fine porcelain figurine, Damon thought appreciatively, unable to tear his gaze from the delicate beauty of her face. Her classically sculpted features were perfect, the tilt of her wide mouth offering a sensual invitation he longed to accept.

It was impossible to travel anywhere in the world without seeing her face on a billboard or featured in a glossy magazine. He'd read somewhere that the cosmetic house she represented had offered her a new contract worth several million pounds and it was easy to see why. With her pale blonde hair drawn back into a sleek chignon and her huge eyes defined by carefully applied make-up, she was every woman's style-icon and every red-blooded male's fantasy.

As his gaze dropped to the soft curve of her mouth he felt his body's involuntary reaction to the sight of her scarlet lips, glistening and moist and so damn sexy that heat surged through him.

He'd wanted her since the moment he'd first seen her on Zathos, but his godson's christening had hardly been the place to indulge his carnal desires. Anna had obviously thought so, too. She had treated him with a cool indifference that had both amused and intrigued him, particularly when her prim air had been unable to disguise her fierce awareness of him.

He'd noted with interest the way her cheeks suffused with colour whenever he approached her. Doubtless it was all part of a clever act, but the innocence of her rosy blush added to her sensual allure and he'd had to forcibly restrain himself from taking her in his arms and exploring her tantalisingly soft, full lips with his own.

He had received the phone call requesting his urgent presence at one of the Kouvaris developments with uncharacteristic regret. For as long as he could remember, work had been his overriding mistress, coming a close second to his family. But for once he'd felt frustrated that he could not spend longer on Zathos to woo the elegant, slender-limbed blonde who dominated his thoughts.

He'd spent much of the last two months in Athens attending to the necessary task of rearranging his personal life, and in particular ending the affair with his mistress. He wanted no messy loose ends to mar his pursuit of Anna and had viewed Filia's tears with irritation. It was not as if Filia had been in love with *him,* but rather his wallet, he acknowledged cynically.

He'd made it clear from the start, as he always did, that he wasn't looking for love and commitment, and could offer neither. Filia had eventually been consoled by several expensive gifts and now he was free and eager to discover if the chemistry he'd felt between him and Anna on Zathos would live up to its explosive promise.

Anna was speaking to him and with an effort he dragged

his mind from the erotic fantasy of exploring her slim body. He guessed from her clipped tone that he had riled her and his lips twitched at the flash of fire in her eyes.

'I fail to see that my eating habits are any of your business, but, if you must know, I have a normal, healthy diet,' she told him indignantly.

'I'm glad to hear it. In that case you'll be able to have dinner with me tomorrow night. I'll pick you up at seven.'

Another guest caught his attention and he smiled as he responded to the query about where exactly in Athens he was based. Beside him Anna seethed silently, waiting for the opportunity to tell him that she was unavailable tomorrow night, or any other night for the foreseeable future.

How dared he just assume that she would jump at his invitation? To her over-sensitive mind it seemed to be another example of his belief that she was a dumb blonde who couldn't think for herself. He was the most arrogant man she had ever met and as soon as she could get a word in edgeways she would turn him down flat.

To her chagrin Damon paid her scant attention for the remainder of the meal and she had drained the last of her coffee and was debating whether Kezia would be offended if she pleaded a headache and went home when he turned to her again.

'Is there anywhere in particular you'd like to go tomorrow night?' he queried casually, as if they had been dating for months. Anna gave him one of her cool smiles guaranteed to freeze the most ardent admirer and swallowed her desire to tell him exactly where she'd like him to go.

'I'm afraid I must turn down your kind offer, tempting though it is,' she said with barely concealed sarcasm. 'I'm busy tomorrow night.'

'That's not a problem,' he assured her blandly. 'We'll make it the following evening.'

'I'm busy then, too.'

'And the next night?' His brows lifted, his tone faintly sardonic now, as if he was growing bored of the game that she was playing.

'I'm afraid not.'

'I had no idea that modelling made such demands on your time.'

'I didn't say I was working,' she snapped, feeling thoroughly hot and flustered. Was his ego so inflated that he couldn't take a simple no for an answer? 'Had it not occurred to you that I could be dating someone else at the moment?'

He paused and reflected for a moment. 'Are you?'

Anna was aware that conversation around the table had lulled and they were attracting attention, Kezia's in particular. It was tempting to lie to him, but innate honesty made her shake her head. 'No,' she admitted ungraciously, her tone sharp. She knew she was overreacting, but she had never felt so acutely aware of a man in her life and she was terrified that he would realise the effect he was having on her.

'So what *are* you doing every evening this week?' Damon enquired silkily, although she wasn't fooled by his indolent tone when she caught the glint of battle in his eyes.

Damn him. How had he managed to turn the conversation around so that she felt guilty for declining what was, in all honesty, a simple request to join him for dinner? She had no reason to feel guilty, she assured herself. If he was conceited enough to believe she was his for the taking, like a ripe plum ready to fall into his hands, he deserved to be disappointed.

'I'm washing my hair,' she snapped, not bothering to disguise the asperity in her tone. She glared at him, quivering with tension as she waited for his response.

'You obviously lead a full life,' he murmured lazily, his mouth curving into a smile that made no effort to hide his

amusement. He turned away from her to speak to the guest on the other side of him, leaving Anna with the distinct impression that she had lost the first round.

She was aware of the faintly embarrassed, pitying glances from around the table and knew that her cheeks were scarlet. She'd got what she wanted, hadn't she? Damon could not have made it plainer that he had lost interest in her and the idea of taking her to dinner. So why did she feel so put out?

She didn't want to have dinner with him, she reminded herself irritably, but the words sounded as unconvincing to her own ears as they did when Kezia demanded an explanation later in the evening.

'I thought you liked Damon,' her friend muttered, after insisting that Anna accompany her upstairs to check on Theo. 'He only asked you out to dinner, Anna; it's not as if he issued an invitation to leap into bed with him.'

'I had the impression that one was merely a prelude to the other,' Anna replied dryly. 'You said yourself that Damon Kouvaris is a notorious womaniser and I have no intention of becoming another notch on his bedpost.'

'More's the pity,' Kezia muttered beneath her breath, but Anna's keen ears caught the comment and her eyes narrowed.

'Meaning what, exactly?'

'Meaning that you cannot spend your whole life pushing people away through fear.'

'I'm not afraid of Damon,' Anna replied fiercely, although not entirely truthfully. The enigmatic Greek disturbed her more than she cared to admit.

Kezia glanced at Anna's tense expression and sighed. 'When will you accept that the sins of your father won't necessarily be repeated by every man you meet? Not every man out there is a serial adulterer.'

'Are you honestly suggesting that Damon would be a

committed and faithful lover?' Anna queried tightly. 'His track record is appalling. I know his type, Kezia. I meet men like him every day and, trust me, he's only interested in one thing.

'Well, he's not getting it from me,' she hissed. She followed Kezia out of the nursery, her steps slowing when a figure emerged from the shadows.

'Damon! You startled us,' Kezia murmured while Anna prayed that a hole would appear beneath her feet.

'Forgive me—Nik said you were checking on Theo and I was wondering if I could take a peep at my godson. I hope I didn't disturb you,' he replied, his smile encompassing them both but his gaze fixed firmly on Anna.

'Not at all, we were just…chatting,' she mumbled, her face flaming at the sardonic expression in his eyes.

'So I heard.' Damon's tone was bland but his smile did not reach his eyes. Anna had been prickly and defensive all evening. He'd assumed she was playing the well-known game of hard to get and he had even been prepared to go along with it for a while. Often, the thrill of the chase proved to be the most enjoyable part of a relationship, he acknowledged cynically.

But the snatches of conversation he had overheard between Anna and Kezia threw a different light on her attitude. The media had exaggerated his reputation as a playboy, but he had never professed to be a saint, he admitted ruefully.

He knew nothing of Anna's family situation, but if her father really had been a serial adulterer then perhaps it explained her unwillingness to acknowledge the attraction that had first flared between them on Zathos. The attraction was, however, undeniably still there; if he'd had any doubts before, he had none now, having noted how she had been unable to keep her eyes off him throughout dinner.

CHAPTER TWO

'IT'S been a wonderful evening, Kezia, but I really must go home,' Anna announced firmly when she followed her friend down the sweeping staircase leading from the nursery. Call her a coward, but she doubted her ability to cope with Damon Kouvaris's unsettling presence for a minute longer. 'I've a busy couple of days ahead,' she murmured by way of excuse.

Damon was waiting at the bottom of the stairs. His brows rose quizzically at her words. 'Yes, all that hair-washing must be exhausting,' he commented dulcetly.

Kezia valiantly hid her smile at Anna's furious expression. 'Of course I don't mind. I'll just fetch your jacket,' she choked as she disappeared into the cloakroom, leaving Anna alone with Damon.

The silence stretched between them until Anna was sure he must be able to hear the erratic thud of her heart. She searched her mind for something to say. She spent her life making witty small talk but it seemed that her brain had decamped and all she could think of were stupid inanities that would probably reinforce his belief that she was a brainless blonde.

'So, you're going to be tied up all week? A punishing schedule in the beauty salon, no doubt,' he drawled, his laconic comment inciting her instant wrath.

'Actually I shall be training all week,' she told him stiffly, wishing that the sight of him in his black dinner suit didn't affect her so strongly. She felt as gauche as a teenager and was aware that her voice sounded breathless and girly when she wanted to impress him with the fact that she was a so-phisticated woman of the world.

'Training for what?' Damon couldn't disguise his scepti-cism.

'I'm running a half-marathon around Hyde Park next weekend. The event is to raise money for a number of charities and I'm supporting a charity that is trying to raise funds for a children's hospice. Perhaps you'd like to sponsor me?' she added, lowering her guard slightly. He was reputed to be a multimillionaire and the charity needed all the support it could get. This wasn't the time for pride.

'I'd be delighted. How many miles are you planning to run?'

'Thirteen,' she admitted, her hesitant tone betraying her doubts. Her training schedule hadn't gone quite to plan and it had come as a shock to realise that the race was only a week away. She had a naturally slender, athletic build and worked out in the gym regularly, but thirteen miles suddenly seemed an awfully long way.

'So how far do you run on your training sessions?'

'About half that distance,' she mumbled, 'give or take the odd mile.'

'Ah.' There was a wealth of amusement in his dark eyes. He plainly didn't think she could do it and his scepticism brought her chin up defiantly. She'd show him.

'I'm pretty fit and I don't anticipate any problems,' she told him coolly, crossing her fingers behind her back as she spoke.

Damon stared at her speculatively for a few moments. 'Nik is a devoted father and I imagine he's pledged a large

donation in support of the children's charity. I'll match his offer.'

'Are you sure…? I mean, it's a six-figure sum,' she argued faintly.

'Are you saying you don't think the charity could make use of the money?'

'Of course it could.' It might even mean that the children's hospice could open earlier than planned, she acknowledged as she worried her bottom lip with her teeth. 'But are you sure you would be prepared to sponsor me for such a huge amount?' There had to be a catch. She didn't believe for a minute that he would make such a generous offer, even if he hadn't initially realized how much Nik's donation was, without demanding something in return.

She felt his dark gaze skim over her, hovering on the delicate swell of her breasts before sliding lower to her narrow hips and long, slender legs encased in sheer black stockings. The heat in his gaze made her quiver with a mixture of outrage and undeniable awareness. If he dared to make the vile suggestion that she sleep with him in return for sponsoring her, she would be out of the front door before he could blink, having first told him precisely where he could stick his donation.

'I'm in the fortunate position to be able to donate to many charities,' he told her. 'But, tell me, why do you support this particular cause?'

Anna shrugged and tore her gaze from his face. 'It's heartbreaking to think of children's lives blighted by illness. I used to visit Kezia while she was undergoing chemotherapy,' she added. 'She was so brave, as all the sick children I've met since are. If I can use my—' she broke off and laughed deprecatingly '—celebrity status to raise money for the charity, then I'm prepared to do anything.'

Well, almost anything, she amended silently when he

moved closer and lifted his hand to smooth a stray tendril of hair back from her face. It was a curiously intimate gesture and she stiffened, her breath catching in her throat as she inhaled his seductive male scent.

'So, I'll make a significant donation to your good cause and in return you'll run thirteen miles—and...' His sudden smile took her breath away and she found that she was unable to drag her gaze from the sensual curve of his mouth.

'And I'll what?' she demanded suspiciously. She'd known there had to be a catch.

'And you'll agree to have dinner with me,' he completed blandly, the gleam in his eyes telling her that he could read her mind and was aware of her misgivings. 'What are you afraid of, Anna? I promise I don't slurp my soup,' he assured her gravely.

He was openly teasing her and she felt her cheeks burn with a mixture of embarrassment and, God forbid, disappointment. She should feel relieved that he hadn't demanded the right to assuage the desire she had glimpsed in his eyes. Instead she felt thoroughly disconcerted. Maybe she'd read the signs wrong. Perhaps she had been so intent on fighting her awareness of him that she had been mistaken in her belief that the attraction was mutual?

He made the most of her hesitation to slide his hand beneath her chin, tilting her face to his so that she had no option but to meet his gaze. 'Do we have a deal?'

'I suppose so,' she muttered, blushing once more when he grimaced.

'And so graciously accepted,' he drawled, 'it should be an evening to remember.'

Anna resisted the urge to slap him and jerked out of his hold. His arrogance was infuriating and she longed to dent his pride. 'I've just remembered that I don't have a free evening for weeks,' she informed him sweetly.

'That's a pity, because no dinner means no donation,' Damon replied hardly, seemingly unperturbed by the flash of fury in her blue eyes.

'Are you saying that, even if I complete the race, you'll only give your donation after I've had dinner with you?' she queried heatedly, needing to have him spell it out. 'That's blackmail!'

'That's the deal,' he stated with ominous finality. 'Don't look so downhearted, *pedhaki mou*. Who knows? You might even enjoy it.'

'I wouldn't count on it.' She bit back the rest of her angry words and took a hasty step away from him when Kezia returned from the cloakroom, holding her jacket.

'Sorry I was so long,' Kezia murmured, her gaze swinging from Anna's mutinous face to Damon's closed expression.

Anna gave her friend a tight-lipped smile. 'Lovely dinner—will you pass on my compliments to Mrs Jessop, and say good night to Nik for me,' she said briskly.

'Be careful. I wish you weren't driving down those dark country lanes on your own,' Kezia replied concernedly, her frown clearing when Damon waved his car keys in the air.

'Don't worry, I'll be following close behind and I'll see that Anna reaches home safely,' he promised. 'I need to put in a couple of hours work tonight, before a meeting tomorrow morning,' he explained apologetically. 'Many thanks for a delightful evening, Kezia.'

'But I thought…' Anna glared at him, incensed by his faintly proprietorial air. She didn't need a bodyguard, for heaven's sake. 'I assumed you were staying here, at Otterbourne,' she muttered as she followed him down the front steps of the house.

'No, it's easier for me to be based in central London. And besides, Nik and Kezia are so wrapped up in each other that I feel like a cuckoo in the love nest,' he added with a grin that caused her insides to melt.

'Well, I hope you're not cutting your evening short because of some misguided belief that you need to escort me home,' she said crisply as she unlocked her low-slung sports car and slid behind the wheel. 'I'm perfectly capable of taking care of myself.'

'I'm sure you are, *pedhaki mou.*' The sudden sultriness of his tone caught her attention and her irritation increased when she discovered that his gaze was focused intently on the way her skirt had ridden up, exposing a length of slender thigh. 'Drive carefully, Anna. I'll be in touch,' he added mockingly, causing her to slam the door so forcefully that the car shook.

'Terrific,' she muttered beneath her breath. She could hardly wait. She swung out of the drive, her mood as black as the pitch-dark lanes, and her temper was not improved by the gleam of his headlights following at a safe distance behind her. It was yet another example of Damon's arrogance, she brooded. She had taken care of herself for most of her life and she valued her independence. She didn't need an overbearing, damnably sexy Greek to suddenly muscle in.

Once on the motorway she pressed her foot down on the accelerator and felt the familiar thrill of pleasure as the car surged forwards. Her top-of-the-range, bright red sports car was an extravagance, especially when she spent most of her time driving around town, where it drank petrol. But here on the open road she could indulge her passion for speed and with luck lose her would-be protector.

Goodbye, Damon! With a satisfied smile she selected a CD and turned up the volume. She flew along in the fast lane and reached her junction in record time, slowing as she turned onto the slip-road leading from the motorway before stopping at the red light. A car pulled up in the next lane and when she turned her head her smile faded. Damn him! He must have been right behind her the whole way, she realised, glaring at him when he gave a mocking salute.

Even from this distance she was aware of the challenging gleam in his eyes and as their gazes clashed she found it impossible to turn away. It was dark but she could make out his profile— the sharp angle of his cheekbones and that square chin that hinted at a stubborn determination.

The only softness about his appearance was the way his thick hair curled onto his collar. He was the most gorgeous, sensual man she had ever met, she conceded, her reverie rudely shattered by an impatient hooting from behind that warned her the lights had changed to green. Thoroughly flummoxed and hot cheeked, she crunched the gears before finally pulling away.

He really was the bitter end, she thought irritably some ten minutes later when she turned into the parking area outside her flat and he drew up beside her. What was he waiting for now—a medal, or an invitation up to her flat for coffee? He was out of luck on both counts but innate good manners made her walk over to his car.

'Thanks for seeing me back,' she murmured politely.

'No problem. I'll wait until you're safely inside.'

She was often fearful of who could be lurking in the bushes on either side of the communal front door and hated the short trip across the car park in the dark, but Damon's tone irritated her 'I'm a big girl now and I really can look after myself, you know,' she drawled.

'I'm not convinced, *pedhaki mou*. For one thing, you drive too fast,' he replied bluntly, the note of censure in his tone causing her hackles to rise.

'I'm an excellent driver,' she snapped indignantly. 'I might drive fast, but I'm always careful.'

He surveyed her silently with his dark, brooding gaze. His eyes were hooded, giving no clue to his thoughts, but somehow he made her feel about six years old.

'So, occasionally I like to live dangerously,' she bit out

belligerently, placing her hands on her hips in a gesture of silent challenge.

His low chuckle caused her to grind her teeth in irritation. 'Then I can only hope that our dinner date is one of those occasions. Now off you go, before I decide to escort you up to your flat,' he warned softly, ignoring her indignant gasp. 'Good night, Anna, and sweet dreams.'

The sound of his mocking laughter followed her across the car park, but Anna refused to award him another glance and marched up the front steps, her back ramrod-straight. Damon Kouvaris was the devil incarnate, but if he thought she would allow him to disturb her calm, well-ordered life, he'd better think again.

Unfortunately the memory of Damon's ruggedly handsome face disturbed her dreams to the extent that she woke the following morning feeling as though she had barely slept at all. Ahead of her lay a week of serious training for the half-marathon, but the thought of spending the day at the local sports centre, pounding the running track, held little appeal and with a groan she burrowed beneath the duvet.

It was late morning before she arrived at the track, spurred on by the knowledge that she had promised the children's charity her support and couldn't let them down. Even discounting Damon's incredible sponsorship offer, she was set to raise many thousands of pounds for the charity. The event was to be televised, with many celebrities taking part, all hoping to raise public awareness, as well as funds for their chosen cause. Pride dictated that she didn't make a complete fool of herself in front the cameras, and, although she hated to admit it—in front of Damon.

An hour later her pride was distinctly shaky, as were her legs. The early June sunshine was surprisingly warm and she was hot and breathless as she strove to keep her pace. The

other runners on the track had all lapped her effortlessly and she sighed at the sound of footsteps behind her. How did they make it look so easy? she wondered despairingly.

'How's the training going? Have you run thirteen miles yet?' The familiar honeyed tones caused her to miss her footing and she stumbled and would have tripped if a strong hand hadn't quickly reached out to save her.

'What are *you* doing here?' she demanded crossly, irritated at the way her body was reacting with humiliating eagerness to the sight of Damon. Last night he had looked stunning in a formal dinner suit but today, in running shorts and black vest-top, he was spectacular.

Her eyes made a fleeting inspection of his broad shoulders and impressive, muscle-bound chest before sliding lower, over his shorts before coming to rest on his powerful thighs and long, tanned legs. His athletic build and superb muscle definition caused a peculiar weakness in the pit of her stomach. Cramp, she told herself irritably as she tore her eyes from his brooding gaze and stared along the track. 'How did you know I was here?'

'You told me last night that you intended to put in some training this week, and when I called at your flat your neighbour informed me that she'd seen you leave, carrying a kit bag. It didn't take much to work out that you were probably at the nearest sports centre,' he answered dryly, his eyes raking over her so that Anna felt acutely conscious that she must look a mess. She could feel the beads of sweat that had formed above her top lip and tried to capture them with the tip of her tongue, hoping to hide the evidence that she was exhausted.

'Quite the Sherlock Holmes, aren't you?' she snapped sarcastically, watching the way his eyes narrowed as they focused on the frantic movements of her tongue. 'Well, now that you've found me, what do you want? You're interrupting my training.'

'Do all forms of physical exercise make you so grumpy?' he queried with a grin, seemingly unconcerned by her un-friendly attitude. 'I do hope not,' he added dulcetly, his eyes glinting with amusement at her furious glare. 'You look tired, *pedhaki mou.* I think you should take a break.'

'I'm fine for several more laps yet,' she lied. She shook her thick plait over her shoulder and started to jog once more. 'Why have you decided to appoint yourself as my nanny?'

'Oh, I have my reasons,' he murmured, keeping pace beside her with infuriating ease. She felt his gaze trawl over her crop-top and the smooth expanse of her flat stomach before sliding lower to her tight, Lycra running shorts that clung to her hips and moulded her neat bottom. 'Although I prefer to think of myself as your personal trainer.'

'I don't need a trainer. I need you to leave me alone.' Her voice came out as a wail of frustration and she swung her head round to stare at him, thought better of it and kept on running. 'Look, Damon, you've already blackmailed me into having dinner with you. Let's just leave it at that,' she muttered breathlessly. 'I don't want to see you, I don't want to spend time with you, and I don't date.'

'You don't date. *Theos!* Hardly a week goes by without a photo of you and your latest celebrity boyfriend posing for the tabloids,' he retorted sardonically, unable to disguise his impatience. 'Reports of your love life fill more newspaper columns than any political intrigue. What's the real issue here, Anna? Is it the fact that I'm not some suitably famous TV soap star? I can assure you, I'm more of a man than any of the pretty boys you seem to favour.'

'Oh, for heaven's sake.' She halted in the middle of the track and glared at him in impotent fury. His arrogance would be funny if she hadn't recognised the intrinsic truth of his last statement. Damon's flagrant, raw masculinity un-settled her more than any other man she'd met.

Nothing would induce her to reveal that her alleged lovers were simply friends who for their own reasons found it useful to act the role of her escort. Living in the media spotlight was akin to living in a goldfish bowl and over the years she had learned to dismiss most of the rubbish that was written about her and her so-called wild love life. Now, as she stared at Damon she felt sickened by the hint of contempt in his eyes.

'How dare you turn up here and…harass me?' she exploded, 'I'm not some blonde bimbo and, despite what you might have read in the tabloids, I am not an easy lay.'

She was shocked by the force of her emotions, the feeling of hurt, and blinked hard to dispel the stupid tears that had gathered in her eyes. She rarely cried, and never over a man. Years of witnessing her mother's disastrous love life and subsequent slide into depression had taught her they weren't worth it.

After her parents' bitter divorce she had vowed never to be emotionally or financially dependent on anyone. The Ice Princess had a heart of glass and she felt a shaft of genuine fear that Damon seemed to possess the power to shatter it.

'Did you really think you could just click your fingers and I would be yours for the taking?' she demanded stiffly. 'Because if so, I've got news for you.'

'Credit me with a little more finesse, Anna,' he replied lazily. 'But I can't deny I hoped for the chance to explore the awareness between us that we both recognised on Zathos. And why not?' he continued. 'We're both consenting adults. Why shouldn't we indulge in a mutually enjoyable affair?'

'You mean sex without the inconvenience of messy emotions?' she said scathingly, ignoring the devil in her head that was asking the question—why not? At least Damon was being honest. He wasn't trying to woo her with

meaningless romantic gestures and promises that they both knew he wouldn't keep. Why not follow the dictates of her body for once rather than listen to the cool voice of common sense?

She sensed instinctively that Damon would be a passionate yet sensitive lover. But he would also be her first. It would almost be worth it, just to see the shock on his face when he realised she was a virgin, she brooded darkly. It was obvious that he believed every piece of tittle-tattle written about her and assumed that she led an active and varied sex life. She could imagine his disappointment when he discovered her inexperience.

Would he offer to tutor her? she wondered, heat coursing through her veins at the mental image of his hands gliding over her body, teaching her the language of love.

Stifling a gasp, she tore her gaze from his darkly handsome face. His heavy brows were drawn into a frown, his eyes hooded, hiding his thoughts, but she was aware of the electricity between them—an invisible force that set her nerve endings on fire and increased her acute consciousness of every breath he took.

What was she thinking of? She must be mad to have considered even for a second, becoming involved with him. In Damon Kouvaris she saw her father—handsome, charismatic and unable to remain faithful to one woman for more than five minutes. She would not repeat the mistakes her mother had made, she assured herself fiercely and she tilted her chin and stared at him coolly.

'I'm sorry to disappoint you but I have no intention of indulging in any kind of a relationship with you, certainly not a casual fling while you happen to be in London. You must be mistaken about Zathos,' she added airily. 'I don't remember there being anything between us. In fact I'd practically forgotten you.'

'Is that so?' Beneath his indolent, faintly amused tone, she detected anger and steeled herself to fight him off when he caught hold of her shoulder and spun her round to face him. His dark eyes were mesmerising and she found herself trapped by the sensual heat of his gaze as he slowly lowered his head.

He was going to kiss her. Her brain sent out an urgent warning telling her to jerk free of his grasp, but she was boneless, enveloped in a haze of quivering anticipation as she waited for his lips to claim hers.

She had wanted this since she had first met him on Zathos, she admitted silently, unwittingly parting her lips in readiness. She needed him to take control, to tear down her defences and capture her mouth in a hungry, elemental kiss that would ignore her token resistance. Time seemed to be suspended as she waited, her eyes closed against the glare of the sun. She could feel his warm breath fan her cheek and as her desperation increased she swayed towards him, her senses leaping when she inhaled his clean, seductive scent.

'In that case I suppose I'll just have to content myself with overseeing your training.' His calm, matter-of-fact voice shattered the spell he had cast over her and her eyes flew open to clash with his glinting gaze. Colour scalded her cheeks and she felt sick with humiliation when he released her and stepped away, his bland smile telling her he was aware of her disappointment. She had offered herself up like…like a sacrificial virgin, she acknowledged furiously, and he had rejected her.

'I don't need any help. I prefer to train on my own,' she muttered, her voice thick with mortification. Spinning round on her heels, she set off at a pace that was impossible to maintain. She was going too fast, too soon, her coach would have advised her, but right now all she could think of was putting some space between her and the most infuriating

man she had ever met. 'Just go away, Damon, and leave me alone,' she flung over her shoulder.

Damon watched her disappear along the track and felt the familiar ache in his groin as he admired her impossibly long, tanned legs and the tantalising sway of her *derrière*. If only it were that easy to let her go, he thought grimly.

He'd been intrigued from the first—drawn not just by her beauty, but by the woman herself. At first glance Anneliese Christiansen appeared every inch the glamorous, sophisticated supermodel who featured regularly in the gossip columns. But he was beginning to realise that the real Anna was a far more complex mixture of emotions.

For a start she was not as worldly as he had expected. She reminded him of a young colt, skittish and nervy, and ready to back away the minute he came near. Persuading her into his bed was not going to be as easy as he had first assumed. It would take time and patience to win her trust and he had a short supply of both.

Common sense told him to walk away. The world was full of stunning blondes and he preferred women who required little emotional maintenance. But for the past two months Anna had filled his mind to the exclusion of almost everything else, even business.

It was a new experience for him and one that he didn't enjoy, which was why he had decided to make use of his time in England to take his desire for her to its logical conclusion. He hadn't anticipated such a robust rebuttal, he acknowledged wryly, but Anna's determination to ignore the chemistry between them only served to further his interest.

He wanted her. And whatever Damon Kouvaris wanted, he invariably got.

CHAPTER THREE

ANNA kept on running until her heart felt as though it would burst. Even then she pushed herself on, lap after lap, and every time she completed a circuit she glanced hopefully over to where she had left her kit bag by the side of the track, praying that Damon would have gone.

He was still there, sprawled on the grass, the sun gilding his bronzed shoulders and strong, muscular thighs revealed below the hem of his running shorts. Not that he had done much running, she noted irritably. He had simply sat there, sunning himself—a demigod in designer shades, watching her run until she was near to the point of collapse.

With a muttered oath she slowed her steps and headed across the track. If his presence as spectator was a battle of wills, she was ready to admit defeat. Her legs felt like jelly— a fact that had nothing to do with the sight of him, she assured herself when she reached the spot where she had dumped her bag.

Affecting an air of supreme uninterest, she ignored him and reached into her bag for her water bottle. The few mouthfuls of liquid remaining in the bottle did nothing to quench her thirst but the thought of walking back to the sports complex to refill it was beyond her and she sank to the ground, burying her face in the sweet-smelling grass.

'If you intend to run at that pace for the whole race, you'll never make it past the halfway mark,' Damon commented idly.

'Go to hell.' The fact that he was right did nothing to improve her temper and she turned her head to glare at him, further incensed as she watched him drink from his own water canister. There was something innately earthy and sensual about the way he gulped thirstily and her eyes focused on the convulsive movement of his throat when he swallowed.

'Here.' He must have felt her eyes on him and handed her the canister. Desperation overcame pride and she sat up and took it from him, put it to her lips and drank. 'You should bring more water with you; one small bottle isn't enough in this heat. Although it defies common sense to train during the hottest part of the day anyway,' he added, as if he were speaking to a small child.

'Anything else?' she drawled sarcastically. She lay back in the grass and allowed her eyes to drift shut. He was the most arrogant, overbearing man she had ever met and she wanted to tell him to get lost, but she was too exhausted to speak, and, anyway, she doubted he would listen.

The running track was set far back from the road and all she could hear was the piercingly sweet song of a skylark hovering high above. It was the sound of summer, she thought sleepily, turning her face to the sun, but as a shadow fell across her she opened her eyes again to find Damon leaning over her.

'You shouldn't lie out in the full glare of the sun without protection. I'm just making sure you don't burn,' he added equably when she frowned at the close proximity of his body next to hers.

He was lying on his side, propped up on one elbow so that his upper body shielded her from the sun. He had removed

his sunglasses so that she could see the fine lines around his
eyes, although his thoughts were concealed behind impossibly long black lashes. A lock of hair had fallen forwards
onto his brow and she resisted the urge to reach up and run
her fingers through the gleaming black silk.

He was too much, and right now she was too tired to do
battle with him, she conceded weakly, dragging her eyes
from the sight of his broad chest, barely covered by his
black sleeveless sports vest. He must spend hours in the
gym developing those biceps, she thought derisively, but
somehow she couldn't imagine him wasting his time lifting
weights.

'What kind of sport do you enjoy?' she queried, blushing
furiously at the wicked glint in his eyes. There was no
doubting the form of physical exercise he liked best.

'I like to play squash. I find it more challenging than
tennis. Other than that I enjoy swimming in the pool at my
villa back home, and when I was younger I belonged to a
boxing club and was junior national champion for three
years running,' he told her on a note of quiet pride.

'You enjoyed fighting?' Anna wrinkled her nose. 'I hate
that kind of aggressive, contact sport.'

'Actually boxing requires extreme discipline and mental
agility, not just brute strength,' he said with a smile. 'It's an
excellent way for boys and young men to release the build-
up of testosterone.'

'I imagine you had more than your fair share of that,' she
muttered dryly. Even at an early age he must have attracted
female attention like bees to honey. She could picture him
as a swaggering, cocky youth, hell-bent on having his own
way. 'You must have driven your parents to distraction.'

'Probably,' he agreed cheerfully, 'but my father curbed
my excesses by sending me to work on building projects. I
may have been the heir to a multimillion-pound fortune but

he believed that I should start at the bottom and earn my place in Kouvaris Construction. He taught me a lot,' he added softly and Kezia caught the note of affection and respect in his voice.

'I'm sure your parents are very proud of you,' she said, recalling a recent newspaper article detailing the astounding success of the Kouvaris Construction group under his directorship. 'Where are they now—do they live near you in Greece?'

'Sadly they've both passed away. My father died ten years ago and my mother followed soon after. He was her reason for living and she simply couldn't bear to be without him,' he added quietly.

'I'm sorry.' She sat up, feeling suddenly restless. Maybe it was the talk about happy families, she thought bleakly. Damon had spoken with such conviction of the love his parents had shared for each other, but she found it unsettling.

She would never award a man so much power over her that he became her reason for living, she vowed fiercely. She had witnessed firsthand the damage such strong emotions could wreak. Her father had been the centre of her mother's universe and his infidelities had almost destroyed her.

'So, do you have any other family—brothers and sisters?' she asked as curiosity won over her initial wariness of him.

'One sister, Catalina.' He rolled onto his back and tucked his arms behind his head so that Anna's eyes were drawn unwittingly to the way his vest top had ridden up, revealing a sprinkling of black hairs that arrowed down over his taut stomach.

'She was only eighteen when my parents died and we're very close. In fact we share a villa just outside Athens. Fortunately a very large villa, which is divided into two separate homes now that Catalina is married and has her own family,' he added with a laugh. 'We frequently all meet up for

meals in the communal courtyard, but I admit I like my own space.'

He paused, as if he was about to say something else, and Anna waited expectantly, but then he shook his head. 'That's enough about me. Now it's your turn.' He stretched out a hand and caught hold of her long, pale gold plait. 'I assume from your colouring and name that you were born in Scandinavia?'

'No, my father is Swedish but my mother's English and I was born here in London. I used to visit my grandparents in Stockholm when I was a child, but I haven't seen them for a long time,' she explained, adding quietly, 'not since my parents split up. The divorce was acrimonious and caused a huge rift in the family.'

'That's a pity; you must miss them. Are you close to your parents?'

'Not particularly.' She jumped up and busied herself with collecting her water bottle and zipping up her bag. 'I was sent away to boarding-school when I was thirteen and I didn't see them that much.' She gave him a brisk smile, indicating her desire to change the subject.

'You didn't enjoy living away from home, I take it?' he asked softly, studying her closed expression speculatively.

'On the contrary, I loved it. It taught me to be independent and stand on my own two feet. The most valuable lesson I've ever learned is never to rely on anyone else.' She swung her bag over her shoulder and began to walk away from him. 'I have to go now,' she stated bluntly, her tone clearly indicating that she didn't expect him to join her.

It was plain that even the most innocent enquiries about her personal life, and, in particular, her family, were off limits, Damon realised. He jumped to his feet and strolled after her. Beneath her bravado he had detected a note of real pain in her voice when she'd spoken of her parents' divorce.

Thirteen was a notoriously difficult age, particularly for girls, he mused, remembering his sister during her teenage years.

He had been lucky enough to enjoy an idyllic childhood, brought up in a happy and stable environment by parents whose love for each other and their children had never been in doubt. Perhaps Anna's childhood experiences had caused real emotional damage and contributed towards her fiercely defended independence?

From the articles about her in the press, he had imagined her to be shallow and spoilt, exchanging one handsome actor boyfriend for another with startling regularity. Equality between the sexes suited him fine, he acceded, his eyes focusing on her endlessly long, slender legs as she marched on ahead of him. He was happy to admit that he wasn't looking for the commitment of a long-term relationship.

Everything he'd read about Anna confirmed that she was a sophisticated woman of the world and he was impatient to take her to bed. But, meeting her again, he had glimpsed an air of vulnerability about her that was as disturbing as it was unexpected. Beneath her ice-cool beauty there lurked a deep well of emotions and to his astonishment he was aware of a tug of protectiveness of her.

'So, are you an only child?' he queried. 'Or are there other, equally stunning Christiansens waiting to take the modelling world by storm?'

Anna paused fractionally, her impatient glare saying louder than words that her private life was none of his business. 'I have a couple of stepsisters from my father's second marriage, but we're not close.'

She almost choked on the understatement. As a teenager she had hated the fact that her adored father preferred to live with his new wife's children rather than her. Her jealousy had caused friction on her monthly visits to see him and had

finally led Lars Christiansen to break off all but the most cursory contact. Her feeling of rejection had been unbearable, but it had been a salutary life lesson, she acknowledged grimly.

'Do you still keep in contact with your father?' Damon asked curiously.

'Christmas cards, the occasional birthday card if he remembers,' she replied shortly. 'He lives in Sweden now and is currently going through his third divorce. My mother has recently married again for the third time, although I can't imagine why. The whole concept of marriage leaves me cold.'

'Perhaps your parents' experiences are the reason why none of your relationships last longer than a few weeks,' Damon mused. 'Your childhood has left you with a fear of commitment. Is that why you flit from one partner to another?'

They had reached the entrance to the sports centre and Anna swung round, almost incandescent with fury. She balanced on the top step, her eyes glinting with temper. Once again his blithe assumption that the tabloid reports concerning her love life were true hurt more that it should. Why should she give a damn what he thought? And why should she listen to his amateur psychobabble about the effects of her childhood?

'You're hardly one to talk about commitment, Damon,' she snapped scathingly. 'Your reputation as a playboy is well documented—a multimillionaire womaniser with the morals of an alley cat, or so I've heard,' she added, ignoring the flash of anger in his dark eyes. 'Rumour has it that you take what you want and who you want with a ruthless disregard for other people's emotions, but I warn you now, you're not having me!'

She spun on her heels and marched across the foyer

towards the changing rooms before he had time to reply. Damon's expression of stunned surprise was almost comical—she doubted he had ever been spoken to with such brutal honesty before, but she had never felt less like laughing. He had practically accused her of being a tart, she remembered when she stood beneath the shower and allowed her angry tears to fall.

As one of the world's most photographed women, she had grown used to the constant gossip and speculation that surrounded her private life. It was a side to her job that she loathed and occasionally her legal team would demand a retraction from the press or threaten to sue over a particularly scurrilous article.

But for the most part she had learned to live with the fact that, in the media's eyes, she was public property and she treated their intrusion with an air of cool disdain. Hiding her true feelings had become a matter of pride and she couldn't understand why Damon's opinion, of all people, mattered so much.

After showering, she slipped into slim fitting jeans and white T-shirt, donned a pair of strappy sandals and combed her hair loose so that it could dry naturally. She strolled through the foyer and paused to inspect the day's menu displayed on the blackboard outside the cafeteria despite her awareness of the mountain of paperwork awaiting her at home. Fortunately there was no sight of Damon and as her tension eased she was aware that she was starving.

'Anna, are you going to eat with us today?'

She turned at the sound of the distinctive Italian accent and smiled at Roberto, the manager of the cafeteria. Under his directorship, the cafeteria had developed into an innovative restaurant with an excellent reputation for fresh, beautifully prepared food. In the summer she often ate her lunch

outside on the terrace, close to the stream that meandered through the grounds of the sports complex.

'I admit I'm tempted,' she replied, discarding the idea of a sandwich back at her flat in favour of one of Roberto's delicacies.

'I've prepared your favourite—Salade Niçoise,' Roberto informed her with a grin. 'Your friend is already waiting at your usual table.'

'Oh, *is* he.' Her appetite instantly vanished, to be replaced with simmering annoyance, but she liked Roberto and had no option but to follow him out onto the terrace.

Damon was sitting at the table beside the stream. *Her* table, she noted irritably, her smile slipping the moment Roberto had gone. 'Why are you here? I thought I'd made it plain that I didn't want to see you again,' she snapped, mindful of the other guests who were enjoying lunch alfresco.

'You need to eat properly after all that exercise,' Damon replied calmly, seemingly unperturbed by the storm brewing in her navy blue eyes. 'And I don't mean just a snatched sandwich while you're catching up on your paperwork.'

Was the man a mind-reader? She sincerely hoped not, Anna thought darkly as she absorbed the impact of him in cream chinos and a black polo shirt, unfastened at the neck to reveal the tanned column of his throat. He was seriously sexy but she would rather die than give him the satisfaction of knowing how much he affected her.

'I don't want to have lunch with you,' she muttered fiercely, placing her hands on her hips and glaring at him. Damon seemed determined to challenge her and she felt like stamping her foot in temper.

'Are you always so childish?' he queried mildly.

'Are you always so pigheaded?'

They seemed to have reached checkmate, but as she

stood, glowering at him, Roberto appeared, his face beaming as he brought out their lunch.

'You're causing a scene. For your friend's sake why don't you be a good girl and sit down?' Damon instructed, the hint of steel beneath his indolent tone causing her to subside into a chair.

'That wasn't a scene—trust me, I can do much better than that,' she growled warningly before pinning a smile on her face to greet Roberto. 'That looks divine, Roberto—as usual,' she complimented approvingly when the chef set her meal before her.

'Enjoy,' Roberto said happily. 'I see you are training hard for the race. Now you need to eat.' He winked at Damon. 'Anna has the face of an angel, huh? But I tell you, she has a big heart. She's always busy raising money for different charities. Are you going to watch her run the marathon?'

'I wouldn't miss it for the world,' Damon assured the other man, carefully avoiding Anna's poisonous glare. 'I'll be there supporting her the whole way.'

The thought was enough to ruin Anna's appetite but she couldn't leave her meal without hurting Roberto's feelings and so she picked up her fork. Damon ignored her while he concentrated on his own meal and after a few mouthfuls she found herself slowly start to relax. The food was heavenly and she ate with enjoyment, her senses soothed by the gentle trickling sound of the stream.

'Better than a sandwich?' The gentle query brought her head up and she discovered that Damon had finished his meal and was quietly watching her.

'Much, although the paperwork is still waiting,' she admitted with a rueful smile. She was not by nature a sulker and, aided by Roberto's culinary skill, her anger had gradually melted away. 'I hadn't realised how hungry I was,' she said awkwardly. 'Thank you.'

'My pleasure.'

It was amazing how two little words could evoke such a fevered reaction within her, she thought despairingly as heat suffused her whole body. She was so agonisingly aware of Damon that it seemed as if nothing else existed. The voices of the other diners faded and the air seemed so still that she was conscious of every breath he took.

'How long do you plan to stay in England?' she burst out, wincing as her voice sounded over-loud to her ears.

'I'm not entirely sure—it depends on a number of things,' he replied obliquely, his smile causing Anna's heart to thud erratically. She felt an irrational urge to snatch his sunglasses from his face in order to read his thoughts but had to content herself with reaching into her bag for her own shades. It might be cowardly but she felt measurably safer with them on. Damon seemed to have the disturbing knack of reading her mind and she preferred to keep her thoughts to herself.

'How about you? Do you have any plans to travel in the near future?'

'I have assignments in New York coming up but I purposefully kept the next couple of weeks clear. Time to prepare for the charity race and time afterwards to recover from it,' she added with a sudden, disarming grin.

It was her smile that did it for him, Damon acknowledged silently, his eyes focusing on the tilt of her wide mouth. When she smiled her face lit up and she was transformed from classically beautiful to simply breathtaking.

He wondered what she would do if he gave into the urge to lean across the table and claim her lips with his own—and to hell with the other diners. Most women of his acquaintance would giggle and lower their lashes, perhaps wind their arms around his neck to respond to his kiss. Anna would undoubtedly throw the coffee-pot at his head, he accepted with a wry

smile as he sought to bring his rampaging hormones under control.

'What led you to choose modelling as a career?' he queried. 'Apart from the obvious, of course.'

'The obvious?' Anna frowned, clearly puzzled.

'Your looks—I'm sure I'm not the first man to tell you that the combination of your features is utterly exquisite.'

The words were uttered with an air of clinical detachment that made Anna shiver. It was true that she received countless compliments—none of which affected her in the slightest. Why then did Damon's cool assessment send a quiver of fierce pleasure through her?

She wanted to say something flippant but her mouth was suddenly dry and she reached for her glass of water with a hand that shook slightly.

'I never made a conscious decision to become a model,' she told him when she could trust herself to speak. 'When I left school, most of my friends, including Kezia, went to university, but I had no clear idea of what I wanted to do with my life. When I was "spotted", walking down the Kings Road, it seemed like a godsend—I'd fallen behind with the rent on my bedsit and had no idea how I was going to pay it.' She shrugged her shoulders expressively. 'To be honest, I thought I'd give modelling a go for a couple of months, until I was back on my feet financially. I never expected it to become a career.'

'Yet your success is astounding,' Damon commented. 'Do you enjoy modelling?'

'I enjoy the money,' she replied bluntly. 'I enjoy the fact that I'm financially independent and don't have to rely on anyone else for anything.'

For anyone else, read any man, Damon guessed. What had happened in her past to make her so mistrustful of relationships? A broken love affair perhaps—or did her wariness

stem from events in her childhood? 'Financial security is obviously important to you, but isn't the predicted career-span of even an internationally successful model such as yourself notoriously short?'

'Hopefully I'll continue to work for a few more years and I already have a significant property portfolio, which I plan to extend. The buy-to-let market in London is booming, as I'm sure you know, and I enjoy being a landlord much more than a tenant.'

'So, behind that angelic face lies the brain of a ruthless businesswoman,' Damon teased lightly.

'I know what it's like to be at rock-bottom,' she replied seriously. 'The few months between when I left school and was taken on by the modelling agency were hellish. I had no job, no money and often had to rely on friends for somewhere to stay.'

'But surely you could have lived with one of your parents after you'd left boarding-school?' Damon demanded, unable to disguise his shock. She had been little more than a child and yet it sounded as though her family had abandoned her. No wonder she was so desperate for financial security.

'My father was busy with his new family. We had already grown apart and his wife made it clear that she didn't view a difficult teenager as a welcome addition to the household,' Anna revealed, unable to disguise the hint of bitterness in her voice. 'My mother was married to her second husband by then and...' she hesitated fractionally before admitting quietly '...there were reasons why I had to leave home.'

Something in her voice caught Damon's attention. He wanted to ask what those reasons were but even across the width of the table he could feel her tension.

The sun was shining as brightly as ever but, despite its warmth, Anna shivered. She felt as though a black cloud had settled over her, suffocating her with the disturbing

memories she would rather forget. Her stepfather's sly, leering face filled her mind and she felt the familiar feeling of nausea sweep over her when she remembered his hot breath on her skin…his hands touching her at every casual opportunity.

'Anna, are you all right?' Damon's voice seemed to sound from a long way off and she blinked and forced her mind back to the present. He was watching her, his dark brows drawn into a frown of concern.

'I'm fine, just a little tired, that's all,' she quickly reassured him, managing a shaky smile. 'I mustn't keep you. I'm sure you're a busy man, Damon,' she added briskly as she stood up. 'Thank you again for lunch.'

'Where are you parked? I'll see you to your car.' He had already walked round the table to pick up her bag, and before she realised his intention he slid a supporting arm around her waist. 'You look very pale, *pedhaki mou*. I don't think you should drive.'

'I don't intend to. My flat's not far from here and I walked through the park this morning. Damon, I'm perfectly okay,' she said sharply. She was so intent on fighting her reaction to the brush of his thigh against hers that she did not notice that he had led her over to his car.

'Here we are—in you get,' he said cheerfully.

She glared at him when he opened the passenger door. 'I've told you, I'll walk.'

'Do you want to fight about it?' He stood, blocking her path, his arms folded resolutely across his chest in a stance that told her she wasn't going anywhere.

She had lost that sickly pallor, Damon noted with satisfaction. Something had seriously bothered her back there, but now wasn't the time to try and draw the truth from her. Instead he had hoped to focus her mind back on the present by deliberately provoking her temper and, from the hectic

colour staining her cheeks, it appeared that he had succeeded.

'You are the most infuriating man I have ever met,' she snapped furiously as she conceded defeat and subsided into the car. She turned her head when he slid behind the wheel and pointedly ignored him for the short journey back to her flat. It was only when he turned into the car park and cut the engine that she swung back to face him, her eyes wide and suspiciously bright.

'What do you want from me?' she demanded huskily, the tremor in her voice causing a peculiar pain in Damon's stomach. The naked vulnerability in her eyes disturbed him more than he cared to admit.

'A little of your time, a chance to get to know one another better and explore what we started on Zathos,' he replied quietly.

'We didn't start anything.' Her fierce rejection of his words was instant and laced with panic as she fumbled to release her seat belt. 'Your imagination must have been playing tricks on you, Damon. There was nothing.'

'No?' He moved before she had time to react, curving his hand around her neck to cup her nape before lowering his head to capture her mouth in a brief, hard kiss.

The moment he touched her Anna tensed, waiting for the familiar feeling of revulsion to fill her. It didn't come. Instead of reliving unpleasant memories from the past, her mind seemed to be a blank canvas where nothing existed except the warm pleasure of his mouth on hers. His tongue explored the shape of her lips with delicate precision; an unhurried, evocative tasting that caused a trembling to start deep inside her. To her astonishment she found herself wanting more, but as she parted her lips he broke the kiss and drew back to stare into her wide, shell-shocked eyes.

'In my imagination?' he taunted. 'I don't think so, Anna.

The chemistry between us on Zathos was white hot, and it still burns—for both of us. The question is, what are we going to do about it?'

CHAPTER FOUR

ANNA spent the rest of the day scrubbing and polishing her flat, hoping that frenzied activity would prevent her from thinking about Damon. She could no longer deny that she was attracted to him but fear had seen her flee from his car as if the devil himself were in pursuit.

The memory of his kiss lingered, however. She couldn't forget the feel of his mouth on hers, the pleasure his warm, firm lips had evoked, and she was shocked by the realisation that she hadn't wanted him to stop.

She spent the evening ploughing through a mountain of paperwork, but, despite the fact that it was past midnight before she crawled into bed, she slept badly for the second night in succession.

It was Damon's fault, she thought grumpily the next morning, pulling on her trainers and running gear ready for another session at the sports track. He had stormed into her life like a tornado, ripping down her fragile defences and leaving her emotions in tatters.

The doorbell pealed as she was gulping down a second cup of coffee and she opened the door to be presented with an exquisite bouquet of cream roses.

'I was told to give you these,' the delivery boy muttered, handing her two large bottles of spring-water. 'The Greek

bloke said I was to be sure to tell you to take them to the track with you.' He shrugged his shoulders indifferently. 'I guess the message means more to you than it does to me.'

Murmuring her thanks, Anna closed the door and carried the flowers back to the kitchen before ripping open the attached envelope with fingers that shook slightly.

'Keep up with the training—I'm looking forward to seeing you cross the finish line,' Damon had written, the sight of his bold signature causing her heart to flip in her chest. His arrogance was insufferable, she thought furiously. For a second she seriously debated stuffing the flowers into the rubbish bin. His note was a subtle reminder that he intended to hold her to her agreement to have dinner with him after the charity race, but to her intense irritation she was unable to repress a little shiver of anticipation at the thought of seeing him again.

The word *no* did not seem to feature in Damon Kouvaris's vocabulary, she decided as she rammed the bottles of water into her kit bag. It was about time someone told him he couldn't always have his own way. But as she inhaled the delicate perfume of the blooms she could not bring herself to destroy them and placed them in a vase on the dining table—a visual reminder of the man she would rather forget.

He phoned mid-afternoon. She had run a bath—hoping to soothe her aching muscles after her run—and was blissfully immersed in scented bubbles when she heard the telephone. After the tenth ring she could stand it no longer, cursing as she wrapped a towel around her before padding barefoot down the hall, leaving a trail of foam in her wake.

The caller was annoyingly persistent, which meant that it was probably her mother, she thought grimly. It was less than six months since Judith had phoned from her home in France and dropped the bombshell that she had just married for the third time. Was it too soon for her mother to be

ringing to announce her divorce? Anna wondered cynically as she snatched up the receiver.

'Anna, I hope I haven't disturbed you,' a familiar, heavily accented voice sounded in her ear, causing goose-bumps to prickle her skin so that she twitched her towel firmly in place.

'I was in the bath,' she replied shortly, 'and now I'm dripping water all over the carpet.'

In his hotel room Damon stretched out on the bed and closed his eyes as he pictured Anna—damp, pink-cheeked and wrapped in a towel. Possibly not even a towel, he mused, feeling the familiar stirring in his loins. Those gorgeous, lissom limbs would be satin-smooth, perhaps glistening with a few stray droplets of moisture. Her blonde hair would be piled on top of her head while stray tendrils framed her face. Hunger flared as he imagined himself releasing the pins so that it fell in a swathe of gold silk over her breasts. 'I'm sorry. Do you want to go and put something on?'

'It's all right; I've got a towel round me.'

'Ah, bath-sheet or hand-towel?' he enquired throatily.

'Does it matter?' Anna inhaled sharply and fought to control the quiver that ran through her at the sound of his sexy drawl. 'Did you want something, Damon—other than a description of the size of my towel?'

It was tempting to spell out in glorious detail *precisely* what he wanted, but Damon restrained himself. 'I have two tickets for the Royal Ballet tonight. I wondered if you would care to join me?'

His voice was deliberately light and neutral, as if he feared that she would accuse him of pressurising her. It was tempting, Anna admitted silently. He was tempting. She hesitated, her eyes drawn along the hallway to the dining room, where the roses he had sent her were reflected in the polished mahogany table. She felt as though she were

balanced on the edge of a precipice and one wrong move could send her hurtling to her destruction.

'Why did you send me flowers?' she demanded huskily.

'They remind me of you—fragrant, fragile and infinitely beautiful,' he replied seriously. 'Don't you like them?'

'Of course I do—what woman doesn't love flowers?' she whispered as her body reacted to the smoky sensuality of his voice. But the thought of all the other women in his life sent her skidding back down to earth. Damon was well practised in the art of seduction. Did he send flowers to every blonde he was interested in? He must have an enormous florists' bill, she thought sardonically as common sense reasserted itself.

'I'm afraid I promised to babysit for a friend tonight and I can't let her down,' she lied. It seemed a foolproof excuse and she was just congratulating herself on her quick thinking when he spoke again.

'Perhaps I could help out? I'm good with children.'

Too late she recalled the gentle patience he'd shown on Zathos towards his little godson Theo. She'd been struck by his natural affinity with children and surprised by the idea that he would make a good father.

Next thing she would be canonising him, she thought impatiently.

'I don't think that would be a good idea, and I'm sure you don't want to waste your tickets. You'll have to flick through your little black book and find another partner for the evening. You must have several willing candidates to choose from,' she added cattily, dismayed at how much she hated the idea that she was just one in a long list of blondes in his phone book.

'Dozens,' he assured her blandly, 'but you're currently top of the list.'

'Lucky me,' she replied every bit as blandly, gently

placing the phone down before he had the chance to reply, and then spent the next ten minutes hovering in the hallway in case he should ring again. He didn't, and, berating herself for being a fool, she returned to her rapidly cooling bath water, any idea of relaxing blown to pieces.

She had been right to turn him down, she assured herself for the hundredth time. Instinct warned her that Damon was out of her league and although he fascinated her, she refused to risk her emotional security on a man who regarded women as nothing more than sexual playmates.

Several hours later she was beginning to wish she had accepted Damon's invitation.

'Hey, Anna, why aren't you drinking?'

The question was slurred and indistinct and Anna turned her head sharply to avoid a wave of alcoholic fumes. Tonight was rapidly turning into the evening from hell, she brooded darkly when Jack Bailey, star of a series of commercials for a popular brand of jeans, slid into the seat next to her.

'Here, waiter, more champagne,' Jack demanded. 'Do you know who this is?' he asked the waiter in a loud voice that caused heads to turn. 'This is Anna Christiansen, the most beautiful woman in the world—isn't that right, Anna?' He leered at her, his handsome face flushed from the effects of too much wine, and Anna stifled a groan.

Having refused Damon's invitation to the ballet, she'd been left facing a long, lonely evening and had jumped when her phone had rung again just after six, her frisson of anticipation quickly dissipating when she'd discovered that the call was from one of the models she had worked with in South Africa.

Dinner with friends, even if they were acquaintances rather than close confidantes, was better than a night in front of the TV, she had decided. And at least it would focus her mind on something other than a certain enigmatic Greek.

But at the restaurant it soon became apparent that the quiet meal she'd anticipated had developed into a full-blown social event. Friends of friends joined the party, the wine flowed and the group grew louder, attracting attention from other diners. Jack's drunken attempts to climb inside her dress were the last straw and she gave him an icy glare.

'Shut up, Jack,' she muttered irritably. 'Don't you think you've had enough to drink?'

Her acerbic comments merely caused the young actor to grin wolfishly and while she was endeavouring to remove his hand from her cleavage she felt a shiver run the length of her spine. It was the same feeling that she remembered from Kezia's dinner party and filled with foreboding, she slowly lifted her head.

Damon was sitting at a table some distance away. Even though her view was partly obscured by other diners, Anna instantly recognised him and her heart lurched as her gaze slid to his attractive companion. Was the woman number two on his list? she wondered bleakly as she stared at the stunning redhead by his side.

It was late in the evening and she guessed that Damon and his companion had come to the restaurant straight from the theatre. Doubtless the Royal Ballet's performance of *Swan Lake* had been spectacular she mused bleakly, wishing that she had found the courage to accept his invitation.

The fact that he'd had no problem finding another partner for the evening proved that she had been wise to decline, she told herself firmly. But she could not tear her eyes from him and she held her breath when he suddenly stiffened and glanced across the busy restaurant.

Even from a distance she registered his brief flare of surprise when he caught sight of her and she blushed, re-membering her earlier excuse that she was babysitting for a friend tonight. It was obvious that Damon was also recall-

ing her lie. His gaze slid to Jack Bailey, who was slumped in a drunken stupor beside her, and his mouth curled into a dark smile before he deliberately returned his attention to his companion.

Damn him, she thought furiously. He wasn't her keeper. And so what if she had lied? Maybe now he would get the message that she didn't want to have anything to do with him.

But to her chagrin she found that she couldn't prevent her eyes from straying in his direction. He looked gorgeous— lean, dark and simmering with his own lethal brand of sexual magnetism. She wasn't the only woman in the room to have noticed him, either, she noted grimly as a quick scan of the restaurant revealed that most female eyes were focused on one man.

At that moment he looked up and trapped her gaze with his brooding stare. The hubbub of voices became muted and the other diners seemed to fade to the periphery of her vision, leaving nothing but Damon and the powerful electric current that flared between them.

Her reaction was instant and shockingly basic as heat coursed through her veins. Her breasts ached and a horrified glance revealed that her nipples were clearly visible through her clingy jersey top. He couldn't see from that distance, she consoled herself, but the sudden tension apparent in his shoulders warned her that he was well aware of the effect he had on her.

'Anna, we're going on to a club. Do you want to come?' Jack Bailey's voice sounded in her ear—as annoyingly persistent as a wasp, it at least gave her the excuse to break free from the spell that Damon had cast over her.

'No, thanks, I've had enough and I'm going home,' she replied curtly.

'Come on, don't be such a bore,' Jack muttered sulkily.

He staggered after her as she picked a route through the restaurant that carefully avoided going anywhere near Damon and his gorgeous dinner date. Outside it was bedlam. The restaurant was currently one of the most popular venues in London and the paparazzi had gathered in droves, desperate to snap shots of any celebrities.

The last thing she wanted was for pictures of her and Jack to be plastered across the front pages of tomorrow's tabloids, Anna thought grimly. For some reason the press were fascinated by her love life but she refused to be a pawn in their stupid game.

She retreated into a corner of the lobby, but Jack must have noticed and a moment later he joined her, his eyes glazed and his shirt buttons half undone as he trapped her against a wall with his arms on either side of her head.

'Okay, forget the club. We'll have our own private party, just you and me, baby. Do you want to come back to my place?' He swayed unsteadily and slumped forwards so that his full weight pinioned Anna against the wall. His breath was hot on her skin as he ground his lips on hers and his hands seemed to be everywhere, damp with sweat as they edged beneath her top.

Instantly she was transported back in time. Instead of Jack, it was her stepfather pushing her against the wall, laughing at her as she struggled to prevent him from touching her.

'Jack, get off me! Leave me alone.' Overwhelmed by panic and a growing feeling of claustrophobia, she gave a shrill cry and lashed out, her hand making sharp contact with his cheek.

'Bloody hell, you little vixen, what did you do that for?' Jack reared back, easing the pressure on her chest, and she gulped for air, her breath coming in short, shallow gasps. 'Everyone says you're a frigid bitch and now I know why,'

he taunted, his sneering smile fading when a hand landed heavily on his shoulder.

'Do you need any help, Anna?'

Damon materialised in front of her, his dark eyes cold and merciless as he gripped Jack's arm, restraining the younger man with insulting ease. Anna would like to have made some flippant remark and shrugged off the incident but instead she nodded wordlessly.

She felt sick with a mixture of shame and fear. Nothing could have happened, she reminded herself impatiently. They were in the lobby of a busy restaurant and Jack couldn't have hurt her—forced her... She shuddered and closed her mind to the memories that had resurfaced. She didn't want to think, not now.

The restaurant manager appeared, frowning as he took in the scene. 'Shall I call the police?' he addressed Damon.

'No!' Anna's eyes were unconsciously pleading. The story would be fodder for the gutter press and she couldn't bear the humiliation of reading about her supposed relationship with Jack in tomorrow's downmarket papers.

'I don't think that will be necessary,' Damon answered, his gaze not leaving Anna's pale face. 'I'll leave you to deal with *him*.' He threw a scathing glance at Jack, whose initial bravado had disappeared and who was now swaying unsteadily on his feet. 'Plenty of black coffee, or a bucket of water over his head—I know which one I'd choose,' he told the manager with a grim smile. 'Is there another way out? The world's press seem to be camped on the front steps.'

'You can leave through the kitchens,' the manager said quickly. 'Come this way.'

'It's all right, I can take care of myself,' Anna muttered as her eyes flew from Damon to his beautiful redheaded companion who was plainly bemused by the scene.

The look on his face said it all. 'Do you really want to

step out there—' he gestured to the front of the restaurant where the paparazzi were assembled on the pavement '—looking like that?'

Before she could reply he spun her round and she gasped at the sight of her reflection in the mirror. Her hair had escaped its once-neat chignon and was hanging in rats' tails around her face, her lipstick was smeared over her chin, but it was her eyes, wild and overbright with unshed tears that gave away the fact that she was near breaking-point.

'The press would have a field day,' Damon told her tersely. He took his phone from his pocket. 'I'll have my driver meet us out back.'

She had no option but to comply, Anna acknowledged when Damon ushered her through the door leading to the kitchens. She half turned to say something but found that he had hung back and was speaking in a quiet undertone to his companion.

What must the other woman be thinking? She bit her lip and followed the restaurant manager through the back door, out into a narrow alley where they had to squeeze past the rubbish bins. She was so embarrassed she wanted to die and could not bring herself to look at Damon or his friend when a car pulled up in the alleyway and a uniformed chauffeur sprang out.

'There was really no need for you to end your evening,' she muttered. 'Ask your driver to drop me off on the main road and I'll take a cab home.'

It was Damon's companion who answered. 'It's really not a problem. I promised my husband that I would be back before midnight anyway,' she added with a smile. 'We don't want to upset him, do we, Damon?'

'Certainly not. Friend or not, I think Marc would feel justified in thumping me if I did not bring you back safely and on time,' he replied, his eyes glinting with amusement at

Anna's obvious confusion. 'Anna, I'd like to introduce you
to Elaine Sotiriou. Her husband and I were at school together
and I was lucky enough to persuade Marc to lend me his wife
for the evening.'

'Yes, the ballet was wonderful. It's such a pity you'd
already arranged to meet your friends,' Elaine said sympa-
thetically. The car pulled up in a mews of tall Georgian
houses and she leaned forwards to brush her lips against
Damon's cheek. 'You're welcome to come in for coffee—
both of you,' she added, giving Anna a gentle smile. 'My
husband would love to meet you.'

'Another time perhaps,' Damon replied. 'I need to get
Anna home.'

Anna opened her mouth to tell him that she was not his
responsibility, remembered her ravaged appearance and
thought better of it. If she was honest she couldn't wait to
reach the quiet sanctuary of her flat. The incident with Jack
had been unpleasant rather than traumatic but it had evoked
memories of her stepfather that even now, after all this time,
still had the power to disturb her.

She was silent for the twenty-minute drive across town,
her body as tense as a coiled spring as she waited for Damon
to comment on the fact that she had lied to him earlier. He
said nothing, seemingly lost in his thoughts, and as the limousine swung into the parking area outside her flat she
released her breath on a shaky sigh.

'Thanks for bringing me home and…everything.' Everything included rescuing her from Jack Bailey's drunken
advances but she was too embarrassed to spell it out and slid
out of the car with as much dignity as she could muster.

'I'll see you up.'

'There's no need.'

Reaction was setting in and she was unable to repress a
shiver. Damon's mouth tightened. Did she have any idea how

vulnerable she looked? he wondered. Her eyes were wide; the expression in their depths *bruised,* he noted grimly. He placed his hand lightly on her shoulder to guide her towards the steps and felt her flinch.

Surely she didn't think he would leap on her as her drunken dinner date had done? The thought was enough for him to remove his hand and he contented himself with following her closely up the two flights of stairs to her flat.

At the front door she paused and he took the key from her trembling fingers.

'Damon.'

He caught the note of desperation in her voice and his jaw tensed. 'I'll make the coffee while you repair the damage your lover inflicted. And then I promise I'll go,' he said steadily.

'Jack's not my lover.' Far from it, she thought with a shudder of revulsion. 'He's just a friend. Not even that really,' she admitted honestly. 'Dinner with a crowd of acquaintances seemed a safer option than…'

'Spending the evening with me,' Damon finished for her, watching the way her cheeks flooded with colour. Once again he was aware of a curious tug of protectiveness. Anneliese Christiansen was reputed to be worldly-wise and sophisticated—the Ice Princess who lured her many lovers with her cool beauty. But the woman standing before him reminded him of a frightened child and he had to restrain himself from drawing her into his arms.

Instinct warned him that if he touched her she would lash out like a cornered wildcat and he carefully kept his distance as he followed her into her flat and down the narrow passageway to the kitchen.

'Coffee, and then you have to go,' she told him, unable to keep the tremor from her voice as she filled the kettle and reached into the cupboard for cups. One slipped through her

fingers and as it shattered on the floor she gave a cry and knelt to gather up the pieces.

'Leave it.'

She jumped at the harshness of his tone and stared up at him, blinking furiously. Damon caught the glint of her tears and felt his gut tighten.

'Go and get cleaned up,' he bade her quietly, taking her hand and drawing her to her feet. She still had a trace of lipstick smeared across her face and he wiped it with his thumb pad.

The moment he'd stepped into the lobby and seen her struggling in the arms of that drunken lout, who'd been pawing her all evening, he'd wanted to commit murder. He couldn't understand where this edge of possessiveness had come from, this urge to take care of her as if she were infinitely precious to him.

He barely knew her, he reminded himself impatiently as he pushed her gently out of the kitchen. Common sense warned him that Anna spelt trouble, in more ways than one. But for the last two months he'd been unable to forget her and even now, when she was ashen and achingly vulnerable, he still desired her more than any woman he'd ever known.

Anna tore her gaze from Damon and shot into the bathroom where she quickly locked the door behind her. She felt dirty, sullied by Jack Bailey's touch, and with swift, almost desperate movements she stripped out of her clothes and dived into the shower.

She quickly scrubbed her body, all the while conscious of faint noises from the kitchen. Damon was probably making coffee as promised.

Suddenly she was fifteen again, listening to the sound of her stepfather's footsteps outside the bathroom door and knowing that he would be there, lurking on the landing when she emerged. He had always had a legitimate reason, of

course, but she shuddered at the memory of his sly grin and the way his eyes had followed her when she'd fled to her bedroom.

This had to stop, she told herself sharply. She stepped out of the shower cubicle and huddled in the folds of a towel. She wasn't fifteen any more, she was twenty-five—a grown woman with a successful career and no one could hurt her, certainly not her mother's second husband Philip Stone.

'You're such a pretty girl, Annie. Not even a girl any more. I've noticed how you're developing into a woman.'

'Shut up, Phil, or I'll tell Mum.'

'Tell her what, Annie? I was only saying that you've blossomed into a real stunner. I bet lots of men like to look at you. I know I do.'

No! Anna's eyes flew open and she stared at herself in the mirror, her face twisted with revulsion at the memories of her stepfather. Phil was in the past. She hadn't seen him since she'd left home at seventeen—preferring to struggle on her own rather than live under the same roof as her tormentor. Her stepfather's sly sexual innuendos had sickened her but when he had started to try and touch her—a hand on her thigh or a playful pat on her bottom, carried out in the guise of jolly Uncle Phil—she'd known that she had to leave.

Confiding in her mother had never been an option. After years of depression brought about by the failure of her first marriage, Judith had finally been happy again and Anna had been unable to bring herself to ruin that happiness. Instead she'd kept quiet about Phil's unhealthy fascination with his stepdaughter and had assured Judith that she was moving into a flat with friends. Life had been tough for a while, but she'd survived and along the way she'd learned that trust was for fools.

Her mother's marriage to Phil had eventually also ended in divorce. She didn't know the reasons why and had never

asked. Despite Judith's pleadings, she'd refused to return home to the house that she had come to hate. She had a new life, earning the kind of money she'd only ever dreamed of, and she'd made a solemn vow that she would never give up her independence for anyone.

'Anna, your coffee's getting cold.' Damon's terse voice sounded through the bathroom door, his tone laced with an underlying concern.

'All right—I'm just coming.' Her thick towelling robe fell past her knees, concealing her curves. She wanted no opportunity for misunderstanding, she thought grimly as she belted it tightly around her waist. She might have allowed Damon into her flat, but coffee was the only thing on offer.

He was the most gorgeous, sexy, charismatic man she had ever met and she was still reeling from her unexpected reaction to his kiss. But forewarned was forearmed and in the spirit of her self-preservation she was determined that it wouldn't happen again.

CHAPTER FIVE

WHEN Anna entered the sitting room she found Damon sprawled on the sofa, his long legs stretched out in front of him and his arms folded behind his head. He had discarded his jacket and tie and unfastened the top couple of shirt buttons to reveal a sprinkling of wiry black chest hair.

To Anna's mind he seemed to dominate the small sitting room, his brazen masculinity a stark contrast to the ultra feminine décor of her flat.

'I see you've made yourself at home,' she commented pithily as she retreated to the armchair furthest away from him. He had switched on the stereo player and the CD he'd selected was one of her current favourites—easy listening that soothed her rattled nerves. He looked as though he was settled for the night, she noted darkly, her senses suddenly on high alert when he gave her one of his devastating smiles.

'Your coffee's here,' he murmured, gesturing to the tray he had set on the low table in front of him. 'And I made some sandwiches. I noticed you didn't eat much at the restaurant.'

'My God, don't tell me you were spying on me. I can look after myself, you know.'

'Yes, I noticed.'

The softly spoken comment caused her to blush as she recalled how he had rescued her from Jack Bailey's clutches.

Anxious to avoid his quizzical gaze, she lifted the napkin from the tray and discovered a pile of sandwiches neatly arranged on a plate.

He'd even taken the trouble to trim off the crusts, she noted. She was so used to fending for herself that the simple gesture caused a prickling sensation behind her eyelids. It was a long time since she'd felt cared for and for some ridiculous reason she felt like crying. With a faint air of desperation she bit into a sandwich. It was true that she had barely touched her dinner and she was surprised to find she was hungry.

'I can't manage all of them,' she muttered stubbornly when she lifted her eyes to find him watching her eat, a look of smug satisfaction on his face. Was he always right? Damn him.

'Come and sit over here and I'll help you out,' he replied, patting the empty space on the sofa. It seemed churlish to refuse and she reluctantly moved next to him, perching awkwardly on the edge of the cushion, her body tensed and ready for instant flight.

'I had no idea you were so domesticated,' she commented coolly as she helped herself to another sandwich.

Damon shrugged. 'I don't have a problem dealing with the mundane things in life. Like you, I value my independence and at home I employ the minimum of staff.' He paused fractionally and then added, 'My wife was a great believer in equality between the sexes and she made it clear from day one of our marriage that she wouldn't run around after me like a traditional Greek wife.'

Anna was aware of a peculiar buzzing sensation in her ears. The room tilted alarmingly and she inhaled sharply, desperate to drag oxygen into her lungs. She couldn't faint; it would be so...pathetic, she told herself furiously. Her sandwich suddenly seemed to be made of cardboard and she had to force herself to swallow her mouthful.

'I didn't know you had a wife,' she said sharply when she could trust herself to speak. She felt physically sick as a variety of emotions threatened to overwhelm her, chiefly anger, she acknowledged grimly. If he was married, what was he doing here in her flat, and why had he kissed her?

God, did he really think he was so irresistible that she would agree to become his mistress, knowing that he had a wife in the background?

'She died eight years ago.' The statement was flat and unemotional and Anna's startled gaze flew to his face.

'I'm sorry, I didn't know,' she mumbled, unaware that he could read each fleeting emotion that crossed her face—shock and confusion mixed with sympathy and a faint hint of relief. 'Was it an accident, or was she ill?'

'A tragic mix of both—Eleni suffered from asthma but it was controlled by medication, or so we believed. There was no indication in the days before her death that her condition had worsened. She was her usual, vibrant self when I left on a business trip,' Damon explained. 'She was an artist and it seems that while she was alone in her studio at the top of the house she suffered a particularly severe attack and couldn't get to her inhaler in time. By the time the house-keeper found her it was too late, she was already dead.'

'Oh, God! How awful. You must miss her,' Anna whispered.

'It was a long time ago,' he offered quietly. 'Life moves on—it has to. But it took a long time to come to terms with the tragedy of a young life so cruelly taken, especially when Eleni had so much to live for.' He hesitated fractionally, as if he was about to say something else, but then continued—'Perhaps losing her so unexpectedly is the reason that I'm de-termined to seize every opportunity. Life isn't a dress rehearsal,' he murmured, staring at her intently with eyes that were so dark she felt as though she could drown in their depths.

'I'm so sorry,' she repeated helplessly. The words seemed totally inadequate and, overwhelmed by emotion, she placed her hand on his arm, wanting to comfort him. Damon reached out and ran a finger lightly down her cheek before cupping her chin and tilting her face to his.

'Don't,' he bade huskily as a solitary tear over-spilled and slid down her face. 'You have an unexpectedly compassionate heart, *pedhaki mou.*'

He couldn't disguise the faint note of surprise in his tone and she jerked back as if he had slapped her.

'What did you expect—that I was the spoilt, haughty supermodel the press like to portray?' she demanded sharply. 'The Ice Princess with a retinue of willing lovers? Is that why you're here, Damon— You assumed I'd agree to a meaningless sexual liaison with no messy emotions to screw it up?'

She broke off, unable to hide the hurt in her voice. Damon had earned a reputation as a playboy with a penchant for nubile blondes, and she was just one in a long line of women who had attracted his passing interest. But beneath the surface he was obviously a man capable of deep emotions. She didn't doubt that he had loved his wife. She'd heard evidence of it in his voice when he'd spoken of Eleni; had seen it in the sudden softening of his expression when he'd mentioned her name.

It was ridiculous to feel so *betrayed,* she told herself angrily. And obscene to feel jealous of the young Greek girl who had captured Damon's heart and whose life had been cut so tragically short.

'If I'd simply wanted sex, there are a number of options I could have chosen,' he growled, the rigid line of his jaw warning her that he was struggling to keep his anger in check. He didn't add that any one of those options would have been easier than pursuing a woman who seemed hell-bent on rejecting him.

If he was frank, he *had* believed that Anna would succumb to the undeniable attraction between them with a minimum of effort on his part. He had been guilty as charged of believing the gossip about her numerous, short-lived affairs and he was honest enough to accept that initially he'd simply wanted to take her to bed.

Okay, he still did, he acknowledged impatiently. His desire for Anna was fast becoming an obsession. He would like nothing better than to unfasten the belt of her robe, part the bulky material and discover her slender curves with his hands and mouth.

Instinct told him that her resistance would be minimal. Even now, the anger mirrored in her stunning blue eyes was mixed with a shimmer of awareness that she could not hide. It would be easy to close the distance between them and capture her mouth, initiate a sensual exploration until her defences crumbled and she responded to his kiss with the desire that he sensed matched his own.

Something held him back; the shadows in her eyes and the slight tremor of her bottom lip that she sought to control by catching the soft flesh with her teeth. On a physical level there was no doubt in his mind that Anna would respond to him. In his thirty-eight years he had enjoyed numerous sexual liaisons, some casual and others that had meant more to him. His marriage had meant the world, but Eleni was dead and in the years since her death he had found no reason to deny himself the pleasure of female company.

He knew without conceit that he possessed both the skill and sensitivity to ensure Anna's sexual pleasure, but mentally she would withdraw even further behind the barriers she had erected. A small voice in his head urged him to simply take what he wanted and to hell with the consequences, but he glimpsed the naked vulnerability in her eyes and realised with a jolt of surprise that he would hate to hurt her.

'We seem to have got off to a bad start,' he ventured quietly. 'I think we both harboured preconceived ideas about each other. Can't we wipe the slate clean and start again?'

Anna stared at him, unable to disguise her confusion. 'Why do you want to?' she demanded suspiciously.

'Because you intrigue me more than any woman I've ever met,' he replied honestly. He trapped her gaze, his eyes clear and candid as if he wanted to prove that he had no hidden agenda. 'And because you are so very lovely, Anna *mou,* that I can't keep my eyes off you. Even when I'm not with you, you dominate my thoughts.'

How did she respond to that? Anna wondered wildly as her heart lurched in her chest. He was practised in the art of seduction but his words held a ring of sincerity about them, rather than a glib statement designed to fool her. Dared she trust him? Wasn't he just the same as every other man she'd met— fascinated by her image but uninterested in the real Anna?

'Someone once told me that men would only ever want me for one thing,' she burst out, her stark admission taking them both by surprise. She didn't know what had induced her to reveal the poison that festered in her brain and her eyes darkened when she recalled her stepfather's taunts.

'You're a little sex-pot Annie, the embodiment of every male fantasy. Forget that rubbish about respecting your mind—every man who ever looks at you will only be interested in your body.'

'You don't believe that, surely?' Damon demanded. The *someone* she'd spoken of had obviously set out to wreck her self-esteem and it seemed they'd done a good job. 'Your looks are only one part of you, teamed with intelligence, wit and an obvious compassion for others.' He cupped her face once more and stared into her eyes. 'Who was he?' he demanded harshly. 'Who hurt you so badly that he made you doubt your self-worth?'

'It doesn't matter,' Anna mumbled, desperately trying to evade his gaze that seemed to burn into her soul. 'He's in the past.'

'Yet he still exerts power over you. Was he a lover who resented it when you ended the relationship and sought to destroy your confidence?' Damon saw the shudder that ran through her, glimpsed the trace of fear in her eyes and his jaw tightened. 'Did he *hurt* you—physically?'

The thought was enough to make him want to commit murder. He was shocked by the strength of his fury, but the idea that anyone could lay a finger on her in anger filled him with revulsion.

'Just leave it, Damon; it's not important.' Anna jerked out of his grasp and jumped to her feet, sending the contents of her coffee-cup flying. 'Damn it, now see what you've made me do,' she snapped as she attempted to blot the pool of coffee with a napkin. 'I think it's time you left.'

She didn't want to talk about the past and was already re-gretting her impulsive statement. How could she convince Damon that she was in control of her emotions when she'd allowed him to glimpse the chinks in her armour?

Damon wisely said no more as he slung his jacket over his shoulder and followed her along the hallway to the front door. He sensed the fierce tension that gripped her, noted the way her eyes seemed too big for her heart-shaped face, and once again he was overwhelmed with the urge to protect her. Far from being the Ice Princess that the press portrayed, she was near to breaking-point, so emotionally fragile that he could not prevent himself from reaching out to smooth her hair back from her temple.

'I mean you no harm, Anna, I swear it,' he vowed in a low tone.

The shimmer of tears caused his gut to clench and he watched as she waged a silent battle in her head. Murmuring

a husky imprecation, he halted the trail of moisture that trickled down her cheek with his thumb pad and lowered his head to brush his lips gently across hers.

She stiffened but did not pull away and he deepened the kiss a little, allowing his tongue to make a tender exploration of the contours of her mouth. Still she didn't reject him, but neither did she respond—just stood, trembling, her body poised for flight.

His one thought was to ease the rigid tension that gripped her. She'd had one hell of a night, he acknowledged grimly as he recalled her struggles with the drunken lout in the restaurant. No wonder she looked as though she would shatter at the lightest touch.

With infinite care he stroked his tongue against the tight line of her lips and felt a quiver run through her. He hadn't expected her to respond, but to his delight she hesitantly opened her mouth to allow him access to the sweetness within. Triumph flooded through him, tempered with a degree of caution. It was tempting to wrap his arms around her and draw her close but he forced himself to clench his hands by his sides so that the only contact between them was mouth on mouth, the gentle sweep of his tongue as he deepened the kiss until it became a sensual tasting that he wanted never to stop.

When at last he lifted his head, Anna could only stare at him, too stunned to utter a word. She was shaking; not through fear or revulsion, but with the desperate need to have him draw her up against the hard wall of his chest. She wanted to feel him, wanted to revel in the brush of his thighs against hers. She wanted to touch him and have him touch her, but now he was stepping away from her, ending the kiss that had shattered her belief that she would never feel sexual desire.

'I'm going to be out of the country for a few days and it's

possible I may not be back in time for your race, so I'll wish you good luck now,' he said in a matter-of-fact tone as he turned and opened the front door.

'Thank you—I'll see you…some time,' Anna murmured dazedly.

'You can count on it, *pedahaki mou.*'

The gleam in his eyes promised her they were at the start of a journey that could only have one destination. The knowledge should have sent her running for cover but instead she was filled with a strange sense of anticipation.

She wanted him, she admitted, feeling a tremor run through her. But it was so new and unexpected after all the years when she had convinced herself she was cold and passionless. Damon had just proved that she was neither, but the barriers in her head had built up over a long time and the thought of lowering them terrified her.

She waited until he had disappeared down the stairs and then closed the door, returned to the sitting room and collected the tray as if she were running on autopilot. A glance at the clock showed that it was past midnight.

She had a magazine shoot booked for early the next morning, followed by another training session at the track. Sleep was imperative but proved elusive as she tossed and turned beneath the sheets. Damon, and her response to his kiss, filled her mind. But her dreams were fractured with images of him as a loving husband whose heart belonged for ever to his tragic young wife.

The charity half-marathon around Hyde Park attracted fevered media interest, due mainly to the number of celebrities taking part. Spurred on by the cheering crowd, Anna crossed the finish line in under three hours and felt euphoric at the knowledge that she had raised a huge amount of money for the children's charity.

She spent the next day quietly relaxing and only ventured out to the health spa for a massage, which worked wonders on her aching muscles. Early evening saw her indulging in a long, hot soak until her peace was shattered by the strident peal of the doorbell. She was half inclined to ignore it and lay back and closed her eyes, but the caller was persistent and, cursing beneath her breath, she hauled herself out of the bath, wrapped a towel around her, sarong-style, and marched down the hall.

'You have a habit of getting me out of the bath,' she snapped, fighting to control the frantic race of her pulse when she opened the door a fraction and discovered Damon leaning indolently against the frame.

'If only that were true, *pedhaki mou,*' he murmured throatily, his dark eyes glinting with amusement and another more disturbing emotion as his gaze slid over her damp body, barely concealed beneath the towel. 'But it's a habit I'd very much like to acquire.'

Damn him. He was incorrigible, Anna thought, unable to prevent her lips from twitching. She had never met anyone like him before and, although she was loath to admit it, she'd missed him.

'What do you want, Damon?'

'To offer my congratulations,' he said blandly. 'I only arrived back in England an hour ago and I've come straight from the airport, but I heard the news of your success in the charity race and I'm delighted to be able to give you this.'

He handed her a cheque made out to the charity and Anna's eyes widened as she stared at the figure scrawled in black ink.

'You weren't joking, then?' she questioned faintly.

'Did you honestly doubt my commitment?'

There was no answer to that and Anna was suddenly conscious that she couldn't expect him to remain on the doorstep

indefinitely. Slowly she opened the door wider for him to enter and clutched her towel to her as if it were a life raft thrown to a drowning man.

He'd made no mention of her joining him for dinner, as he'd threatened when he'd first agreed to sponsor her. Perhaps he had forgotten, or was no longer interested, she thought a shade bleakly.

'The charity will be overwhelmed by your generosity,' she told him huskily as she glanced again at the cheque. 'I can't quite believe it, but I'm surprised you've given it to me now.'

'Before I've held you to your agreement to have dinner with me, you mean?' His expression was one of gentle amusement, as if he understood the reasons for her uncertainty. 'I was rather hoping that you would agree to dine with me because you want to, rather than seeing it as a form of blackmail,' he added, plainly remembering her furious accusation on the night of Kezia's dinner party.

Sneaky didn't begin to describe him. It was little wonder that he had a reputation as the most wily man ever to set foot inside a boardroom, she thought darkly. In the interests of self-preservation she ought to tell him to get lost but the words wouldn't come and instead she stared up at him, the inner battle she was waging evident in the sapphire darkness of her eyes.

'Dinner seems the least I can do when you've been so incredibly…kind,' she responded at last, colour stealing into her cheeks at the way his eyebrows lifted quizzically. His look told her that *kind* was not a word usually associated with Damon Kouvaris, yet she didn't doubt his compassion.

'I'm glad to hear it. You've got half an hour,' he told her cheerfully, striding down the hall and into the sitting room as if he owned the place.

'Do you mean…you want us to have dinner *tonight?*' She

padded down the hall after him, a frown forming on her brow. 'But I'm still recovering from the race. I'm too tired!'

'It's only dinner, *pedhaki mou,* unless you were planning something a little more *energetic?*'

'Slapping you is the only thing that springs to mind,' she said grittily, her cheeks on fire. 'Tonight will be fine. At least it gets it out of the way.' With that she gripped her towel tightly round her and stormed out of the room, her temper not improved by the sound of his mocking laughter following her along the hall.

CHAPTER SIX

IN AN effort to disguise her nervousness, Anna selected a midnight-blue couture dress for her dinner date with Damon. The stark simplicity of the style conveyed the impression of cool sophistication, especially when teamed with a few discreet pieces of jewellery—sapphire and diamond earrings and a matching bracelet on her wrist.

With her hair swept into an elegant chignon and the addition of killer heels, she looked every inch the confident career woman. She could only pray that nobody would notice the slight tremor of her hands when she followed Damon across the foyer of his hotel.

'Where are we going?' she queried with a frown when he ushered her into the lift. 'I assumed the dining room is on the ground floor.'

'It is, but we're not eating there,' he replied with a smile that did nothing to allay her apprehension.

Anna surveyed him suspiciously as the lift whisked them towards the upper floors. She had already made her feelings clear when he'd informed her that they would be dining at his hotel rather than a restaurant. Now what? Perhaps the hotel had a dining area in the roof garden, she pondered, but she didn't relish the prospect of sitting in the rain.

'I need to shower and change, and then I thought we'd

dine in the privacy of my suite,' he explained cheerfully as he led the way along a corridor and threw open the door leading to a large, luxuriously appointed room.

Anna glanced around warily, noting the elegant furnishings and the small dining table set for two. At the far end of the room was a door, which she guessed led to Damon's bedroom. It was that last thought that caused her to stop dead.

Damon glanced at her, his smile fading as he noticed her icy expression. 'Do you have any objections?'

'Dozens, the main one being that you tricked me.'

'In what way?' he demanded forcefully. 'You agreed to have dinner with me of your own free will.'

'I assumed we would be spending the evening in a busy restaurant, not in your room.'

'It's the penthouse suite, not the broom cupboard. What's the real issue, here Anna?' he demanded, his eyes narrowing when she shied away from him. 'Do you honestly think I brought you here with the intention of seducing you?'

'Didn't you?'

He was silent for so long that she lifted her eyes to stare at him, wondering what he was thinking. Too late she realised that the rigid set of his jaw gave a clue to the level of his anger. He was furious, his nostrils flaring as he sought to control his temper, and Anna realised with growing unease that she had insulted him unforgivably.

'Damon, I—' She broke off and extended her hand in a helpless gesture of contrition.

'Why don't you go back down and wait for me in the main lounge?' he suggested, his clipped tone indicating that he couldn't care less if she caught the next bus home. 'I'll meet you in twenty minutes and we'll have a drink while you're deciding whether you're willing to risk sitting in a public restaurant with me.'

He swung round and strode away from her, pausing briefly in the doorway leading to his room. 'Tell me, Anna, what are you so afraid of?'

There was no simple answer to that and she shook her head in silence, utterly beyond speech. How could she possibly begin to explain the mental damage her stepfather had inflicted? The misery of every school holiday spent trying to evade a man who had delighted in taunting her with revolting suggestions of what he would like to do to her.

She had moved out as soon as possible, before Phil had had a chance to carry out the abuses he'd threatened. But, as she'd been an impressionable teenager, her imagination had proved her worst enemy and the nightmares had haunted her for years.

'Are you afraid of me?' His voice was so gruff that she could almost believe she had hurt him.

Damon was nothing like her stepfather, she acknowledged. He might have a reputation as a playboy, but she knew instinctively that he would never physically harm her. Emotionally it was a different matter, but she couldn't bear the troubled look in his eyes and sought to reassure him.

'No,' she replied quietly.

He said no more, but she sensed a release in the fierce tension that gripped him. With a curt nod he entered his bedroom and closed the door firmly behind him.

Anna spent the next few minutes torn with indecision. Should she go downstairs and wait for him as he had suggested, or stay until he emerged from his room and try to seek his forgiveness? She had been unbelievably rude, she accepted grimly. This was a man who had just donated an astonishing amount of money to the children's hospice and she'd treated him as if he were Jack the Ripper.

A discreet knock on the door made the decision for her. 'I've come to clear away the table. Mr Kouvaris phoned

down to say that it's no longer required,' the bellboy explained.

'Wait. Actually there's been another change of plan and we'd like to have dinner up here after all,' Anna said. 'Is that still possible?'

'Anything's possible for Mr Kouvaris,' the bellboy replied seriously. 'Will the order be the same as before?'

'Yes, thank you.' She didn't know what dishes Damon had selected from the menu and, if she was honest, she didn't care. She just prayed she was doing the right thing and that her actions wouldn't further incite his anger.

She spent another ten minutes anxiously pacing the carpet while her tension increased to screaming pitch. A waiter arrived pushing a loaded trolley and she watched as he rearranged the cutlery and opened the wine, his precise attention to detail shredding her nerves. The faint snick of the door had her swinging round, her eyes wide with a mixture of uncertainty and bravado when Damon strolled through from his bedroom.

'Would you like me to pour the wine?' The waiter's eyes moved from her to Damon and in the ensuing pause, which seemed to last a lifetime, she discovered that she was holding her breath.

'I thought it would be nice to eat here after all,' she said quickly, flushing beneath Damon's quizzical stare.

'Good,' he murmured at last and nodded to the waiter to fill their glasses. He moved purposefully towards her, tall, dark and utterly devastating in superbly tailored black trousers and matching shirt. His hair was still damp from his shower and Anna noted the way it curled onto his collar. He exuded a simmering, sexual magnetism and she quivered when he came to stand in front of her, the scent of his cologne mixed with the fresh tang of soap, setting her senses on fire.

'What made you change your mind?'

She couldn't begin to tell him of the war that was waging inside her and shook her head helplessly.

'I thought it was a woman's prerogative?' she whispered, unaware of the stark vulnerability in her eyes.

He waited a heartbeat, his eyes dark and unfathomable while he studied her tense expression, and then he nodded and smiled at her so that his teeth gleamed white against his olive gold skin.

'Of course it is, *pedhaki mou*. I don't know about you, but I'm starving. Let's eat.'

It quickly became apparent that Damon was not a man to hold a grudge. He had every right to be annoyed with her, Anna acknowledged, but from the moment they took their places at the table he seemed determined to help her relax.

Witty, amusing and fiercely intelligent, he could charm the birds from the trees, she thought wryly. Dinner had been out of this world. She'd already eaten more than she should, but he tempted her to dessert—cheesecake with fresh raspberries and a summer berry coulis that tantalised her taste buds.

He kept their conversation deliberately light. They discussed the latest film release from a director they both admired and discovered a shared taste in modern authors. It was a long time since she had felt so at ease on a date, Anna mused as she finished her wine and shook her head when he offered to refill her glass.

She rarely drank alcohol and the glass of Chablis had left her feeling mellow and just the tiniest bit light-headed. It wasn't an unpleasant feeling, but she was wary of losing the tight grip on her control, especially with Damon around. Not that she did not trust him, she acceded; it was herself and her wayward response to the undisguised hunger in his eyes that worried her.

'Are you sure I can't persuade you to indulge in another slice of cheesecake?'

'Absolutely not!' She had a feeling that he could persuade her to indulge in a number of things that she wouldn't have dreamed of with any other man, but her slender figure was her fortune and she was grateful for her iron will-power. 'I can see that I'm going to have to run another thirteen miles tomorrow as it is,' she quipped lightly.

She left him pouring the coffee and wandered over to the window to stare out at the view of Marble Arch and Hyde Park beyond. The park was shrouded in black velvet but the surrounding streets were teeming with traffic, the car headlights winking like frenetic fireflies in the darkness. It was home, the sights and sounds comfortingly familiar, and Anna gave an unconscious sigh of pleasure.

'Do you enjoy living in London?'

She turned to find that Damon had moved to stand beside her and her senses leapt when he placed his hand lightly on the small of her back. The gesture was in no way threatening and a quiver ran through her. To her astonishment she realised that she longed for him to slide his arm around her waist and draw her up against the hard length of his body.

'I love it,' she replied hastily. 'Even during the bad times, after I'd left school and was struggling to find somewhere to live, I never considered moving away. It's a wonderful city and I'm proud that it's my home.'

'So where did you spend your childhood?' he asked, captivated by her enthusiasm.

'When my parents were together we lived in a house in Notting Hill,' she explained, wistfully recalling the past. 'It was an incredibly happy time. I used to think that my dad was the cleverest, funniest, most wonderful person in the world; he was so charming and good-looking. Unfortunately I wasn't the only female to think so,' she added dryly. 'After

the divorce Mum couldn't keep up with the mortgage repayments and the house had to be sold. She and I moved into a flat and Lars lived a few streets away with his new wife and her children.'

'I suppose it at least meant you were able to see your father as often as you liked.'

'The access agreement was once a month, but Marion, Dad's second wife, didn't like me going to their house,' she told him flatly. 'She said I unsettled her two little girls but what she really meant was that I unsettled her. She couldn't stand the fact that I had a place in Dad's life.

'In my experience the whole step-parent, stepchild relationship is a minefield of resentment and jealousy,' she burst out, surprising them both with her sudden bitterness. 'If I'm sure of one thing, it's that I will never get involved with a man who has baggage.'

'Baggage?'

'Children,' she elaborated when Damon frowned. 'My stepmother did her best to destroy my relationship with my father, although ultimately he was the one who decided to break off contact. But I never want to be in the position where someone I care about feels that he has to choose between me and any children he might have from a previous relationship.'

'But surely there are thousands of couples in that situation for whom it works well?' Damon argued. 'Just because your own experiences were unhappy, it doesn't mean that it can't work with a little give and take on all sides.'

'Perhaps,' Anna said with a shrug, 'but it can also be a breeding ground for misery and heartache. I'm sorry, but, as you've probably guessed, it's a subject I feel strongly about,' she murmured huskily when Damon stared at her. He had tensed, his face as hard as if it had been sculpted from marble, but she had no idea what had disturbed him so strongly.

'Your childhood obviously left some serious scars—understandably when you lost your father and your home at such an impressionable age,' he said quietly. 'What about your mother—were you happy living with her? I imagine your financial circumstances were reduced.'

'We were broke,' Anna said with a harsh laugh. 'Before her marriage, my mother had been a brilliant musician with a promising career ahead of her, but she gave it all up to support my father in his various, and mostly unsuccessful, business ventures.

'She sacrificed everything for him,' she added bitterly. 'When he left us, she couldn't cope. She had some sort of breakdown and that's when I was sent away to school. Fortunately my grandmother had left an annuity to pay for my schooling.

'I loved my time at Braebourne Ladies College. I felt safe there,' she admitted, so quietly that he only just caught her words.

It was a strange thing to say and Damon frowned. Had there been times during her childhood when she hadn't felt safe? And whom had she been afraid of? Not her father, surely? From the way she had spoken of him, he guessed that she had adored Lars Christiansen and been devastated by his cruel desertion.

It was small wonder that she had such an issue with trust, he thought grimly. She was prickly and defensive but her father's seeming rejection of her in favour of his new wife and children had seeded the expectation that all men would let her down. Already she was edging away from him, clearly regretting the impulse that had led her to confide in him.

He wanted to draw her into his arms and hold her close, Damon acknowledged. He wanted to reassure her that he would never knowingly hurt her in any way.

The realisation caused him to frown. What was he thinking? His whole reason for coming to England and seeking her out had been to persuade her into his bed and keep her there until his hunger for her had been satiated. And how could he possibly hope to win her trust now, when there were issues in his life that he had deliberately kept from her?

It wasn't that he had set out to deceive her, he brooded when he joined her on the sofa and took a gulp of his coffee. But in the years since Eleni's death he had made a conscious decision to keep his private life separate from his family situation. He had never found the need to explain his commitments to his various mistresses; his life was neatly compartmentalised and he liked it that way.

He didn't even understand why he had told Anna about his marriage. Perhaps it was because he wanted to prove that there was more to him than his reputation as a wealthy playboy portrayed? But if that was the reason, it hadn't worked. He was no nearer to winning her trust and if he was scrupulously honest, he didn't deserve it when his motives had been triggered solely by lust.

Stifling an impatient sigh, he leaned back against the cushions and felt her stiffen. He could feel her watching him; surreptitious little glances when she thought he wasn't looking. But he was aware of the way her gaze focused on his mouth, aware of how her small, pink tongue suddenly darted out to moisten her lips. Desire pierced him, so savage that every muscle in his body clenched, and he strove to control the urge to plunder those soft lips with his own.

Walking away while he still had the chance no longer seemed to be an option, he acknowledged heavily. He'd never felt like this before; it was new and faintly terrifying, which was another alien emotion to him. He had never been afraid in his life, but as he recalled her fierce avowal that she would never become involved with a man with *baggage* his

gut twisted and he tore his gaze from her to stare moodily at the blank television screen.

Anna drained her coffee and shifted edgily on the sofa. Damon seemed to be lost in his thoughts and, from the strained silence that had fallen, she could only assume that those thoughts were not happy ones. She was relieved when he activated the remote to switch on the television. At least forcing her brain to concentrate on the late evening news programme prevented her from dwelling on the intoxicating warmth of his thigh pressing lightly against hers.

The final part of the bulletin was devoted to coverage of the charity marathon and the work of the charity she had raised money for and she leaned forward slightly, her heart leaping when the presenter explained that the children's hospice was set to open ahead of target, thanks to the huge amount of funds raised from the race. The film then showed the vast crowd that had congregated in Hyde Park for the race the day before and she grimaced when her image flashed onto the screen.

'Oh, God, I hadn't realised that my running shorts were so, well…*short*,' she groaned, hectic colour flooding her cheeks. 'Over a thousand competitors took part, yet the cameraman seems to have spent the entire race fixated with my derrière.'

Beside her she felt Damon relax and she watched in fascination as his mouth curved into a slow smile.

'I have a certain amount of sympathy with him; he's only human, after all,' he said dulcetly, 'and it is a particularly delightful derrière, Anna *mou*.'

At his words, she snapped her head round, indignation warring with a strong desire to burst out laughing. He was the most outrageous flirt she had ever met, but the urge to slap him was lost before the lambent warmth of his gaze.

The tension between them returned with a vengeance, but

now it was laced with a degree of sexual awareness that she could neither ignore nor deny. Her breath caught in her throat and she could feel the erratic jerk of her pulse when he trailed a finger lightly down her cheek.

'Exquisite,' he breathed softly, suddenly sounding very Greek. He lowered his head, almost as if he had no control over his movements, and Anna watched, wide-eyed, as his mouth descended to claim her lips in a sweetly evocative caress.

This was dangerous, her brain warned when he lifted his head almost immediately and stared into her eyes. This was the very scenario she had hoped to avoid, and the reason she had wanted to dine in a restaurant rather than in Damon's private suite. Her experiences with her stepfather had taught her to avoid situations where she could be at risk, but, although she was alone with Damon, it wasn't fear that made her tremble.

She surveyed him warily when he slid his hand to her nape and released the clip that secured her chignon. Her hair fell in a heavy swathe of pale gold silk around her shoulders and she heard his low murmur of appreciation as he threaded his fingers through the silky strands. Far from terrifying her, the burning heat of his gaze filled her with a wild sense of excitement, and when he lowered his head once more she parted her lips to welcome the gentle exploration of his tongue.

It was soft and sensuous, but it wasn't enough. For the first time in her life she wanted more and she urged closer, winding her arms around his neck in the desperate hope that he would deepen the kiss.

Damon hesitated fractionally, afraid that he was rushing her, but the tentative stroke of her tongue against his lips shattered the remnants of his self-control and he increased the pressure of his mouth on hers to a level that was fla-

grantly erotic. He was aware of the slight tremor that ran through her and half expected her to draw back, but she leaned into him, one hand sliding down to rest over his heart thudding painfully in his chest.

She could hardly fail to realise the effect she was having on him, he acknowledged derisively. Not when his arousal was a throbbing, burgeoning force pushing against her hip. He needed to exert control over his rampaging hormones, but she had tormented his every waking thought for the past couple of months, invaded his dreams so that he'd woken hard and hot and as frustrated as hell. Who could blame him for seizing the sudden glimpse of heaven she was now offering?

Anna offered no resistance when Damon wrapped his arms around her and hauled her up against the hard wall of his chest. Desire was a potent force, she acknowledged with the tiny part of her brain still capable of conscious thought. She was overwhelmed by the feelings flooding through her. After so many years of imposing a rigid control over her emotions, it was a relief to discover that she was a normal woman, with normal sexual urges, although rather more disturbing to realise that it was only Damon who was able to arouse them.

When his hand skimmed her ribcage and then gently cupped her breast, heat flooded her and she closed her eyes, blotting out everything but the feel of his mouth on hers. The stroke of his thumb pad across her nipple caused an exquisite sensation that was new and wondrous and made her long for him to slide her dress from her shoulders. She wanted to feel him, skin on skin, his mouth to follow the path of his hands, and with a little murmur of frustration she cupped his face and kissed him with all the pent up passion that she had tried so hard to deny.

She had been created for this, she thought wildly when

he eased one strap of her dress down her arm, lower and lower until her small, creamy breast was fully exposed to his gaze. Amazingly she felt neither fear nor revulsion, just a languorous ache deep inside. The feel of his palm against her naked flesh sent a quiver through her and she held her breath when he gently stroked the dusky pink nipple so that it hardened to a throbbing peak.

As she stared at his head, bent low over her breast, she wondered what he would say if she admitted that this was the first time she had allowed any man to touch her so intimately? Undoubtedly he would be shocked, possibly disbelieving. He assumed that the press rumours about her active love life were true and presumably expected her to be sexually experienced.

Only she knew that nothing could be further from the truth.

Damon's breath was warm on her skin and she trembled as he trailed his lips from her collar-bone, down over the soft swell of her breast. With infinite care he stroked his tongue around the darker skin of her aureole, painting moist circles as he edged ever closer to the sensitive tip.

'You don't know how often I've fantasised about doing this,' he murmured before his mouth closed fully around her nipple. Sensation arrowed through her, so intense that it seemed to rip through her entire body, and she arched and clung to him while his words slowly penetrated the sensual haze that enveloped her.

'I want to make love to you, my sweet Annie.'

'Don't!' Her reaction was instant and violent as she jerked out of his arms. 'Don't *ever* call me that.'

'You don't know how often I fantasise about you, Annie— shall I tell you what I'd like to do to you?'

She stumbled to her feet and wrenched the strap of her dress back over her shoulder, so forcefully that her nails left

angry weals on her skin. Her stepfather's mocking voice sounded in her head and for a moment it was not Damon sitting on the sofa, but Philip Stone, laughing at her as she struggled to ignore his taunts and get on with her homework.

'My name is *Anna;* do you hear me?'

'I hear, but I sure as hell don't understand,' Damon growled, his bewilderment and frustration clearly visible on his face. 'What's the matter with you? *Theos,* one minute you are warm and willing in my arms, and the next you're a spitting she-cat—with razor sharp claws,' he added slowly when he caught sight of the self-inflicted scratches on her arm. 'Tell me, Anna,' he pleaded huskily, 'what did I do wrong? If I offended you…'

'You didn't…you didn't do anything wrong. It's me—' She broke off and shook her head as the feeling of nausea gradually lessened. 'I'm no good at all this,' she muttered, waving her hand expressively towards the sofa, where minutes before she had responded to his kisses with such fervour.

'You seemed pretty good to me,' he ventured wryly. 'You wanted me, Anna. The desire was not all on one side.' He made a move towards her and then lifted his hands placatingly when she shied away from him. 'Something frightened you,' he said broodingly, 'but I can't help you if you won't confide in me, *pedhaki mou.*'

'I don't need help!' She glared at him, her cheeks burning as she acknowledged that he was probably right. He must believe her to be a head-case. Maybe she was. Her reaction to his lovemaking certainly wasn't normal and yet for a few moments in his arms she had gloried in the pleasurable sensations his caresses evoked.

The strident, repetitive sound of his cell-phone shattered the fragile silence and she frowned when he made no move to answer it.

'Shouldn't you get that?'

'It can wait. This is more important. You and me,' he elaborated grimly, the determination in his eyes filling her with panic.

'There is no you and me. Can't you understand, Damon? I don't want you.' His phone had finally stopped ringing and her voice sounded painfully shrill and over-loud to her ears.

'That's not the message your body was sending out.'

'Well, it's been outvoted. I'm not in the market for casual sex.'

Damon's jaw tightened as he fought to control his anger and Anna quailed at the coldness in his eyes.

'Not from what I've heard,' he commented silkily.

His scathing taunt tore at her already brittle emotions and she couldn't stifle her gasp of distress. His phone rang again but this time she welcomed its intrusion as she forced her arms into her jacket with jerky, uncoordinated movements.

'I have to go,' she muttered numbly.

'Anna…forgive me—that was uncalled for.'

'Forget it.' She clawed back a little of her self-possession and swung away from him. 'And for pity's sake answer your phone and put whoever is so desperate to speak to you out of their misery.'

'We need to talk.' As he spoke Damon snatched up his phone, intent on switching it off, but he glanced at the caller display and hesitated. 'I'm sorry, but I have to take this.'

'I'd like to use the bathroom,' she mumbled.

'Through there,' he indicated the door at the far end of the sitting room, and, without awarding him another glance, Anna hurried across the room.

The door led to his bedroom and she carried on into the *en suite* bathroom where she filled the sink and splashed her face with ice-cold water. Dear God, what was happening to

her? She stared into the mirror, looking for answers, but the face looking back at her was ravaged, her eyes full of shadows.

What must Damon think of her? She closed her eyes briefly as if she could somehow shut out her thoughts. She didn't want to think, she just wanted to go home to the safe cocoon of her flat and hide away until she had reassembled her defences.

Her head fell forwards to lean against the mirror and she took several deep breaths in an effort to compose herself before she crossed Damon's bedroom once more. The door leading to the sitting room was slightly ajar and she could hear the deep resonance of his voice as he spoke into his cell-phone. He was speaking in his native tongue; she could pick out the odd Greek word and she wondered who had been so eager to talk to him.

From her view of him through the gap in the door, she guessed that the caller was someone with whom he shared a close relationship. His voice was soft and intimate and his body language was relaxed, in stark contrast to the tension that had gripped him a few minutes earlier.

Did he have a mistress back in Greece? she wondered bleakly. Doubtless some dark-eyed, curvaceous beauty who offered uncomplicated sex and wasn't besieged with hang-ups.

Tears stung her eyes and she blinked fiercely as her gaze fell on the vast king-sized bed that dominated the room. If things had been different, if *she* had been different, would Damon have made love to her on that bed? Would he have peeled her dress from her body, laid her down on the sheets and continued his devastating exploration of every sensitive curve and pulse point?

More than anything she wished that she could be the woman he wanted her to be. Cool, confident Anneliese

Christiansen—style icon and experienced seductress who would match him, caress, for caress, and send him wild with desire. She longed to be a teasing temptress but her stepfather had inflicted irreparable damage to her self-esteem and with it her chance of a normal, loving relationship.

Swallowing the sudden lump in her throat, she peered round the door. Damon was still talking, but any minute now he would finish his call and he had every right to demand an explanation for her behaviour. The thought of a post-mortem was unbearable and she crossed swiftly to the other door that she prayed led straight from his bedroom, out to the main corridor.

Minutes later she stepped out of the lift and hurried over to the reception desk where she requested a taxi. There was no point in prolonging her misery and certainly no point in hoping for some sort of relationship with him when she'd just proved that she was incapable of responding to him like a normal, sexually confident woman.

As she raced down the hotel steps she half expected to turn and see Damon striding across the foyer after her. Only when the taxi sped off through the rain did she finally release her breath. She was unaware that he had arrived downstairs seconds too late and could do nothing but watch her go.

CHAPTER SEVEN

'Why do you have to go to New York, Papa?'

Damon lifted his gaze from the report that he had been vainly trying to concentrate on for the past half-hour and glanced at his daughter.

Ianthe was sitting on the opposite side of his desk and had covered his once-neat piles of paperwork with her books and a collection of unlikely coloured plastic horses.

'Business, I'm afraid—nothing very exciting.' Which did not explain why his stomach lurched at the thought of the imminent trip, he acknowledged derisively.

The little girl had drawn a picture and was now busy colouring it in. To Damon's technical eye, the pencilled lines of her house were alarmingly crooked but he wisely refrained from pointing it out and watched as she carefully blocked in the roof with a crayon.

'How long will you be away?'

'A week—ten days at the most. Aunt Tina will take care of you as usual.'

There was no pause in the movement of her crayon and he smiled at the sight of her tongue peeping out while she concentrated on keeping the colour within the outline of her drawing.

'Will you be back for my birthday?'

'You think I would miss the most important event of the year?'

Now she looked up and awarded him a grin that spoke of her absolute confidence that he would be there for her special day.

'Remember, I'm going to be nine.'

'I haven't forgotten, *agapetikos*.' Although it seemed hard to believe. His daughter's birth was an event that would be imprinted on his brain for ever. He would never forget his feeling of awe when he had first held her in his arms and looked down at her tiny, screwed-up face.

Eleni had been equally overjoyed at the birth of their first baby—unaware that Ianthe would be her only child. Thankfully they'd had no inkling of the tragedy that would befall ten months later.

Throughout the dark days after Eleni's death, Ianthe had provided his only motivation to get out of bed each day, and now here she was, all pansy-brown eyes and velvet curls, about to celebrate nine years that, despite the loss of her mother, had been filled with happiness.

His daughter was the most important person in his life, Damon acknowledged. Ianthe had no recollection of her mother but she was a confident, well-adjusted child, which was due in no small part to the devotion of his sister. Catalina had willingly stepped in to provide her little niece with a mother figure and even now, despite her marriage and the birth of three children in quick succession, she still treated Ianthe as if she were her own child.

Ianthe finished her artwork and surveyed him solemnly. 'Will you come swimming with me, or are you too busy?' she asked with a theatrical sigh.

Nine years old and already she was adept at winding him around her little finger, Damon thought wryly as he switched

off his computer. 'I'm never too busy for you, Ianthe *mou*. Last one in the pool has to swim ten lengths.'

Ianthe sped from the room, squealing with laughter. It was a familiar sound that brought joy to Damon's heart. His daughter laughed a lot and once again he congratulated himself for ensuring that her childhood had not been complicated by a succession of 'aunts'.

He kept his love life strictly separate from his family, fearing that Ianthe might form an attachment to whoever he happened to be dating and be left disappointed when the affair ended. He'd never felt the need to provide her with a stepmother and purposefully avoided telling his various mistresses that he had a child.

Call him a cynic, but he'd learned early on that any mention of the fact that he was a single father encouraged most women in the belief that he must be looking for a replacement wife, when in fact nothing could be further from the truth.

The arrangement worked well and he could see no reason to change it, he brooded as he headed out to the pool. After the disastrous dinner date with Anna, he had returned to Greece determined to forget her. But he was incensed to find that he could not dismiss her from his thoughts. She intrigued him more than any woman he had ever met and, despite her rejection of him, his desire for her was as fierce as ever.

The timing of his business trip to New York was more than a happy coincidence. He was still desperate to discover if the chemistry between them could develop into an affair. But did that necessitate revealing that he had a child?

It was not as if he was planning a long-term relationship with Anna, he reminded himself. He wanted her in his bed, that was all—a series of mutually enjoyable sexual encounters whenever their schedules happened to coincide. But he

couldn't forget the visible torment on her face when he had last seen her in London.

She had been pale and tense, her beautiful blue eyes inexplicably full of fear, yet only moments before she had responded to him with a degree of passion that had fuelled his hunger. What the hell had caused her to retreat from him in such panic? And did she respond in similar fashion to the other men she dated, or was he the only man to evoke such an intense reaction?

He didn't even know what he wanted any more, he thought savagely. She'd got him so wound up that he couldn't think straight. With a muttered oath he plunged into the pool and surfaced to find Ianthe bobbing next to him.

'I beat you!' she told him gleefully. 'Never mind, Papa, you'll just have to try harder next time.'

Valuable advice from the mouth of a child, he acknowledged wrily. But as far as Anna was concerned, it was his wisest course of action.

London might be her favourite city in the world, but New York came a close second, Anna decided as she stared out of her hotel window and absorbed the noise and bustle of Times Square. She was a city girl at heart and loved the frenetic pace of the metropolis that never slept.

Since her arrival a week ago, she had lived a punishing schedule of photo shoots and publicity events to mark the twenty-fifth anniversary of the cosmetic house she represented, culminating in last night's lavish party. She'd arrived back at her hotel in the early hours, slept until late and spent an enjoyable afternoon shopping on 5th Avenue.

Not that she needed another pair of shoes, but retail therapy provided her with a much-needed distraction from a certain charismatic Greek who invaded her thoughts with disturbing regularity.

Don't go there, she told herself fiercely and sought to banish the image of Damon's ruggedly handsome face. It had been two weeks since their disastrous date at his London hotel. Two weeks, three days and eighteen hours she amended dismally. She hadn't heard from him in that time and in all honesty could hardly have expected to. Since her hysterical outburst when he'd attempted to make love to her, followed by her ignominious departure, he had doubtless lost all patience with her.

She'd tried telling herself she didn't care. Why on earth would she want an arrogant, overbearing, alpha male in her life? Never mind that he was also a gorgeous Greek demigod. But she hadn't expected to miss him so much that it was a constant, nagging ache around her heart.

Not that she would cry, she vowed fiercely. Never! And if her face was wet even before she stepped into the shower, it was her secret.

Two hours later her façade of ice-cool elegance gave no sign of her inner turmoil as she stood in the wings, waiting for her cue to step out onto the catwalk. The fashion show was another charity event, sponsored by some of the world's top designers and attended by New York's social élite.

'God, there's not an empty seat out there,' one of the younger models whispered after taking a peep at the packed audience. 'Aren't you nervous? I feel sick.'

'Remember to look straight ahead, not at the audience,' Anna advised with an encouraging smile. Gina couldn't be more than sixteen—it was her first show and she was plainly overawed by the star-studded event. 'That's our cue. Come on—time to go.'

With no visible hint of nerves Anna squared her shoulders and strode onto the runway. As usual the lights blinded her for a few seconds but after eight years on the circuit she knew how to show off the stunning evening gown she was

modelling to its best advantage and she walked on confidently. Four more steps, pause for a moment and then turn—the pattern was familiar and afterwards she wondered what had caused her to ignore her own advice and cast her gaze over the audience.

The formidable width of his shoulders and the proud angle of his head were unmistakable and for a brief, stomach-churning second she lost her footing and stumbled. It was only the thought of her utter humiliation should she fall into Damon's lap that enabled her to regain her composure.

Snatching a sharp breath, she tore her startled gaze from his face and swung round to saunter back up the runway. What was he doing here? It must be a coincidence, she reassured herself frantically. It was impossible to believe he had deliberately sought her out after her violent rejection of him the last time they'd met.

From then on the evening became a test of nerve and it was only her professionalism combined with sheer, dogged determination that saw her complete the show.

She refused to glance at Damon again, although every time she neared the end of the catwalk her heart thudded painfully in her chest. But now, as she joined the other models for the finale, her eyes were drawn to him and the ache inside intensified.

He was a playboy and a philanderer—no better than her father. So what madness was it that insisted he was the other half of her soul?

'Hell, I could do with a drink,' one of the other models announced when they fought their way through the backstage chaos. 'Are you staying for the after-show party, Anna?'

Not if she could help it, Anna thought grimly. But her presence at the party was expected and once again her pro-

fessionalism saw her pin a smile on her face and join the throng of guests.

She noticed Damon the moment she entered the ballroom. In a room full of tall, dominant males, he stood out above the rest. Wealth and power were strong aphrodisiacs and when they were combined with his lethal brand of sexual magnetism it was hardly surprising that he was the subject of intense interest from every female present.

The woman at his side seemed intent on signifying ownership with her hand on his arm and her head tilted slightly so that it was almost resting on his shoulder. God forbid that she should ever appear so desperate, Anna thought scathingly as she fought the corrosive jealousy that burned in her chest. Luisa Mendoza was well-known on the modelling circuit as a man-eater. With her golden skin and mass of luscious black curls she was exquisitely beautiful—an exotic temptress who had obviously wasted no time in hooking her claws into Damon.

She couldn't give a damn whom he dated, Anna told herself impatiently. But the sight of Luisa rubbing herself sensuously, and very unsubtly, against him made her feel sick. At that moment Damon glanced across the room. As his eyes trailed over her she blushed, furious at having been caught staring at him. He held her gaze for a second and then gave a brief nod of recognition before returning his attention to his companion.

He could not have made his lack of interest any plainer and to her horror Anna felt her eyes glaze with tears. She would not break down in public, she told herself fiercely. She longed to return to her hotel but it was her job to chat with the guests who had attended the fashion show and so she gritted her teeth and began to circulate.

The following two hours passed agonisingly slowly but at least she managed to evade Damon and she felt a huge

sense of relief when she finally slipped out into the foyer of the fabulous art deco hotel. She had almost reached the main doors when a voice stopped her in her tracks.

'Running away, Anna? You seem to have a habit of sneaking out of hotels.'

'I am not *sneaking* anywhere.'

She swung round, trembling with outrage and fierce awareness when Damon strolled towards her. In his charcoal-coloured suit, grey shirt and burgundy silk tie he was breathtaking. Anna's feet seemed to be rooted to the floor and she swallowed when he halted in front of her, so close that she could almost see the sparks of electricity that arced between them.

'I'm finished here tonight. Duty done. There's no reason for me to stay,' she added pointedly as she allowed her gaze to trawl over him. 'What are you doing here, Damon? Are you interested in fashion?'

'Not in the slightest,' he replied blandly. 'But you know why I'm here, Anna *mou.*' The glint in his eyes warned her that beneath the façade of urbane charm, his hot temper was simmering like volcanic lava waiting to erupt. 'Why did you run out on me in London?'

'My God, you flew all the way across the Atlantic to ask me that? And why now, after no contact for over two weeks?'

'I returned to Greece with the intention of putting you out of my mind,' he admitted grimly.

'From the way you were pawing Luisa Mendoza tonight, you were obviously successful.'

'Unfortunately that intention did not go to plan,' he continued, as if she hadn't spoken. 'And with no disrespect to Miss Mendoza—she was pawing me. I'm not interested in her or any other woman. I have been unable to forget you, Anna—any more than I suspect you've been able to forget me.'

'Did anyone ever tell you that a swollen head is not attractive?' she queried sarcastically, desperate to hide the effect his words were having on her. She tossed her head so that her hair flew around her face in a halo of gold silk. 'What makes you think I've spent the past two weeks pining for you?'

'This,' he said simply before he swooped and captured her mouth in a devastatingly possessive kiss that should have appalled her. Instead it breached her fragile defences so that she could do nothing but stand helplessly in his arms while he continued his flagrant assault of her senses.

His tongue forced entry between her lips to make a skilful exploration, while one hand slid to her nape to angle her head so that he could deepen the caress to a level that was shamelessly erotic. He ran his other hand restlessly over her body, from her waist, over her hip and down to cup her bottom.

Anna gasped when he hauled her close. The unmistakable feel of his arousal pushing against her stomach was new and shocking; yet fiercely exciting as for the first time in her life she became aware of the power of her femininity. There was no doubt that Damon wanted her with a hunger that should have terrified her, but instead of fear she gloried in the irrefutable proof of his desire.

Part of her wanted the kiss never to end and it was only when he lifted his head to stare down at her with a faintly triumphant gleam in his eyes that reality intruded with a vengeance.

'How dare you?' she snapped, her face flaming when she realised that they were incurring curious stares from a number of onlookers. 'If you don't take your hands off me right now, I'll call for Security.'

'Let's spare ourselves such an embarrassing scenario,' Damon drawled, plainly unperturbed by her fury. 'My car's waiting out front.'

'Then I suggest you get in it. I have my own driver, thanks.'

'Not any more—I told him you wouldn't be requiring his services tonight.'

'You've got a bloody cheek!'

Damon was already striding towards the door and Anna hurried after him as fast as her three-inch stiletto heels would allow, determined to give him a piece of her mind.

'There's no need to run. I promise I won't leave without you, *pedhaki mou*,' he mocked gently when she stumbled on the front steps. Before she could think of a suitably blistering retort, he slid his arm around her waist and ushered her over to his limousine.

'This is ridiculous—you can't just kidnap me. I demand that you take me straight to my hotel,' she said in a loud voice intended to alert his driver. The car pulled away from the kerb and she shifted along the seat away from Damon.

'Relax,' he told her idly. 'That's where we're going.'

'But you don't know where I'm staying.'

His slow smile reminded her of a wolf inspecting its prey. Of course he knew where she was staying, she realised shakily. He would have made it his business to find out.

'I can't believe you came all this way just to torment me,' she whispered, unable to keep the faint tremor from her voice.

'I hate to disillusion you but I have a number of important business meetings in New York. When Kezia mentioned that you were here, it seemed a good opportunity to meet up and discover the answer to several pertinent questions—the most important of which, you've already confirmed,' he added with a satisfied smile as his gaze focused on her mouth.

Once again Anna was aware of the sizzling chemistry between them. Raw, primitive, sexual attraction at its most

basic, she registered as she felt her nipples harden to tight
buds that strained against the soft jersey-silk of her dress.
Her frisson of fear was not of what Damon might do, but
what she wanted him to do, and she was thankful when the
car pulled up outside her hotel.

'I'm sorry to curtail such a fascinating conversation, but
it's been a long day,' she said icily. 'There's no need for you
to escort me inside.' Her irritation trebled when he slid out
of the car and followed her to the door. His amused smile
made her want to hit him, her frustration a tangible force as
realisation slowly dawned. 'You're staying here, too, aren't
you?'

'As a matter of fact, I've been here for the past two days.
I'm surprised we didn't bump into each other at breakfast.'

'You really are the most infuriating man I've ever met,'
Anna informed him bitterly when he followed her across the
reception area and into the lift. *Two days.* He'd been staying
here in her hotel for two whole days and hadn't bothered to
let her know. It certainly put her in her place, she thought
bleakly, unaware that he could decipher every expression
that flitted across her face.

'I told you I had urgent business to take care of. But now
I'm all yours, *Anna mou,*' he breathed softly. The lift
suddenly seemed airless and she inhaled sharply, her eyes
locked with his dark velvet gaze.

'You'll forgive me if I don't jump for joy,' she croaked,
her attempt at sarcasm lost beneath the huskiness of her
tone. The lift halted at her floor and she hurried along the
corridor, intent on reaching the sanctuary of her room before
he caught up with her. Of course it was hopeless—his long
stride easily outmatched hers and she paused outside her
door.

'What is it exactly that you want, Damon?'

'Who used to call you Annie? Your father?' he pressed,

when she failed to answer. 'Did he ever hit you, *pedhaki mou?*'

'Of course not.' Anna opened her door and stumbled inside. She was so startled by his question that she didn't register he had followed her into her room until it was too late. 'My father wasn't like that—he was kind and…and funny and I loved him.'

The shimmer of her tears made Damon's gut twist and he had to force himself to continue.

'So who upset you so badly that the mere mention of his nickname for you caused you to react the way you did in London?'

'It doesn't matter. It's none of your business.' Shock, fear, shame—all the emotions her stepfather had once evoked surged through her.

Phil used to accuse her of deliberately leading him on. He'd said it was her fault that he couldn't keep his hands off her and, although common sense told her she had done nothing wrong, there was a part of her that wondered if she had somehow deserved his attention.

Maybe her stepfather was right and she was intrinsically bad. She was an adult now but the fears of an impressionable teenager were still locked inside her head. She would die of shame if Damon ever learned of the things Phil had said to her, the suggestions that even now made her shudder with revulsion. Maybe Damon would believe she had encouraged her stepfather.

With a low cry she spun away from him, her shoulders rigid with tension.

'Go away, Damon. Didn't you get the message when we were in London? I don't want to have anything to do with you.'

'You're lying.'

It wasn't a question but a statement delivered with his usual arrogance.

'My God, what do I have to do to get through to you?' she cried, her eyes wide and despairing when she turned back to face him. 'Leave me alone.'

'How can I when you are inside my head every minute of the day and night?' he growled. 'How can I forget you when you respond to me with such passion? You *feel* it, Anna, the same as I do. There's something between us—chemistry, awareness, call it what you will. All I know is that I have never felt this way about any other woman.'

As he spoke he jerked her into his arms, his dark eyes burning with desire and frustration and a degree of tenderness that made her ache inside. The tears that she had fought to hold back since she had first set eyes on him at the fashion show slid unchecked down her face.

'You don't understand,' she sobbed, beating her hands wildly against his chest.

'Then make me understand.' He ignored the blows she dealt him and tightened his arms inexorably around her until she gave up and crumpled against him, her shoulders heaving. 'I want to have a relationship with you, Anna,' he told her quietly. He tilted her chin and stared down at her. 'Friends, as well as lovers,' he added steadily when she shook her head in fierce negation of the suggestion. 'And I think I understand why you find the issue of trust so difficult.'

She sincerely doubted it, Anna thought grimly. No-one knew the secrets locked inside her head. She had been unable to confide in anyone about her stepfather's unnatural fixation with her and had never spoken about his taunts or the way he had tried to touch her—not even to Kezia.

'Why won't you accept that I'm just not attracted to you?' she muttered as she struggled out of his hold and endeavoured to put some space between them. He seemed to dominate the room and her eyes were drawn to the for-

midable width of his shoulders and the proud angle of his head. Helplessly she focused on his mouth, remembering the way it had felt on hers, and her lips parted in an unconscious invitation.

'I believe you are as captive to the attraction that burns between us as I am,' he told her seriously. When I hold you—kiss you—your body tells me what you refuse to admit. You want me, Anna, with a passion that matches mine. But events in your childhood—and your father's betrayal in particular—have left you wary of giving in to your emotions.'

'What has Lars got to do with this? I told you, I adored my dad.'

'And he deserted you. He rejected you and chose his second wife's children over you. I understand how devastating that must have been for you, *pedhaki mou.*'

'I doubt it,' Anna muttered wearily. 'My father was a serial adulterer who broke my mother's heart. You can hardly blame me for wanting to avoid the same fate.' She swung away from him, wishing he would just go and leave her in peace. 'I'm tired, and I don't want to talk about it,' she muttered, stiffening when he came up behind her and placed his hands on her shoulders.

'I can't help you until you learn to have some faith in me,' he said gently.

'I don't *need* help, damn it! If ever I do want an analyst, I'll let you know,' she shot back, her attempt at sarcasm lost amid the tears that clogged her throat.

Damon made no reply as he began to massage the tight knot of muscles at the base of her neck. Anna knew she should move, put some space between them, but the feel of his hands on her skin was heaven. He kneaded her flesh with firm, yet gentle expertise, easing her tension so that she gradually felt herself relax.

'Better?' His warm breath feathered her cheek and a soft sigh escaped her. She offered no resistance when he turned her in his arms, her eyes widening a little as she absorbed the warmth in his. Common sense dictated that she should step away from him and demand that he leave. Instead she tilted her head and waited with a curious sense of inevitability for him to capture her mouth in a slow, sensual kiss that demolished her resistance.

This was where she wanted to be, she acknowledged as she wound her arms around his neck. He knew it and there seemed little point in trying to deny it any longer. She knew it was ridiculous, but when Damon held her she felt safe.

She parted her lips, eager to accept the probing warmth of his tongue as he took the kiss to a deeper level of intimacy. Suddenly nothing else mattered—not her father who had destroyed her trust in all men, or her stepfather who had wrecked her self-esteem. All that was important was the feel of Damon's lips on her skin as he trailed a line of kisses along her jaw and found the sensitive pulse point at the base of her throat.

When he lifted his head a fraction she traced her lips over his cheek, paused at the corner of his mouth before initiating a tentative exploration with her tongue. For long moments he allowed her to take control, until his hunger for her became an overwhelming need that saw him slide his fingers into her hair to hold her fast while he took the kiss to a level that was blatantly erotic.

'Damon.' She gave a soft cry when he suddenly swung her into his arms and strode purposefully towards her bedroom. Alarm bells rang faintly in her head but she ignored them. For years her stupid hang-ups had prevented her from exploring her sexuality—but not any more. She wanted Damon to make love to her. She wanted him to release her from her prison of fear and prove that she was a normal, sexually responsive woman.

When he placed her on the bed she clung tightly to him as if she feared that he would withdraw from her.

'Easy, *pedhaki mou*—there's no rush,' he murmured gently when she gripped his shoulders and pulled him down on top of her.

He didn't understand, she thought wildly. She had to do this *now,* while her nerve still held. With a muttered cry she sought his mouth while her fingers scrabbled with his shirt buttons. When she finally freed them she pushed the material aside to run her hands over his chest.

He had an incredible body—lean and powerful, the hard muscles of his abdomen clearly visible beneath his olive-gold skin. His body hair felt slightly abrasive against her palms and she trembled as she imagined how it would feel against the tender flesh of her breasts.

'My turn,' he teased softly as his hand moved to untie the straps of her halter neck. He must be a mind-reader, Anna decided feverishly when he slowly peeled the material down her body to leave her pale breasts exposed to his gaze. She watched the way his eyes darkened, recognised the elemental hunger in his gaze and gave a soft moan when he lowered himself onto her so that they lay together, skin on skin.

His lips trailed a sensual path from her mouth, down her throat to nestle briefly in the valley between her breasts. Anna held her breath when he cupped each soft mound in his palms before he lowered his head to stroke his tongue across one sensitive peak and then the other. Exquisite sensation flooded through her and she slid her fingers into his hair, silently urging him to continue working his magic.

Perhaps understanding her desperation, he drew one nipple fully into his mouth and suckled her until she arched beneath him and rocked her hips against his with devastating effect.

'*Theos,* Anna, I don't think I can wait,' he muttered

hoarsely. He lifted his head for a second, his face a taut mask of desire, before he flicked his tongue over her other tight bud, watching with apparent fascination as it hardened to a throbbing peak that begged for his attention.

Anna closed her eyes and gave herself up to the wondrous sensations Damon was arousing within her. Her body felt as though it were on fire and the dull ache in the pit of her stomach intensified until it was a clamouring need. She shifted her hips restlessly as molten heat pooled between her thighs and even when she felt him tug her dress down, over her hips, she was still utterly certain that this was what she wanted to do.

The brush of his hand on her inner thigh made her quiver with excitement. Her only covering now was a tiny triangle of lace and she inhaled sharply when she felt his fingers dip beneath the waistband to stroke gently through the downy curls at the apex of her thighs.

This was still good, she told herself frantically as the first doubts crept into her head. She was aware of his fingers sliding lower, knew instinctively that any second now he would part her and touch her where she wanted him most.

Oh, God, she wanted him to continue, wanted it desperately, but the heat was draining from her body. Where she had been wet and ready for him, now she was dry, her muscles rigid with tension as the image of her stepfather's leering smile pushed into her mind.

'Shall I tell you where I'd like to touch you, Annie?'

'What is it, Anna *mou?'* Damon lifted his head to smile down at her with tender passion. She stared at him wildly, willing herself to relax, but she couldn't do it. As his fingers gently stroked her she jerked her legs together and pushed her hands against his chest.

'No, *no!* I can't. Please, Damon, let me up. Please,' she whispered, unconsciously pleading for his forgiveness as she

watched his face tighten until his skin seemed to be stretched over the sharp angle of his cheekbones. 'I'm sorry. I can't do this. I'm sorry.'

As he rolled away from her she snatched her robe from the end of the bed and thrust her arms into it before dragging it tightly over her breasts. She felt sick. Any minute now she would actually throw up. It would be the final humiliation and she snatched air into her lungs—great, gasping breaths that made her chest heave.

She could hardly bear to look at Damon, sure that she would see both disgust and contempt in his gaze. But when she dared to peep at him, she saw neither. He simply looked weary and curiously deflated. She could almost believe that she had hurt him and the thought made her crumple.

'You must hate me.' She was determined not to cry in front of him but was powerless to prevent the tears that slid down her face. She heard his heavy sigh and crossed her arms over her chest when he stood and walked towards her. He had refastened his shirt buttons in the wrong holes and the mistake was a telling indication of his inner torment that made her tears flow faster.

'Why must I hate you?' he queried gently.

'You must think I'm a tease—that I deliberately led you on and then—' She broke off and shook her head, unable to continue.

'Is that what you were doing, Anna? Were you deliberately taunting me?' His tone was flat and so devoid of any emotion that she had no idea what he was thinking. Did he really despise her? The thought was unbearable and she lifted her head to stare into his eyes.

'No. I wanted you. I thought I could do it. I honestly thought I could go through with it,' she whispered huskily.

It was a peculiar phrase and Damon frowned. She had responded to him with such passion that he had believed she

wanted to make love with him. The idea that she had been steeling herself to 'go through with *it*' was repugnant to him. Did she really view him as some sort of ogre? Yet she had seemed so eager when he had first carried her into the bedroom.

He'd known he was rushing her and was furious with himself. He'd planned to take it slow and had come to New York with the intention of wooing her until he won her trust. Instead he'd acted with all the finesse of Neanderthal man. It was little wonder she was staring at him so fearfully, he told himself impatiently.

The naked vulnerability in her eyes made him long to draw her into his arms and hold her close but he restrained himself and reached out to smooth her hair back from her face.

'I don't hate you, Anna—far from it. But I admit, I don't always understand you,' he added ruefully. 'In my eagerness to make love to you, I mistook your response to me as an invitation to take you to bed.

'I fear I am not as patient as your previous lovers,' he groaned, his frustration with himself evident in the darkness of his eyes. 'But I appreciate your need to feel that you can trust me before we take our relationship any further.'

His gentle understanding tore at Anna's fragile emotions. From the first he had been honest about what he wanted from her and it was about time she returned that honesty.

'My previous lovers—who would they be, Damon?'

He shrugged, a faint stain of colour running along his cheekbones. 'Your affairs are headline news, but I'm not criticising you, *pedhaki mou,* I can hardly claim to have lived like a monk myself.' He raked his hand through his hair, unable to disguise his frustration as he struggled to understand her. 'Have your other boyfriends let you down? Is that what this is about?'

'There haven't been any other boyfriends—not in the way you mean,' she whispered, her heart thudding painfully in her chest as she absorbed his stunned expression. 'I've never had a lover.'

'But what of the other men in your life…the numerous love affairs reported in the tabloids?'

'Gossip and speculation by editors desperate to boost sales of their rags,' she explained with a harsh laugh. 'For some reason my photo on the front cover of magazines increases sales, and an article concerning my supposed sex life sells even better. Some of the men I've been linked with are friends, nothing more. Others I've barely met, but they believe that having their name linked with mine will be a good career move. I warned you not to believe every trashy article about me,' she taunted, trying to sound flippant to disguise her hurt.

'Are you telling me you're a *virgin?*'

In different circumstances the utter disbelief in his voice would have been comical but Anna had never felt less like laughing.

'It's not a crime, you know.' To her horror she felt her eyes glaze with tears and she swung away from him, desperate to hide her distress. 'I'd like you to leave now. I'm tired and I want to go to bed.' Her eyes fell on the rumpled sheets where a few moments ago she had *ached* with desire for him. Now the ache was around her heart but she would rather die than suffer the humiliation of having him pity her.

'Anna, I…' He reached out to her but she jerked away and fled towards the bathroom.

'Just go, Damon,' she begged brokenly. 'Accept that I am not the woman you thought I was—the experienced seductress you want me to be. I'm sure there must be a dozen blondes in your little black book who can offer uncomplicated sex,' she choked as she scrubbed her wet face with her hand. 'Trust me, you're wasting your time with me.'

CHAPTER EIGHT

WHEN Anna finally found the courage to emerge from the bathroom she was relieved to discover that Damon had gone. She crawled into bed and cried until there were no more tears left, before falling into a restless sleep.

Next morning she woke feeling like death and stumbled into the bathroom to stare at her blotchy face and puffy eyes. She'd read somewhere that crying was supposed to be cathartic, a natural purging of emotions, but all it had done was leave her with a murderous headache.

It took several minutes for her to realise that the knocking sound was coming from the door, rather than someone performing a clog dance inside her head. Muttering a curse, she went to answer it and stared in bemusement at the smiling waiter.

'Room service,' he announced breezily as he steered his trolley past her.

'There must be some mistake. I didn't order anything,' she protested. 'You must have the wrong room.'

'Number 158, breakfast for two,' he insisted. He began to unload the contents of the trolley onto the table. 'We have orange juice, coffee, eggs, hash browns, bagels...'

'All I want is a couple of aspirin and a cup of tea,' she muttered weakly, her stomach churning at the thought of food.

'Yes, you do look a bit rough this morning. It's lucky the editors of *Vogue* magazine can't see you right now,' a familiar accented voice sounded from the doorway. 'That will be all, thanks,' Damon dismissed the waiter and strolled into the room, his lips twitching at the sight of Anna's outraged glare.

'I've spent the night from hell. Is it any wonder I look *a bit rough?*' she demanded furiously. Having believed that she would never have the courage to meet his gaze again, she was now seriously tempted to throw a bagel at his head, followed by the coffee-pot.

She placed her hands on her hips, quivering with rage and another; rather more disturbing emotion when he crossed the room and gently tilted her chin.

'You will always be the most beautiful woman in the world to me, *Anna mou*.'

'Don't.' The inherent tenderness in his tone brought fresh tears to her eyes and her lashes fell.

'I'm sorry you had a bad night. If it's any consolation, mine was possibly worse.'

She lifted her head to study his face and noted the faint lines around his eyes and the deeper grooves on either side of his mouth. Bad night or not, he still looked gorgeous, she thought numbly when his mouth curved into a soft smile that melted the ice around her heart.

'I understand you're free today,' he said cheerfully. Although he did not offer an explanation of how he knew, Anna noted irritably. 'I thought we'd have a lazy breakfast and then spend the rest of the day exploring the city—maybe take a cruise around Manhattan. The full trip takes about three hours and guarantees excellent views of all the famous landmarks.'

'Why?' Anna queried huskily, trying hard not to get caught up in his enthusiasm. Her most sensible course of

action would be to catch the next flight home and try to forget she had ever met Damon Kouvaris.

'Why take the boat trip? It seems a more relaxing way of seeing the sights than by road, but there are plenty of bus tours if you'd prefer.'

'That's not what I meant, and you know it. You don't have to spend the day with me. It won't change anything,' she said awkwardly, her cheeks suffusing with colour at his quizzical glance.

'I'm not expecting you to leap into bed with me as payment for an entertaining day out,' he informed her dryly. 'I would simply like to spend some time with you, Anna,' he added softly as he cupped her jaw and lifted her face to his.

His kiss was sweetly evocative, his lips as light as gossamer on hers before he lifted his head to stare into her eyes. 'I don't know what happened in your past, *pedhaki mou,* and, without resorting to thumbscrews, I can't force you to confide in me. Something—someone obviously hurt you so badly that you're afraid to put your trust in anyone. But I'm not simply going to walk away from you.'

'Even knowing that I'll never be able to make love with you?' she whispered. 'Because I can't, Damon. Last night, I thought it would be all right. I wanted you so much,' she admitted with a raw honesty that shook him. 'But when it came to it, I just…froze.' Tears filled her eyes and she blinked furiously. What was it about this man that left her emotions in tatters?

Damon slid his arms around her and she felt him brush his lips against her hairline. 'Never is a long time. Let's just take it one day at a time. You froze last night because I rushed you and you weren't ready. I understand how important trust is to you, Anna. You need to feel confident that I won't hurt you or let you down. All I'm asking for is a chance to prove that you can have faith in me.'

He was impossible to resist, Anna thought weakly as she laid her head on his chest and absorbed his strength. Where she had expected him to be angry with her, or at least impatient, he had shown her nothing but understanding and kindness. It was a long time since she had felt cared for and she feared it could become addictive.

Damon dropped a light kiss on the tip of her nose and led her over to the table. 'I hope you're hungry. This is breakfast New York style,' he smiled as he surveyed the laden table.

'I'm starving,' Anna replied, surprised to find it was true. After a night of utter misery she'd thought she would never be able to eat again, but to her amazement she discovered that her appetite had returned. She sat down and heaped a pile of fluffy scrambled eggs onto her plate. 'Aren't you going to join me?'

Her tentative smile caused a curious pain in Damon's gut. With her face scrubbed free of make-up and her hair caught up in a pony-tail, she looked young and painfully innocent. Although he was still reeling at the thought of just how innocent, he acknowledged grimly.

He didn't doubt for a second that she had spoken the truth when she'd admitted her complete lack of sexual experience. He only wondered how he had missed the signs for so long. He had been guilty of believing all the trash written about her, but her determination to raise money for the children's hospice should have told him she was nothing like her image of a spoilt supermodel.

Anna was beautiful inside and out, but she was also emotionally fragile and haunted by demons from her past. He'd spent a hellish night wrestling with his conscience, knowing that he had neither the time nor the capability to help her. He had commitments she knew nothing about—*baggage* in the form of a child who would always be his first priority.

When *was* a good time to drop into the conversation that you had an eight-year-old daughter? he brooded darkly. The situation had never arisen before. In the years since Eleni's death, he'd never felt the slightest inclination to deepen his relationship with any of his mistresses to the level where Ianthe became an issue.

But Anna was different. He…*cared,* he accepted as he responded to her smile and watched the way her cheeks flushed with pleasure. He didn't understand how, or why, it had happened, he just knew that he wanted her in his life.

Sex was obviously a problem for her, but rather than lessening his desire it only made him want her more. He wanted to help her overcome her fears. He wanted to tutor her and watch her as she experienced sexual pleasure for the first time. She stirred feelings within him that were primitive and deeply possessive and he was prepared to wait for as long as it took until she felt ready to give herself completely to him.

He took his place at the table and helped himself to food, although his appetite had deserted him. How the hell could he ask her to trust him when he was guilty of keeping a fundamental part of his life from her? He had to tell her about Ianthe, and sooner rather than later.

'…Damon.'

He was suddenly aware that Anna was speaking to him and forced himself to focus.

'It's fine if you've changed your mind about today,' she murmured, unable to hide her uncertainty. 'I'm sure you have better things to do than spend the day with me.'

'No,' he replied with simple honesty, 'there's nothing I would rather do than be with you.' He paused for a heartbeat and then added, 'How long do you plan to spend in New York?'

'You mean you haven't already checked my diary?'

Her brows arched in a look that was pure Anneliese
Christiansen—ice-cool and disdainful—before her face
broke into an impish smile that was the real Anna. 'I have a
photo shoot booked for next week, but there's little point in
flying home between now and then. Besides, I'm quite
happy to have some free time here. How about you?' she
queried hesitantly. 'I assume you have to return to Greece
soon.'

'I am my own master and I can do whatever I choose,' he
told her with a flash of his outrageous arrogance. 'And I
choose to stay until next week.' His eyes gleamed with
sensual heat as he trapped her gaze. 'So, here we are, two
people alone in Manhattan. I suggest we team up for the next
few days. Safety in numbers and all that,' he added with a
grin.

'Are you saying I'd be safe with you?'

'You have my word, *pedhaki mou.*' His voice lost its
teasing edge and he regarded her steadily, noting the betraying tremor of her mouth. 'You can trust me, Anna *mou.*'

Anna had always believed that New York was an amazing
city but with Damon it became truly magical. As he had suggested, they boarded a cruise boat at the harbour and enjoyed
a leisurely trip around Manhattan, their eyes drawn to the
towering skyscrapers that dominated the horizon.

He was an attentive and tactile companion. On the boat
he stood behind her and slid his arms around her waist to
draw her against the solid strength of his chest. The steady
thud of his heart was strangely comforting and although
Anna stared determinedly at the view, she was overwhelmed
with longing to turn and bury her face in his shirt.

After lunch they took the ferry from Battery Park across
to the Statue of Liberty. As they strolled around the base of
the great monument he threaded his fingers through hers

with an easy familiarity that dismantled her defensive
barriers one by one. She didn't understand what he wanted
from her—why he was here—but suddenly she no longer
cared.

When he paused and drew her into his arms, she stared
up at him, silently willing him to cover her mouth with his
own. He aroused feelings within her that she'd never experienced with any other man. The knowledge should have terrified her but she was tired of being scared.

Damon had given his word that he wouldn't attempt to rush
her into a sexual relationship before she was ready, and she
knew with complete certainty that he would never try and
force her.

She had never believed she could trust any man but
maybe, just maybe, he was different.

As the week slipped past she realised with growing certainty that Damon was unlike any man she had ever met. To
the outside world he was a successful, powerful and undoubtedly ruthless businessman at the top of his game. But
there was another side to him that she guessed few people
outside his immediate family were privileged to meet.

Only a truly confident man could team strength with
gentleness and a tender consideration that made her want
to weep. Damon had the ability to make her feel like a
princess. She adored the way he treated her as if she were
infinitely precious to him, even though she knew in her
heart that it could not be so.

He could have any woman he wanted. Why on earth was
he wasting his time with a sexually inexperienced novice
who was incapable of satisfying him?

It was a question that increasingly demanded an answer
the more time she spent with him.

'You're very quiet, *pedhaki mou*. Are you tired?'

'A little—but it's been a wonderful day. My head's still buzzing from everything we saw today.' They had spent several hours at the 'Met'—the world famous Metropolitan Museum of Art—and Anna felt as though her senses had overdosed on the visual feast of fantastic exhibits. Tonight they had dined at one of New York's finest restaurants and afterwards Damon had surprised her with a romantic carriage ride through Central Park.

Now they were back at their hotel and he had accepted her invitation to join her for a nightcap in her suite. The natural conclusion to the magical evening they'd spent together was for him to sweep her into his arms and carry her through to the bedroom, where they would spend the night making love.

If she was a *normal* woman, she would saunter over to him, link her arms around his neck and issue him with a bold invitation to take her to bed. But she was not normal, Anna brooded miserably. She was frigid—unable to enjoy or bestow sexual pleasure, even with the man who was fast capturing her heart.

'What is it, Anna? Do you want me to go?'

She was standing by the window, staring unseeingly at the myriad neon lights that lit up Times Square. As Damon spoke he moved to stand behind her and slid his arms around her waist to draw her up against the solid wall of his chest.

'I guess you should…it's getting late,' she whispered, helpless to disguise the tears that clogged her voice. She offered no resistance when he turned her to face him, and watched the way his eyes darkened as he caught the trickle of moisture with his thumb pad. 'I wish things could be different,' she admitted despairingly. 'You've been so kind to me these past few days and I feel I should…'

'Sleep with me? Offer yourself like a sacrificial virgin because I've been *kind* to you? Anna, when you come to me

it will be because you want to make love with me, not because you feel obligated,' he assured her.

'But what if that day never comes? How can you be so sure? There must be literally dozens of women willing to fall into your bed,' she muttered, fighting a wave of nausea at the mental image of him holding another woman in his arms.

'I only want you, Anna *mou*. No one else will do. And you are not completely immune to me,' he added softly as his arms tightened around her. 'You simply need time to feel comfortable with me before we can enjoy a fully intimate relationship.'

Comfortable! Dear God, she felt anything but. Comfortable conjured up an image of easy familiarity that was a million miles away from the fierce tension that suddenly gripped her. The sensual heat in Damon's eyes sent fire coursing through her veins and she trembled with anticipation rather than fear when he lowered his head.

He had kissed her several times during the past week—gentle, tender kisses that were bound by the tight restraint he exerted over his emotions. Anna had appreciated his sensitivity. He'd promised not to rush her and was obviously determined to honour that promise, but there was a part of her that had longed for him to lose control and kiss her with the fierce passion she glimpsed in his simmering gaze.

Now that passion was a force he could no longer deny and he claimed her lips with uncompromising hunger. It felt so right, she thought wonderingly as she parted her lips and revelled in the masterful sweep of his tongue. With Damon she didn't feel dirty or ashamed. He brought her to life so that every nerve ending quivered to his touch.

For the first time in her life she relished the feeling that she was a sensual, sensuous creature. Her body seemed to have been created solely for the purpose of giving and receiving pleasure and she exalted in the thrusting proof of his arousal pushing against her stomach.

She followed blindly when he led her over to the sofa and drew her down onto his lap. He captured her mouth again in a slow, seductive kiss that drugged her senses so that she was mindless to everything but the feel of his hands on her body, and she shivered with excitement when he began to unfasten the tiny pearl buttons at the front of her top. She remembered how it had felt when he had caressed her breasts and already her nipples had hardened in anticipation of the pleasure to come.

Damon freed the final button, but to Anna's disappointment he made no move to slide the soft satin from her shoulders. She stirred restlessly in his lap and he groaned and clamped her hips to prevent her from moving.

'I am not made of stone, *pedhaki mou*. If you don't keep still, I'm likely to do something that will shock you and embarrass me.'

She stared at him wordlessly, her cheeks flaming at the erotic images his words evoked. She didn't want him to stop, she acknowledged with a sense of wonderment. She wanted him to kiss her again, touch her where she ached to be touched, and she swayed towards him, her eyes unconsciously pleading.

'I don't think you could shock me,' she told him seriously. 'I feel safe with you, Damon, and I want you to kiss me… touch me,' she admitted huskily.

She felt his chest heave—as if he were a drowning man snatching for air—and she noted that the hand he used to stroke her hair back from her face was not quite steady. His eyes had darkened to the colour of mahogany, lit by a flame of desire that made her tremble with an answering passion.

'You are so beautiful, Anna *mou*. I have never hungered for any woman the way I hunger for you,' he muttered rawly. 'But I won't rush you, or hurt you, and I give you my word that I'll stop the moment you ask me to.'

Maybe she wouldn't want him to stop, Anna thought as he claimed her lips once more in a fierce, hard kiss. Hope surged through her and she opened her mouth to accept the bold sweep of his tongue. She trusted Damon to keep his word, but maybe she would be so caught up in the pleasure he evoked that her fears would remain in the far recess of her mind.

The fine boning of her top provided sufficient support for her small breasts without the need for a bra. She gave a murmur of approval when he pushed the material aside and cupped each pale mound in his big hands. The brush of his thumbs across her swollen nipples sent sensation flooding through her and she moaned softly and allowed her head to fall back so that her breasts were fully exposed to his gaze.

Damon trailed his lips down her throat and continued an inexorable path lower, to stroke his tongue over one tight peak until it throbbed for his full possession. Anna shifted on his lap and slid her hands into his hair to hold him to his task, whimpering when his lips finally closed around her nipple and he suckled her.

By the time he transferred his attention to her other breast she was shaking with a combination of shock that what he was doing to her could feel so good, and a burgeoning need for more. There was nothing in her mind other than a feverish desire for him to assuage the ache that was building inside her and when he slid his hand beneath the hem of her skirt she quivered at the butterfly touch of his fingers skimming the sensitive flesh of her inner thigh.

He paused, mistaking the little gasp she gave as a request for him to cease his gentle exploration of her body. 'Is it too much, Anna? Do you want me to stop?' he whispered, his breath grazing her shoulder as he lifted his head to look into her eyes.

Slowly she shook her head in negation and watched the

smouldering heat in his gaze when she leaned towards him and initiated a tremulous kiss that stirred his soul. For a moment he allowed her to maintain control before he deepened the kiss to another level that was flagrantly erotic. His tongue was an instrument of sensual delight and he explored her with a thoroughness that left his desire for her in no doubt.

Anna was aware of his hand sliding higher and higher beneath her skirt but the pressure of his mouth on hers was creating such havoc with her emotions that she felt neither fear nor revulsion when he gently stroked his fingers over the tiny triangle of lace at the junction of her thighs. Desire flooded her, leaving her hot and slick, and she held her breath when he eased his fingers beneath her knickers to initiate an intimate exploration that was new and utterly beautiful.

She parted for him like a rose opening its velvety petals to the sun and with infinite care he slid in deep, feeling her muscles spasm around his finger. She was tighter than he had expected and he was desperate not to cause her pain, but rather than wanting him to withdraw she seemed intent on urging him to continue caressing her.

Anna closed her eyes; her whole body focused on the incredible sensations Damon was arousing. Her body felt on fire, with the brightest flame burning at her central core. She wasn't even sure what she wanted, just knew that it was there, hovering, and with a little cry of frustration she rocked her hips and pushed herself against his hand.

Damon seemed to sense the tumultuous sensations that were building inside her and began to move his finger with little pulsing strokes. At the same time he rubbed the tip of his thumb over the acutely sensitive nub of her clitoris, and Anna's world exploded.

Spasm after spasm ripped through her so that she

trembled in his arms. It was frighteningly new and yet so utterly exquisite that she wasn't afraid. She threw her head back and cried out; unaware of the pleasure he took from watching her climax for the very first time.

An emotion that was deeply primitive surged through Damon. Anna was his woman and his alone. No other man had ever caressed her so intimately or made her cry out with the pleasure of sexual release.

She was his and he would treasure her always, he vowed as he felt her tremors gradually lessen. Whatever had happened in her past still haunted her. There was still some way to go before she would feel confident enough to give herself to him completely. But he could wait, God help him. He would use his iron will-power to control the desire that threatened to overwhelm him and one day his patience would be rewarded and he would be able to penetrate her fully so that their bodies were joined as one.

The thought was enough to make his penis strain uncomfortably against the restriction of his trousers and with one swift movement he stood with her still in his arms. The pressure of her pert bottom rubbing against him was enough to tempt a saint but he had promised not to rush her and he would keep that promise, even though he would probably spend the rest of the night beneath a cold shower.

Anna opened her eyes as the room swayed alarmingly, and discovered that Damon was carrying her purposefully towards her bedroom. He had given her more pleasure than she had believed it was possible to experience. Even now, little quivers of aftershock were spiralling through her. It was only fair that he should want to experience the same sexual ecstasy, she told herself as she tried to ignore her frisson of apprehension.

When he placed her on the bed, she stared at him silently, unaware of the stark vulnerability in her eyes when she gave

him a tremulous smile. He would be gentle; she knew it. She trusted him. He wasn't a barbarian and he certainly wasn't the balding, sweaty, middle-aged excuse for a man that her stepfather had been.

Damon would never mock her or make her feel tainted, she frantically reminded herself. But as he leaned over her she felt her breath catch in her throat so that her chest jerked unevenly.

'I'll give you some privacy to get undressed,' he said in a matter-of-fact tone that brought her crashing back to reality.

She blinked at him in bemusement when he gathered up her nightshirt and handed it to her and his next sentence added to her confusion.

'Can I get you something—a cup of tea perhaps?'

Tea! He wanted to calmly sit and drink tea as if they were at a vicarage tea party before he threw her down on the bed and made passionate love to her. If she hadn't been terrified out of her wits at the thought of the passionate lovemaking, Anna would have found the situation hysterical.

'I'm fine, thanks,' she croaked, clutching her nightshirt in front of her naked breasts like a talisman. Damon gave her a brief smile before he strolled into the sitting room and it was only when he had closed the door between them that she released her breath.

She had no idea how long her reprieve would last and shot into the bathroom where she scrambled out of her skirt and into the nightshirt, washed her face and brushed her teeth, all in record time.

She could do this, she told her reflection, desperately trying to ignore the fact that every last vestige of desire that Damon had aroused in her earlier had disappeared. Her nerves were at screaming point, and the sensual heat that had flooded between her thighs had gone, leaving her as dry and barren as a desert. But she could do this.

For a second, her stepfather's face leered back at her and she blinked hard to dispel his image from her mind. She heard faint sounds from the bedroom. Damon was waiting for her and sick fear lurched in the pit of her stomach. She couldn't remain a virgin for the rest of her life. Better to get the first time over with. And at least she trusted him enough to know he would be patient.

She looked like a small lamb at the gates of the slaughterhouse, Damon thought grimly when Anna emerged from the bathroom. Her voluminous white cotton nightshirt, decorated with yellow daisies, was curiously childlike and he wanted to draw her into his arms and simply hold her close. Instead he turned back the bed sheets with brisk efficiency and patted the mattress.

'Come on, in you get. You look all in, *pedhaki mou.*'

Fighting the urge to flee from the room, Anna obediently climbed into bed and lay down. Damon was still fully clothed. Perhaps he intended to strip in front of her, she speculated frantically, and squeezed her eyes shut to block out the image of him peeling the clothes from his body.

She felt him draw the covers over her and when the mattress dipped she dared to peep between her lashes to discover him sitting, still clothed, on the edge of the bed.

'I thought we could try and get tickets for a Broadway show tomorrow—if you'd like to?'

'That sounds…nice,' she muttered stiffly, finding it hard to make plans for the next day when there was still the night to get through.

Damon stood up but made no effort to remove his clothes. 'Good. I'll make enquiries at Reception in the morning. Sleep well, Anna.' He leaned over and brushed his lips over hers in a gentle benediction before he strolled across to the door.

'But I thought…' She jerked upright and stared at him in

bewilderment. 'I assumed you were going to stay the night.' Faced with his silence, she chewed on her bottom lip, her cheeks scarlet as she ploughed on. 'Earlier, when we…when I—' oh, God, this was difficult '—I didn't satisfy you.'

'On the contrary, Anna *mou,* the fact that I was able to give you pleasure gave me more joy than I've ever known,' he told her gravely. 'Soon I hope to make love to you fully, but only when you're ready—only when you trust me enough to give yourself to me without fear or reservation.

'Until then I will sleep in my own bed, although it may be necessary to spend most of the night beneath a very cold shower,' he admitted with a wry smile that tugged at her heart.

'Sweet dreams, Anna. I'll see you at breakfast,' he bade her softly, before he stepped out of her room and closed the door behind him.

CHAPTER NINE

ANNA slept fitfully and woke at dawn to spend the next couple of hours rehearsing what she wanted to say to Damon. After showering, she blow-dried her hair so that it fell in a sleek gold veil around her shoulders before selecting white linen trousers and a lacy top from the wardrobe. The finished effect was cool and elegant, and hopefully masked the fact that inside she was a seething mass of emotions.

At eight she could wait no longer and took the lift to his floor, her heart hammering in her chest when she headed down the corridor to his suite. The patience and understanding he'd shown the previous night had proved irrefutably that she could trust him. She accepted that they would never have a proper relationship until she told him about her stepfather and now she was ready to confide in him.

Perhaps Damon would be able to dismiss the fears that Philip Stone had put into her head—the idea that sex was grubby and disgusting. Common sense told her that making love was a perfectly natural act but she needed Damon's strength and sensitivity to convince her.

'I know it's early, but I couldn't wait to see you,' she said shyly when he answered his door. 'I thought we could have breakfast together...' She tailed to a halt and stared at his grim face.

He looked terrible. His face was haggard, with deep lines etched around his mouth. His grey suit was impeccably tailored but he'd obviously not found time to shave, and his jaw was shaded with black stubble.

'Damon, what's wrong?'

'I have to go home. Today. Now.' His accent was very pronounced—an indication of his stress levels—and as he strode across to his bedroom he spoke into the cell phone clamped to his ear, in terse, voluble Greek.

'I'm sorry, Anna,' he said when he finished the call and turned to find her hovering uncertainly in the doorway. 'It's an emergency. I can't get on a damn flight for hours, so I've chartered a private jet.' As he spoke he bundled several bespoke, Egyptian cotton shirts into his case with as much care as if they were rags, before drawing the zip shut. With a final glance around the room, he snatched up his jacket and headed for the door, frowning when she continued to block his path.

'I'll call you,' he promised distractedly, but it was only when she put her hand on his arm that he seemed to really register her presence.

'What's happened? What sort of emergency? Please—don't shut me out, Damon,' she pleaded. 'Maybe I can help?'

He took a deep breath, as if he had to force himself to be patient with her. 'There's been an accident back in Greece. Everything's under control and there's nothing you can do. I just need to get home as quickly as possible.'

'But who…a member of your family—why is it such a secret?' Anna broke off, appalled by the thought that had suddenly struck her. 'Do you have a mistress in Greece? Is that why you won't tell me?'

'*Theos,* why do you always think the worst?' he growled savagely. 'I don't have a mistress—in Greece or anywhere else.'

'Then who has been hurt in an accident?' she demanded. 'I thought we were friends, Damon—that there was something between us. Surely you can tell me?'

For a moment he looked as if he would ignore her. His face was a tight mask, his eyes shadowed and unfathomable, but then he turned—his hand already on the door handle—and stared at her.

'My daughter has fallen off her bike and is in hospital with concussion. Tests have detected a slight swelling on the brain. That's why I have to go.'

The silence in the room vibrated with tension as Anna struggled to assimilate his words. He had to be making some sort of cruel joke, she decided numbly. This was Damon, the man whom, during the long hours of the night, she had decided that she could trust with her life. How could he have a child and not have told her?

'Your daughter?' she said thickly, desperately trying to moisten her parched lips. 'You have a daughter? But when…how?' She shook her head. 'I don't understand.'

'It's quite simple,' he said brusquely. The look of shocked disbelief in her eyes made his gut twist, but there was no time to break the news gently when his adored little girl was lying injured in a hospital bed. 'My wife gave birth to our daughter, Ianthe, ten months before her death.'

'So she…your daughter, she's eight years old?'

'Nearly nine—' He broke off and raked a hand through his hair. 'Look, I realise it must have come as a shock, but I really don't have time to talk about it—her—now.' He pulled open the door, his big body taut with impatience and the need for action. 'I'll call you, *pedhaki mou.*'

'*Don't!*' Anna gave a harsh laugh. 'Don't call me that. In fact, don't call me at all. I never want to hear from you again, Damon.'

'Don't be ridiculous.' On the point of striding out of the

room, he halted and swung back to stare at her ashen face. 'We need to talk, Anna,' he added more gently when she lifted her bewildered, pain-filled eyes to him. 'But right now my first priority is Ianthe. You must see that.'

Anna stared at him as if she were truly seeing him for the first time and the contempt in her eyes drove a knife through his heart. 'She should always be your first priority, Damon. My God! She's an eight-year-old, motherless child and you left her alone in Greece while you flew to the other side of the world to try and persuade me into your bed. What kind of a father does that make you?'

'I did not leave her alone,' he snapped furiously, outraged that she should question his abilities as a parent. 'Ianthe has always spent a great deal of time with my sister and her family. She regards Catalina as a surrogate mother and is as close to her cousins as if they were her own brothers.'

'It's not the same,' Anna told him fiercely. 'You are her father, her only parent, and you left her to be with me. I *know* how it feels to be abandoned. To be overlooked in favour of another woman. You're just the same as my father and I can't *believe* I was so stupid as to have actually started to trust you.'

'When have I ever given you cause to doubt my word?' Damon demanded, his eyes smouldering with angry fire.

'You have a child!' Anna yelled at him. 'A child you've never seen fit to mention despite the fact that you urged me to trust you. Why didn't you tell me?' she whispered brokenly, her anger draining away as the enormity of his deception hit her.

Damon looked as though he had been sculpted from marble, his skin stretched taut over the sharp contours of his face. Suddenly he seemed frighteningly distant and remote and she realised with a sickening lurch that she really didn't know him at all. 'In the general scheme of things, I'm not important to you, am I, Damon?'

'At first, no, you were not,' he admitted bluntly. 'I have always kept my private life separate from Ianthe. It's amazing how many women view a multimillionaire single father as prime husband material. And I was not looking for a wife.'

'Are you saying you didn't tell me about your daughter because you feared I would use her as a means to engineer a permanent place in your life? My God, your arrogance is beyond belief.'

Anna fought the wave of nausea that swept over her. Her heart felt as though it had been rent in two but she wouldn't give him the satisfaction of seeing how much he had hurt her. 'You know my feelings on the whole step-parent issue.'

'Which is precisely why I couldn't find the courage to broach the subject,' Damon replied quietly. 'I have known for some time that you are different to my previous mistresses.'

'Yes, I've got a major hang-up about sex. I don't imagine it's a problem that your numerous exes have ever suffered from,' she flung at him bitterly.

'I meant that I…feel differently about you. You mean more to me than any other woman has done since Eleni died,' he admitted slowly.

Incredibly for Damon Kouvaris, he seemed awkward and unsure of himself—a first, surely, for Mr Confidence, Anna thought darkly. The tide of colour that stained his cheekbones was all the more endearing because it was in such contrast to his usual arrogance.

But his embarrassment was probably caused by guilt that he had been caught out, she told herself fiercely as she hardened her heart against him. All the time he had been urging her to trust him, he had been deliberately deceiving her. He was no better than every other man she'd met. No better than her father.

It belatedly occurred to her that somewhere on the other side of the world a frightened little girl was lying alone in hospital with possibly life-threatening injuries. Now was not the time for bitter recriminations. Damon's daughter needed him and the most important thing right now was for him to be by her side.

'Just…go, Damon. Go home to your little girl. Trust me,' she whispered thickly, 'the only person she wants at the moment is her daddy. No one else will do.'

Damon nodded, his face darkening when he moved jerkily towards her and saw her flinch. The silent plea in his eyes tore at Anna's heart but her composure was held together by the most fragile of threads and she knew that if he touched her, it would snap.

She watched as he stepped into the lift, her gaze locked with his until the doors silently closed between them. And then he was gone. Stifling a sob, she hurried back to her room and bolted the door before she gave in to the maelstrom of emotions that hit her with the force of a tornado.

Athens in August was as hot as Hades. During the short walk across the airport car park, Anna had felt the intense heat of the sun on her skin and was glad to climb into the cool interior of the air-conditioned limousine that was waiting to collect her.

The roads leading from the airport were teeming with traffic. The chauffeur seemed unconcerned by the cacophony of hooting from impatient taxi drivers but Anna held her breath when one of the literally hundreds of motorcyclists on the road veered in front of them.

'Have you visited Athens before?' enquired the young woman who was sitting beside her in the back of the car.

'I've worked here a few times but I've never really explored Athens properly, and fortunately I've never had to

drive on its roads,' Anna replied dryly. 'Is the studio far from here?'

'We're actually going to my private villa, which is about twenty minutes out of town. I have a workshop and design studio there and I think it will be an ideal place for the photo shoot,' the woman explained, her Greek accent not detracting from the fact that she spoke excellent English. 'I've booked Fabien Valoise. I know you've worked with him before and I was very impressed with the pictures he took of you.'

Anna's brows rose. Tina Theopoulis was obviously sparing no expense in the marketing of her range of exclusive, hand-crafted jewellery. Fabien Valoise was one of the best photographers around and she knew that his diary was booked up for months in advance.

When her agent had first contacted her with details of the assignment in Greece, she had turned it down flat, stating with complete honesty that she would rather fly to the moon than travel to Athens. But Tina Theopoulis—or her financial backers—had been adamant that Anna's cool, Nordic beauty would provide a perfect backdrop for the Aphrodite collection.

It was not the eye-opening financial incentive offered that had finally made her decide to take the job, Anna acknowledged as she stared out at the busy streets. She had no interest in money or her career—no interest in life itself.

For the past month—ever since she had returned from New York—she'd felt as though she were slowly dying inside. She couldn't sleep, and certainly couldn't eat. It was unheard of for a model to be too thin, but her clothes were hanging off her and her eyes looked too big for her gaunt face. She could only hope Fabien Valoise would work his magic with the camera and transform the dull-eyed stick insect she had become into the iconic Anneliese Christiansen that Tina Theopoulis was expecting.

The only reason she had come to Athens was because Damon was here, and, although she hated to admit it, she'd been unable to resist the opportunity to be near him. Not that she expected to actually see him, she conceded miserably. Athens was a big and overcrowded city and the chances of bumping into him were practically zero. But this was Damon's home and her bruised heart took some comfort from knowing that he was near.

The car eventually reached the outskirts of the city and headed out towards the Olympic Village before the road climbed into the mountains.

'Here we are,' Tina murmured when they turned into a driveway and halted in front of a white-walled villa.

'Goodness, what a spectacular place,' Anna commented, her unhappiness momentarily forgotten as she stared up at the villa. 'It's huge, and absolutely beautiful. How many storeys are there—five?'

'Six counting the basement, and there's underground parking beneath that,' Tina replied with a smile. 'We're on the slopes of Mount Parnitha, hence the wonderful view. On a clear day it's even possible to see the island of Aegina.'

'Do you live here alone?' Anna asked curiously when she followed her hostess up the front steps and into a vast, marble-floored entrance hall. Before Tina could reply, three small boys hurtled into the lobby. The oldest couldn't be more than five years old, Anna guessed, while the youngest was little more than a baby, with chubby limbs and an adorable smile.

'Hardly alone, as you can see,' Tina laughed, 'although I sometimes think I would be more productive in my work if I did not have the children.'

'But you wouldn't be without them,' Anna guessed, feeling an unexpected pang of longing when she watched Tina lift the youngest child into her arms. She'd never given

much thought to having a family of her own. It was something she'd vaguely imagined for her future—and would only be possible if she ever overcame the seemingly insurmountable problem of trusting a man enough to have a physical relationship with him.

For a brief time she'd believed she could trust Damon, she thought bitterly. But even if by some miracle they met again and embarked on an affair—that was all it would be. Damon had a child who was, rightly, the main priority in his life, and he'd made it clear that he wasn't looking for a permanent relationship with any woman.

'The villa is arranged as two separate residences,' Tina explained as she ushered Anna over to the lift. 'My husband, Kosta, and I live with the boys in the lower rooms and my bro…' she paused, suddenly flustered and pink cheeked, before quickly adding '…and other family members occupy the top floors. My workshop is in the basement. If you'd like to go down, I'll take the children to their nanny and join you in a few minutes.'

The three boys were running boisterously around the lobby. Tina certainly had her hands full, Anna noted when an older child—a girl—suddenly peered over the banister of the ornate central staircase. Four children and a successful career as a jewellery designer—it was an enviable lifestyle, she mused when Tina spoke in Greek to her daughter.

The girl was a few years older than her brothers, with the same dark eyes and black silky curls. She was exceptionally pretty but seemed shy compared to the bold little boys and stared at Anna curiously for a few seconds, before darting off up the stairs again.

'The lift will take you down to the basement where Fabien is already waiting,' Tina murmured, seeming curiously tense. Perhaps she was anxious to make a start, Anna decided as she stepped into the lift. The photo shoot must

be costing a fortune and, for a small business such as Theopoulis Jewellery Design, time was money.

As Tina had promised, Fabien Valoise had already arrived. With the help of his lighting engineer, he had turned the design room into a photographic studio and was waiting with the make-up artist, hairdresser and stylist.

'Anna! It's good to see you, *chérie*. How are you?' Fabien greeted her warmly.

Anna dredged up a smile for the thin, angular man, dressed from head to toe in black. She'd worked with him several times in the past and they had become good friends. 'Fabien—it's good to see you, too. I'm fine.'

'Something tells me you're lying, *ma petite*.' Fabien cast a professional eye over her before strolling across the room to greet her with a kiss on both cheeks. 'You've lost weight since I last worked with you. Are you ill, or in love?'

'Isn't one the cause of the other?' Anna queried bitterly. 'Perhaps I'm suffering from a sickness of the heart.'

'Ah! Do you want to talk about it, or do you simply need a shoulder to cry on?' the Frenchman asked with gentle sympathy.

'Neither—I can deal with it,' Anna replied. 'Shall we get to work?'

'Just a couple more shots, *chérie*. Look to the left and lift your chin a little more. Perfect—now look straight at the camera…'

Anna followed Fabien's instructions and moved her head obediently. They had been working for several hours and the hot studio lights had made her feel thirsty, but she knew Fabien hated interruptions and so she ignored the prickling dryness of her throat.

Tina Theopoulis was clearly a gifted artist and jeweller. Anna was impressed with every piece she had modelled, but

the wedding collection—comprising a white gold and diamond necklace and drop earrings—was simply exquisite. Diamonds as beautiful as these were almost worth risking marriage for, she thought cynically as she glanced down at the floor-length, oyster silk dress the stylist had chosen for her to wear with the jewellery.

'Okay, *chérie,* we'll take a break,' Fabien murmured.

Anna gave a sigh of relief and stretched her aching muscles, but as she lifted her head her attention was caught by a figure standing at the back of the room. Her heart rate accelerated and she felt sick and dizzy. She must be seeing things! It could not possibly be Damon—was her last conscious thought before the walls closed in and she slid into oblivion.

She opened her eyes to find that her face was pressed against a solid wall of muscle.

'Damon?' she whispered, when a furtive peep upwards revealed a square jaw and the chiselled facial bone structure of a sculpted masterpiece.

He speared her with a brief, furious glance. 'Who else were you expecting?' he demanded curtly.

'Certainly not you—you're the last person I expected or wanted to see. Where are you taking me?' she added sharply as she slowly became aware of her surroundings. At that moment the lift halted and the doors opened into an enormous marble-floored room with huge windows on three sides, which allowed sunlight to pour in.

Damon strode across the room, ignoring her attempts to wriggle out of his arms.

'Will you put me down? You have no right to…to man-handle me,' she cried, her breath leaving her body on a sharp gasp when he dropped her unceremoniously onto one of the wide sofas, scattered with brightly coloured cushions, that were grouped beneath the main window.

Instantly she struggled to sit up, her cheeks the same shade of scarlet as the sofa. 'How dare you interrupt my photo shoot? I'm supposed to be working for Tina Theopoulis—whatever will she think? And what are you doing here? Did you know I would be here?'

'Of course I knew. It's taken me two weeks of constantly badgering your agent to arrange the shoot,' he growled.

He loomed over her, big and powerful and so utterly gorgeous that Anna's heart contracted and she felt the familiar sting of tears. Damn him! For a woman who'd once vowed never to cry over a man, she had shed an ocean over him and she hated herself for her weakness.

Nothing horrified her more than the idea that she was turning into the woman her mother had once been—wasting her life and her emotions on a man who didn't deserve them. But she'd missed Damon so much this past month that every day without him had been more agonising than the last. How could she have let it happen? she wondered as she edged off the sofa. How could she have been stupid enough to fall in love with him?

That last thought was so terrifying that she jumped up, only to have him haul her back down onto his lap and imprison her with arms of steel.

'What did you mean when you said you arranged the photo shoot?' she demanded, hastily dragging her eyes from his face. He was too close for comfort. She could feel the warmth emanating from him and the familiar tang of his cologne set her senses alight. 'Are you Tina Theopoulis's financial backer?'

'Yes, but I'm also her brother. Catalina, or Tina as she is sometimes known, is incredibly talented—don't you think?' He absorbed her look of stunned comprehension and gave a wolfish smile, his eyes gleaming with the familiar heated desire that made Anna tremble. 'Diamonds suit you, *pedhaki*

mou,' he murmured softly, sliding his fingers over the ornate necklace at her throat before tipping her head back to claim her mouth in a brief, hard kiss that drove her to the edge of sanity.

Common sense told her she should resist him, but, as was usual when she was in Damon's arms, her brain seemed to lose all power of rational thought and she became a wanton creature, desperately seeking the pleasure his mouth evoked.

Sensing her capitulation, he deepened the kiss until it became a sensual feast that demolished her mental barriers and had her clinging to him, her lips parting helplessly beneath the demanding sweep of his tongue. Finally he lifted his head and stared down at her swollen lips, noting the expression of stunned despair in her eyes. There was still a hell of a way to go, he accepted grimly. But at least she was here, in his arms, and this time he was determined not to let her go.

'Why did you go to such lengths to bring me here?' Anna croaked. She tried to ease off his lap, needing to put some space between her and the temptation he aroused to fasten her mouth on his and lose herself in the exquisite ecstasy of his kiss.

She quickly discovered that her attempts to escape him were futile when he clamped his hands around her like a vice and forced her to remain balanced on his thighs.

'I want some answers—and, as you refused to take any of my calls, kidnapping you was my only alternative,' he told her bluntly.

'Kidnap! You can't possibly believe you can keep me here against my will…' She tailed to a halt, the look in his dark eyes warning her that he intended to do just that. 'My agent will wonder where I am if I don't contact her.'

'I told her to clear your diary for the next month.'

'You've got a damn nerve. This is my career we're talking about.'

'No, our future relationship is the only subject up for discussion,' he said mildly, earning himself a look of such wrath that he had to hide his smile. Angry was good—at least she looked more alive than the pale waif who had looked as though she would snap in the slightest breeze.

'I did answer your first call,' Anna snapped. 'I was glad to hear that your daughter's head injury was not as serious as first believed and that she was recovering well from her bike accident.' She inhaled sharply as a thought struck her. 'The little girl downstairs—that was Ianthe, wasn't it?'

'She's been very excited about your visit ever since I told her about you and she couldn't resist taking a peep,' Damon explained. 'She thinks you look like a princess.'

'But why did you tell her about me? I don't understand what game you're playing, Damon, but it's a dangerous one,' Anna warned. 'I told you the last time we spoke that I won't be drawn into a relationship with you now that I know about your daughter.

'I don't want to be responsible for hurting her like I was hurt when my father walked out,' she added painfully. 'Ianthe is a little girl who needs your full attention and commitment. You have to be there for her and make sure she knows how much you love her. You have to protect her,' she told him fiercely, 'and you can't do that if you're constantly flitting between London and Athens, trying to maintain a long distance affair with me.'

She wiped her hand over her face and was startled to find that her cheeks were wet. Damon had stilled—she could feel the tension in him as he tilted her chin and forced her to meet his gaze.

'Ianthe is in no doubt of my love for her. I would gladly give my life for my daughter. But your father didn't protect you, did he, Anna? That's what all this is about.'

'I don't know what you mean,' Anna lied thickly. She

tried to pull away from him but he cupped her face in his big hand and gently wiped away her tears.

'I spoke to your mother about you.'

'You did *what?*' Anna's eyes flew open. 'How dare you harass members of my family—how did you even know where to find her?'

'It was relatively simple for my private detective to discover that she's living in France with her third husband,' Damon revealed steadily. 'You've never met Charles Aldridge, have you? Your mother couldn't hide her disappointment that you've never visited.' He paused for a moment and then added, 'He seems to be a decent man.'

'Good,' Anna muttered, remembering the promises she'd made to visit her mother's French home, and the last-minute excuses that had prevented her from going.

'A far better choice than her second husband,' Damon said softly. He didn't know what sort of reaction to expect and was unprepared for Anna's violent struggle as she scrambled out of his lap. The patent distress in her navy-blue eyes told him what he already suspected. He knew now who had called her Annie, but for both their sakes he had to make her face her demons.

'Did you know that Philip Stone served a jail sentence for downloading illicit images of young girls onto his computer? I guessed not,' Damon murmured when Anna silently shook her head. 'Your mother left him after he was arrested and immediately started divorce proceedings. She explained that you had already left home by then and, because she didn't want to upset you, she never told you the truth about him. But you knew what he was like, didn't you, *pedhaki mou?* And that was the reason you chose to struggle to live independently at such a young age, rather than return home.'

She was silent for so long that he thought she wouldn't answer, but suddenly she lifted her head. The utter desola-

tion in her eyes made his heart clench and he longed to draw her into his arms, but he knew she would reject him.

'He used to watch me,' she whispered, 'all the time; whatever I was doing in the house, he'd be there, staring at me. At first I thought I was imagining it. I only saw him when I came home from boarding school and I thought maybe I was just being silly.'

She took a deep breath and forced herself to continue. 'But then he started saying things, making personal comments about how my body was developing. I didn't like it, of course—it was embarrassing—but he only did it when we were alone and when Mum was there he was always just normal and friendly.'

'Is that why you didn't say anything to your mother?' Damon asked gently.

'I knew Phil would laugh it off or make out that I was over-imaginative. And Mum was happy. For the first time since my father had left us I actually saw her laughing, after years of watching her crying all the time. I couldn't destroy that happiness,' Anna told him fiercely. 'I would have done anything to see her smile, and my stepfather knew it.

'That was when he started trying to touch me,' she revealed, her face twisting with revulsion as long-buried memories re-surfaced. 'He didn't sexually abuse me in the full sense, but he used to brush against me as if by accident and he delighted in telling me, in grotesque detail, exactly what he'd like to do to me.'

'Where was your real father while all this was going on?' Damon queried tightly, fighting to disguise the anger in his voice that anyone could have treated a vulnerable young girl on the brink of womanhood so appallingly.

'He was busy with his new wife and family,' Anna replied quietly. 'I barely had any contact with him and I was afraid he would accuse me of trying to stir up trouble to gain his attention.'

'So the man you should have been able to depend on most failed to protect you,' Damon murmured, quietly. Suddenly everything made sense. Her father had abandoned her and hadn't been there when she'd desperately needed him. She had been forced to cope alone with her stepfather's foul sexual advances. It was little wonder that she was afraid to trust any man.

Despite the late-evening sunshine spilling into the room, Anna was cold and she wrapped her arms defensively around her body as if to prevent herself from falling apart. This was the first time in her life that she had ever spoken about the trauma she'd suffered at the hands of her stepfather. It was as if the floodgates had opened and the words spilled out of her. 'Philip made me feel dirty,' she admitted huskily. 'He made me believe that sex was disgusting, and, although the sensible part of me knows that can't be true, I still hear his voice in my head.

'When you touch me, try to make love to me, I imagine his hands on my body and I can't bear the knowledge that he's out there somewhere, thinking all those disgusting things about me.'

'But he's not, *pedhaki mou*.' Damon stood and swiftly crossed the room to pull her into his arms. Instantly she stiffened but he held her against the broad strength of his chest and stroked his hand through her hair. 'Philip Stone was killed in a car accident two years ago. Whatever happened in the past is over and he can never hurt you again.'

CHAPTER TEN

'ANNA, are you awake?'

Anna opened her eyes and frowned at the sound of the disembodied voice—before she remembered where she was. 'It's all right, Ianthe, you can come in,' she murmured, smiling sleepily when her bedroom door was cautiously pushed open.

'Papa said I wasn't to wake you,' Damon's daughter admitted anxiously, in the fluent English that she spoke as easily as Greek, 'but we're going to Poros today and I can't wait!'

The little girl flung herself on the bed, her riotous mass of black curls dancing on her shoulders and her dark eyes sparkling with excitement. 'It's going to be great. We're going on Papa's boat and when we get to the island we can go swimming in the sea. You will come swimming with me, won't you?'

'Of course,' Anna promised. Ianthe's enthusiasm was impossible to resist. 'I'm all packed. I'll have a quick shower and then I'll be ready. What's the time?'

'Almost nine o'clock,' Ianthe informed her. 'I wanted to wake you earlier, but Papa said you were tired because sometimes you have bad dreams.' She hopped off the bed and followed Anna into the *en suite* bathroom. 'I used to have

bad dreams about a monster, but Papa told me not to be scared because he would chase all the monsters away. Do you dream about monsters, Anna?'

Anna stared at her reflection in the mirror and realised that her eyes were no longer full of shadows. 'I used to,' she replied honestly, 'but your papa chased my monster away, too.'

'Papa's the best,' Ianthe stated with a degree of adoration in her voice that tugged at Anna's heart. She remembered a time when she'd believed that her father was the most wonderful person in the world, and her feeling of devastation when he'd walked out and left her behind.

Damon was nothing like her father, she acknowledged. He would never abandon his child. It was a week since she had arrived in Greece and discovered that the modelling assignment for Tina Theopoulis had partly been a trick to lure her to Damon's home. In that time she had quickly come to realise that Damon's daughter was a happy, well-adjusted child who was utterly confident of her father's love.

Ianthe would always be Damon's first priority and Anna admired and respected him for his dedication to his daughter. She would never be jealous of his love for his little girl. But the ghost of his dead wife was another matter.

'Are you going to have a very *long* shower?' Ianthe asked in a tone that told Anna she was struggling to hide her impatience.

'Five minutes max,' Anna assured her. 'Where is your papa?'

'Waiting on the terrace. I'll tell him you're almost ready.' Ianthe bounded out of the room and threw a final plea over her shoulder. '*Hurry up,* Anna!'

Ten minutes later Anna had managed to shower, blow-dry her hair and slip into a pair of white jeans and lemon yellow strap top. If she was honest, she was almost as excited about the coming trip as Ianthe and she quickly applied the

minimum of make-up and sprayed her wrists with her favourite perfume before heading for the lift.

She had spent the first few days since Damon's revelation that Philip Stone was dead in a state of shock. It was
hard to accept that the man who had caused her such misery
and mental anguish was gone for good.

Even though she hadn't seen her stepfather for years, the
idea that he was still enjoying his disgusting fantasises about
her had filled her with revulsion. Damon's news had created
a heady sense of relief. She felt as though she had been
released from a life sentence, and the mental barriers that
had prevented her from having a sexual relationship were
slowly disappearing.

As the week had progressed she'd realised that the past
was finally buried and she could look to the future with a
new optimism. The thought of making love with Damon no
longer filled her with fear. Indeed, every time he kissed her
she responded with an eager passion that she hoped would
show him that she was ready for them to become lovers.

But to her frustration he had made no move to take her
to bed. At first she'd thought that the gentle sensitivity he'd
shown her all week was his way of giving her time to come
to terms with the news of her stepfather's death. He was obviously determined not to rush her, she decided, when each
night he escorted her to her room and kissed her until she
was senseless with longing, before politely bidding her good
night and retreating to his own room.

However, as the days and nights slipped past her doubts
grew and she wondered if his seeming reluctance to deepen
their relationship was for another reason. Damon's wife was
dead, but her memory lived on. Every room in the villa was
adorned with her artwork—vibrantly beautiful paintings and
exquisite sculptures that were a lasting legacy to Eleni's incredible talent.

How tragic that the pretty and gifted young woman pictured in the photographs that Ianthe had proudly shown her had died so young, and when she'd had so much to live for, Anna brooded. She didn't doubt that Damon had been deeply in love with his wife, and in Ianthe—who was the image of her mother—he had a visual reminder of all that he had lost.

Eleni was a hard act for any woman to follow and she had no intention of even trying, she accepted when she reached the terrace and saw Damon sitting beneath the shade of the pergola. He'd even admitted that he wasn't looking for another wife. But as her senses flared at the sight of him she wondered if she could cope with a brief affair and emerge unscathed.

'Good morning, Anna—did you sleep well?'

Damon lowered his newspaper and subjected her to a slow appraisal that brought a flush of colour to her cheeks. Although she was one of the most photographed women in the world, her self-confidence was shaky and she couldn't help thinking that she must look pale and uninteresting compared to Eleni's exotic beauty.

'Too well, I'm afraid,' she murmured apologetically. For the first time in years she was able to sleep without fear of the nightmares that had so often plagued her. 'I had no idea it was so late, but I'm ready now,' she added with a smile when she watched Ianthe hop impatiently from foot to foot.

'Good—we'll leave as soon as you've had breakfast.'

'Oh, I'm not hungry,' she said quickly.

'Well, we're not going anywhere until you've eaten, *pedhaki mou*,' Damon told her implacably. 'If you don't wish to disappoint Ianthe, I suggest you sit down and have some fruit and yoghurt.'

'Has anyone ever told you you're the bossiest man in the world?' Anna snapped as she took her place at the table and

forced a smile for the maid who had set a cup of coffee in front of her.

'No one else has ever dared,' Damon admitted with one of the devastating smiles that took her breath away. 'Trust you to break the mould, Anna *mou*.'

The note of gentle affection in his voice, teamed with the warmth in his eyes, made her heart lurch and she hastily tore her gaze from him and helped herself to a selection of fresh fruit.

In faded denims that clung lovingly to his thighs, and a black T-shirt stretched taut over his broad chest, he was awesome. Anna was filled with a crazy urge to lean across the table, snatch his newspaper out of his hands and claim his mouth with her own, in a kiss that would leave him in no doubt of what she wanted.

Now was not the time, she conceded—and with Ianthe present, certainly not the place. She forced herself to swallow a segment of orange but when she dared to glance up again she was shocked by the stark hunger in Damon's eyes before his expression was hidden behind the veil of his thick black lashes.

His heart might belong to Eleni, but he could not disguise his desire for *her*. The knowledge caused liquid heat to course through Anna's veins and she was conscious that her breasts had tightened so that her nipples strained against her thin cotton top. If she had any sense, she would refuse to go to his farmhouse retreat on Poros and instead catch the next flight home. But when had good sense ever triumphed over love? she brooded grimly.

After weeks of desperately trying to ignore her feelings, she could no longer deny the truth. She loved Damon with an intensity that terrified her and, although she knew she should leave while her heart was still intact, the thought of walking away from him was unbearable. Besides, she reassured herself, there was Ianthe to consider.

From the moment Damon had introduced her to his daughter, she'd felt an immediate bond with the little girl. She'd still been reeling from Damon's shocking revelation that Philip Stone was dead, her emotions had been raw, and the innocence of Ianthe's smile had brought home to her the loss of her own childhood at the hands of her stepfather.

She would do everything in her power to protect this child, she realised. But the fact that Ianthe had come to mean so much to her in such a short space of time was something of a shock, and she was aware of an ache of maternal longing that six months ago would have astounded her.

'Would you like another slice of melon, Anna?' Ianthe's voice broke into her thoughts.

'No, thank you, I've had enough breakfast, and I'm sure you've had enough of waiting for me. Shall we see if we can persuade your papa to take us on his boat now?' Anna gave the little girl a conspiratorial wink and pushed her empty bowl towards Damon.

'Satisfied?' she queried.

'Not yet, *pedhaki mou,* but I live in hope,' he replied softly, the gleam in his eyes sending liquid heat scalding through her veins.

He was the Devil's own, she decided as she jumped to her feet, praying that Ianthe would not comment on her scarlet cheeks. But, dear God, she couldn't resist his smouldering sexual promise for much longer and perhaps on Poros— away from this house that was a shrine to his dead wife— she wouldn't have to.

Three days later Anna was willing to believe that she had died and gone to heaven. The island of Poros was a green paradise set in an azure blue sea, and yet it was little more than an hour's boat ride away from noisy, bustling Athens. Damon's holiday retreat was a rustic farmhouse that clung

to a hillside and commanded spectacular views over the island and the sea beyond.

Anna loved the simplicity of the house, which was comfortable but basic, with cool stone floors and whitewashed walls. Unlike the villa in Athens, there were no staff at the farmhouse and she enjoyed the intimacy of helping Damon to prepare their meals while Ianthe set the rough wooden table with cutlery and napkins, and a vase of wild flowers that she had collected.

Playing at families was better than she could ever have anticipated, Anna acknowledged—but playing was all it was. In another few days they would return to Athens. Damon could not take time away from his business indefinitely, and neither could she. There were assignments booked for Australia and the Far East, commitments she must honour, and it was ridiculous to wish for time to stand still so that she could live here with Damon for ever.

With a sigh, she closed her book and rolled over onto her stomach. She had spent the morning on the beach with Ianthe, while Damon put in a couple of hours' work on his laptop. The heat of the midday sun was making her feel sleepy, the sound of the waves lapping the shore hypnotic.

'I hope you're wearing plenty of sunscreen?' A familiar voice sounded in her ear while at the same time something cold hit her back. Uttering a yelp of surprise, she opened her eyes to find Damon kneeling beside her with a bottle of lotion in his hands.

'I can do it myself,' she muttered breathlessly as her senses leapt into vibrant life at the feel of his hands on her sun-warmed skin.

'But you don't have to, *pedhaki mou,* when I'm happy to do it for you,' Damon said equably. 'Hold still, I don't want to get cream on your bikini.' He deftly released the clasp of her bikini top and Anna buried her face in her

arms to stifle a groan when he began to massage cream into her skin.

'Damon!'

He splayed his fingers on her back and then over her ribcage until he reached the soft swell of her breast. For a few mindless seconds she was tempted to turn over so that he could cup her breasts fully in his big hands. Maybe he would stroke his fingers across her nipples, or even push her bikini aside to take one engorged peak into his mouth.

Heat pooled between her thighs. She felt hot with desire. Did he have any idea what he was doing to her? She opened her eyes and noted the savage hunger in his with an element of satisfaction. This desperate longing was not hers alone. The sexual chemistry that had smouldered between them since their arrival on Poros was at combustion point, but this was a public beach and Ianthe was about.

'It's hell, isn't it?' Damon murmured in a matter of fact voice that was at variance with the slumberous sensuality of his gaze. He refastened her bikini with hands that shook slightly. 'I'm just thankful that the sea is so cold. As you may have noticed, Anna *mou*, I spend a lot of time in it, trying to exorcise my more basic desires.'

Anna sat up and calmly met his gaze. The patience and sensitivity he'd shown her since she'd confided in him about her stepfather was humbling. He would never hurt her—or not physically, at any rate. Emotionally was a different matter. He didn't love her and never would, but he cared for her, she would swear by it. She meant more to him than his previous mistresses. The very fact that he had introduced her to Ianthe and the rest of his family was proof of that.

He had sworn that he would not rush her, and even here on Poros, where they had spent every waking minute of each day consumed with a blistering awareness of each

other, he was still waiting for her to give him some sign that she was ready to take their relationship to a physical level.

She stared at his face, noting the slant of his heavy brows, the strong nose and the sensual curve of his mouth. Love had caught her unawares and trapped her in its silken web. She didn't want to love him. She'd spent her life vowing that she would never repeat the mistakes her mother had made and leave herself open to the anguish of rejection. But love, she had discovered, had a will of its own.

If she walked away from him now, she would leave her heart behind. She had spent the years since she'd left home meticulously planning every aspect of her life, until Damon had crashed into it. He had torn down her defences, but she was no longer afraid to admit that she needed him.

He would be her first and only lover. How could any other man come close to him? It was time to be daring, to live for the here and now and stop looking to the future where almost inevitably, one day, they would part.

Acting on impulse, she swung her legs round so that she was kneeling on the sand in front of him and gave him an impish smile. 'I can think of several other ways of exorcising those desires, Damon,' she told him softly. 'And none of them involve swimming in the cold sea.'

For a moment he stiffened and she watched the way his broad chest heaved with the effort of drawing air into his lungs. 'Would you care to elaborate, *pedhaki mou?*'

He had lowered his head so that his mouth hovered millimetres from hers and, uttering a low cry, she closed the space between them to claim his lips in a kiss that pierced his soul. For the first time Anna held nothing back. She wanted no more doubts or misunderstandings and she responded to the tentative sweep of his tongue by parting her lips and drawing him into her.

Passion ripped through them with the ferocity of a flame set to tinder. She heard Damon mutter something in Greek before his arms closed around her and he dragged her up against the solid wall of his chest. One hand tangled in her hair while the other roamed up and down her spine, forcing her hips into burning contact with his so that she was made achingly aware of the power of his arousal.

Finally, when she didn't think she could withstand much more without dragging him down onto the sand and begging him to take her, he eased the pressure of his mouth on hers until the kiss was a gentle caress on her swollen lips.

'Are you sure, Anna?' he demanded rawly, the huskiness of his tone warning her of his tenuous hold on his self-control. 'We don't have to rush. I'm prepared to wait—'

'But I'm not,' she interrupted him softy, placing her finger across his lips. 'I want you, Damon. When you encouraged me to talk about what happened with my stepfather, and then revealed that he can no longer hurt me, or any other vulnerable young girl—you set me free. I no longer feel dirty or ashamed. I feel beautiful, not because of my life in front of the camera, but because you make me feel beautiful. I want to thank you,' she whispered. She linked her arms around his neck but Damon gripped her wrists.

'You don't have to thank me—certainly not like this,' he told her fiercely, his eyes so dark that she thought she would drown in their depths. 'When we make love, I want it to be because you are *hungry* with desire for me, not because you feel you owe me the pleasure of your body to repay a debt.'

The raw emotion in his gaze made her heart clench with love. Even now, when his big, powerful body was trembling with need for her, he was still determined to protect her. She had to bite her lip to prevent herself from spilling out how

much he meant to her and instead she ran her hand over his chest, following the path of dark hairs that arrowed over his stomach, until she reached the waistband of his shorts.

'I'm hungry now, Damon,' she whispered provocatively and heard him growl deep in his throat. His face was a taut mask, desire etched onto every sharp angle and plane, but instead of taking up the invitation of her soft lips he reached out and smoothed her hair back from her temple.

'Your timing leaves a lot to be desired, Anna *mou*,' he teased gently. Ianthe's voice drifted towards them on the breeze and Anna watched as the desire in his gaze slowly faded and was replaced with rueful amusement.

'When are we having lunch, Papa? I'm starving,' Ianthe announced as she threw herself down on the sand, blithely unaware of the simmering tension in the air.

'Me, too,' Damon murmured beneath his breath so that only Anna heard the heartfelt words. Suddenly the sun seemed to shine brighter and the sea was a more intense blue. Her senses were acutely aware of the salt tang in the air, the mew of a seagull circling above them and the lambent warmth in Damon's eyes.

'There's plenty of time,' she whispered, feeling as though her heart would burst when he lifted her hand to his mouth and grazed his lips across her knuckles.

'All the time in the world,' he promised with a smile that filled her with joy and a tiny flame of hope that she could actually mean something to him.

After lunch they took the boat out on a leisurely cruise around the island before mooring in a tiny, deserted cove where Ianthe could swim to her heart's content. They returned to the farmhouse as the sun was setting and Anna showered and changed into a delicate chiffon dress with narrow shoulder straps and a tiered skirt in soft shades of

green. The colour looked good against her golden tan and she felt a thrill of feminine pleasure when she stood back to inspect her reflection.

The sun had lightened her hair to platinum blonde and she caught it up in a loose knot on top of her head, leaving a few tendrils to frame her face. A coat of mascara to darken her lashes and a touch of pink gloss on her lips was the only make-up she needed, and she was spraying perfume on her pulse points when there was a tap on her door.

'You look…exquisite.' Damon paused in the doorway, unable to hide his reaction to her as streaks of colour ran along the sharp line of his cheekbones. She had never seen him looking anything other than supremely self-confident and the realisation that he too could be feeling vulnerable and unsure tore at her heart.

'Thank you—you're looking pretty good yourself. Almost good enough to eat,' she added, her eyes dancing with mischief and another emotion that made Damon long to forget dinner and simply draw her into his arms.

'Hold that thought,' he bade her urgently. 'I thought just the two of us could go out tonight. The family in the beach-front house are old friends who are happy for Ianthe to stay with them for a couple of hours.'

'Have you asked Ianthe what she'd like to do?' Anna walked over to him and calmly met his gaze. 'I know she will always be the most important person in your life, Damon. It's as it should be and I wouldn't want it any other way. I certainly don't want her to feel that I'm pushing her out. I know how that feels,' she added huskily. 'I think it would be nice if we all dined out together.'

'You take my breath away, do you know that?' he replied quietly, his eyes darkening with admiration. 'You suffered a hellish childhood, but instead of being bitter and resentful you spend much of your time and energy raising money for

children's charities. You have incredible patience with my daughter and I thank you, *pedhaki mou.*' He dropped a brief, tantalising kiss on her mouth and moved towards the door. 'I'd better tell Ianthe to get changed. She's been desperate for an opportunity to wear her new dress.'

They ate in a little taverna overlooking the harbour. Anna had dined in exclusive restaurants around the world, but she'd never enjoyed a meal more than in the friendly ambience of the family-run taverna.

Conscious of Ianthe's presence, she kept her conversation with Damon light and innocuous, but she was aware of the far more intimate message in his eyes and her excitement grew. Tonight she would give herself to him completely. The thought no longer filled her with fear, but a heady sense of anticipation that made her eyes sparkle and brought a flush of rosy colour to her cheeks.

'Would you like more wine?' he asked towards the end of the meal.

'I'd better not; it makes me sleepy.'

'Definitely not in that case—I want you wide awake and conscious of every kiss and stroke and lick and bite when I make love to you.'

'Damon!' Anna gasped. Ianthe had jumped down from the table and was watching the boats bobbing in the harbour, but she was afraid the little girl might overhear. 'You're embarrassing me.'

'I hope not,' he replied, suddenly serious. 'There is nothing embarrassing or disgusting about the act of love, *pedhaki mou.* I want to honour you with my body and give you more pleasure than you've ever known.'

His words caused a delicious shiver to run the length of Anna's spine and she moistened her suddenly dry lips with her tongue. 'Right—actually, shall we go? Ianthe seems to

have finished and I couldn't eat another thing,' she said hurriedly, trying to ignore Damon's soft chuckle.

They walked hand in hand back across the beach while Ianthe ran on ahead, laughing as she dodged the waves.

'Straight up to bed, young lady,' Damon bade his daughter when they reached the farmhouse. 'Say good night to Anna.'

In reply, Ianthe wrapped her arms around Anna's waist and squeezed. 'I'm glad you're here, Anna. We're having a lovely time, aren't we?'

'We certainly are,' Anna agreed. 'Good night, darling, I'll see you in the morning.'

Damon followed Ianthe up the narrow stairs to her bedroom in the eaves. The master bedroom and guest room were on the floor below and Anna hesitated on the landing, her heart thudding in her chest as she debated which room to enter, before she made her decision.

Ten minutes later Damon found her in his room, staring out over the bay where the moonlight dappled the sea with silvery fingers. 'She was asleep the moment her head touched the pillow,' he murmured.

'I'm not surprised after all the swimming she's done today.' A little of Anna's tension eased and she smiled fondly at the thought of the child whom she was quickly growing to love. She was aware of Damon crossing the room to slide his arms around her waist and draw her up against his chest. He trailed a line of kisses along her neck and she gasped when she felt him nip her earlobe.

'You see, I told you biting can be pleasurable,' he teased. He turned her in his arms and trapped her gaze, the gentle warmth in his eyes demolishing her nerves. 'I understand the legacy of fear your stepfather inflicted on you and you have my word that I won't demand more of you than you are prepared to give,' he promised. 'The moment you want me to stop, just say so, Anna.'

His mouth hovered above hers, tantalisingly close. She wasn't worried about him stopping, she just wanted him to start, Anna thought desperately as she wound her arms around his neck. 'Just kiss me, Damon,' she muttered, and he needed no further encouragement.

He captured her mouth and initiated a sensual exploration that left her in no doubt of his hunger for her. Helplessly she tipped her head back and welcomed the thrust of his tongue between her lips while he dragged her hard up against his thighs and made her aware of the throbbing power of his arousal.

Slowly he slid the strap of her dress over her shoulder, followed by the other, and then peeled the material down to reveal her breasts. Anna could not repress a shiver when he cupped each soft mound in his palms and held her breath when he delicately stroked his thumb pads over her tight nipples.

Sensation flooded through her and she moaned when he trailed his lips over the pulse that was beating frantically at the base of her throat, down, down until finally he was where she wanted him to be. The stroke of his tongue sent pleasure spiralling through her and she clutched his hair and held his head against her breast while he took her nipple into his mouth.

By the time he had metered the same exquisite punishment on its twin, she was trembling so much that her legs could barely support her. Damon must have sensed it and he swept her into his arms and carried her over to the bed where he carefully laid her on the cool sheets.

Anna watched, wide-eyed, when he unbuttoned his shirt. The sun had darkened his skin to bronze and the hard muscles of his abdomen rippled beneath the covering of wiry black hairs when he shrugged the shirt over his shoulders and dropped it to the floor. He paused fractionally and then moved his hand to the zip of his trousers.

Anna swallowed but could not drag her eyes from him as the trousers joined his shirt and he stood before her, his silk boxers struggling to conceal the jutting length of his manhood.

'Are you afraid of me, Anna?' he queried huskily.

Slowly she shook her head. She was awed, yes. Slightly apprehensive of what was to come, especially when faced with the magnificent proof of how much he desired her. But she did not fear him.

Silently she opened her arms and he moved towards the bed. When he tugged the folds of her dress down, she obligingly lifted her hips, although she hesitated when he hooked his fingers in the waistband of her knickers. He held her gaze as he slowly drew them over her silky smooth thighs, and only when he felt that he had her full confidence did he allow his eyes to move over her naked beauty.

'You are so very lovely, Anna *mou*,' he muttered when he joined her on the bed and claimed her mouth in kiss that quickly became a sensual feast. Anna twisted restlessly beneath him when he trailed a moist path across each breast before sliding lower, over her flat stomach where he paused to dip his tongue into her navel.

The sensations he aroused were new and faintly shocking, and she felt liquid heat pool between her thighs. She inhaled sharply when his dark head moved lower still. Surely he wouldn't…?

He would, and did—gently nudging her legs apart so that he could use his tongue in the most intimate caress she had ever experienced. Anna cried out and frantically tugged his hair, trying to make him stop.

It felt so good. She had never believed it possible to feel such intense pleasure and after a moment she let go of his hair and dug her fingers into his shoulders as if she needed to anchor herself to something solid. She remembered his

teasing comments about licking her. Dear God, she had never expected that he would use his tongue quite so thoroughly.

But her ability to think rationally was disappearing beneath the waves of sensation that were building inexorably, causing her to arch her hips in mute supplication for him to continue his mastery. The ache inside her overwhelmed any other consideration and demolished any lingering fears that her stepfather had induced. She wanted Damon deep inside her. Only he could appease her desperate need.

With a cry of frustration she reached down and sought to drag his boxers over his hips. She wanted to feel him push against her without the barrier of fine silk. But as he moved slightly to aid her a sharp, high-pitched scream shattered the sexual haze that enveloped them.

'Ianthe!' Damon muttered a savage curse in his own tongue and sat up, dragging air into his lungs. Never in his life had he resented his adored daughter, but right now he would happily ignore her fearful cry.

'Papa, Papa, come quickly!'

'I'll have to go to her,' he said harshly as he forced himself to get up from the bed and move away from the temptation of Anna's long, slender limbs that only moments before he had imagined her wrapping around him. 'She's probably had a nightmare.'

Ianthe screamed again and Anna's blood ran cold. She remembered what it felt like to wake in the night, heart pumping with fear as demons haunted her. Something had plainly terrified the little girl and they couldn't leave her.

She swung her legs over the side of the bed, suddenly acutely conscious of her nakedness. Damon had pulled on a robe and she hastily reached for his shirt to cover herself. 'Of course you must go,' she assured him as Ianthe's sobs echoed through the house. 'I'll get her a drink.'

When she entered the attic bedroom a few minutes later, she found Ianthe huddled on the bed and Damon half under it.

'Spider,' he answered her silent query when he lifted his head.

'Have you caught it, Papa?' Ianthe asked tearfully.

'Not yet, *kyria*. I think it's run away. It's probably deaf,' he added, struggling to hide his impatience.

'I don't want to go to sleep when it's under my bed.' More tears fell and he groaned.

'I'll get the torch and have another look,' he muttered and strode out of the bedroom, leaving Anna to deal with Ianthe.

'It was that big,' the little girl assured Anna seriously, spreading her hands to demonstrate the size of the creature. 'I hate spiders and I want to go home.'

Following her natural instincts, Anna wrapped her arms around the sobbing child and gently rocked her until she began to relax. 'I'm sure it's gone now, darling. Let's think about all the lovely things we're going to do tomorrow.' The ploy worked and she watched in satisfaction as Ianthe's eyes grew heavy while she planned the next day's activities.

'Are you feeling better now?' she queried softly. She pulled the sheet up to Ianthe's chin and stroked her curls. 'You don't really want to go home, do you? You love it here on Poros.'

The child gave a sleepy nod. 'Papa loves it here, too. Poros is his favourite place in the whole world—that's why he brought my mama here for their honeymoon. Do you think she liked it here, Anna?'

'I'm sure she did,' Anna replied quietly, fighting to control the sudden feeling of nausea that had swept over her. Unlike at the villa in Athens, there were none of Eleni's paintings or sculptures in the farmhouse. The lack of visual reminders of Damon's first wife was one reason why she had felt so relaxed here, Anna acknowledged sickly. It was a shock to

discover that the farmhouse itself was a shrine to Eleni's memory and the love that Damon had once shared with her.

Ianthe had fallen back to sleep and she tiptoed out of the room to bump into Damon on the landing.

'Sorry I was so long—I couldn't find the damn torch.'

'It's all right. Ianthe's gone to sleep now—and I'd like to do the same.' She could not bring herself to meet his gaze and stared determinedly at the floor. She heard him sigh and sensed the moment he reached out to touch her. *'Don't, please...I can't...not now,'* she pleaded. 'I just want to go to bed—alone.'

'Of course.' Damon's tone was politely neutral but his expression was grim. 'I'm sorry, Anna, but the reality of having a child is that sometimes they need you at the most inopportune moments.'

She paused in the doorway to her room and stared at him. 'I appreciate that.'

'Do you? Are you sure you're not punishing me for putting the concerns of my daughter over you?' he demanded bitterly. 'Because, like it or not, that's the way it has to be. I thought you were different. I thought you understood.'

'I do,' Anna cried, but her words were drowned out by the sound of Damon slamming his bedroom door savagely behind him.

CHAPTER ELEVEN

'ANNA—over here, sweetheart! Give us a smile. Have you got anything to say regarding the rumours about you and the pop star Mitch Travis?'

Anna flicked the photographer an icy stare, guaranteed to freeze even the most determined members of the press pack who were tailing her through Sydney Airport. She was dressed head to toe in designer clothes. Her face was exquisitely made up—her lips coated in a chic pale gloss while her hair was swept up into a severe knot on top of her head. The finished effect was as she had intended; an elegant, aloof Ice Princess who would never reveal to the paparazzi that her heart was breaking.

At the check-in desk she subjected the hapless reporter to a final look of haughty disdain before sweeping into the departure lounge, followed by her entourage of assistants. The past three weeks in Australia had been hell, which was in no way the fault of the vast continent or its people, she conceded grimly.

She would give anything to be back on Poros with Damon, but after their acrimonious parting it was unlikely that he would ever want to see her again.

She had spent the remainder of the night after Ianthe had disturbed them torn between a desperate desire to knock on

Damon's bedroom door and wrestling with the bitter knowledge that she could never compete with the ghost of his dead wife.

Poros would always be a special place for her and Damon—or so she'd believed—a paradise island where they had spent precious time together and first consummated their relationship. Except that they hadn't.

It had hurt immeasurably to discover that he had done it all before. No doubt he had once eaten in the taverna by the harbour with Eleni, and together they would have explored the many coves and beaches of the island. Had he made love to his wife for the first time in the master bedroom of the farmhouse? The same bed where *she* had been so eager to give herself to him. Perhaps he had even been thinking about his honeymoon night while he'd made love to her, and imagined that it was Eleni he was holding in his arms.

Jealousy was a corrosive poison that had scarred much of her mother's life. She could not allow it to ruin hers. If she felt this bad about a ghost, how would she cope when Damon's attention began to stray?

It would kill her, she had accepted bleakly. She loved him so much that the idea of him even looking at another woman would destroy her and she would become clingy and obsessive, just as her mother had been. Walking away from him now, while she still had the strength of will, was the only answer.

But when she had broken the untruth the following morning, that the date of her assignment in Australia had been brought forward, Damon had not bothered to hide his anger.

'You can't just leave,' he hissed furiously, conscious that Ianthe was in earshot. 'Whatever the reason for your change of heart, between the time you were a wild temptress in my arms, and now, I won't let you go.'

'You can't stop me,' she replied, closing her heart to the silent plea in his eyes. 'This is work, Damon, my career, which will always be my first priority, as Ianthe is yours.'

'Is that what this is all about?' he asked scathingly. 'You resent the fact that I have a child now that you've spent time with us and discovered the reality of parenthood.'

'I do not. That's a foul thing to say. I know how much you love her and I...I'm fond of her, too.'

'Then why are you so determined to hurt her? Because you're not just leaving Poros, are you, Anna? You're leaving me for good and running out on our relationship.'

'In all honesty, how can we have a relationship?' Anna flung at him. 'The most we could hope for is a brief fling when our hectic schedules happen to coincide. I don't want to live like that, Damon, and that's why I've decided to end it now.'

For a moment he'd seemed totally stunned. His face was ashen and the torment in his eyes sowed the first seeds of doubt in Anna's mind. Maybe he did care. Maybe she'd got it wrong. 'Do you have any other suggestions?' she asked quietly, knowing that it was ridiculous to wish for some indication of commitment from him, but wishing anyway.

'You could give up modeling, for a start, or at least cut down on your assignments. You don't need to work, *pedhaki mou*. I will take care of you,' he murmured, sliding his arms around her waist and drawing her close.

For an infinitesimal second Anna was tempted to lay her head on his chest and give in—allow him to take over her life. She knew he would do as he said. No doubt he would install her in an elegant Athens apartment, conveniently close to his own home, where he would visit several times a week—perhaps even pop in during his lunch hour for a quickie, she thought cynically. Common sense quickly reasserted itself and she stepped away from him.

'That's your idea of a compromise? I give up everything that I've worked for and you give up what, exactly? I'm sorry, Damon, but I will never give up my career or my financial independence for any man, even you.'

He gave up then, his face seemingly hewn from stone while she bade a heart-wrenching farewell to Ianthe and evaded the issue of when she would be coming back. He was silent on the trip to the harbour but as she was about to step onto the ferry he caught hold of her shoulder and spun her round, sliding a hand beneath her chin to force her to look at him.

'This is not over, Anna,' he told her fiercely. 'I don't know what you want from me. I suspect you don't even know yourself. But when you've worked it out, I'll be waiting for you.'

He swooped before she had time to react, capturing her mouth in a savage, possessive kiss that demanded her response. Anna clung to him helplessly, while her heart splintered into a thousand shards. How could she tell him that she knew exactly what she wanted from him, when it was the one thing he could not give?

His heart belonged to the beautiful, gifted Greek girl who had given birth to his precious daughter. He had chosen Eleni for his wife and even now, years after her death, he surrounded himself with her artwork as if he could not bear to let her go.

She would only ever be a poor second, Anna acknowledged despairingly. And although she loved him more than life—that was something she could not bear.

The flight to Paris seemed to last for ever. Anna was thankful that she was able to travel in business class, which offered a degree of comfort and room to stretch her long legs. First class travel was one of the many perks of her job but over

the last three weeks she'd concluded that she would even be prepared to sacrifice her precious career, if only Damon loved her.

At the airport in Paris she collected a hire car and, having left the city, spent a frustrating few hours trying to negotiate the narrow roads of rural northern France in search of her mother's remote *gîte*. Dusk was falling by the time she pulled up in a small courtyard and stared at the farmhouse that her mother shared with her third husband.

Damon had said that Charles Aldridge was a decent man, and for Judith's sake she hoped he was right, Anna thought as she eased her tired body out of the car. She didn't understand this sudden urgency to see her mother. They hadn't been close for years but she was falling apart and she needed someone to salvage the splinters of her heart.

'Anna! What are you doing here? Not that you're not welcome, of course,' Judith Christiansen—now Aldridge— babbled when she opened the door. 'It's so wonderful to see you, darling. I'd almost given up hope that you would ever visit.' She caught hold of Anna's hand and led her into the house. 'You must meet Charles. He's still working in the garden—I'll just call him.'

Judith turned and gave Anna a joyous smile. 'I suppose that lovely man of yours brought you. He promised he would try and persuade you to visit. Where is he?' As she glanced expectantly at the door Anna frowned.

'Which man?'

'Damon, of course,' her mother replied in a tone that suggested there could be no other man in Anna's life. 'He was so concerned about you when he visited a month or so ago. And he was so sympathetic when I explained about my divorce from your father. He seemed to understand how much it had affected you.' She stared in bemusement at the tears that were streaming down Anna's cheeks. 'What is it, darling?

Have you rowed? I'm sure you can sort it out. Damon loves you very much.'

'He doesn't,' Anna wept, unable to hide her inner anguish any longer. 'He's still in love with his first wife. His house is full of mementoes of her and he even took me to the place where he spent his honeymoon. She was so beautiful and clever, and I can't compete with her memory.'

'Don't be silly. I don't believe you have to compete with anyone,' Judith told her firmly as she put an arm around her shoulders and hugged her. 'I may not have been very successful in the choice of my first two husbands—this may come as a shock, but Philip Stone wasn't the charming man I first thought,' she confided, unaware of the shaft of pain that crossed Anna's face. 'But I do know love when I see it. And I saw it in Damon's eyes when he spoke of you,' she assured Anna firmly.

'Now, come and have something to eat. You're much too thin—I don't suppose you've been eating properly. After that you can have a bath and bed and in the morning you'll see that whatever has happened is just a lovers' tiff. I don't know anything about Damon's first wife, but I'm quite certain that you're the woman he loves now.'

Anna stood in the middle of the kitchen and buried her face in her hands. 'I think I may have made a terrible mistake,' she whispered. 'But I'm so afraid of becoming jealous and possessive like…' She halted abruptly so that her words hovered in the embarrassed silence.

'Like I was,' Judith finished the sentence for her. 'Oh, Anna, there are so many things I should have explained to you,' she said sadly. 'For most of my adult life I've suffered from a severe depressive illness, which thankfully is now controlled by medication. But for many years I struggled to deal with my feelings alone,' she admitted.

'There were times during your childhood when I was

paranoid and obsessive, and your father found it difficult to cope. The truth is, I drove Lars away, but it wasn't until all these years later, and thanks to Charles's wonderful support, that I've been able to accept that I was partly to blame for the collapse of my first marriage.'

Judith wiped her eyes with a hand that shook slightly. The betraying gesture tore at Anna's heart as for the first time she recognised her mother's fragility. She must have been an ideal target for Philip Stone—a vulnerable single mother with a young daughter in tow, Anna acknowledged bitterly.

The realisation lifted the resentment she had felt all these years, that her mother was in some way to blame for what had happened with her stepfather. Judith must have believed she was doing the best for her child by providing her with a father-figure—unaware that the man she had married was a monster. It would destroy her if she ever discovered how Anna had suffered at the hands of jolly Uncle Phil.

She would never tell her mother, Anna vowed. It was in the past and now Phil was dead and could no longer hurt anyone. Damon was the only person to know her secret and it was thanks to him that she had finally overcome the fears her stepfather had instilled in her.

Damon had shown her nothing but patience and incredible sensitivity but she had thrown it back in his face.

'I have to go to Greece,' she muttered dazedly. She didn't know if it was love that Judith had seen in Damon's eyes, but suddenly she didn't care. The last three weeks without him had been so unutterably miserable that she was prepared to risk her pride by admitting how much she loved him.

Maybe he would always care for Eleni, but he couldn't make love to a memory.

'I'm sorry, Mum, but I can't stop. I promise to return soon though. I have to go back to Damon and…'

'And tell him you love him,' her mother agreed gently. 'I

suppose it's useless trying to persuade you to stay the night, so I'd better drive you to the airport.'

The offices of Kouvaris Construction were in the heart of Athens. Anna stepped out of the heat of the late-summer sunshine into the cool interior of the reception area. Her heart was beating in time with the staccato tap of her stiletto heels on the marble floor as she strode past the startled receptionist and into the lift.

She had already elicited from Damon's sister that he was at work and that his office was on the top floor. Tina had also warned that her brother's mood had been grim ever since he'd returned from Poros and suggested that Anna was the only person who could make him smile again.

Somehow that seemed unlikely, Anna brooded when the lift halted at the top floor. She had carefully planned what she wanted to say to him, but now the time was here and her confidence was draining away faster than water down a plug-hole.

Taking a deep breath, she smiled at the elegant woman who she guessed was Damon's secretary, and marched briskly towards his office. The woman said something in Greek that probably translated to Damon did not want to be disturbed, but Anna ignored the warning and pushed open the door.

He looked tired and curiously dejected, with no sign of his usual wonderful arrogance, she noted when she stared greedily at him, feeling her body's instinctive response to his raw masculinity. He must have heard the click of the door but did not bother to lift his head as he growled a terse comment in Greek.

'Hello, Damon.'

She didn't know what she had been expecting and was shocked at the look of savage pain in his eyes, before his

thick lashes fell, concealing his emotions. For those few brief seconds she had looked into his heart and relief crashed over her, making her legs feel decidedly wobbly.

'Anna. What a…pleasant surprise,' he said coolly. 'Why arc you here?'

It was typical of Damon to ignore social niceties and go straight for the kill, Anna acknowledged ruefully. 'Can't you guess?' she asked.

'I gave up trying to fathom the intricacies of your mind long ago. Why don't you just tell me and save time for both of us?' He leaned back in his chair and surveyed her boldly, as if he were a sultan inspecting his latest concubine.

Once Anna would have felt self-conscious, but now she calmly met his gaze. Her skirt was shorter than she normally wore, revealing her long, slender legs in their sheer black hose. She watched in fascination the stain of colour that ran along Damon's cheekbones when his eyes slid all the way down to her heels.

Desire, the fierce chemistry that had always existed between them, still glittered in his dark eyes. It was a start, she thought. Passion was as powerful an emotion as love and if necessary she would use it to tie him to her until he no longer knew where passion ended and love began.

She sauntered across the room, unfastening the buttons of her jacket as she went. 'Perhaps this will give you some clue as to why I'm here,' she murmured. She shrugged the jacket over her shoulders and let it slip to the floor. Beneath it she was wearing nothing but a black lacy bra that cupped the creamy swell of her breasts. She shook back her hair and heard Damon inhale sharply, although his expression remained impassive.

With slow deliberation she unzipped her skirt and wriggled her hips to ease its path down over her thighs. The whole concept of peeling off her layers of clothing was in-

credibly liberating. Damon had freed her from the belief that her body was somehow sinful. She was proud of her breasts and her narrow waist and her endlessly long legs, and from the heat in his gaze he appreciated every one of her feminine curves.

That appreciation was not mirrored in his voice. 'Very nice,' he drawled in a tone of supreme indifference. 'Your Aussie lover is a lucky boy.'

'Who?' Anna stared at him, plainly bemused.

'Midge, or whatever he calls himself. The insect with the long hair and bug eyes.'

'You mean Mitch Travis, lead singer of Australia's biggest pop group.' Anna shook her head as realisation dawned. 'You're jealous!'

Damon did not deign to reply but the fury in his gaze should have sent her running for cover.

'For your information, I happened to be standing next to Mitch at a film première and the press immediately concocted the story that we're having an affair. In my world, it happens all the time.'

'I do not like your world,' Damon growled, sounding very Greek.

'Nothing happened,' she assured him as joy bubbled within her. He was jealous. That had to mean something. 'The only man I'll ever want is you.'

She leaned forwards, caught hold of his tie and pulled him towards her, seeking his mouth with newfound confidence. For a few nerve-racking seconds he remained stiff and unyielding before he wrapped his arms around her and dragged her down onto his knee.

'Anna *mou,* I don't think I can take much more of this,' he groaned when he finally lifted his head to stare at her softly swollen mouth and the slumberous desire in her eyes. 'I love you—' the words were wrenched from his soul

'—more than I believed it possible to love another human being. But my need for you is tearing me apart.'

His face twisted with emotion and Anna traced a shaky hand over his jaw. 'But I thought…' She broke off as joy unfurled within her like the petals of a flower opening to the sun. 'Oh, Damon, I love you, too. With all my heart,' she vowed fiercely, her eyes glistening with the emotions she no longer had to hide.

'Then why did you leave me?' he groaned. 'That night on Poros when Ianthe was frightened by the spider, you were so cold and distant and I knew then that I was losing you. But I can't change the fact that I have a child.'

'I love Ianthe almost as much as I love you,' Anna assured him softly. She flushed shamefacedly. 'I could never resent her, but I found it hard to deal with the fact that you're still in love with her mother.

'Ianthe told me that night that you had spent your honeymoon at the farmhouse on Poros,' she added.

'Did she?' Damon frowned. 'It's true that I took Eleni to Poros, but we stayed at a friend's villa on the other side of the island. I only bought the farmhouse a couple of years ago as somewhere to take Ianthe and I told her about the honeymoon because I think it's important for her to know as many details as possible about her mother.'

'Eleni died a long time ago,' he said quietly. 'For Ianthe's sake I will always remember her, which is why I have all her artwork on display in the villa. I loved her, yes,' he agreed, tightening his arms around Anna to foil her bid for escape. 'She was a sweet girl. We met soon after the death of my parents and I suppose I wanted to recreate a sense of family. But my sadness was for the loss of a young life and when I think of her now, it is with affection. You are the love of my life, *pedhaki mou*. Together with Ianthe you are my reason for living.'

He sought her mouth with tender passion that quickly developed to an inferno of desire. The last three weeks without him had been purgatory, Anna thought as she wound her arms around his neck and parted her lips to savour the wicked sorcery of his tongue.

'I am a man of action rather than words,' Damon growled as his glorious arrogance bounced back. 'I need to show you how much you mean to me before I explode!'

He stood and carried her over to a door on the other side of his office. 'Sometimes if I've been working late, I sleep here,' he told her when he nudged the door open with his shoulder and strode over to the bed. The room was functional rather than decorative and he gave her a rueful glance. 'It's not the most romantic venue for your first time, *pedhaki mou*. If you prefer, we could check into a hotel.'

'No time,' Anna muttered feverishly as she fumbled with his shirt buttons. 'I want you to make love to me now. I can't wait. And I have no intention of lying here admiring the décor.'

The undisguised hunger in her eyes was all the encouragement Damon needed to strip down to his boxers with record speed. He hesitated for a moment and trapped her gaze while his hand moved to the waistband.

'Please, I want to see you,' she whispered, wetting her dry lips with the tip of her tongue.

Her plea almost sent him over the edge and when he shrugged out of his underwear the solid length of his arousal jutted proudly forwards.

'You are so beautiful,' Anna whispered, her faint apprehension fading as she absorbed the latent power of his muscle bound body. He was her Greek god and she was impatient to feel him inside her. Already she could feel the flood of warmth between her thighs and when he stretched out beside her she drew his head down and initiated a kiss that stirred his soul.

He removed her bra with fingers that shook slightly and cradled her breasts with gentle reverence before lowering his head to anoint each nipple with his lips. Anna moaned and arched her back, silently pleading for more. She felt him skim his hand over her flat stomach to the tiny triangle of black lace and lifted her hips so that he could remove her knickers.

Her slender body was naked except for the sheer black stockings that contrasted starkly against her pale flesh. Damon muttered a harsh imprecation and traced the wide band of lace at the junction between her thighs before pushing her legs apart with an edge of roughness that warned of his urgent desire to push deep inside her.

Anna felt no fear, only pleasure when he stroked her and then gently eased his fingers into her to perform an erotic dance that made her tremble. Only when he was sure that she was completely relaxed did he slide his hands beneath her bottom to angle her in readiness to receive him. She felt his hard length rub against the opening to her vagina and stretched her legs wider, eager to be one with the one man who had captured her heart.

'I love you, Anna *mou*.' The words were torn from him as he slowly entered her and then paused when he felt the fragile barrier of her virginity. 'I don't want to hurt you,' he muttered hoarsely, his face a rigid mask as he sought to retain control.

'You won't. I trust you, my love,' she whispered and lifted her hips towards him, tensed for a second and dug her nails into his shoulders as her muscles stretched around him, then relaxed when he eased in deep and filled her.

He claimed her lips with the same tender passion with which he had claimed her body and began to move, slowly at first and then, when she learned his rhythm, faster, deeper so that the sensations he aroused in her grew ever more intense.

'Damon!' She called his name as the waves of pleasure built inexorably, taking her higher and higher until she was poised at the edge of some magical place that she had never known existed. The agonising tension that gripped her was suddenly and shatteringly released in a tumultuous wave of pleasure that seemed impossible to withstand.

In the recesses of her mind she heard Damon cry out, a harsh, feral sound so that she instinctively clung to him as his big body shuddered and he drove into her one last time.

Breathing hard, he rested his forehead against hers and felt the wetness on her cheeks. 'Are you all right?' he asked desperately.

'I love you.' She placed a finger over his lips and blinked away her tears.

'You know I'll never let you go? You'll have to marry me, *agape mou*. Please,' he added huskily when she stared at him with wide, stunned eyes. 'Make me the happiest man in the world? I know your career is important to you and I respect your choice to work, but perhaps you could be based in Athens rather than England. I admit that I'll hate it when you're away on assignments,' he added honestly, 'but I'll be waiting for you every time you come home.'

The last of Anna's lingering doubts disappeared and with it her old fear of not being financially dependent and she smiled at him. 'You didn't use protection, did you?'

'No,' he said slowly, frowning at the sudden change in conversation.

'And I'm not on the pill, so technically I could already be pregnant.'

'Technically I suppose you could.'

The glow of love in her eyes made him catch his breath.

'I think we should give Ianthe a little brother or sister as soon as possible, don't you?' she murmured, sliding her hand down to where their bodies were still joined. 'And if

you leave me any spare time outside of the bedroom, I could always model maternity wear.'

'Be warned, *agape mou,*' he told her, his eyes darkening with desire as he stirred deliciously within her, 'I shall ensure that you have very little spare time!'

Harlequin Presents brings you
a brand-new duet by star author

Sharon Kendrick

THE GREEK BILLIONAIRES' BRIDES

Power, pride and passion—discover how only
the love and passion of two women can reunite
these wealthy, successful brothers,
divided by a bitter rivalry.

Available June 2008:

THE GREEK TYCOON'S
BABY BARGAIN

Available July 2008:

THE GREEK TYCOON'S
CONVENIENT WIFE

Don't miss the brilliant
new novel from

Natalie Rivers

**featuring a dark, dangerous
and decadent Italian!**

THE SALVATORE
MARRIAGE DEAL

Available June 2008
Book #2735

*Look out for more books
from Natalie Rivers coming soon,
only in Harlequin Presents!*

TALL, DARK AND SEXY

The men who never fail—seduction included!

Brooding, successful and arrogant, these men
can sweep any female they desire off her feet.
But now there's only one woman they want—
and they'll use their wealth, power, charm and
irresistibly seductive ways to claim her!

**Don't miss any of the titles in this exciting
collection available June 10, 2008:**

#9 THE BILLIONAIRE'S VIRGIN BRIDE
by HELEN BROOKS

#10 HIS MISTRESS BY MARRIAGE
by LEE WILKINSON

#11 THE BRITISH BILLIONAIRE AFFAIR
by SUSANNE JAMES

#12 THE MILLIONAIRE'S MARRIAGE REVENGE
by AMANDA BROWNING

*Harlequin Presents EXTRA delivers a themed
collection every month featuring 4 new titles.*

REQUEST YOUR FREE BOOKS!

2 FREE NOVELS PLUS 2 FREE GIFTS!

YES! Please send me 2 FREE Harlequin Presents® novels and my 2 FREE gifts (gifts are worth about $10). After receiving them, if I don't wish to receive any more books, I can return the shipping statement marked "cancel". If I don't cancel, I will receive 6 brand-new novels every month and be billed just $4.05 per book in the U.S. or $4.74 per book in Canada, plus 25¢ shipping and handling per book and applicable taxes, if any*. That's a savings of close to 15% off the cover price! I understand that accepting the 2 free books and gifts places me under no obligation to buy anything. I can always return a shipment and cancel at any time. Even if I never buy another book, the two free books and gifts are mine to keep forever.   106 HDN ERRW 306 HDN ERRL

Name	(PLEASE PRINT)	
Address		Apt. #
City	State/Prov.	Zip/Postal Code

Signature (if under 18, a parent or guardian must sign)

Mail to the Harlequin Reader Service:
IN U.S.A.: P.O. Box 1867, Buffalo, NY 14240-1867
IN CANADA: P.O. Box 609, Fort Erie, Ontario L2A 5X3

Not valid to current subscribers of Harlequin Presents books.

Want to try two free books from another line?
Call 1-800-873-8635 or visit www.morefreebooks.com.

* Terms and prices subject to change without notice. N.Y. residents add applicable sales tax. Canadian residents will be charged applicable provincial taxes and GST. Offer not valid in Quebec. This offer is limited to one order per household. All orders subject to approval. Credit or debit balances in a customer's account(s) may be offset by any other outstanding balance owed by or to the customer. Please allow 4 to 6 weeks for delivery. Offer available while quantities last.

Your Privacy: Harlequin Books is committed to protecting your privacy. Our Privacy Policy is available online at www.eHarlequin.com or upon request from the Reader Service. From time to time we make our lists of customers available to reputable third parties who may have a product or service of interest to you. If you would prefer we not share your name and address, please check here. ☐

HP08R

THE BOSS'S MISTRESS

Out of the office…and into his bed

These ruthless, powerful men are used
to having their own way in the office—
and with their mistresses they're also
boss in the bedroom!

**Don't miss any of our fantastic stories
in the July 2008 collection:**

#13 THE ITALIAN TYCOON'S MISTRESS
by CATHY WILLIAMS

#14 RUTHLESS BOSS, HIRED WIFE
by KATE HEWITT

#15 IN THE TYCOON'S BED
by KATHRYN ROSS

#16 THE RICH MAN'S RELUCTANT MISTRESS
by MARGARET MAYO

HARLEQUIN *Presents*

EXTRA

Coming Next Month

Be sure to look out for our *Tall, Dark and Sexy* collection in Harlequin Presents EXTRA

And Coming Next Month in Harlequin Presents

She's cool,
controlled...and ready
to be claimed!

Supermodel Anneliese Christiansen
seems to have it all—but Anna is an
innocent, and has reasons for resisting
Damon Kouvaris's ruthless seduction....

He's Mediterranean, made of money...
and irresistibly marriageable!

Anna proves to be a challenge but Damon always
gets what he wants...and if the prize is good
enough he'll pay the price!

Will the Greek tycoon claim this virgin
to be his bride...?

HARLEQUIN®
Presents®

Seduction and Passion Guaranteed

$4.75 U.S./$5.75 CAN.
ISBN-13:978-0-373-82081-8
ISBN-10:   0-373-82081-X

82081

UPC

Harlequin Presents® EXTR
www.eHarlequin.com

PENGUIN BOOKS

A Christmas Carol

Charles Dickens was born in Portsmouth on 7 February 1812, the second of eight children. Dickens's childhood experiences were similar to those depicted in *David Copperfield*. His father, who was a government clerk, was imprisoned for debt and Dickens was briefly sent to work in a blacking warehouse at the age of twelve. He received little formal education, but taught himself shorthand and became a reporter of parliamentary debates for the *Morning Chronicle*. He began to publish sketches in various periodicals, which were subsequently republished as *Sketches by Boz*. *The Pickwick Papers* was published in 1836–7 and after a slow start became a publishing phenomenon and Dickens's characters the centre of a popular cult. Part of the secret of his success was the method of cheap serial publication he adopted; thereafter, all Dickens's novels were published in serial form. He began *Oliver Twist* in 1837, followed by *Nicholas Nickleby* (1838) and *The Old Curiosity Shop* (1840–41). After finishing *Barnaby Rudge* (1841) Dickens set off for America; he went full of enthusiasm for the young republic but, in spite of a triumphant reception, he returned disillusioned. His experiences are recorded in *American Notes* (1842). *A Christmas Carol*, the first of the hugely popular *Christmas Books*, appeared in 1843, while *Martin Chuzzlewit*, which included a fictionalized account of his American travels, was first published over the period 1843–4. During 1844–6 Dickens travelled abroad and he began *Dombey and Son* while in Switzerland. This and *David Copperfield* (1849–50) were more serious in theme and more carefully planned than his early novels. In later works, such as *Bleak House* (1853) and *Little Dorrit* (1857), Dickens's social criticism became more radical and his comedy more savage. In 1850 Dickens started the weekly periodical

Household Words, succeeded in 1859 by *All the Year Round*; in these he published *Hard Times* (1854), *A Tale of Two Cities* (1859) and *Great Expectations* (1860–61). Dickens's health was failing during the 1860s and the physical strain of the public readings which he began in 1858 hastened his decline, although *Our Mutual Friend* (1865) retained some of his best comedy. His last novel, *The Mystery of Edwin Drood*, was never completed and he died on 9 June 1870. Public grief at his death was considerable and he was buried in the Poets' Corner of Westminster Abbey.

CHARLES DICKENS

A Christmas Carol

PENGUIN BOOKS

PENGUIN BOOKS

Published by the Penguin Group

Penguin Books Ltd, 80 Strand, London WC2R ORL, England

Penguin Group (USA) Inc., 375 Hudson Street, New York, New York 10014, USA

Penguin Group (Canada), 90 Eglinton Avenue East, Suite 700, Toronto, Ontario, Canada M4P 2Y3
(a division of Pearson Penguin Canada Inc.)

Penguin Ireland, 25 St Stephen's Green, Dublin 2, Ireland (a division of Penguin Books Ltd)

Penguin Group (Australia), 250 Camberwell Road, Camberwell, Victoria 3124, Australia
(a division of Pearson Australia Group Pty Ltd)

Penguin Books India Pvt Ltd, 11 Community Centre,
Panchsheel Park, New Delhi – 110 017, India

Penguin Group (NZ), 67 Apollo Drive, Rosedale, North Shore 0632, New Zealand
(a division of Pearson New Zealand Ltd)

Penguin Books (South Africa) (Pty) Ltd, 24 Sturdee Avenue,
Rosebank, Johannesburg 2196, South Africa

Penguin Books Ltd, Registered Offices: 80 Strand, London WC2R ORL, England

www.penguin.com

First published 1843
Published as a Penguin Red Classic 2007

1

All rights reserved

Set in 11.5/13.5 pt PostScript Monotype Dante
Typeset by Rowland Phototypesetting Ltd, Bury St Edmunds, Suffolk
Printed in England by Clays Ltd, St Ives plc

978–0–141–03173–6

www.greenpenguin.co.uk

Penguin Books is committed to a sustainable future
for our business, our readers and our planet.
The book in your hands is made from paper
certified by the Forest Stewardship Council.

Contents

MARLEY'S GHOST

Marley was dead: to begin with. There is no doubt whatever about that. The register of his burial was signed by the clergyman, the clerk, the undertaker, and the chief mourner. Scrooge signed it: and Scrooge's name was good upon 'Change, for anything he chose to put his hand to. Old Marley was as dead as a door-nail.

Mind! I don't mean to say that I know, of my own knowledge, what there is particularly dead about a door-nail. I might have been inclined, myself, to regard a coffin-nail as the deadest piece of ironmongery in the trade. But the wisdom of our ancestors is in the simile; and my unhallowed hands shall not disturb it, or the Country's done for. You will therefore permit me to repeat, emphatically, that Marley was as dead as a door-nail.

Scrooge knew he was dead? Of course he did. How could it be otherwise? Scrooge and he were partners for I don't know how many years. Scrooge was his sole executor, his sole administrator, his sole assign, his sole residuary legatee, his sole friend and sole mourner. And even Scrooge was not so dreadfully cut up by the sad event, but that he was an excellent man of business on the very day of

the funeral, and solemnised it with an undoubted bargain.

The mention of Marley's funeral brings me back to the point I started from. There is no doubt that Marley was dead. This must be distinctly understood, or nothing wonderful can come of the story I am going to relate. If we were not perfectly convinced that Hamlet's Father died before the play began, there would be nothing more remarkable in his taking a stroll at night, in an easterly wind, upon his own ramparts, than there would be in any other middle-aged gentleman rashly turning out after dark in a breezy spot – say Saint Paul's Churchyard for instance – literally to astonish his son's weak mind.

Scrooge never painted out Old Marley's name. There it stood, years afterwards, above the warehouse door: Scrooge and Marley. The firm was known as Scrooge and Marley. Sometimes people new to the business called Scrooge Scrooge, and sometimes Marley, but he answered to both names: it was all the same to him.

Oh! But he was a tight-fisted hand at the grindstone, Scrooge! a squeezing, wrenching, grasping, scraping, clutching, covetous old sinner! Hard and sharp as flint, from which no steel had ever struck out generous fire; secret, and self-contained, and solitary as an oyster. The cold within him froze his old features, nipped his pointed nose, shrivelled his cheek, stiffened his gait; made his eyes red, his thin lips blue; and spoke out shrewdly in his grating

voice. A frosty rime was on his head, and on his eyebrows, and his wiry chin. He carried his own low temperature always about with him; he iced his office in the dog-days; and didn't thaw it one degree at Christmas.

External heat and cold had little influence on Scrooge. No warmth could warm, nor wintry weather chill him. No wind that blew was bitterer than he, no falling snow was more intent upon its purpose, no pelting rain less open to entreaty. Foul weather didn't know where to have him. The heaviest rain, and snow, and hail, and sleet, could boast of the advantage over him in only one respect. They often 'came down' handsomely, and Scrooge never did.

Nobody ever stopped him in the street to say, with gladsome looks, 'My dear Scrooge, how are you? when will you come to see me?' No beggars implored him to bestow a trifle, no children asked him what it was o'clock, no man or woman ever once in all his life inquired the way to such and such a place, of Scrooge. Even the blindmen's dogs appeared to know him; and when they saw him coming on, would tug their owners into doorways and up courts; and then would wag their tails as though they said, 'no eye at all is better than an evil eye, dark master!'

But what did Scrooge care? It was the very thing he liked. To edge his way along the crowded paths of life, warning all human sympathy to keep its distance, was what the knowing ones call 'nuts' to Scrooge.

Once upon a time – of all the good days in the year, on Christmas Eve – old Scrooge sat busy in his counting-house. It was cold, bleak, biting weather: foggy withal: and he could hear the people in the court outside, go wheezing up and down, beating their hands upon their breasts, and stamping their feet upon the pavement-stones to warm them. The city clocks had only just gone three, but it was quite dark already: it had not been light all day: and candles were flaring in the windows of the neighbouring offices, like ruddy smears upon the palpable brown air. The fog came pouring in at every chink and keyhole, and was so dense without, that although the court was of the narrowest, the houses opposite were mere phantoms. To see the dingy cloud come drooping down, obscuring everything, one might have thought that Nature lived hard by, and was brewing on a large scale.

The door of Scrooge's counting-house was open that he might keep his eye upon his clerk, who in a dismal little cell beyond, a sort of tank, was copying letters. Scrooge had a very small fire, but the clerk's fire was so very much smaller that it looked like one coal. But he couldn't replenish it, for Scrooge kept the coal-box in his own room; and so surely as the clerk came in with the shovel, the master predicted that it would be necessary for them to part. Wherefore the clerk put on his white comforter, and tried to warm himself at the candle; in which effort, not being a man of a strong imagination, he failed.

'A merry Christmas, uncle! God save you!' cried a cheerful voice. It was the voice of Scrooge's nephew, who came upon him so quickly that this was the first intimation he had of his approach.

'Bah!' said Scrooge, 'Humbug!'

He had so heated himself with rapid walking in the fog and frost, this nephew of Scrooge's, that he was all in a glow; his face was ruddy and handsome; his eyes sparkled, and his breath smoked again.

'Christmas a humbug, uncle!' said Scrooge's nephew. 'You don't mean that, I am sure?'

'I do,' said Scrooge. 'Merry Christmas! What right have you to be merry? what reason have you to be merry? You're poor enough.'

'Come, then,' returned the nephew gaily. 'What right have you to be dismal? what reason have you to be morose? You're rich enough.'

Scrooge having no better answer ready on the spur of the moment, said, 'Bah!' again; and followed it up with 'Humbug.'

'Don't be cross, uncle,' said the nephew.

'What else can I be' returned the uncle, 'when I live in such a world of fools as this? Merry Christmas! Out upon merry Christmas! What's Christmas time to you but a time for paying bills without money; a time for finding yourself a year older, and not an hour richer; a time for balancing your books and having every item in 'em through a round dozen of months presented dead against you? If I could work my will,' said Scrooge, indignantly, 'every idiot who goes about with "Merry

5

Christmas,'' on his lips, should be boiled with his own pudding, and buried with a stake of holly through his heart. He should!'

'Uncle!' pleaded the nephew.

'Nephew!' returned the uncle, sternly, 'keep Christmas in your own way, and let me keep it in mine.'

'Keep it!' repeated Scrooge's nephew. 'But you don't keep it.'

'Let me leave it alone, then,' said Scrooge. 'Much good may it do you! Much good it has ever done you!'

'There are many things from which I might have derived good, by which I have not profited, I dare say,' returned the nephew: 'Christmas among the rest. But I am sure I have always thought of Christmas time, when it has come round – apart from the veneration due to its sacred name and origin, if anything belonging to it can be apart from that – as a good time: a kind, forgiving, charitable, pleasant time: the only time I know of, in the long calendar of the year, when men and women seem by one consent to open their shut-up hearts freely, and to think of people below them as if they really were fellow-passengers to the grave, and not another race of creatures bound on other journeys. And therefore, uncle, though it has never put a scrap of gold or silver in my pocket, I believe that it *has* done me good, and *will* do me good; and I say, God bless it!'

The clerk in the tank involuntarily applauded:

becoming immediately sensible of the impropriety, he poked the fire, and extinguished the last frail spark for ever.

'Let me hear another sound from *you*' said Scrooge, 'and you'll keep your Christmas by losing your situation. You're quite a powerful speaker, sir,' he added, turning to his nephew. 'I wonder you don't go into Parliament.'

'Don't be angry, uncle. Come! Dine with us to-morrow.'

Scrooge said that he would see him – yes, indeed he did. He went the whole length of the expression, and said that he would see him in that extremity first.

'But why?' cried Scrooge's nephew. 'Why?'

'Why did you get married?' said Scrooge.

'Because I fell in love.'

'Because you fell in love!' growled Scrooge, as if that were the only one thing in the world more ridiculous than a merry Christmas. 'Good afternoon!'

'Nay, uncle, but you never came to see me before that happened. Why give it as a reason for not coming now?'

'Good afternoon,' said Scrooge.

'I want nothing from you; I ask nothing of you; why cannot we be friends?'

'Good afternoon,' said Scrooge.

'I am sorry, with all my heart, to find you so resolute. We have never had any quarrel, to which I have been a party. But I have made the trial in

homage to Christmas, and I'll keep my Christmas humour to the last. So A Merry Christmas, uncle!'

'Good afternoon!' said Scrooge.

'And A Happy New Year!'

'Good afternoon!' said Scrooge.

His nephew left the room without an angry word, notwithstanding. He stopped at the outer door to bestow the greetings of the season on the clerk, who, cold as he was, was warmer than Scrooge; for he returned them cordially.

'There's another fellow,' muttered Scrooge; who overheard him: 'my clerk, with fifteen shillings a-week, and a wife and family, talking about a merry Christmas. I'll retire to Bedlam.'

This lunatic, in letting Scrooge's nephew out, had let two other people in. They were portly gentlemen, pleasant to behold, and now stood, with their hats off, in Scrooge's office. They had books and papers in their hands, and bowed to him.

'Scrooge and Marley's, I believe,' said one of the gentlemen, referring to his list. 'Have I the pleasure of addressing Mr. Scrooge, or Mr. Marley?'

'Mr. Marley has been dead these seven years,' Scrooge replied. 'He died seven years ago, this very night.'

'We have no doubt his liberality is well represented by his surviving partner,' said the gentleman, presenting his credentials.

It certainly was; for they had been two kindred spirits. At the ominous word 'liberality,' Scrooge

frowned, and shook his head, and handed the credentials back.

'At this festive season of the year, Mr. Scrooge,' said the gentleman, taking up a pen, 'it is more than usually desirable that we should make some slight provision for the poor and destitute, who suffer greatly at the present time. Many thousands are in want of common necessaries; hundreds of thousands are in want of common comforts, sir.'

'Are there no prisons?' asked Scrooge.

'Plenty of prisons,' said the gentleman, laying down the pen again.

'And the Union workhouses?' demanded Scrooge. 'Are they still in operation?'

'They are. Still,' returned the gentleman, 'I wish I could say they were not.'

'The Treadmill and the Poor Law are in full vigour, then?' said Scrooge.

'Both very busy, sir.'

'Oh! I was afraid, from what you said at first, that something had occurred to stop them in their useful course,' said Scrooge. 'I'm very glad to hear it.'

'Under the impression that they scarcely furnish Christian cheer of mind or body to the multitude,' returned the gentleman, 'a few of us are endeavouring to raise a fund to buy the Poor some meat and drink, and means of warmth. We choose this time because it is a time, of all others, when Want is keenly felt, and Abundance rejoices. What shall I put you down for?'

'Nothing!' Scrooge replied.

'You wish to be anonymous?'

'I wish to be left alone,' said Scrooge. 'Since ou ask me what I wish, gentlemen, that is my answer. I don't make merry myself at Christmas, and I can't afford to make idle people merry. I help to support the establishments I have mentioned: they cost enough: and those who are badly off must go there.'

'Many can't go there; and many would rather die.'

'If they would rather die,' said Scrooge, 'they had better do it, and decrease the surplus population. Besides – excuse me – I don't know that.'

'But you might know it,' observed the gentleman.

'It's not my business,' Scrooge returned. 'It's enough for a man to understand his own business, and not to interfere with other people's. Mine occupies me constantly. Good afternoon, gentlemen!'

Seeing clearly that it would be useless to pursue their point, the gentlemen withdrew. Scrooge resumed his labours with an improved opinion of himself, and in a more facetious temper than was usual with him.

Meanwhile the fog and darkness thickened so, that people ran about with flaring links, proffering their services to go before horses in carriages, and conduct them on their way. The ancient tower of a church, whose gruff old bell was always peeping slily down at Scrooge out of a gothic window in

the wall, became invisible, and struck the hours and quarters in the clouds, with tremulous vibrations afterwards, as if its teeth were chattering in its frozen head up there. The cold became intense. In the main street, at the corner of the court, some labourers were repairing the gas-pipes, and had lighted a great fire in a brazier, round which a party of ragged men and boys were gathered: warming their hands and winking their eyes before the blaze in rapture. The water-plug being left in solitude, its overflowings sullenly congealed, and turned to misanthropic ice. The brightness of the shops where holly sprigs and berries crackled in the lamp-heat of the windows, made pale faces ruddy as they passed. Poulterers' and grocers' trades became a splendid joke: a glorious pageant, with which it was next to impossible to believe that such dull principles as bargain and sale had anything to do. The Lord Mayor, in the stronghold of the mighty Mansion House, gave orders to his fifty cooks and butlers to keep Christmas as a Lord Mayor's household should; and even the little tailor, whom he had fined five shillings on the previous Monday for being drunk and blood-thirsty in the streets, stirred up to-morrow's pudding in his garret, while his lean wife and the baby sallied out to buy the beef.

Foggier yet, and colder! Piercing, searching, biting cold. If the good Saint Dunstan had but nipped the Evil Spirit's nose with a touch of such weather as that, instead of using his familiar

weapons, then indeed he would have roared to lusty purpose. The owner of one scant young nose, gnawed and mumbled by the hungry cold as bones are gnawed by dogs, stooped down at Scrooge's keyhole to regale him with a Christmas carol: but at the first sound of –

> 'God bless you merry gentleman!
> May nothing you dismay!'

Scrooge seized the ruler with such energy of action, that the singer fled in terror, leaving the keyhole to the fog and even more congenial frost.

At length the hour of shutting up the counting-house arrived. With an ill-will Scrooge dismounted from his stool, and tacitly admitted the fact to the expectant clerk in the Tank, who instantly snuffed his candle out, and put on his hat.

'You'll want all day to-morrow, I suppose?' said Scrooge.

'If quite convenient, sir.'

'It's not convenient,' said Scrooge, 'and it's not fair. If I was to stop half-a-crown for it, you'd think yourself ill used, I'll be bound?'

The clerk smiled faintly.

'And yet,' said Scrooge, 'you don't think *me* ill used, when I pay a day's wages for no work.'

The clerk observed that it was only once a year.

'A poor excuse for picking a man's pocket every twenty-fifth of December!' said Scrooge, buttoning

his great-coat to the chin. 'But I suppose you must have the whole day. Be here all the earlier next morning!'

The clerk promised that he would; and Scrooge walked out with a growl. The office was closed in a twinkling, and the clerk, with the long ends of his white comforter dangling below his waist (for he boasted no great-coat), went down a slide on Cornhill, at the end of a lane of boys, twenty times, in honour of its being Christmas-eve, and then ran home to Camden Town as hard as he could pelt, to play at blindman's-buff.

Scrooge took his melancholy dinner in his usual melancholy tavern; and having read all the newspapers, and beguiled the rest of the evening with his banker's-book, went home to bed. He lived in chambers which had once belonged to his deceased partner. They were a gloomy suite of rooms, in a lowering pile of building up a yard, where it had so little business to be, that one could scarcely help fancying it must have run there when it was a young house, playing at hide-and-seek with other houses, and have forgotten the way out again. It was old enough now, and dreary enough, for nobody lived in it but Scrooge, the other rooms being all let out as offices. The yard was so dark that even Scrooge, who knew its every stone, was fain to grope with his hands. The fog and frost so hung about the black old gateway of the house, that it seemed as if the Genius of the Weather sat in mournful meditation on the threshold.

Now, it is a fact, that there was nothing at all particular about the knocker on the door, except that it was very large. It is also a fact, that Scrooge had seen it night and morning during his whole residence in that place; also that Scrooge had as little of what is called fancy about him as any man in the City of London, even including – which is a bold word – the corporation, aldermen, and livery. Let it also be borne in mind that Scrooge had not bestowed one thought on Marley, since his last mention of his seven-years' dead partner that afternoon. And then let any man explain to me, if he can, how it happened that Scrooge, having his key in the lock of the door, saw in the knocker, without its undergoing any intermediate process of change: not a knocker, but Marley's face.

Marley's face. It was not in impenetrable shadow as the other objects in the yard were, but had a dismal light about it, like a bad lobster in a dark cellar. It was not angry or ferocious, but looked at Scrooge as Marley used to look: with ghostly spectacles turned up upon its ghostly forehead. The hair was curiously stirred, as if by breath or hot-air; and though the eyes were wide open, they were perfectly motionless. That, and its livid colour, made it horrible; but its horror seemed to be, in spite of the face and beyond its control, rather than a part of its own expression.

As Scrooge looked fixedly at this phenomenon, it was a knocker again.

To say that he was not startled, or that his blood

was not conscious of a terrible sensation to which it had been a stranger from infancy, would be untrue. But he put his hand upon the key he had relinquished, turned it sturdily, walked in, and lighted his candle.

He *did* pause, with a moment's irresolution, before he shut the door; and he *did* look cautiously behind it first, as if he half-expected to be terrified with the sight of Marley's pigtail sticking out into the hall. But there was nothing on the back of the door, except the screws and nuts that held the knocker on; so he said 'Pooh, pooh!' and closed it with a bang.

The sound resounded through the house like thunder. Every room above, and every cask in the wine-merchant's cellars below, appeared to have a separate peal of echoes of its own. Scrooge was not a man to be frightened by echoes. He fastened the door, and walked across the hall, and up the stairs: slowly too: trimming his candle as he went.

You may talk vaguely about driving a coach-and-six up a good old flight of stairs, or through a bad young Act of Parliament; but I mean to say you might have got a hearse up that staircase, and taken it broadwise, with the splinter-bar towards the wall, and the door towards the balustrades: and done it easy. There was plenty of width for that, and room to spare; which is perhaps the reason why Scrooge thought he saw a locomotive hearse going on before him in the gloom. Half a dozen gas-lamps out of the street wouldn't have lighted the entry

too well, so you may suppose that it was pretty dark with Scrooge's dip.

Up Scrooge went, not caring a button for that: darkness is cheap, and Scrooge liked it. But before he shut his heavy door, he walked through his rooms to see that all was right. He had just enough recollection of the face to desire to do that.

Sitting-room, bed-room, lumber-room. All as they should be. Nobody under the table, nobody under the sofa; a small fire in the grate; spoon and basin ready; and the little saucepan of gruel (Scrooge had a cold in his head) upon the hob. Nobody under the bed; nobody in the closet; nobody in his dressing-gown, which was hanging up in a suspicious attitude against the wall. Lumber-room as usual. Old fire-guard, old shoes, two fish-baskets, washing-stand on three legs, and a poker.

Quite satisfied, he closed his door, and locked himself in; double-locked himself in, which was not his custom. Thus secured against surprise, he took off his cravat; put on his dressing-gown and slippers, and his nightcap; and sat down before the fire to take his gruel.

It was a very low fire indeed; nothing on such a bitter night. He was obliged to sit close to it, and brood over it, before he could extract the least sensation of warmth from such a handful of fuel. The fireplace was an old one, built by some Dutch merchant long ago, and paved all round with quaint Dutch tiles, designed to illustrate the Scriptures. There were Cains and Abels; Pharaoh's daughters,

Queens of Sheba, Angelic messengers descending through the air on clouds like feather-beds, Abrahams, Belshazzars, Apostles putting off to sea in butter-boats, hundreds of figures to attract his thoughts; and yet that face of Marley, seven years dead, came like the ancient Prophet's rod, and swallowed up the whole. If each smooth tile had been a blank at first, with power to shape some picture on its surface from the disjointed fragments of his thoughts, there would have been a copy of old Marley's head on every one.

'Humbug!' said Scrooge; and walked across the room.

After several turns, he sat down again. As he threw his head back in the chair, his glance happened to rest upon a bell, a disused bell, that hung in the room, and communicated for some purpose now forgotten with a chamber in the highest story of the building. It was with great astonishment, and with a strange, inexplicable dread, that as he looked, he saw this bell begin to swing. It swung so softly in the outset that it scarcely made a sound; but soon it rang out loudly, and so did every bell in the house.

This might have lasted half a minute, or a minute, but it seemed an hour. The bells ceased as they had begun, together. They were succeeded by a clanking noise, deep down below; as if some person were dragging a heavy chain over the casks in the wine-merchant's cellar. Scrooge then remembered to have heard that ghosts in haunted houses were described as dragging chains.

The cellar-door flew open with a booming sound, and then he heard the noise much louder, on the floors below; then coming up the stairs; then coming straight towards his door.

'It's humbug still!' said Scrooge. 'I won't believe it.'

His colour changed though, when, without a pause, it came on through the heavy door, and passed into the room before his eyes. Upon its coming in, the dying flame leaped up, as though it cried 'I know him! Marley's Ghost!' and fell again.

The same face: the very same. Marley in his pig-tail, usual waistcoat, tights, and boots; the tassels on the latter bristling, like his pigtail, and his coat-skirts, and the hair upon his head. The chain he drew was clasped about his middle. It was long, and wound about him like a tail; and it was made (for Scrooge observed it closely) of cash-boxes, keys, padlocks, ledgers, deeds, and heavy purses wrought in steel. His body was transparent: so that Scrooge, observing him, and looking through his waistcoat, could see the two buttons on his coat behind.

Scrooge had often heard it said that Marley had no bowels, but he had never believed it until now.

No, nor did he believe it even now. Though he looked the phantom through and through, and saw it standing before him; though he felt the chilling influence of its death-cold eyes; and marked the very texture of the folded kerchief bound about its head and chin, which wrapper he had not observed

before: he was still incredulous, and fought against his senses.

'How now!' said Scrooge, caustic and cold as ever. 'What do you want with me?'

'Much!' – Marley's voice, no doubt about it.

'Who are you?'

'Ask me who I *was*.'

'Who *were* you then?' said Scrooge, raising his voice. 'You're particular – for a shade.' He was going to say '*to* a shade,' but substituted this, as more appropriate.

'In life I was your partner, Jacob Marley.'

'Can you – can you sit down?' asked Scrooge, looking doubtfully at him.

'I can.'

'Do it then.'

Scrooge asked the question, because he didn't know whether a ghost so transparent might find himself in a condition to take a chair; and felt that in the event of its being impossible, it might involve the necessity of an embarrassing explanation. But the ghost sat down on the opposite side of the fireplace, as if he were quite used to it.

'You don't believe in me,' observed the Ghost.

'I don't,' said Scrooge.

'What evidence would you have of my reality, beyond that of your senses?'

'I don't know,' said Scrooge.

'Why do you doubt your senses?'

'Because,' said Scrooge, 'a little thing affects them. A slight disorder of the stomach makes them

cheats. You may be an undigested bit of beef, a blot
of mustard, a crumb of cheese, a fragment of an
underdone potato. There's more of gravy than of
grave about you, whatever you are!'

Scrooge was not much in the habit of cracking
jokes, nor did he feel, in his heart, by any means
waggish then. The truth is, that he tried to be smart,
as a means of distracting his own attention, and
keeping down his terror; for the spectre's voice
disturbed the very marrow in his bones.

To sit, staring at those fixed, glazed eyes, in
silence for a moment, would play, Scrooge felt, the
very deuce with him. There was something very
awful, too, in the spectre's being provided with an
infernal atmosphere of its own. Scrooge could not
feel it himself, but this was clearly the case; for
though the Ghost sat perfectly motionless, its hair,
and skirts, and tassels, were still agitated as by the
hot vapour from an oven.

'You see this toothpick?' said Scrooge, returning
quickly to the charge, for the reason just assigned;
and wishing, though it were only for a second, to
divert the vision's stony gaze from himself.

'I do,' replied the Ghost.

'You are not looking at it,' said Scrooge.

'But I see it,' said the Ghost, 'notwithstanding.'

'Well!' returned Scrooge. 'I have but to swallow
this, and be for the rest of my days persecuted by a
legion of goblins, all of my own creation. Humbug,
I tell you – humbug!'

At this, the spirit raised a frightful cry, and shook

its chain with such a dismal and appalling noise, that Scrooge held on tight to his chair, to save himself from falling in a swoon. But how much greater was his horror, when the phantom taking off the bandage round its head, as if it were too warm to wear in-doors, its lower jaw dropped down upon its breast!

Scrooge fell upon his knees, and clasped his hands before his face.

'Mercy!' he said. 'Dreadful apparition, why do you trouble me?'

'Man of the worldly mind!' replied the Ghost, 'do you believe in me or not?'

'I do,' said Scrooge. 'I must. But why do spirits walk the earth, and why do they come to me?'

'It is required of every man,' the Ghost returned, 'that the spirit within him should walk abroad among his fellow-men, and travel far and wide; and if that spirit goes not forth in life, it is condemned to do so after death. It is doomed to wander through the world – oh, woe is me! – and witness what it cannot share, but might have shared on earth, and turned to happiness!'

Again the spectre raised a cry, and shook its chain and wrung its shadowy hands.

'You are fettered,' said Scrooge, trembling. 'Tell me why?'

'I wear the chain I forged in life,' replied the Ghost. 'I made it link by link, and yard by yard; I girded it on of my own free will, and of my own free will I wore it. Is its pattern strange to *you*?'

Scrooge trembled more and more.

'Or would you know,' pursued the Ghost, 'the weight and length of the strong coil you bear your-self? It was full as heavy and as long as this, seven Christmas Eves ago. You have laboured on it, since. It is a ponderous chain!'

Scrooge glanced about him on the floor, in the expectation of finding himself surrounded by some fifty or sixty fathoms of iron cable: but he could see nothing.

'Jacob,' he said, imploringly. 'Old Jacob Marley, tell me more. Speak comfort to me, Jacob.'

'I have none to give,' the Ghost replied. 'It comes from other regions, Ebenezer Scrooge, and is con-veyed by other ministers, to other kinds of men. Nor can I tell you what I would. A very little more is all permitted to me. I cannot rest, I cannot stay, I cannot linger anywhere. My spirit never walked beyond our counting-house – mark me! – in life my spirit never roved beyond the narrow limits of our money-changing hole; and weary journeys lie before me!'

It was a habit with Scrooge, whenever he became thoughtful, to put his hands in his breeches pockets. Pondering on what the Ghost had said, he did so now, but without lifting up his eyes, or getting off his knees.

'You must have been very slow about it, Jacob,' Scrooge observed, in a business-like manner, though with humility and deference.

'Slow!' the Ghost repeated.

'Seven years dead,' mused Scrooge. 'And travelling all the time?'

'The whole time,' said the Ghost. 'No rest, no peace. Incessant torture of remorse.'

'You travel fast?' said Scrooge.

'On the wings of the wind,' replied the Ghost.

'You might have got over a great quantity of ground in seven years,' said Scrooge.

The Ghost, on hearing this, set up another cry, and clanked its chain so hideously in the dead silence of the night, that the Ward would have been justified in indicting it for a nuisance.

'Oh! captive, bound, and double-ironed,' cried the phantom, 'not to know, that ages of incessant labour by immortal creatures, for this earth must pass into eternity before the good of which it is susceptible is all developed. Not to know that any Christian spirit working kindly in its little sphere, whatever it may be, will find its mortal life too short for its vast means of usefulness. Not to know that no space of regret can make amends for one life's opportunity misused! Yet such was I! Oh! such was I!'

'But you were always a good man of business, Jacob,' faultered Scrooge, who now began to apply this to himself.

'Business!' cried the Ghost, wringing its hands again. 'Mankind was my business. The common welfare was my business; charity, mercy, forbearance, and benevolence, were, all, my business. The dealings of my trade were but a drop of water

in the comprehensive ocean of my business!'

It held up its chain at arm's length, as if that were the cause of all its unavailing grief, and flung it heavily upon the ground again.

'At this time of the rolling year,' the spectre said, 'I suffer most. Why did I walk through crowds of fellow-beings with my eyes turned down, and never raise them to that blessed Star which led the Wise Men to a poor abode? Were there no poor homes to which its light would have conducted *me!*'

Scrooge was very much dismayed to hear the spectre going on at this rate, and began to quake exceedingly.

'Hear me!' cried the Ghost. 'My time is nearly gone.'

'I will,' said Scrooge. 'But don't be hard upon me! Don't be flowery, Jacob! Pray!'

'How it is that I appear before you in a shape that you can see, I may not tell. I have sat invisible beside you many and many a day.'

It was not an agreeable idea. Scrooge shivered, and wiped the perspiration from his brow.

'That is no light part of my penance,' pursued the Ghost. 'I am here to-night to warn you, that you have yet a chance and hope of escaping my fate. A chance and hope of my procuring, Ebenezer.'

'You were always a good friend to me,' said Scrooge. 'Thank'ee!'

'You will be haunted,' resumed the Ghost, 'by Three Spirits.'

Scrooge's countenance fell almost as low as the Ghost's had done.

'Is that the chance and hope you mentioned, Jacob?' he demanded, in a faultering voice.

'It is.'

'I – I think I'd rather not,' said Scrooge.

'Without their visits,' said the Ghost, 'you cannot hope to shun the path I tread. Expect the first to-morrow, when the bell tolls one.'

'Couldn't I take 'em all at once, and have it over, Jacob?' hinted Scrooge.

'Expect the second on the next night at the same hour. The third upon the next night when the last stroke of twelve has ceased to vibrate. Look to see me no more; and look that, for your own sake, you remember what has passed between us!'

When it had said these words, the spectre took its wrapper from the table, and bound it round its head, as before. Scrooge knew this, by the smart sound its teeth made, when the jaws were brought together by the bandage. He ventured to raise his eyes again, and found his supernatural visitor confronting him in an erect attitude, with its chain wound over and about its arm.

The apparition walked backward from him; and at every step it took, the window raised itself a little, so that when the spectre reached it, it was wide open. It beckoned Scrooge to approach, which he did. When they were within two paces of each other, Marley's Ghost held up its hand, warning him to come no nearer. Scrooge stopped.

Not so much in obedience, as in surprise and fear: for on the raising of the hand, he became sensible of confused noises in the air; incoherent sounds of lamentation and regret; wailings inexpressibly sorrowful and self-accusatory. The spectre, after listening for a moment, joined in the mournful dirge; and floated out upon the bleak, dark night.

Scrooge followed to the window: desperate in his curiosity. He looked out.

The air filled with phantoms, wandering hither and thither in restless haste, and moaning as they went. Every one of them wore chains like Marley's Ghost; some few (they might be guilty governments) were linked together; none were free. Many had been personally known to Scrooge in their lives. He had been quite familiar with one old ghost, in a white waistcoat, with a monstrous iron safe attached to its ankle, who cried piteously at being unable to assist a wretched woman with an infant, whom it saw below, upon a door-step. The misery with them all was, clearly, that they sought to interfere, for good, in human matters, and had lost the power for ever.

Whether these creatures faded into mist, or mist enshrouded them, he could not tell. But they and their spirit voices faded together; and the night became as it had been when he walked home.

Scrooge closed the window, and examined the door by which the Ghost had entered. It was double-locked, as he had locked it with his own

hands, and the bolts were undisturbed. He tried to say 'Humbug!' but stopped at the first syllable. And being, from the emotion he had undergone, or the fatigues of the day, or his glimpse of the Invisible World, or the dull conversation of the Ghost, or the lateness of the hour, much in need of repose; went straight to bed, without undressing, and fell asleep upon the instant.

THE FIRST OF THE
THREE SPIRITS

When Scrooge awoke, it was so dark, that looking out of bed, he could scarcely distinguish the transparent window from the opaque walls of his chamber. He was endeavouring to pierce the darkness with his ferret eyes, when the chimes of a neighbouring church struck the four quarters. So he listened for the hour.

To his great astonishment the heavy bell went on from six to seven, and from seven to eight, and regularly up to twelve; then stopped. Twelve! It was past two when he went to bed. The clock was wrong. An icicle must have got into the works. Twelve!

He touched the spring of his repeater, to correct this most preposterous clock. Its rapid little pulse beat twelve; and stopped.

'Why, it isn't possible,' said Scrooge, 'that I can have slept through a whole day and far into another night. It isn't possible that anything has happened to the sun, and this is twelve at noon!'

The idea being an alarming one, he scrambled out of bed, and groped his way to the window. He was obliged to rub the frost off with the sleeve of his dressing-gown before he could see anything;

and could see very little then. All he could make out was, that it was still very foggy and extremely cold, and that there was no noise of people running to and fro, and making a great stir, as there unquestionably would have been if night had beaten off bright day, and taken possession of the world. This was a great relief, because 'three days after sight of this First of Exchange pay to Mr. Ebenezer Scrooge or his order,' and so forth, would have become a mere United States' security if there were no days to count by.

Scrooge went to bed again, and thought, and thought, and thought it over and over and over, and could make nothing of it. The more he thought, the more perplexed he was; and the more he endeavoured not to think, the more he thought. Marley's Ghost bothered him exceedingly. Every time he resolved within himself, after mature inquiry, that it was all a dream, his mind flew back again, like a strong spring released, to its first position, and presented the same problem to be worked all through, 'Was it a dream or not?'

Scrooge lay in this state until the chimes had gone three quarters more, when he remembered, on a sudden, that the Ghost had warned him of a visitation when the bell tolled one. He resolved to lie awake until the hour was passed; and, considering that he could no more go to sleep than go to Heaven, this was perhaps the wisest resolution in his power.

The quarter was so long, that he was more than

once convinced he must have sunk into a doze unconsciously, and missed the clock. At length it broke upon his listening ear.

'Ding, dong!'

'A quarter past,' said Scrooge, counting.

'Ding, dong!'

'Half past!' said Scrooge.

'Ding, dong!'

'A quarter to it,' said Scrooge.

'Ding, dong!'

'The hour itself,' said Scrooge, triumphantly, 'and nothing else!'

He spoke before the hour bell sounded, which it now did with a deep, dull, hollow, melancholy ONE. Light flashed up in the room upon the instant, and the curtains of his bed were drawn.

The curtains of his bed were drawn aside, I tell you, by a hand. Not the curtains at his feet, nor the curtains at his back, but those to which his face was addressed. The curtains of his bed were drawn aside; and Scrooge, starting up into a half-recumbent attitude, found himself face to face with the unearthly visitor who drew them: as close to it as I am now to you, and I am standing in the spirit at your elbow.

It was a strange figure – like a child: yet not so like a child as like an old man, viewed through some supernatural medium, which gave him the appearance of having receded from the view, and being diminished to a child's proportions. Its hair, which hung about its neck and down its back, was

white as if with age; and yet the face had not a wrinkle in it, and the tenderest bloom was on the skin. The arms were very long and muscular; the hands the same, as if its hold were of uncommon strength. Its legs and feet, most delicately formed, were, like those upper members, bare. It wore a tunic of the purest white; and round its waist was bound a lustrous belt, the sheen of which was beautiful. It held a branch of fresh green holly in its hand; and, in singular contradiction of that wintry emblem, had its dress trimmed with summer flowers. But the strangest thing about it was, that from the crown of its head there sprung a bright clear jet of light, by which all this was visible; and which was doubtless the occasion of its using, in its duller moments, a great extinguisher for a cap, which it now held under its arm.

Even this, though, when Scrooge looked at it with increasing steadiness, was *not* its strangest quality. For as its belt sparkled and glittered now in one part and now in another, and what was light one instant, at another time was dark, so the figure itself fluctuated in its distinctness: being now a thing with one arm, now with one leg, now with twenty legs, now a pair of legs without a head, now a head without a body: of which dissolving parts, no outline would be visible in the dense gloom wherein they melted away. And in the very wonder of this, it would be itself again; distinct and clear as ever.

'Are you the Spirit, sir, whose coming was fore-told to me?' asked Scrooge.

'I am!'

The voice was soft and gentle. Singularly low, as if instead of being so close beside him, it were at a distance.

'Who, and what are you?' Scrooge demanded.

'I am the Ghost of Christmas Past.'

'Long Past?' inquired Scrooge: observant of its dwarfish stature.

'No. Your past.'

Perhaps, Scrooge could not have told anybody why, if anybody could have asked him; but he had a special desire to see the Spirit in his cap; and begged him to be covered.

'What!' exclaimed the Ghost, 'would you so soon put out, with worldly hands, the light I give? Is it not enough that you are one of those whose passions made this cap, and force me through whole trains of years to wear it low upon my brow!'

Scrooge reverently disclaimed all intention to offend, or any knowledge of having wilfully 'bonneted' the Spirit at any period of his life. He then made bold to inquire what business brought him there.

'Your welfare!' said the Ghost.

Scrooge expressed himself much obliged, but could not help thinking that a night of unbroken rest would have been more conducive to that end. The Spirit must have heard him thinking for it said immediately:

'Your reclamation, then. Take heed!'

It put out its strong hand as it spoke, and clasped him gently by the arm.

'Rise! and walk with me!'

It would have been in vain for Scrooge to plead that the weather and the hour were not adapted to pedestrian purposes; that bed was warm, and the thermometer a long way below freezing; that he was clad but lightly in his slippers, dressing-gown, and nightcap; and that he had a cold upon him at that time. The grasp, though gentle as a woman's hand, was not to be resisted. He rose: but finding that the Spirit made towards the window, clasped its robe in supplication.

'I am a mortal,' Scrooge remonstrated, 'and liable to fall.'

'Bear but a touch of my hand *there*,' said the Spirit, laying it upon his heart, 'and you shall be upheld in more than this!'

As the words were spoken, they passed through the wall, and stood upon an open country road, with fields on either hand. The city had entirely vanished. Not a vestige of it was to be seen. The darkness and the mist had vanished with it, for it was a clear, cold, winter day, with snow upon the ground.

'Good Heaven!' said Scrooge, clasping his hands together, as he looked about him. 'I was bred in this place. I was a boy here!'

The Spirit gazed upon him mildly. Its gentle touch, though it had been light and instantaneous, appeared still present to the old man's sense of

feeling. He was conscious of a thousand odours floating in the air, each one connected with a thousand thoughts, and hopes, and joys, and cares long, long, forgotten!

'Your lip is trembling,' said the Ghost. 'And what is that upon your cheek?'

Scrooge muttered, with an unusual catching in his voice, that it was a pimple; and begged the Ghost to lead him where he would.

'You recollect the way?' inquired the Spirit.

'Remember it!' cried Scrooge with fervour – 'I could walk it blindfold.'

'Strange to have forgotten it for so many years!' observed the Ghost. 'Let us go on.'

They walked along the road; Scrooge recognising every gate, and post, and tree; until a little market-town appeared in the distance, with its bridge, its church, and winding river. Some shaggy ponies now were seen trotting towards them with boys upon their backs, who called to other boys in country gigs and carts, driven by farmers. All these boys were in great spirits, and shouted to each other, until the broad fields were so full of merry music, that the crisp air laughed to hear it.

'These are but shadows of the things that have been,' said the Ghost. 'They have no consciousness of us.'

The jocund travellers came on; and as they came, Scrooge knew and named them every one. Why was he rejoiced beyond all bounds to see them! Why did his cold eye glisten, and his heart leap up

as they went past! Why was he filled with gladness when he heard them give each other Merry Christmas, as they parted at cross-roads and bye-ways, for their several homes! What was merry Christmas to Scrooge? Out upon merry Christmas! What good had it ever done to him?

'The school is not quite deserted,' said the Ghost. 'A solitary child, neglected by his friends, is left there still.'

Scrooge said he knew it. And he sobbed.

They left the high-road, by a well-remembered lane, and soon approached a mansion of dull red brick, with a little weathercock-surmounted cupola on the roof, and a bell hanging in it. It was a large house, but one of broken fortunes; for the spacious offices were little used, their walls were damp and mossy, their windows broken, and their gates decayed. Fowls clucked and strutted in the stables; and the coach-houses and sheds were over-run with grass. Nor was it more retentive of its ancient state, within; for entering the dreary hall, and glancing through the open doors of many rooms, they found them poorly furnished, cold, and vast. There was an earthy savour in the air, a chilly bareness in the place, which associated itself somehow with too much getting up by candle-light, and not too much to eat.

They went, the Ghost and Scrooge, across the hall, to a door at the back of the house. It opened before them, and disclosed a long, bare, melancholy room, made barer still by lines of plain deal forms

and desks. At one of these a lonely boy was reading near a feeble fire; and Scrooge sat down upon a form, and wept to see his poor forgotten self as he had used to be.

Not a latent echo in the house, not a squeak and scuffle from the mice behind the panelling, not a drip from the half-thawed water-spout in the dull yard behind, not a sigh among the leafless boughs of one despondent poplar, not the idle swinging of an empty store-house door, no, not a clicking in the fire, but fell upon the heart of Scrooge with a softening influence, and gave a freer passage to his tears.

The Spirit touched him on the arm, and pointed to his younger self, intent upon his reading. Suddenly a man, in foreign garments: wonderfully real and distinct to look at: stood outside the window, with an axe stuck in his belt, and leading an ass laden with wood by the bridle.

'Why, it's Ali Baba!' Scrooge exclaimed in ecstasy. 'It's dear old honest Ali Baba! Yes, yes, I know! One Christmas time, when yonder solitary child was left here all alone, he *did* come, for the first time, just like that. Poor boy! And Valentine,' said Scrooge, 'and his wild brother, Orson; there they go! And what's his name, who was put down in his drawers, asleep, at the Gate of Damascus; don't you see him! And the Sultan's Groom turned upside-down by the Genii; there he is upon his head! Serve him right. I'm glad of it. What business had *he* to be married to the Princess!'

To hear Scrooge expending all the earnestness of his nature on such subjects, in a most extraordinary voice between laughing and crying; and to see his heightened and excited face; would have been a surprise to his business friends in the city, indeed.

'There's the Parrot!' cried Scrooge. 'Green body and yellow tail, with a thing like a lettuce growing out of the top of his head; there he is! Poor Robin Crusoe, he called him, when he came home again after sailing round the island. "Poor Robin Crusoe, where have you been, Robin Crusoe?" The man thought he was dreaming, but he wasn't. It was the Parrot, you know. There goes Friday, running for his life to the little creek! Halloa! Hoop! Halloo!'

Then, with a rapidity of transition very foreign to his usual character, he said, in pity for his former self, 'Poor boy!' and cried again.

'I wish,' Scrooge muttered, putting his hand in his pocket, and looking about him, after drying his eyes with his cuff: 'but it's too late now.'

'What is the matter?' asked the Spirit.

'Nothing,' said Scrooge. 'Nothing. There was a boy singing a Christmas Carol at my door last night. I should like to have given him something: that's all.'

The Ghost smiled thoughtfully, and waved its hand: saying as it did so, 'Let us see another Christmas!'

Scrooge's former self grew larger at the words, and the room became a little darker and more dirty.

The panels shrunk, the windows cracked; fragments of plaster fell out of the ceiling, and the naked laths were shown instead; but how all this was brought about, Scrooge knew no more than you do. He only knew that it was quite correct; that everything had happened so; that there he was, alone again, when all the other boys had gone home for the jolly holidays.

He was not reading now, but walking up and down despairingly. Scrooge looked at the Ghost, and with a mournful shaking of his head, glanced anxiously towards the door.

It opened; and a little girl, much younger than the boy, came darting in, and putting her arms about his neck, and often kissing him, addressed him as her 'Dear, dear brother.'

'I have come to bring you home, dear brother!' said the child, clapping her tiny hands, and bending down to laugh. 'To bring you home, home, home!'

'Home, little Fan?' returned the boy.

'Yes!' said the child, brimful of glee. 'Home, for good and all. Home, for ever and ever. Father is so much kinder than he used to be, that home's like Heaven! He spoke so gently to me one dear night when I was going to bed, that I was not afraid to ask him once more if you might come home; and he said Yes, you should; and sent me in a coach to bring you. And you're to be a man!' said the child, opening her eyes, 'and are never to come back here; but first, we're to be together all the

Christmas long, and have the merriest time in all the world.'

'You are quite a woman, little Fan!' exclaimed the boy.

She clapped her hands and laughed, and tried to touch his head; but being too little, laughed again, and stood on tiptoe to embrace him. Then she began to drag him, in her childish eagerness, towards the door; and he, nothing loth to go, accompanied her.

A terrible voice in the hall cried, 'Bring down Master Scrooge's box, there!' and in the hall appeared the schoolmaster himself, who glared on Master Scrooge with a ferocious condescension, and threw him into a dreadful state of mind by shaking hands with him. He then conveyed him and his sister into the veriest old well of a shivering best-parlour that ever was seen, where the maps upon the wall, and the celestial and terrestrial globes in the windows were waxy with cold. Here he produced a decanter of curiously light wine, and a block of curiously heavy cake, and administered instalments of those dainties to the young people: at the same time, sending out a meagre servant to offer a glass of 'something' to the postboy, who answered that he thanked the gentleman, but if it was the same tap as he had tasted before, he had rather not. Master Scrooge's trunk being by this time tied on to the top of the chaise, the children bade the schoolmaster good-bye right willingly; and getting into it, drove gaily down the garden-sweep:

the quick wheels dashing the hoar-frost and snow from off the dark leaves of the evergreens like spray.

'Always a delicate creature, whom a breath might have withered,' said the Ghost. 'But she had a large heart!'

'So she had,' cried Scrooge. 'You're right. I'll not gainsay it, Spirit. God forbid!'

'She died a woman,' said the Ghost, 'and had, as I think, children.'

'One child,' Scrooge returned.

'True,' said the Ghost. 'Your nephew!'

Scrooge seemed uneasy in his mind; and answered briefly, 'Yes.'

Although they had but that moment left the school behind them, they were now in the busy thoroughfares of a city, where shadowy passengers passed and repassed; where shadowy carts and coaches battled for the way, and all the strife and tumult of a real city were. It was made plain enough, by the dressing of the shops, that here too it was Christmas time again; but it was evening, and the streets were lighted up.

The Ghost stopped at a certain warehouse door, and asked Scrooge if he knew it.

'Know it!' said Scrooge. 'Was I apprenticed here?'

They went in. At sight of an old gentleman in a Welch wig, sitting behind such a high desk, that if he had been two inches taller he must have knocked his head against the ceiling, Scrooge cried in great excitement:

'Why, it's old Fezziwig! Bless his heart; it's Fezziwig alive again!'

Old Fezziwig laid down his pen, and looked up at the clock, which pointed to the hour of seven. He rubbed his hands; adjusted his capacious waistcoat; laughed all over himself, from his shoes to his organ of benevolence; and called out in a comfortable, oily, rich, fat, jovial voice:

'Yo ho, there! Ebenezer! Dick!'

Scrooge's former self, now grown a young man, came briskly in, accompanied by his fellow-'prentice.

'Dick Wilkins, to be sure!' said Scrooge to the Ghost. 'Bless me, yes. There he is. He was very much attached to me, was Dick. Poor Dick! Dear, dear!'

'Yo ho, my boys!' said Fezziwig. 'No more work to-night. Christmas Eve, Dick. Christmas, Ebenezer! Let's have the shutters up,' cried old Fezziwig, with a sharp clap of his hands, 'before a man can say, Jack Robinson!'

You wouldn't believe how those two fellows went at it! They charged into the street with the shutters – one, two, three – had 'em up in their places – four, five, six – barred 'em and pinned 'em – seven, eight, nine – and came back before you could have got to twelve, panting like race-horses.

'Hilli-ho!' cried old Fezziwig, skipping down from the high desk, with wonderful agility. 'Clear away, my lads, and let's have lots of room here! Hilli-ho, Dick! Chirrup, Ebenezer!'

Clear away! There was nothing they wouldn't have cleared away, or couldn't have cleared away, with old Fezziwig looking on. It was done in a minute. Every movable was packed off, as if it were dismissed from public life for evermore; the floor was swept and watered, the lamps were trimmed, fuel was heaped upon the fire; and the warehouse was as snug, and warm, and dry, and bright a ball-room, as you would desire to see upon a winter's night.

In came a fiddler with a music-book, and went up to the lofty desk, and made an orchestra of it, and tuned like fifty stomach-aches. In came Mrs. Fezziwig, one vast substantial smile. In came the three Miss Fezziwigs, beaming and lovable. In came the six young followers whose hearts they broke. In came all the young men and women employed in the business. In came the housemaid, with her cousin, the baker. In came the cook, with her brother's particular friend, the milkman. In came the boy from over the way, who was suspected of not having board enough from his master; trying to hide himself behind the girl from next door but one, who was proved to have had her ears pulled by her Mistress. In they all came, one after another; some shyly, some boldly, some gracefully, some awkwardly, some pushing, some pulling; in they all came, anyhow and everyhow. Away they all went, twenty couples at once, hands half round and back again the other way; down the middle and up again; round and round in various stages of affectionate

grouping; old top couple always turning up in the wrong place; new top couple starting off again, as soon as they got there; all top couples at last, and not a bottom one to help them. When this result was brought about, old Fezziwig, clapping his hands to stop the dance, cried out, 'Well done!' and the fiddler plunged his hot face into a pot of porter, especially provided for that purpose. But scorning rest upon his reappearance, he instantly began again, though there were no dancers yet, as if the other fiddler had been carried home, exhausted, on a shutter; and he were a bran-new man resolved to beat him out of sight, or perish.

There were more dances, and there were forfeits, and more dances, and there was cake, and there was negus, and there was a great piece of Cold Roast, and there was a great piece of Cold Boiled, and there were mince-pies, and plenty of beer. But the great effect of the evening came after the Roast and Boiled, when the fiddler (an artful dog, mind! The sort of man who knew his business better than you or I could have told it him!) struck up 'Sir Roger de Coverley'. Then old Fezziwig stood out to dance with Mrs. Fezziwig. Top couple, too; with a good stiff piece of work cut out for them; three or four and twenty pair of partners; people who were not to be trifled with; people who *would* dance, and had no notion of walking.

But if they had been twice as many: ah, four times: old Fezziwig would have been a match for them, and so would Mrs. Fezziwig. As to *her*, she

was worthy to be his partner in every sense of the term. If that's not high praise, tell me higher, and I'll use it. A positive light appeared to issue from Fezziwig's calves. They shone in every part of the dance like moons. You couldn't have predicted, at any given time, what would become of 'em next. And when old Fezziwig and Mrs. Fezziwig had gone all through the dance; advance and retire, hold hands with your partner; bow and curtsey; corkscrew; thread-the-needle, and back again to your place; Fezziwig 'cut' – cut so deftly, that he appeared to wink with his legs, and came upon his feet again without a stagger.

When the clock struck eleven, this domestic ball broke up. Mr. and Mrs. Fezziwig took their stations, one on either side the door, and shaking hands with every person individually as he or she went out, wished him or her a Merry Christmas. When everybody had retired but the two 'prentices, they did the same to them; and thus the cheerful voices died away, and the lads were left to their beds; which were under a counter in the back-shop.

During the whole of this time, Scrooge had acted like a man out of his wits. His heart and soul were in the scene, and with his former self. He corroborated everything, remembered everything, enjoyed everything, and underwent the strangest agitation. It was not until now, when the bright faces of his former self and Dick were turned from them, that he remembered the Ghost, and became

conscious that it was looking full upon him, while the light upon its head burnt very clear.

'A small matter,' said the Ghost, 'to make these silly folks so full of gratitude.'

'Small!' echoed Scrooge.

The Spirit signed to him to listen to the two apprentices, who were pouring out their hearts in praise of Fezziwig: and when he had done so, said,

'Why! Is it not? He has spent but a few pounds of your mortal money: three or four, perhaps. Is that so much that he deserves this praise?'

'It isn't that,' said Scrooge, heated by the remark, and speaking unconsciously like his former, not his latter, self. 'It isn't that, Spirit. He has the power to render us happy or unhappy; to make our service light or burdensome; a pleasure or a toil. Say that his power lies in words and looks; in things so slight and insignificant that it is impossible to add and count 'em up: what then? The happiness he gives, is quite as great as if it cost a fortune.'

He felt the Spirit's glance, and stopped.

'What is the matter?' asked the Ghost.

'Nothing particular,' said Scrooge.

'Something, I think?' the Ghost insisted.

'No,' said Scrooge, 'No. I should like to be able to say a word or two to my clerk just now! That's all.'

His former self turned down the lamps as he gave utterance to the wish; and Scrooge and the Ghost again stood side by side in the open air.

'My time grows short,' observed the Spirit. 'Quick!'

This was not addressed to Scrooge, or to any one whom he could see, but it produced an immediate effect. For again Scrooge saw himself. He was older now; a man in the prime of life. His face had not the harsh and rigid lines of later years; but it had begun to wear the signs of care and avarice. There was an eager, greedy, restless motion in the eye, which showed the passion that had taken root, and where the shadow of the growing tree would fall.

He was not alone, but sat by the side of a fair young girl in a mourning-dress: in whose eyes there were tears, which sparkled in the light that shone out of the Ghost of Christmas Past.

'It matters little,' she said, softly. 'To you, very little. Another idol has displaced me; and if it can cheer and comfort you in time to come, as I would have tried to do, I have no just cause to grieve.'

'What Idol has displaced you?' he rejoined.

'A golden one.'

'This is the even-handed dealing of the world!' he said. 'There is nothing on which it is so hard as poverty; and there is nothing it professes to condemn with such severity as the pursuit of wealth!'

'You fear the world too much,' she answered, gently. 'All your other hopes have merged into the hope of being beyond the chance of its sordid reproach. I have seen your nobler aspirations fall off one by one, until the master-passion, Gain, engrosses you. Have I not?'

'What then?' he retorted. 'Even if I have grown so much wiser, what then? I am not changed towards you.'

She shook her head.

'Am I?'

'Our contract is an old one. It was made when we were both poor and content to be so, until, in good season, we could improve our worldly fortune by our patient industry. You *are* changed. When it was made, you were another man.'

'I was a boy,' he said impatiently.

'Your own feeling tells you that you were not what you are,' she returned. 'I am. That which promised happiness when we were one in heart, is fraught with misery now that we are two. How often and how keenly I have thought of this, I will not say. It is enough that I *have* thought of it, and can release you.'

'Have I ever sought release?'

'In words. No. Never.'

'In what, then?'

'In a changed nature; in an altered spirit; in another atmosphere of life; another Hope as its great end. In everything that made my love of any worth or value in your sight. If this had never been between us,' said the girl, looking mildly, but with steadiness, upon him; 'tell me, would you seek me out and try to win me now? Ah, no!'

He seemed to yield to the justice of this supposition, in spite of himself. But he said, with a struggle, 'You think not.'

'I would gladly think otherwise if I could,' she answered, 'Heaven knows! When I have learned a Truth like this, I know how strong and irresistible it must be. But if you were free to-day, to-morrow, yesterday, can even I believe that you would choose a dowerless girl – you who, in your very confidence with her, weigh everything by Gain: or, choosing her, if for a moment you were false enough to your one guiding principle to do so, do I not know that your repentance and regret would surely follow? I do; and I release you. With a full heart, for the love of him you once were.'

He was about to speak; but with her head turned from him, she resumed.

'You may – the memory of what is past half makes me hope you will – have pain in this. A very, very brief time, and you will dismiss the recollection of it, gladly, as an unprofitable dream, from which it happened well that you awoke. May you be happy in the life you have chosen!'

She left him; and they parted.

'Spirit!' said Scrooge, 'show me no more! Conduct me home. Why do you delight to torture me?'

'One shadow more!' exclaimed the Ghost.

'No more!' cried Scrooge. 'No more. I don't wish to see it. Show me no more!'

But the relentless Ghost pinioned him in both his arms, and forced him to observe what happened next.

They were in another scene and place: a room, not very large or handsome, but full of comfort.

Near to the winter fire sat a beautiful young girl, so like the last that Scrooge believed it was the same, until he saw *her*, now a comely matron, sitting opposite her daughter. The noise in this room was perfectly tumultuous, for there were more children there, than Scrooge in his agitated state of mind could count; and, unlike the celebrated herd in the poem, they were not forty children conducting themselves like one, but every child was conducting itself like forty. The consequences were uproarious beyond belief; but no one seemed to care; on the contrary, the mother and daughter laughed heartily, and enjoyed it very much; and the latter, soon beginning to mingle in the sports, got pillaged by the young brigands most ruthlessly. What would I not have given to be one of them! Though I never could have been so rude, no, no! I wouldn't for the wealth of all the world have crushed that braided hair, and torn it down; and for the precious little shoe, I wouldn't have plucked it off, God bless my soul! to save my life. As to measuring her waist in sport, as they did, bold young brood, I couldn't have done it; I should have expected my arm to have grown round it for a punishment, and never come straight again. And yet I should have dearly liked, I own, to have touched her lips; to have questioned her, that she might have opened them; to have looked upon the lashes of her downcast eyes, and never raised a blush; to have let loose waves of hair, an inch of which would be a keepsake beyond price: in short, I should have liked,

I do confess, to have had the lightest licence of a child, and yet been man enough to know its value.

But now a knocking at the door was heard, and such a rush immediately ensued that she with laughing face and plundered dress was borne towards it the centre of a flushed and boisterous group, just in time to greet the father, who came home attended by a man laden with Christmas toys and presents. Then the shouting and the struggling, and the onslaught that was made on the defenceless porter! The scaling him with chairs for ladders, to dive into his pockets, despoil him of brown-paper parcels, hold on tight by his cravat, hug him round the neck, pommel his back, and kick his legs in irrepressible affection! The shouts of wonder and delight with which the development of every package was received! The terrible announcement that the baby had been taken in the act of putting a doll's frying-pan into his mouth, and was more than suspected of having swallowed a fictitious turkey, glued on a wooden platter! The immense relief of finding this a false alarm! The joy, and gratitude, and ecstasy! They are all indescribable alike. It is enough that by degrees the children and their emotions got out of the parlour and by one stair at a time, up to the top of the house; where they went to bed, and so subsided.

And now Scrooge looked on more attentively than ever, when the master of the house, having his daughter leaning fondly on him, sat down with

her and her mother at his own fireside; and when he thought that such another creature, quite as graceful and as full of promise, might have called him father, and been a spring-time in the haggard winter of his life, his sight grew very dim indeed.

'Belle,' said the husband, turning to his wife with a smile, 'I saw an old friend of yours this afternoon.'

'Who was it?'

'Guess!'

'How can I? Tut, don't I know,' she added in the same breath, laughing as he laughed. 'Mr. Scrooge.'

'Mr. Scrooge it was. I passed his office window; and as it was not shut up, and he had a candle inside, I could scarcely help seeing him. His partner lies upon the point of death, I hear; and there he sat alone. Quite alone in the world, I do believe.'

'Spirit!' said Scrooge in a broken voice, 'remove me from this place.'

'I told you these were shadows of the things that have been,' said the Ghost. 'That they are what they are, do not blame me!'

'Remove me!' Scrooge exclaimed. 'I cannot bear it!'

He turned upon the Ghost, and seeing that it looked upon him with a face, in which in some strange way there were fragments of all the faces it had shown him, wrestled with it.

'Leave me! Take me back. Haunt me no longer!'

In the struggle, if that can be called a struggle in which the Ghost with no visible resistance on its own part was undisturbed by any effort of its

adversary, Scrooge observed that its light was burning high and bright; and dimly connecting that with its influence over him, he seized the extinguisher-cap, and by a sudden action pressed it down upon its head.

The Spirit dropped beneath it, so that the extinguisher covered its whole form; but though Scrooge pressed it down with all his force, he could not hide the light: which streamed from under it, in an unbroken flood upon the ground.

He was conscious of being exhausted, and overcome by an irresistible drowsiness; and, further, of being in his own bedroom. He gave the cap a parting squeeze, in which his hand relaxed; and had barely time to reel to bed, before he sank into a heavy sleep.

THE SECOND OF
THE THREE SPIRITS

Awaking in the middle of a prodigiously tough snore, and sitting up in bed to get his thoughts together, Scrooge had no occasion to be told that the bell was again upon the stroke of One. He felt that he was restored to consciousness in the right nick of time, for the especial purpose of holding a conference with the second messenger despatched to him through Jacob Marley's intervention. But, finding that he turned uncomfortably cold when he began to wonder which of his curtains this new spectre would draw back, he put them every one aside with his own hands; and lying down again, established a sharp look-out all round the bed. For he wished to challenge the Spirit on the moment of its appearance, and did not wish to be taken by surprise and made nervous.

Gentlemen of the free-and-easy sort, who plume themselves on being acquainted with a move or two, and being usually equal to the time-of-day, express the wide range of their capacity for adventure by observing that they are good for anything from pitch-and-toss to manslaughter; between which opposite extremes, no doubt, there lies a tolerably wide and comprehensive range of sub-

jects. Without venturing for Scrooge quite as hardily as this, I don't mind calling on you to believe that he was ready for a good broad field of strange appearances, and that nothing between a baby and a rhinoceros would have astonished him very much.

Now, being prepared for almost anything, he was not by any means prepared for nothing; and, consequently, when the Bell struck One, and no shape appeared, he was taken with a violent fit of trembling. Five minutes, ten minutes, a quarter of an hour went by, yet nothing came. All this time, he lay upon his bed, the very core and centre of a blaze of ruddy light, which streamed upon it when the clock proclaimed the hour; and which being only light, was more alarming than a dozen ghosts, as he was powerless to make out what it meant, or would be at; and was sometimes apprehensive that he might be at that very moment an interesting case of spontaneous combustion, without having the consolation of knowing it. At last, however, he began to think – as you or I would have thought at first; for it is always the person not in the predica- ment who knows what ought to have been done in it, and would unquestionably have done it too – at last, I say, he began to think that the source and secret of this ghostly light might be in the adjoining room: from whence, on further tracing it, it seemed to shine. This idea taking full possession of his mind, he got up softly and shuffled in his slippers to the door.

The moment Scrooge's hand was on the lock, a strange voice called him by his name, and bade him enter. He obeyed.

It was his own room. There was no doubt about that. But it had undergone a surprising transformation. The walls and ceiling were so hung with living green, that it looked a perfect grove, from every part of which, bright gleaming berries glistened. The crisp leaves of holly, mistletoe, and ivy reflected back the light, as if so many little mirrors had been scattered there; and such a mighty blaze went roaring up the chimney, as that dull petrification of a hearth had never known in Scrooge's time, or Marley's, or for many and many a winter season gone. Heaped up on the floor, to form a kind of throne, were turkeys, geese, game, poultry, brawn, great joints of meat, sucking-pigs, long wreaths of sausages, mince-pies, plum-puddings, barrels of oysters, red-hot chestnuts, cherry-cheeked apples, juicy oranges, luscious pears, immense twelfth-cakes, and seething bowls of punch, that made the chamber dim with their delicious steam. In easy state upon this couch, there sat a jolly Giant, glorious to see; who bore a glowing torch, in shape not unlike Plenty's horn, and held it up, high up, to shed its light on Scrooge, as he came peeping round the door.

'Come in!' exclaimed the Ghost. 'Come in! and know me better, man!'

Scrooge entered timidly, and hung his head before this Spirit. He was not the dogged Scrooge

he had been; and though the Spirit's eyes were clear and kind, he did not like to meet them.

'I am the Ghost of Christmas Present,' said the Spirit. 'Look upon me!'

Scrooge reverently did so. It was clothed in one simple deep green robe, or mantle, bordered with white fur. This garment hung so loosely on the figure, that its capacious breast was bare, as if disdaining to be warded or concealed by any artifice. Its feet, observable beneath the ample folds of the garment, were also bare; and on its head it wore no other covering than a holly wreath, set here and there with shining icicles. Its dark brown curls were long and free: free as its genial face, its sparkling eye, its open hand, its cheery voice, its unconstrained demeanour, and its joyful air. Girded round its middle was an antique scabbard; but no sword was in it, and the ancient sheath was eaten up with rust.

'You have never seen the like of me before!' exclaimed the Spirit.

'Never,' Scrooge made answer to it.

'Have never walked forth with the younger members of my family; meaning (for I am very young) my elder brothers born in these later years?' pursued the Phantom.

'I don't think I have,' said Scrooge. 'I am afraid I have not. Have you had many brothers, Spirit?'

'More than eighteen hundred,' said the Ghost.

'A tremendous family to provide for!' muttered Scrooge.

The Ghost of Christmas Present rose.

'Spirit,' said Scrooge submissively, 'conduct me where you will. I went forth last night on compulsion, and I learnt a lesson which is working now. To-night, if you have aught to teach me, let me profit by it.'

'Touch my robe!'

Scrooge did as he was told, and held it fast.

Holly, mistletoe, red berries, ivy, turkeys, geese, game, poultry, brawn, meat, pigs, sausages, oysters, pies, puddings, fruit, and punch, all vanished instantly. So did the room, the fire, the ruddy glow, the hour of night, and they stood in the city streets on Christmas morning, where (for the weather was severe) the people made a rough, but brisk and not unpleasant kind of music, in scraping the snow from the pavement in front of their dwellings, and from the tops of their houses: whence it was mad delight to the boys to see it come plumping down into the road below, and splitting into artificial little snow-storms.

The house fronts looked black enough, and the windows blacker, contrasting with the smooth white sheet of snow upon the roofs, and with the dirtier snow upon the ground; which last deposit had been ploughed up in deep furrows by the heavy wheels of carts and waggons; furrows that crossed and re-crossed each other hundreds of times where the great streets branched off, and made intricate channels, hard to trace, in the thick yellow mud and icy water. The sky was gloomy, and the shortest

streets were choked up with a dingy mist, half thawed, half frozen, whose heavier particles descended in a shower of sooty atoms, as if all the chimneys in Great Britain had, by one consent, caught fire, and were blazing away to their dear hearts' content. There was nothing very cheerful in the climate or the town, and yet was there an air of cheerfulness abroad that the clearest summer air and brightest summer sun might have endeavoured to diffuse in vain.

For the people who were shovelling away on the housetops were jovial and full of glee; calling out to one another from the parapets, and now and then exchanging a facetious snowball – better-natured missile far than many a wordy jest – laughing heartily if it went right, and not less heartily if it went wrong. The poulterers' shops were still half open, and the fruiterers' were radiant in their glory. There were great round, pot-bellied baskets of chestnuts, shaped like the waistcoats of jolly old gentlemen, lolling at the doors, and tumbling out into the street in their apoplectic opulence. There were ruddy, brown-faced, broad-girthed Spanish Onions, shining in the fatness of their growth like Spanish Friars; and winking from their shelves in wanton slyness at the girls as they went by, and glanced demurely at the hung-up mistletoe. There were pears and apples, clustered high in blooming pyramids; there were bunches of grapes, made in the shopkeepers' benevolence to dangle from conspicuous hooks, that people's mouths might water gratis as they

passed; there were piles of filberts, mossy and brown, recalling, in their fragrance, ancient walks among the woods, and pleasant shufflings ankle deep through withered leaves; there were Norfolk Biffins, squab and swarthy, setting off the yellow of the oranges and lemons, and, in the great compactness of their juicy persons, urgently entreating and beseeching to be carried home in paper bags and eaten after dinner. The very gold and silver fish, set forth among these choice fruits in a bowl, though members of a dull and stagnant-blooded race, appeared to know that there was something going on; and, to a fish, went gasping round and round their little world in slow and passionless excitement.

The Grocers''! oh the Grocers''! nearly closed, with perhaps two shutters down, or one; but through those gaps such glimpses! It was not alone that the scales descending on the counter made a merry sound, or that the twine and roller parted company so briskly, or that the canisters were rattled up and down like juggling tricks, or even that the blended scents of tea and coffee were so grateful to the nose, or even that the raisins were so plentiful and rare, the almonds so extremely white, the sticks of cinnamon so long and straight, the other spices so delicious, the candied fruits so caked and spotted with molten sugar as to make the coldest lookers-on feel faint and subsequently bilious. Nor was it that the figs were moist and pulpy, or that the French plums blushed in modest

tartness from their highly-decorated boxes, or that everything was good to eat and in its Christmas dress: but the customers were all so hurried and so eager in the hopeful promise of the day, that they tumbled up against each other at the door, clashing their wicker baskets wildly, and left their purchases upon the counter, and came running back to fetch them, and committed hundreds of the like mistakes in the best humour possible; while the Grocer and his people were so frank and fresh that the polished hearts with which they fastened their aprons behind might have been their own, worn outside for general inspection, and for Christmas daws to peck at if they chose.

But soon the steeples called good people all, to church and chapel, and away they came, flocking through the streets in their best clothes, and with their gayest faces. And at the same time there emerged from scores of bye streets, lanes, and nameless turnings, innumerable people, carrying their dinners to the bakers' shops. The sight of these poor revellers appeared to interest the Spirit very much, for he stood with Scrooge beside him in a baker's doorway, and taking off the covers as their bearers passed, sprinkled incense on their dinners from his torch. And it was a very uncommon kind of torch, for once or twice when there were angry words between some dinner-carriers who had jostled each other, he shed a few drops of water on them from it, and their good humour was restored directly. For they said, it was a shame to quarrel

upon Christmas Day. And so it was! God love it, so it was!

In time the bells ceased, and the bakers' were shut up; and yet there was a genial shadowing forth of all these dinners and the progress of their cooking, in the thawed blotch of wet above each baker's oven; where the pavement smoked as if its stones were cooking too.

'Is there a peculiar flavour in what you sprinkle from your torch?' asked Scrooge.

'There is. My own.'

'Would it apply to any kind of dinner on this day?' asked Scrooge.

'To any kindly given. To a poor one most.'

'Why to a poor one most?' asked Scrooge.

'Because it needs it most.'

'Spirit,' said Scrooge, after a moment's thought, 'I wonder you, of all the beings in the many worlds about us, should desire to cramp these people's opportunities of innocent enjoyment.'

'I!' cried the Spirit.

'You would deprive them of their means of dining every seventh day, often the only day on which they can be said to dine at all,' said Scrooge. 'Wouldn't you?'

'I!' cried the Spirit.

'You seek to close these places on the Seventh Day?' said Scrooge. 'And it comes to the same thing.'

'I seek!' exclaimed the Spirit.

'Forgive me if I am wrong. It has been done in

your name, or at least in that of your family,' said Scrooge.

'There are some upon this earth of yours,' returned the Spirit, 'who lay claim to know us, and who do their deeds of passion, pride, ill-will, hatred, envy, bigotry, and selfishness in our name, who are as strange to us and all our kith and kin, as if they had never lived. Remember that, and charge their doings on themselves, not us.'

Scrooge promised that he would; and they went on, invisible, as they had been before, into the suburbs of the town. It was a remarkable quality of the Ghost (which Scrooge had observed at the baker's) that notwithstanding his gigantic size, he could accommodate himself to any place with ease; and that he stood beneath a low roof quite as gracefully and like a supernatural creature, as it was possible he could have done in any lofty hall.

And perhaps it was the pleasure the good Spirit had in showing off this power of his, or else it was his own kind, generous, hearty nature, and his sympathy with all poor men, that led him straight to Scrooge's clerk's; for there he went, and took Scrooge with him, holding to his robe; and on the threshold of the door the Spirit smiled, and stopped to bless Bob Cratchit's dwelling with the sprinkling of his torch. Think of that! Bob had but fifteen 'Bob' a-week himself; he pocketed on Saturdays but fifteen copies of his Christian name; and yet the Ghost of Christmas Present blessed his four-roomed house!

Then up rose Mrs. Cratchit, Cratchit's wife, dressed out but poorly in a twice-turned gown, but brave in ribbons, which are cheap and make a goodly show for sixpence; and she laid the cloth, assisted by Belinda Cratchit, second of her daughters, also brave in ribbons; while Master Peter Cratchit plunged a fork into the saucepan of potatoes, and getting the corners of his monstrous shirt-collar (Bob's private property, conferred upon his son and heir in honour of the day) into his mouth, rejoiced to find himself so gallantly attired, and yearned to show his linen in the fashionable Parks. And now two smaller Cratchits, boy and girl, came tearing in, screaming that outside the baker's they had smelt the goose, and known it for their own; and basking in luxurious thoughts of sage and onion, these young Cratchits danced about the table, and exalted Master Peter Cratchit to the skies, while he (not proud, although his collars nearly choked him) blew the fire, until the slow potatoes bubbling up, knocked loudly at the saucepan-lid to be let out and peeled.

'What has ever got your precious father then,' said Mrs. Cratchit. 'And your brother, Tiny Tim; and Martha warn't as late last Christmas Day by half-an-hour!'

'Here's Martha, mother!' said a girl, appearing as she spoke.

'Here's Martha, mother!' cried the two young Cratchits. 'Hurrah! There's *such* a goose, Martha!'

'Why, bless your heart alive, my dear, how late

you are!' said Mrs. Cratchit, kissing her a dozen times, and taking off her shawl and bonnet for her, with officious zeal.

'We'd a deal of work to finish up last night,' replied the girl, 'and had to clear away this morning, mother!'

'Well! Never mind so long as you are come,' said Mrs. Cratchit. 'Sit ye down before the fire, my dear, and have a warm, Lord bless ye!'

'No no! There's father coming,' cried the two young Cratchits, who were everywhere at once. 'Hide Martha, hide!'

So Martha hid herself, and in came little Bob, the father, with at least three feet of comforter exclusive of the fringe, hanging down before him; and his thread-bare clothes darned up and brushed, to look seasonable; and Tiny Tim upon his shoulder. Alas for Tiny Tim, he bore a little crutch, and had his limbs supported by an iron frame!

'Why, where's our Martha?' cried Bob Cratchit looking round.

'Not coming,' said Mrs. Cratchit.

'Not coming!' said Bob, with a sudden declension in his high spirits; for he had been Tim's blood horse all the way from church, and had come home rampant. 'Not coming upon Christmas Day!'

Martha didn't like to see him disappointed, if it were only in joke; so she came out prematurely from behind the closet door, and ran into his arms, while the two young Cratchits hustled Tiny Tim,

and bore him off into the wash-house, that he might hear the pudding singing in the copper.

'And how did little Tim behave?' asked Mrs. Cratchit, when she had rallied Bob on his credulity and Bob had hugged his daughter to his heart's content.

'As good as gold,' said Bob, 'and better. Somehow he gets thoughtful sitting by himself so much, and thinks the strangest things you ever heard. He told me, coming home, that he hoped the people saw him in the church, because he was a cripple, and it might be pleasant to them to remember upon Christmas Day, who made lame beggars walk and blind men see.'

Bob's voice was tremulous when he told them this, and trembled more when he said that Tiny Tim was growing strong and hearty.

His active little crutch was heard upon the floor, and back came Tiny Tim before another word was spoken, escorted by his brother and sister to his stool before the fire; and while Bob, turning up his cuffs – as if, poor fellow, they were capable of being made more shabby – compounded some hot mixture in a jug with gin and lemons, and stirred it round and round and put it on the hob to simmer; Master Peter, and the two ubiquitous young Cratchits went to fetch the goose, with which they soon returned in high procession.

Such a bustle ensued that you might have thought a goose the rarest of all birds; a feathered phenomenon, to which a black swan was a matter

of course; and in truth it was something very like it in that house. Mrs. Cratchit made the gravy (ready beforehand in a little saucepan) hissing hot; Master Peter mashed the potatoes with incredible vigour; Miss Belinda sweetened up the apple-sauce; Martha dusted the hot plates; Bob took Tiny Tim beside him in a tiny corner at the table; the two young Cratchits set chairs for everybody, not forgetting themselves, and mounting guard upon their posts, crammed spoons into their mouths, lest they should shriek for goose before their turn came to be helped. At last the dishes were set on, and grace was said. It was succeeded by a breathless pause, as Mrs. Cratchit, looking slowly all along the carving-knife, prepared to plunge it in the breast; but when she did, and when the long expected gush of stuffing issued forth, one murmur of delight arose all round the board, and even Tiny Tim, excited by the two young Cratchits, beat on the table with the handle of his knife, and feebly cried Hurrah!

There never was such a goose. Bob said he didn't believe there ever was such a goose cooked. Its tenderness and flavour, size and cheapness, were the themes of universal admiration. Eked out by the apple-sauce and mashed potatoes, it was a sufficient dinner for the whole family; indeed, as Mrs. Cratchit said with great delight (surveying one small atom of a bone upon the dish), they hadn't ate it all at last! Yet every one had had enough, and the youngest Cratchits in particular, were steeped in sage and onion to the eyebrows! But now, the plates being

changed by Miss Belinda, Mrs. Cratchit left the room alone – too nervous to bear witnesses – to take the pudding up, and bring it in.

Suppose it should not be done enough! Suppose it should break in turning out! Suppose somebody should have got over the wall of the back-yard, and stolen it, while they were merry with the goose: a supposition at which the two young Cratchits became livid! All sorts of horrors were supposed.

Hallo! A great deal of steam! The pudding was out of the copper. A smell like a washing-day! That was the cloth. A smell like an eating-house, and a pastry cook's next door to each other, with a laundress's next door to that! That was the pudding. In half a minute Mrs. Cratchit entered: flushed, but smiling proudly: with the pudding, like a speckled cannon-ball, so hard and firm, blazing in half of half-a-quartern of ignited brandy, and bedight with Christmas holly stuck into the top.

Oh, a wonderful pudding! Bob Cratchit said, and calmly too, that he regarded it as the greatest success achieved by Mrs. Cratchit since their marriage. Mrs. Cratchit said that now the weight was off her mind, she would confess she had had her doubts about the quantity of flour. Everybody had something to say about it, but nobody said or thought it was at all a small pudding for a large family. It would have been flat heresy to do so. Any Cratchit would have blushed to hint at such a thing.

At last the dinner was all done, the cloth was cleared, the hearth swept, and the fire made up. The

compound in the jug being tasted, and considered perfect, apples and oranges were put upon the table, and a shovel-full of chestnuts on the fire. Then all the Cratchit family drew round the hearth, in what Bob Cratchit called a circle, meaning half a one; and at Bob Cratchit's elbow stood the family display of glass; two tumblers, and a custard-cup without a handle.

These held the hot stuff from the jug, however, as well as golden goblets would have done; and Bob served it out with beaming looks, while the chestnuts on the fire sputtered and crackled noisily. Then Bob proposed:

'A Merry Christmas to us all, my dears. God bless us!'

Which all the family re-echoed.

'God bless us every one!' said Tiny Tim, the last of all.

He sat very close to his father's side, upon his little stool. Bob held his withered little hand in his, as if he loved the child, and wished to keep him by his side, and dreaded that he might be taken from him.

'Spirit,' said Scrooge, with an interest he had never felt before, 'tell me if Tiny Tim will live.'

'I see a vacant seat,' replied the Ghost, 'in the poor chimney corner, and a crutch without an owner, carefully preserved. If these shadows remain unaltered by the Future, the child will die.'

'No, no,' said Scrooge. 'Oh no, kind Spirit! say he will be spared.'

'If these shadows remain unaltered by the Future, none other of my race,' returned the Ghost, 'will find him here. What then? If he be like to die, he had better do it, and decrease the surplus population.'

Scrooge hung his head to hear his own words quoted by the Spirit, and was overcome with penitence and grief.

'Man,' said the Ghost, 'if man you be in heart, not adamant, forbear that wicked cant until you have discovered What the surplus is, and Where it is. Will you decide what men shall live, what men shall die? It may be, that in the sight of Heaven, you are more worthless and less fit to live than millions like this poor man's child. Oh God! to hear the Insect on the leaf pronouncing on the too much life among his hungry brothers in the dust!'

Scrooge bent before the Ghost's rebuke, and trembling cast his eyes upon the ground. But he raised them speedily, on hearing his own name.

'Mr. Scrooge!' said Bob; 'I'll give you Mr. Scrooge, the Founder of the Feast!'

'The Founder of the Feast indeed!' cried Mrs. Cratchit, reddening. 'I wish I had him here. I'd give him a piece of my mind to feast upon, and I hope he'd have a good appetite for it.'

'My dear,' said Bob, 'the children; Christmas Day.'

'It should be Christmas Day, I am sure,' said she, 'on which one drinks the health of such an odious, stingy, hard, unfeeling man as Mr. Scrooge. You

know he is, Robert! Nobody knows it better than you do, poor fellow!'

'My dear,' was Bob's mild answer, 'Christmas Day.'

'I'll drink his health for your sake and the Day's,' said Mrs. Cratchit, 'not for his. Long life to him! A merry Christmas and a happy new year! – he'll be very merry and very happy, I have no doubt!'

The children drank the toast after her. It was the first of their proceedings which had no heartiness in it. Tiny Tim drank it last of all, but he didn't care twopence for it. Scrooge was the Ogre of the family. The mention of his name cast a dark shadow on the party, which was not dispelled for full five minutes.

After it had passed away, they were ten times merrier than before, from the mere relief of Scrooge the Baleful being done with. Bob Cratchit told them how he had a situation in his eye for Master Peter, which would bring in, if obtained, full five-and-sixpence weekly. The two young Cratchits laughed tremendously at the idea of Peter's being a man of business; and Peter himself looked thoughtfully at the fire from between his collars, as if he were deliberating what particular investments he should favour when he came into the receipt of that bewildering income. Martha, who was a poor apprentice at a milliner's, then told them what kind of work she had to do, and how many hours she worked at a stretch, and how she meant to lie a-bed tomorrow morning for a good long rest; to-morrow being a

holiday she passed at home. Also how she had seen a countess and a lord some days before, and how the lord 'was much about as tall as Peter'; at which Peter pulled up his collars so high that you couldn't have seen his head if you had been there. All this time the chestnuts and the jug went round and round; and bye and bye they had a song, about a lost child travelling in the snow, from Tiny Tim; who had a plaintive little voice, and sang it very well indeed.

There was nothing of high mark in this. They were not a handsome family; they were not well dressed; their shoes were far from being water-proof; their clothes were scanty; and Peter might have known, and very likely did, the inside of a pawnbroker's. But they were happy, grateful, pleased with one another, and contented with the time; and when they faded, and looked happier yet in the bright sprinklings of the Spirit's torch at parting, Scrooge had his eye upon them, and especially on Tiny Tim, until the last.

By this time it was getting dark, and snowing pretty heavily; and as Scrooge and the Spirit went along the streets, the brightness of the roaring fires in kitchens, parlours, and all sorts of rooms, was wonderful. Here, the flickering of the blaze showed preparations for a cosy dinner, with hot plates baking through and through before the fire, and deep red curtains, ready to be drawn, to shut out cold and darkness. There, all the children of the house were running out into the snow to meet their

married sisters, brothers, cousins, uncles, aunts, and be the first to greet them. Here, again, were shadows on the window-blind of guests assembling; and there a group of handsome girls, all hooded and fur-booted, and all chattering at once, tripped lightly off to some near neighbour's house; where, woe upon the single man who saw them enter – artful witches: well they knew it – in a glow!

But if you had judged from the numbers of people on their way to friendly gatherings, you might have thought that no one was at home to give them welcome when they got there, instead of every house expecting company, and piling up its fires half-chimney high. Blessings on it, how the Ghost exulted! How it bared its breadth of breast, and opened its capacious palm, and floated on, outpouring, with a generous hand, its bright and harmless mirth on everything within its reach! The very lamplighter, who ran on before dotting the dusky street with specks of light, and who was dressed to spend the evening somewhere, laughed out loudly as the Spirit passed: though little kenned the lamplighter that he had any company but Christmas!

And now, without a word of warning from the Ghost, they stood upon a bleak and desert moor, where monstrous masses of rude stone were cast about, as though it were the burial-place of giants; and water spread itself wheresoever it listed – or would have done so, but for the frost that held it prisoner; and nothing grew but moss and furze, and

coarse, rank grass. Down in the west the setting sun had left a streak of fiery red, which glared upon the desolation for an instant, like a sullen eye, and frowning lower, lower, lower yet, was lost in the thick gloom of darkest night.

'What place is this?' asked Scrooge.

'A place where Miners live, who labour in the bowels of the earth,' returned the Spirit. 'But they know me. See!'

A light shone from the window of a hut, and swiftly they advanced towards it. Passing through the wall of mud and stone, they found a cheerful company assembled round a glowing fire. An old, old man and woman, with their children and their children's children, and another generation beyond that, all decked out gaily in their holiday attire. The old man, in a voice that seldom rose above the howling of the wind upon the barren waste, was singing them a Christmas song; it had been a very old song when he was a boy; and from time to time they all joined in the chorus. So surely as they raised their voices, the old man got quite blithe and loud; and so surely as they stopped, his vigour sang again.

The Spirit did not tarry here, but bade Scrooge hold his robe, and passing on above the moor, sped whither? Not to sea? To sea. To Scrooge's horror, looking back, he saw the last of the land, a frightful range of rocks, behind them; and his ears were deafened by the thundering of water, as it rolled, and roared, and raged among the dreadful caverns

it had worn, and fiercely tried to undermine the earth.

Built upon a dismal reef of sunken rocks, some league or so from shore, on which the waters chafed and dashed, the wild year through, there stood a solitary lighthouse. Great heaps of sea-weed clung to its base, and storm-birds – born of the wind one might suppose, as sea-weed of the water – rose and fell about it, like the waves they skimmed.

But even here, two men who watched the light had made a fire, that through the loophole in the thick stone wall shed out a ray of brightness on the awful sea. Joining their horny hands over the rough table at which they sat, they wished each other Merry Christmas in their can of grog; and one of them: the elder, too, with his face all damaged and scarred with hard weather, as the figure-head of an old ship might be: struck up a sturdy song that was like a Gale in itself.

Again the Ghost sped on, above the black and heaving sea – on, on – until, being far away, as he told Scrooge, from any shore, they lighted on a ship. They stood beside the helmsman at the wheel, the look-out in the bow, the officers who had the watch; dark, ghostly figures in their several stations; but every man among them hummed a Christmas tune, or had a Christmas thought, or spoke below his breath to his companion of some bygone Christmas Day, with homeward hopes belonging to it. And every man on board, waking or sleeping, good or bad, had had a kinder word for another on that

day than on any day in the year; and had shared to some extent in its festivities; and had remembered those he cared for at a distance, and had known that they delighted to remember him.

It was a great surprise to Scrooge, while listening to the moaning of the wind, and thinking what a solemn thing it was to move on through the lonely darkness over an unknown abyss, whose depths were secrets as profound as Death: it was a great surprise to Scrooge, while thus engaged, to hear a hearty laugh. It was a much greater surprise to Scrooge to recognise it as his own nephew's, and to find himself in a bright, dry, gleaming room, with the Spirit standing smiling by his side, and looking at that same nephew with approving affability!

'Ha, ha!' laughed Scrooge's nephew. 'Ha, ha, ha!'

If you should happen, by any unlikely chance, to know a man more blest in a laugh than Scrooge's nephew, all I can say is, I should like to know him too. Introduce him to me, and I'll cultivate his acquaintance.

It is a fair, even-handed, noble adjustment of things, that while there is infection in disease and sorrow, there is nothing in the world so irresistibly contagious as laughter and good-humour. When Scrooge's nephew laughed in this way: holding his sides, rolling his head, and twisting his face into the most extravagant contortions: Scrooge's niece, by marriage, laughed as heartily as he. And their

assembled friends being not a bit behindhand, roared out, lustily.

'Ha, ha! Ha, ha, ha, ha!'

'He said that Christmas was a humbug, as I live!' cried Scrooge's nephew. 'He believed it too!'

'More shame for him, Fred!' said Scrooge's niece, indignantly. Bless those women; they never do anything by halves. They are always in earnest.

She was very pretty: exceedingly pretty. With a dimpled, surprised-looking, capital face; a ripe little mouth, that seemed made to be kissed – as no doubt it was; all kinds of good little dots about her chin, that melted into one another when she laughed; and the sunniest pair of eyes you ever saw in any little creature's head. Altogether she was what you would have called provoking, you know; but satisfactory too. Oh, perfectly satisfactory!

'He's a comical old fellow,' said Scrooge's nephew, 'that's the truth: and not so pleasant as he might be. However, his offences carry their own punishment, and I have nothing to say against him.'

'I'm sure he is very rich, Fred,' hinted Scrooge's niece. 'At least you always tell *me* so.'

'What of that, my dear!' said Scrooge's nephew. 'His wealth is of no use to him. He don't do any good with it. He don't make himself comfortable with it. He hasn't the satisfaction of thinking – ha, ha, ha! – that he is ever going to benefit Us with it.'

'I have no patience with him,' observed Scrooge's

niece. Scrooge's niece's sisters, and all the other ladies, expressed the same opinion.

'Oh, I have!' said Scrooge's nephew. 'I am sorry for him; I couldn't be angry with him if I tried. Who suffers by his ill whims! Himself, always. Here, he takes it into his head to dislike us, and he won't come and dine with us. What's the consequence? He don't lose much of a dinner.'

'Indeed, I think he loses a very good dinner,' interrupted Scrooge's niece. Everybody else said the same, and they must be allowed to have been competent judges, because they had just had dinner; and, with the dessert upon the table, were clustered round the fire, by lamplight.

'Well! I'm very glad to hear it,' said Scrooge's nephew, 'because I haven't great faith in these young housekeepers. What do *you* say, Topper?'

Topper had clearly got his eye upon one of Scrooge's niece's sisters, for he answered that a bachelor was a wretched outcast, who had no right to express an opinion on the subject. Whereat Scrooge's niece's sister – the plump one with the lace tucker: not the one with the roses – blushed.

'Do go on, Fred,' said Scrooge's niece, clapping her hands. 'He never finishes what he begins to say! He is such a ridiculous fellow!'

Scrooge's nephew revelled in another laugh, and as it was impossible to keep the infection off; though the plump sister tried hard to do it with aromatic vinegar; his example was unanimously followed.

'I was going to say,' said Scrooge's nephew, 'that

the consequence of his taking a dislike to us, and not making merry with us, is, as I think, that he loses some pleasant moments, which could do him no harm. I am sure he loses pleasanter companions than he can find in his own thoughts, either in his mouldy old office, or his dusty chambers. I mean to give him the same chance every year, whether he likes it or not, for I pity him. He may rail at Christmas till he dies, but he can't help thinking better of it – I defy him – if he finds me going there, in good temper, year after year, and saying Uncle Scrooge, how are you? If it only puts him in the vein to leave his poor clerk fifty pounds, *that's* something; and I think I shook him, yesterday.'

It was their turn to laugh now, at the notion of his shaking Scrooge. But being thoroughly good-natured, and not much caring what they laughed at, so that they laughed at any rate, he encouraged them in their merriment, and passed the bottle, joyously.

After tea, they had some music. For they were a musical family, and knew what they were about, when they sung a Glee or Catch, I can assure you: especially Topper, who could growl away in the bass like a good one, and never swell the large veins in his forehead, or get red in the face over it. Scrooge's niece played well upon the harp; and played among other tunes a simple little air (a mere nothing: you might learn to whistle it in two minutes), which had been familiar to the child who fetched Scrooge from the boarding-school, as he

had been reminded by the Ghost of Christmas Past. When this strain of music sounded, all the things that the Ghost had shown him, came upon his mind; he softened more and more; and thought that if he could have listened to it often, years ago, he might have cultivated the kindnesses of life for his own happiness with his own hands, without resorting to the sexton's spade that buried Jacob Marley.

But they didn't devote the whole evening to music. After a while they played at forfeits; for it is good to be children sometimes, and never better than at Christmas, when its mighty Founder was a child himself. Stop! There was first a game at blind-man's buff. Of course there was. And I no more believe Topper was really blind than I believe he had eyes in his boots. My opinion is, that it was a done thing between him and Scrooge's nephew; and that the Ghost of Christmas Present knew it. The way he went after that plump sister in the lace tucker, was an outrage on the credulity of human nature. Knocking down the fire-irons, tumbling over the chairs, bumping against the piano, smothering himself among the curtains, wherever she went, there went he. He always knew where the plump sister was. He wouldn't catch anybody else. If you had fallen up against him, as some of them did, and stood there; he would have made a feint of endeavouring to seize you, which would have been an affront to your understanding; and would instantly have sidled off in the direction of the

plump sister. She often cried out that it wasn't fair; and it really was not. But when at last, he caught her; when, in spite of all her silken rustlings, and her rapid flutterings past him, he got her into a corner whence there was no escape; then his conduct was the most execrable. For his pretending not to know her; his pretending that it was necessary to touch her head-dress, and further to assure himself of her identity by pressing a certain ring upon her finger, and a certain chain about her neck; was vile, monstrous! No doubt she told him her opinion of it, when, another blind-man being in office, they were so very confidential together, behind the curtains.

Scrooge's niece was not one of the blind-man's buff party, but was made comfortable with a large chair and a footstool, in a snug corner, where the Ghost and Scrooge were close behind her. But she joined in the forfeits, and loved her love to admiration with all the letters of the alphabet. Likewise at the game of How, When, and Where, she was very great, and to the secret joy of Scrooge's nephew, beat her sisters hollow: though they were sharp girls too, as Topper could have told you. There might have been twenty people there, young and old, but they all played, and so did Scrooge; for wholly forgetting in the interest he had in what was going on, that his voice made no sound in their ears, he sometimes came out with his guess quite loud, and very often guessed quite right, too; for the sharpest needle, best Whitechapel, warranted

not to cut in the eye, was not sharper than Scrooge: blunt as he took it in his head to be.

The Ghost was greatly pleased to find him in this mood, and looked upon him with such favour that he begged like a boy to be allowed to stay until the guests departed. But this the Spirit said could not be done.

'Here's a new game,' said Scrooge. 'One half hour, Spirit, only one!'

It was a Game called Yes and No, where Scrooge's nephew had to think of something, and the rest must find out what; he only answering to their questions yes or no as the case was. The brisk fire of questioning to which he was exposed, elicited from him that he was thinking of an animal, a live animal, rather a disagreeable animal, a savage animal, an animal that growled and grunted sometimes, and talked sometimes, and lived in London, and walked about the streets, and wasn't made a show of, and wasn't led by anybody, and didn't live in a menagerie, and was never killed in a market, and was not a horse, or an ass, or a cow, or a bull, or a tiger, or a dog, or a pig, or a cat, or a bear. At every fresh question that was put to him, this nephew burst into a fresh roar of laughter; and was so inexpressibly tickled, that he was obliged to get up off the sofa and stamp. At last the plump sister, falling into a similar state, cried out:

'I have found it out! I know what it is, Fred! I know what it is!'

'What is it?' cried Fred.

'It's your Uncle Scro-o-o-o-oge!'

Which it certainly was. Admiration was the universal sentiment, though some objected that the reply to 'Is it a bear?' ought to have been 'Yes;' inasmuch as an answer in the negative was sufficient to have diverted their thoughts from Mr. Scrooge, supposing they had ever had any tendency that way.

'He has given us plenty of merriment, I am sure,' said Fred, 'and it would be ungrateful not to drink his health. Here is a glass of mulled wine ready to our hand at the moment; and I say "Uncle Scrooge!"'

'Well! Uncle Scrooge!' they cried.

'A Merry Christmas and a Happy New Year to the old man, whatever he is!' said Scrooge's nephew. 'He wouldn't take it from me, but may he have it, nevertheless. Uncle Scrooge!'

Uncle Scrooge had imperceptibly become so gay and light of heart, that he would have pledged the unconscious company in return, and thanked them in an inaudible speech, if the Ghost had given him time. But the whole scene passed off in the breath of the last word spoken by his nephew; and he and the Spirit were again upon their travels.

Much they saw, and far they went, and many homes they visited, but always with a happy end. The Spirit stood beside sick beds, and they were cheerful; on foreign lands, and they were close at home; by struggling men, and they were patient in their greater hope; by poverty, and it was rich. In

alms-house, hospital, and jail, in misery's every refuge, where vain man in his little brief authority had not made fast the door, and barred the Spirit out, he left his blessing, and taught Scrooge his precepts.

It was a long night, if it were only a night; but Scrooge had his doubts of this, because the Christmas Holidays appeared to be condensed into the space of time they passed together. It was strange, too, that while Scrooge remained unaltered in his outward form, the Ghost grew older, clearly older. Scrooge had observed this change, but never spoke of it, until they left a children's Twelfth Night party, when, looking at the Spirit as they stood together in an open place, he noticed that its hair was gray.

'Are spirits' lives so short?' asked Scrooge.

'My life upon this globe, is very brief,' replied the Ghost. 'It ends to-night.'

'To-night!' cried Scrooge.

'To-night at midnight. Hark! The time is drawing near.'

The chimes were ringing the three quarters past eleven at that moment.

'Forgive me if I am not justified in what I ask,' said Scrooge, looking intently at the Spirit's robe, 'but I see something strange, and not belonging to yourself, protruding from your skirts. Is it a foot or a claw!'

'It might be a claw, for the flesh there is upon it,' was the Spirit's sorrowful reply. 'Look here.'

From the foldings of its robe, it brought two children; wretched, abject, frightful, hideous, miserable. They knelt down at its feet, and clung upon the outside of its garment.

'Oh, Man! look here. Look, look, down here!' exclaimed the Ghost.

They were a boy and girl. Yellow, meagre, ragged, scowling, wolfish; but prostrate, too, in their humility. Where graceful youth should have filled their features out, and touched them with its freshest tints, a stale and shrivelled hand, like that of age, had pinched, and twisted them, and pulled them into shreds. Where angels might have sat enthroned, devils lurked; and glared out menacing. No change, no degradation, no perversion of humanity, in any grade, through all the mysteries of wonderful creation, has monsters half so horrible and dread.

Scrooge started back, appalled. Having them shown to him in this way, he tried to say they were fine children, but the words choked themselves, rather than be parties to a lie of such enormous magnitude.

'Spirit! are they yours?' Scrooge could say no more.

'They are Man's,' said the Spirit, looking down upon them. 'And they cling to me, appealing from their fathers. This boy is Ignorance. This girl is Want. Beware them both, and all of their degree, but most of all beware this boy, for on his brow I see that written which is Doom, unless the writing

be erased. Deny it!' cried the Spirit, stretching out its hand towards the city. 'Slander those who tell it ye! Admit it for your factious purposes, and make it worse. And bide the end!'

'Have they no refuge or resource?' cried Scrooge.

'Are there no prisons?' said the Spirit, turning on him for the last time with his own words. 'Are there no workhouses?'

The bell struck twelve.

Scrooge looked about him for the Ghost, and saw it not. As the last stroke ceased to vibrate, he remembered the prediction of old Jacob Marley, and lifting up his eyes, beheld a solemn Phantom, draped and hooded, coming, like a mist along the ground, towards him.

THE LAST OF THE SPIRITS

The Phantom slowly, gravely, silently, approached. When it came near him, Scrooge bent down upon his knee; for in the very air through which this Spirit moved it seemed to scatter gloom and mystery.

It was shrouded in a deep black garment, which concealed its head, its face, its form, and left nothing of it visible save one outstretched hand. But for this it would have been difficult to detach its figure from the night, and separate it from the darkness by which it was surrounded.

He felt that it was tall and stately when it came beside him, and that its mysterious presence filled him with a solemn dread. He knew no more, for the Spirit neither spoke nor moved.

'I am in the presence of the Ghost of Christmas Yet To Come?' said Scrooge.

The Spirit answered not, but pointed onward with its hand.

'You are about to show me shadows of the things that have not happened, but will happen in the time before us,' Scrooge pursued. 'Is that so, Spirit?'

The upper portion of the garment was contracted

for an instant in its folds, as if the Spirit had inclined its head. That was the only answer he received.

Although well used to ghostly company by this time, Scrooge feared the silent shape so much that his legs trembled beneath him, and he found that he could hardly stand when he prepared to follow it. The Spirit paused a moment, as observing his condition, and giving him time to recover.

But Scrooge was all the worse for this. It thrilled him with a vague uncertain horror, to know that behind the dusky shroud, there were ghostly eyes intently fixed upon him, while he, though he stretched his own to the utmost, could see nothing but a spectral hand and one great heap of black.

'Ghost of the Future!' he exclaimed, 'I fear you more than any Spectre I have seen. But as I know your purpose is to do me good, and as I hope to live to be another man from what I was, I am prepared to bear you company, and do it with a thankful heart. Will you not speak to me?'

It gave him no reply. The hand was pointed straight before them.

'Lead on!' said Scrooge. 'Lead on! The night is waning fast, and it is precious time to me, I know. Lead on, Spirit!'

The Phantom moved away as it had come towards him. Scrooge followed in the shadow of its dress, which bore him up, he thought, and carried him along.

They scarcely seemed to enter the city; for the city rather seemed to spring up about them, and

encompass them of its own act. But there they were, in the heart of it; on 'Change, amongst the merchants; who hurried up and down, and chinked the money in their pockets, and conversed in groups, and looked at their watches, and trifled thoughtfully with their great gold seals; and so forth, as Scrooge had seen them often.

The Spirit stopped beside one little knot of business men. Observing that the hand was pointed to them, Scrooge advanced to listen to their talk.

'No,' said a great fat man with a monstrous chin, 'I don't know much about it, either way. I only know he's dead.'

'When did he die?' inquired another.

'Last night, I believe.'

'Why, what was the matter with him?' asked a third, taking a vast quantity of snuff out of a very large snuff-box. 'I thought he'd never die.'

'God knows,' said the first, with a yawn.

'What has he done with his money?' asked a red-faced gentleman with a pendulous excrescence on the end of his nose, that shook like the gills of a turkey-cock.

'I haven't heard,' said the man with the large chin, yawning again. 'Left it to his Company, perhaps. He hasn't left it to *me*. That's all I know.'

This pleasantry was received with a general laugh.

'It's likely to be a very cheap funeral,' said the same speaker; 'for upon my life I don't know of

anybody to go to it. Suppose we make up a party and volunteer?'

'I don't mind going if a lunch is provided,' observed the gentleman with the excrescence on his nose. 'But I must be fed, if I make one.'

Another laugh.

'Well, I am the most disinterested among you, after all,' said the first speaker, 'for I never wear black gloves, and I never eat lunch. But I'll offer to go, if anybody else will. When I come to think of it, I'm not at all sure that I wasn't his most particular friend; for we used to stop and speak whenever we met. Bye, bye!'

Speakers and listeners strolled away, and mixed with other groups. Scrooge knew the men, and looked towards the Spirit for an explanation.

The Phantom glided on into a street. Its finger pointed to two persons meeting. Scrooge listened again, thinking that the explanation might lie here.

He knew these men, also, perfectly. They were men of business: very wealthy, and of great importance. He had made a point always of standing well in their esteem: in a business point of view, that is; strictly in a business point of view.

'How are you?' said one.

'How are you?' returned the other.

'Well!' said the first. 'Old Scratch has got his own at last, hey?'

'So I am told,' returned the second. 'Cold, isn't it?'

'Seasonable for Christmas time. You're not a skaiter, I suppose?'

'No. No. Something else to think of. Good morning!'

Not another word. That was their meeting, their conversation, and their parting.

Scrooge was at first inclined to be surprised that the Spirit should attach importance to conversations apparently so trivial; but feeling assured that they must have some hidden purpose, he set himself to consider what it was likely to be. They could scarcely be supposed to have any bearing on the death of Jacob, his old partner, for that was Past, and this Ghost's province was the Future. Nor could he think of any one immediately connected with himself, to whom he could apply them. But nothing doubting that to whomsoever they applied they had some latent moral for his own improvement, he resolved to treasure up every word he heard, and everything he saw; and especially to observe the shadow of himself when it appeared. For he had an expectation that the conduct of his future self would give him the clue he missed, and would render the solution of these riddles easy.

He looked about in that very place for his own image; but another man stood in his accustomed corner, and though the clock pointed to his usual time of day for being there, he saw no likeness of himself among the multitudes that poured in through the Porch. It gave him little surprise, however; for he had been revolving in his mind a change

of life, and thought and hoped he saw his new-born resolutions carried out in this.

Quiet and dark, beside him stood the Phantom, with its outstretched hand. When he roused himself from his thoughtful quest, he fancied from the turn of the hand, and its situation in reference to himself, that the Unseen Eyes were looking at him keenly. It made him shudder, and feel very cold.

They left the busy scene, and went into an obscure part of the town, where Scrooge had never penetrated before although he recognised its situation, and its bad repute. The ways were foul and narrow; the shops and houses wretched; the people half-naked, drunken, slipshod, ugly. Alleys and arch-ways, like so many cesspools, disgorged their offences of smell, and dirt, and life, upon the strag-gling streets; and the whole quarter reeked with crime, with filth, and misery.

Far in this den of infamous resort, there was a low-browed, beetling shop, below a pent-house roof, where iron, old rags, bottles, bones, and greasy offal, were bought. Upon the floor within, were piled up heaps of rusty keys, nails, chains, hinges, files, scales, weights, and refuse iron of all kinds. Secrets that few would like to scrutinise were bred and hidden in mountains of unseemly rags, masses of corrupted fat, and sepulchres of bones. Sitting in among the wares he dealt in, by a charcoal-stove, made of old bricks, was a gray-haired rascal, nearly seventy years of age; who had screened himself from the cold air without, by a frousy curtaining of

miscellaneous tatters, hung upon a line; and smoked his pipe in all the luxury of calm retirement.

Scrooge and the Phantom came into the presence of this man, just as a woman with a heavy bundle slunk into the shop. But she had scarcely entered, when another woman, similarly laden, came in too; and she was closely followed by a man in faded black, who was no less startled by the sight of them, than they had been upon the recognition of each other. After a short period of blank astonishment, in which the old man with the pipe had joined them, they all three burst into a laugh.

'Let the charwoman alone to be the first!' cried she who had entered first. 'Let the laundress alone to be the second; and let the undertaker's man alone to be the third. Look here, old Joe, here's a chance! If we haven't all three met here without meaning it.'

'You couldn't have met in a better place,' said old Joe, removing his pipe from his mouth. 'Come into the parlour. You were made free of it long ago, you know; and the other two an't strangers. Stop till I shut the door of the shop. Ah! How it skreeks! There an't such a rusty bit of metal in the place as its own hinges, I believe; and I'm sure there's no such old bones here, as mine. Ha, ha! We're all suitable to our calling, we're well matched. Come into the parlour. Come into the parlour.'

The parlour was the space behind the screen of rags. The old man raked the fire together with an old stair-rod, and having trimmed his smoky lamp

(for it was night), with the stem of his pipe, put it in his mouth again.

While he did this, the woman who had already spoken threw her bundle on the floor and sat down in a flaunting manner on a stool; crossing her elbows on her knees, and looking with a bold defiance at the other two.

'What odds then! What odds, Mrs. Dilber?' said the woman. 'Every person has a right to take care of themselves. *He* always did!'

'That's true, indeed!' said the laundress. 'No man more so.'

'Why then, don't stand staring as if you was afraid, woman; who's the wiser? We're not going to pick holes in each other's coats, I suppose?'

'No, indeed!' said Mrs. Dilber and the man together. 'We should hope not.'

'Very well, then!' cried the woman. 'That's enough. Who's the worse for the loss of a few things like these? Not a dead man, I suppose.'

'No, indeed,' said Mrs. Dilber, laughing.

'If he wanted to keep 'em after he was dead, a wicked old screw,' pursued the woman, 'why wasn't he natural in his lifetime? If he had been, he'd have had somebody to look after him when he was struck with Death, instead of lying gasping out his last there, alone by himself.'

'It's the truest word that ever was spoke,' said Mrs. Dilber. 'It's a judgment on him.'

'I wish it was a little heavier one,' replied the woman; 'and it should have been, you may depend

upon it, if I could have laid my hands on anything else. Open that bundle, old Joe, and let me know the value of it. Speak out plain. I'm not afraid to be the first, nor afraid for them to see it. We knew pretty well that we were helping ourselves, before we met here, I believe. It's no sin. Open the bundle, Joe.'

But the gallantry of her friends would not allow of this; and the man in faded black, mounting the breach first, produced *his* plunder. It was not extensive. A seal or two, a pencil-case, a pair of sleeve-buttons, and a brooch of no great value, were all. They were severally examined and appraised by old Joe, who chalked the sums he was disposed to give for each, upon the wall, and added them up into a total when he found there was nothing more to come.

'That's your account,' said Joe, 'and I wouldn't give another sixpence, if I was to be boiled for not doing it. Who's next?'

Mrs. Dilber was next. Sheets and towels, a little wearing apparel, two old-fashioned silver tea-spoons, a pair of sugar-tongs, and a few boots. Her account was stated on the wall in the same manner.

'I always give too much to ladies. It's a weakness of mine, and that's the way I ruin myself,' said old Joe. 'That's your account. If you asked me for another penny, and made it an open question, I'd repent of being so liberal and knock off half-a-crown.'

'And now undo *my* bundle, Joe,' said the first woman.

Joe went down on his knees for the greater convenience of opening it, and having unfastened a great many knots, dragged out a large and heavy roll of some dark stuff.

'What do you call this?' said Joe. 'Bed-curtains!'

'Ah!' returned the woman, laughing and leaning forward on her crossed arms. 'Bed-curtains!'

'You don't mean to say you took 'em down, rings and all, with him lying there?' said Joe.

'Yes I do,' replied the woman. 'Why not?'

'You were born to make your fortune,' said Joe, 'and you'll certainly do it.'

'I certainly shan't hold my hand, when I get anything in it by reaching it out, for the sake of such a man as He was, I promise you, Joe,' returned the woman coolly. 'Don't drop that oil upon the blankets, now.'

'His blankets?' asked Joe.

'Whose else's do you think?' replied the woman. 'He isn't likely to take cold without 'em, I dare say.'

'I hope he didn't die of anything catching? Eh?' said old Joe, stopping in his work, and looking up.

'Don't you be afraid of that,' returned the woman. 'I an't so fond of his company that I'd loiter about him for such things, if he did. Ah! you may look through that shirt till your eyes ache; but you won't find a hole in it, nor a thread-bare place. It's

the best he had, and a fine one too. They'd have wasted it, if it hadn't been for me.'

'What do you call wasting of it?' asked old Joe.

'Putting it on him to be buried in, to be sure,' replied the woman with a laugh. 'Somebody was fool enough to do it, but I took it off again. If calico an't good enough for such a purpose, it isn't good enough for anything. It's quite as becoming to the body. He can't look uglier than he did in that one.'

Scrooge listened to this dialogue in horror. As they sat grouped about their spoil, in the scanty light afforded by the old man's lamp, he viewed them with a detestation and disgust, which could hardly have been greater, though they had been obscene demons, marketing the corpse itself.

'He, ha!' laughed the same woman, when old Joe, producing a flannel bag with money in it, told out their several gains upon the ground. 'This is the end of it, you see! He frightened every one away from him when he was alive, to profit us when he was dead! Ha, ha, ha!'

'Spirit!' said Scrooge, shuddering from head to foot. 'I see, I see. The case of this unhappy man might be my own. My life tends that way, now. Merciful Heaven, what is this!'

He recoiled in terror, for the scene had changed, and now he almost touched a bed: a bare, uncurtained bed: on which, beneath a ragged sheet, there lay a something covered up, which, though it was dumb, announced itself in awful language.

The room was very dark, too dark to be observed with any accuracy, though Scrooge glanced round it in obedience to a secret impulse, anxious to know what kind of room it was. A pale light, rising in the outer air, fell straight upon the bed; and on it, plundered and bereft, unwatched, unwept, uncared for, was the body of this man.

Scrooge glanced towards the Phantom. Its steady hand was pointed to the head. The cover was so carelessly adjusted that the slightest raising of it, the motion of a finger upon Scrooge's part, would have disclosed the face. He thought of it, felt how easy it would be to do, and longed to do it; but had no more power to withdraw the veil than to dismiss the spectre at his side.

Oh cold, cold, rigid, dreadful Death, set up thine altar here, and dress it with such terrors as thou hast at thy command: for this is thy dominion! But of the loved, revered, and honoured head, thou canst not turn one hair to thy dread purposes, or make one feature odious. It is not that the hand is heavy and will fall down when released; it is not that the heart and pulse are still; but that the hand was open, generous, and true; the heart brave, warm, and tender; and the pulse a man's. Strike, Shadow, strike! And see his good deeds springing from the wound, to sow the world with life immortal!

No voice pronounced these words in Scrooge's ears, and yet he heard them when he looked upon the bed. He thought, if this man could be raised

up now, what would be his foremost thoughts? Avarice, hard dealing, griping cares? They have brought him to a rich end, truly!

He lay, in the dark empty house, with not a man, a woman, or a child, to say that he was kind to me in this or that, and for the memory of one kind word I will be kind to him. A cat was tearing at the door, and there was a sound of gnawing rats beneath the hearth-stone. What *they* wanted in the room of death, and why they were so restless and disturbed, Scrooge did not dare to think.

'Spirit!' he said, 'this is a fearful place. In leaving it, I shall not leave its lesson, trust me. Let us go!'

Still the Ghost pointed with an unmoved finger to the head.

'I understand you,' Scrooge returned, 'and I would do it, if I could. But I have not the power, Spirit. I have not the power.'

Again it seemed to look upon him.

'If there is any person in the town, who feels emotion caused by this man's death,' said Scrooge quite agonised, 'show that person to me, Spirit, I beseech you!'

The Phantom spread its dark robe before him for a moment, like a wing; and withdrawing it, revealed a room by daylight, where a mother and her children were.

She was expecting someone, and with anxious eagerness; for she walked up and down the room; started at every sound; looked out from the

window; glanced at the clock; tried, but in vain, to work with her needle; and could hardly bear the voices of the children in their play.

At length the long-expected knock was heard. She hurried to the door, and met her husband; a man whose face was care-worn and depressed, though he was young. There was a remarkable expression in it now; a kind of serious delight of which he felt ashamed, and which he struggled to repress.

He sat down to the dinner that had been hoarding for him by the fire; and when she asked him faintly what news (which was not until after a long silence), he appeared embarrassed how to answer.

'Is it good,' she said, 'or bad?' – to help him.

'Bad,' he answered.

'We are quite ruined?'

'No. There is hope yet, Caroline.'

'If *he* relents,' she said, amazed, 'there is! Nothing is past hope, if such a miracle has happened.'

'He is past relenting,' said her husband. 'He is dead.'

She was a mild and patient creature if her face spoke truth; but she was thankful in her soul to hear it, and she said so, with clasped hands. She prayed forgiveness the next moment, and was sorry; but the first was the emotion of her heart.

'What the half-drunken woman whom I told you of last night, said to me, when I tried to see him and obtain a week's delay; and what I thought was a mere excuse to avoid me; turns out to have been

quite true. He was not only very ill, but dying, then.'

'To whom will our debt be transferred?'

'I don't know. But before that time we shall be ready with the money; and even though we were not, it would be bad fortune indeed to find so merciless a creditor in his successor. We may sleep to-night with light hearts, Caroline!'

Yes. Soften it as they would, their hearts were lighter. The children's faces, hushed and clustered round to hear what they so little understood, were brighter; and it was a happier house for this man's death! The only emotion that the Ghost could show him, caused by the event, was one of pleasure.

'Let me see some tenderness connected with a death,' said Scrooge; 'or that dark chamber, Spirit, which we left just now, will be for ever present to me.'

The Ghost conducted him through several streets familiar to his feet; and as they went along, Scrooge looked here and there to find himself, but nowhere was he to be seen. They entered poor Bob Cratchit's house; the dwelling he had visited before; and found the mother and the children seated round the fire.

Quiet. Very quiet. The noisy little Cratchits were as still as statues in one corner, and sat looking up at Peter, who had a book before him. The mother and her daughters were engaged in sewing. But surely they were very quiet!

' "And He took a child, and set him in the midst of them." '

Where had Scrooge heard those words? He had not dreamed them. The boy must have read them out, as he and the Spirit crossed the threshold. Why did he not go on?

The mother laid her work upon the table, and put her hand up to her face.

'The colour hurts my eyes,' she said.

The colour? Ah, poor Tiny Tim!

'They're better now again,' said Cratchit's wife. 'It makes them weak by candle-light; and I wouldn't show weak eyes to your father when he comes home, for the world. It must be near his time.'

'Past it rather,' Peter answered, shutting up his book. 'But I think he's walked a little slower than he used, these few last evenings, mother.'

They were very quiet again. At last she said, and in a steady, cheerful voice, that only faultered once:

'I have known him walk with – I have known him walk with Tiny Tim upon his shoulder, very fast indeed.'

'And so have I,' cried Peter. 'Often.'

'And so have I!' exclaimed another. So had all.

'But he was very light to carry,' she resumed, intent upon her work, 'and his father loved him so, that it was no trouble – no trouble. And there is your father at the door!'

She hurried out to meet him; and little Bob in his comforter – he had need of it, poor fellow –

came in. His tea was ready for him on the hob, and they all tried who should help him to it most. Then the two young Cratchits got upon his knees and laid, each child a little cheek, against his face, as if they said, 'Don't mind it, father. Don't be grieved!'

Bob was very cheerful with them, and spoke pleasantly to all the family. He looked at the work upon the table, and praised the industry and speed of Mrs. Cratchit and the girls. They would be done long before Sunday, he said.

'Sunday! You went to-day then, Robert?' said his wife.

'Yes, my dear,' returned Bob. 'I wish you could have gone. It would have done you good to see how green a place it is. But you'll see it often. I promised him that I would walk there on a Sunday. My little, little child!' cried Bob. 'My little child!'

He broke down all at once. He couldn't help it. If he could have helped it, he and his child would have been farther apart perhaps than they were.

He left the room, and went up stairs into the room above, which was lighted cheerfully, and hung with Christmas. There was a chair set close beside the child, and there were signs of some one having been there, lately. Poor Bob sat down in it, and when he had thought a little and composed himself, he kissed the little face. He was reconciled to what had happened, and went down again quite happy.

They drew about the fire, and talked; the girls and mother working still. Bob told them of the

extraordinary kindness of Mr. Scrooge's nephew, whom he had scarcely seen but once, and who, meeting him in the street that day, and seeing that he looked a little – 'just a little down you know' said Bob, inquired what had happened to distress him. 'On which,' said Bob, 'for he is the pleasantest-spoken gentleman you ever heard, I told him. "I am heartily sorry for it, Mr. Cratchit," he said, "and heartily sorry for your good wife." By the bye, how he ever knew *that* I don't know.'

'Knew what, my dear?'

'Why, that you were a good wife,' replied Bob.

'Everybody knows that!' said Peter.

'Very well observed, my boy!' cried Bob. 'I hope they do. "Heartily sorry," he said, "for your good wife. If I can be of service to you in any way," he said, giving me his card, "that's where I live. Pray come to me." Now, it wasn't,' cried Bob, 'for the sake of anything he might be able to do for us, so much as for his kind way, that this was quite delightful. It really seemed as if he had known our Tiny Tim, and felt with us.'

'I'm sure he's a good soul!' said Mrs. Cratchit.

'You would be surer of it, my dear,' returned Bob, 'if you saw and spoke to him. I shouldn't be at all surprised, mark what I say, if he got Peter a better situation.'

'Only hear that, Peter,' said Mrs. Cratchit.

'And then,' cried one of the girls, 'Peter will be keeping company with some one, and setting up for himself.'

'Get along with you!' retorted Peter, grinning.

'It's just as likely as not,' said Bob, 'one of these days; though there's plenty of time for that, my dear. But however and whenever we part from one another, I am sure we shall none of us forget poor Tiny Tim – shall we – or this first parting that there was among us?'

'Never, father!' cried they all.

'And I know,' said Bob, 'I know, my dears, that when we recollect how patient and how mild he was; although he was a little, little child; we shall not quarrel easily among ourselves, and forget poor Tiny Tim in doing it.'

'No, never, father!' they all cried again.

'I am very happy,' said little Bob, 'I am very happy!'

Mrs. Cratchit kissed him, his daughters kissed him, the two young Cratchits kissed him, and Peter and himself shook hands. Spirit of Tiny Tim, thy childish essence was from God!

'Spectre,' said Scrooge, 'something informs me that our parting moment is at hand. I know it, but I know not how. Tell me what man that was whom we saw lying dead?'

The Ghost of Christmas Yet To Come conveyed him, as before – though at a different time, he thought: indeed, there seemed no order in these latter visions, save that they were in the Future – into the resorts of business men, but showed him not himself. Indeed, the Spirit did not stay for anything, but went straight on, as to the end just

now desired, until besought by Scrooge to tarry for a moment.

'This court,' said Scrooge, 'through which we hurry now, is where my place of occupation is, and has been for a length of time. I see the house. Let me behold what I shall be, in days to come.'

The Spirit stopped; the hand was pointed elsewhere.

'The house is yonder,' Scrooge exclaimed. 'Why do you point away?'

The inexorable finger underwent no change.

Scrooge hastened to the window of his office, and looked in. It was an office still, but not his. The furniture was not the same, and the figure in the chair was not himself. The Phantom pointed as before.

He joined it once again, and wondering why and whither he had gone, accompanied it until they reached an iron gate. He paused to look round before entering.

A churchyard. Here, then, the wretched man whose name he had now to learn, lay underneath the ground. It was a worthy place. Walled in by houses; overrun by grass and weeds, the growth of vegetation's death, not life; choked up with too much burying; fat with repleted appetite. A worthy place!

The Spirit stood among the graves, and pointed down to One. He advanced towards it trembling. The Phantom was exactly as it had been, but he dreaded that he saw new meaning in its solemn shape.

'Before I draw nearer to that stone to which you point,' said Scrooge, 'answer me one question. Are these the shadows of the things that Will be, or are they shadows of things that May be, only?'

Still the Ghost pointed downward to the grave by which it stood.

'Men's courses will foreshadow certain ends, to which, if persevered in, they must lead,' said Scrooge. 'But if the courses be departed from, the ends will change. Say it is thus with what you show me!'

The Spirit was immovable as ever.

Scrooge crept towards it, trembling as he went; and following the finger, read upon the stone of the neglected grave his own name, EBENEZER SCROOGE.

'Am I that man who lay upon the bed?' he cried, upon his knees.

The finger pointed from the grave to him, and back again.

'No, Spirit! Oh, no, no!'

The finger still was there.

'Spirit!' he cried, tight clutching at its robe, 'hear me! I am not the man I was. I will not be the man I must have been but for this intercourse. Why show me this, if I am past all hope?'

For the first time the hand appeared to shake.

'Good Spirit,' he pursued, as down upon the ground he fell before it: 'Your nature intercedes for me, and pities me. Assure me that I yet may change

these shadows you have shown me, by an altered life!'

The kind hand trembled.

'I will honour Christmas in my heart, and try to keep it all the year. I will live in the Past, the Present, and the Future. The Spirits of all Three shall strive within me. I will not shut out the lessons that they teach. Oh, tell me I may sponge away the writing on this stone!'

In his agony, he caught the spectral hand. It sought to free itself, but he was strong in his entreaty, and detained it. The Spirit, stronger yet, repulsed him.

Holding up his hands in a last prayer to have his fate reversed, he saw an alteration in the Phantom's hood and dress. It shrunk, collapsed, and dwindled down into a bedpost.

THE END OF IT

Yes! and the bedpost was his own. The bed was his own, the room was his own. Best and happiest of all, the Time before him was his own, to make amends in!

'I will live in the Past, the Present, and the Future!' Scrooge repeated, as he scrambled out of bed. 'The Spirits of all Three shall strive within me. Oh Jacob Marley! Heaven, and the Christmas Time be praised for this! I say it on my knees, old Jacob; on my knees!'

He was so fluttered and so glowing with his good intentions, that his broken voice would scarcely answer to his call. He had been sobbing violently in his conflict with the Spirit, and his face was wet with tears.

'They are not torn down,' cried Scrooge, folding one of his bed-curtains in his arms, 'they are not torn down, rings and all. They are here: I am here: the shadows of the things that would have been, may be dispelled. They will be. I know they will!'

His hands were busy with his garments all this time: turning them inside out, putting them on upside down, tearing them, mislaying them, making them parties to every kind of extravagance.

'I don't know what to do!' cried Scrooge, laughing and crying in the same breath; and making a perfect Laocoön of himself with his stockings. 'I am as light as a feather, I am as happy as an angel, I am as merry as a school-boy. I am as giddy as a drunken man. A merry Christmas to everybody! A happy New Year to all the world! Hallo here! Whoop! Hallo!'

He had frisked into the sitting-room, and was now standing there: perfectly winded.

'There's the saucepan that the gruel was in!' cried Scrooge, starting off again, and frisking round the fire-place. 'There's the door, by which the Ghost of Jacob Marley entered! There's the corner where the Ghost of Christmas Present, sat! There's the window where I saw the wandering Spirits! It's all right, it's all true, it all happened. Ha ha ha!'

Really, for a man who had been out of practice for so many years, it was a splendid laugh, a most illustrious laugh. The father of a long, long line of brilliant laughs!

'I don't know what day of the month it is!' said Scrooge. 'I don't know how long I've been among the Spirits. I don't know anything. I'm quite a baby. Never mind. I don't care. I'd rather be a baby. Hallo! Whoop! Hallo here!'

He was checked in his transports by the churches ringing out the lustiest peals he had ever heard. Clash, clang, hammer, ding, dong, bell. Bell, dong, ding, hammer, clang, clash! Oh, glorious, glorious!

Running to the window, he opened it, and put

out his head. No fog, no mist; clear, bright, jovial, stirring, cold; cold, piping for the blood to dance to; Golden sunlight; Heavenly sky; sweet fresh air; merry bells. Oh, glorious. Glorious!

'What's to-day?' cried Scrooge, calling downward to a boy in Sunday clothes, who perhaps had loitered in to look about him.

'Eh?' returned the boy, with all his might of wonder.

'What's to-day, my fine fellow?' said Scrooge.

'To-day!' replied the boy. 'Why, Christmas Day.'

'It's Christmas Day!' said Scrooge to himself. 'I haven't missed it. The Spirits have done it all in one night. They can do anything they like. Of course they can. Of course they can. Hallo, my fine fellow!'

'Hallo!' returned the boy.

'Do you know the Poulterer's, in the next street but one, at the corner?' Scrooge inquired.

'I should hope I did,' replied the lad.

'An intelligent boy!' said Scrooge. 'A remarkable boy! Do you know whether they've sold the prize Turkey that was hanging up there? Not the little prize Turkey: the big one?'

'What, the one as big as me?' returned the boy.

'What a delightful boy!' said Scrooge. 'It's a pleasure to talk to him. Yes, my buck!'

'It's hanging there now,' replied the boy.

'Is it?' said Scrooge. 'Go and buy it.'

'Walk-er!' exclaimed the boy.

'No, no,' said Scrooge, 'I am in earnest. Go and

buy it, and tell 'em to bring it here, that I may give them the direction where to take it. Come back with the man, and I'll give you a shilling. Come back with him in less than five minutes, and I'll give you half-a-crown!'

The boy was off like a shot. He must have had a steady hand at a trigger who could have got a shot off half so fast.

'I'll send it to Bob Cratchit's!' whispered Scrooge, rubbing his hands, and splitting with a laugh. 'He shan't know who sends it. It's twice the size of Tiny Tim. Joe Miller never made such a joke as sending it to Bob's will be!'

The hand in which he wrote the address was not a steady one, but write it he did, somehow, and went down stairs to open the street door, ready for the coming of the poulterer's man. As he stood there, waiting his arrival, the knocker caught his eye.

'I shall love it, as long as I live!' cried Scrooge, patting it with his hand. 'I scarcely ever looked at it before. What an honest expression it has in its face! It's a wonderful knocker! – Here's the Turkey. Hallo! Whoop! How are you! Merry Christmas!'

It *was* a Turkey! He never could have stood upon his legs, that bird. He would have snapped 'em short off in a minute, like sticks of sealing-wax.

'Why, it's impossible to carry that to Camden Town,' said Scrooge. 'You must have a cab.'

The chuckle with which he said this, and the chuckle with which he paid for the Turkey, and

the chuckle with which he paid for the cab, and the chuckle with which he recompensed the boy, were only to be exceeded by the chuckle with which he sat down breathless in his chair again, and chuckled till he cried.

Shaving was not an easy task, for his hand continued to shake very much; and shaving requires attention, even when you don't dance while you are at it. But if he had cut the end of his nose off, he would have put a piece of sticking-plaister over it, and been quite satisfied.

He dressed himself 'all in his best', and at last got out into the streets. The people were by this time pouring forth, as he had seen them with the Ghost of Christmas Present; and walking with his hands behind him, Scrooge regarded every one with a delighted smile. He looked so irresistibly pleasant, in a word, that three or four good-humoured fellows said, 'Good morning, sir! A merry Christmas to you!' And Scrooge said often afterwards, that of all the blithe sounds he had ever heard, those were the blithest in his ears.

He had not gone far, when coming on towards him he beheld the portly gentleman, who had walked into his counting-house the day before and said, 'Scrooge and Marley's, I believe?' It sent a pang across his heart to think how this old gentleman would look upon him when they met; but he knew what path lay straight before him, and he took it.

'My dear sir,' said Scrooge, quickening his pace,

and taking the old gentleman by both his hands. 'How do you do? I hope you succeeded yesterday. It was very kind of you. A merry Christmas to you, sir!'

'Mr. Scrooge?'

'Yes,' said Scrooge. 'That is my name, and I fear it may not be pleasant to you. Allow me to ask your pardon. And will you have the goodness' – here Scrooge whispered in his ear.

'Lord bless me!' cried the gentleman, as if his breath were gone. 'My dear Mr. Scrooge, are you serious?'

'If you please,' said Scrooge. 'Not a farthing less. A great many back-payments are included in it, I assure you. Will you do me that favour?'

'My dear sir,' said the other, shaking hands with him. 'I don't know what to say to such munifi –'

'Don't say anything, please,' retorted Scrooge. 'Come and see me. Will you come and see me?'

'I will!' cried the old gentleman. And it was clear he meant to do it.

'Thank'ee,' said Scrooge. 'I am much obliged to you. I thank you fifty times. Bless you!'

He went to church, and walked about the streets, and watched the people hurrying to and fro, and patted children on the head, and questioned beggars, and looked down into the kitchens of houses, and up to the windows; and found that everything could yield him pleasure. He had never dreamed that any walk – that anything – could give

him so much happiness. In the afternoon, he turned his steps towards his nephew's house.

He passed the door a dozen times, before he had the courage to go up and knock. But he made a dash, and did it:

'Is your master at home, my dear?' said Scrooge to the girl. Nice girl! Very.

'Yes, sir.'

'Where is he, my love?' said Scrooge.

'He's in the dining-room, sir, along with mistress. I'll show you up stairs, if you please.'

'Thank'ee. He knows me,' said Scrooge, with his hand already on the dining-room lock. 'I'll go in here, my dear.'

He turned it gently, and sidled his face in, round the door. They were looking at the table (which was spread out in great array); for these young housekeepers are always nervous on such points, and like to see that everything is right.

'Fred!' said Scrooge.

Dear heart alive, how his niece by marriage started! Scrooge had forgotten, for the moment, about her sitting in the corner with the footstool, or he wouldn't have done it, on any account.

'Why bless my soul!' cried Fred, 'who's that?'

'It's I. Your uncle Scrooge. I have come to dinner. Will you let me in, Fred?'

Let him in! It is a mercy he didn't shake his arm off. He was at home in five minutes. Nothing could be heartier. His niece looked just the same. So did Topper when *he* came. So did the plump sister,

when *she* came. So did every one when *they* came. Wonderful party, wonderful games, wonderful unanimity, won-der-ful happiness!

But he was early at the office next morning. Oh, he was early there. If he could only be there first, and catch Bob Cratchit coming late! That was the thing he had set his heart upon.

And he did it; yes, he did! The clock struck nine. No Bob. A quarter past. No Bob. He was full eighteen minutes and a half, behind his time. Scrooge sat with his door wide open, that he might see him come into the Tank.

His hat was off, before he opened the door; his comforter too. He was on his stool in a jiffy; driving away with his pen, as if he were trying to overtake nine o'clock.

'Hallo!' growled Scrooge, in his accustomed voice as near as he could feign it. 'What do you mean by coming here at this time of day?'

'I am very sorry, sir,' said Bob. 'I *am* behind my time.'

'You are?' repeated Scrooge. 'Yes. I think you are. Step this way, if you please.'

'It's only once a year, sir,' pleaded Bob, appearing from the Tank. 'It shall not be repeated. I was making rather merry yesterday, sir.'

'Now, I'll tell you what, my friend,' said Scrooge, 'I am not going to stand this sort of thing any longer. And therefore,' he continued, leaping from his stool, and giving Bob such a dig in the waistcoat that he staggered back into the Tank

again: 'and therefore I am about to raise your salary!'

Bob trembled, and got a little nearer to the ruler. He had a momentary idea of knocking Scrooge down with it; holding him; and calling to the people in the court for help and a strait-waistcoat.

'A merry Christmas, Bob!' said Scrooge, with an earnestness that could not be mistaken, as he clapped him on the back. 'A merrier Christmas, Bob, my good fellow, than I have given you, for many a year! I'll raise your salary, and endeavour to assist your struggling family, and we will discuss your affairs this very afternoon, over a Christmas bowl of smoking bishop, Bob! Make up the fires, and buy another coal-scuttle before you dot another i, Bob Cratchit!'

Scrooge was better than his word. He did it all, and infinitely more; and to Tiny Tim, who did NOT die, he was a second father. He became as good a friend, as good a master, and as good a man, as the good old city knew, or any other good old city, town, or borough, in the good old world. Some people laughed to see the alteration in him, but he let them laugh, and little heeded them; for he was wise enough to know that nothing ever happened on this globe, for good, at which some people did not have their fill of laughter in the outset; and knowing that such as these would be blind anyway, he thought it quite as well that they should wrinkle up their eyes in grins, as have the malady in less

attractive forms. His own heart laughed: and that was quite enough for him.

He had no further intercourse with Spirits, but lived upon the Total Abstinence Principle, ever afterwards; and it was always said of him, that he knew how to keep Christmas well, if any man alive possessed the knowledge. May that be truly said of us, and all of us! And so, as Tiny Tim observed, God bless Us, Every One!

PENGUIN RED CLASSICS

GREAT EXPECTATIONS
CHARLES DICKENS

Pip doesn't expect much from life …

His sister makes it clear that her orphaned little brother is nothing but a burden on her. But suddenly things begin to change. Pip's narrow existence is blown apart when he finds an escaped criminal, is summoned to visit a mysterious old woman and meets the icy beauty Estella. Most astoundingly of all, an anonymous person gives him money to begin a new life in London.

Are these events as random as they seem? Or does Pip's fate hang on a series of coincidences he could never have expected?

'Fascinating and disturbing' *Independent*

'Beneath a veneer of old-fashioned English storytelling is the most nakedly haunted book Dickens ever wrote' *Guardian*

'Impresses me more deeply with every read' Sarah Waters

For more classic fiction, read Red
www.penguinclassics.com/reds

PENGUIN RED CLASSICS

HARD TIMES
CHARLES DICKENS

Mr Gradgrind the school-owner cares about nothing but facts, facts, facts.

He despises emotions and imagination. His great ambition is to break the spirits of his pupils and turn them into human cogs in a huge industrial machine.

These strict teachings also apply to his own children, obedient Louisa and rebellious Tom. Can they free themselves from his heartless regime? Or are they doomed to live without love and freedom? And will Gradgrind himself learn the error of his ways and come to value the human heart?

'His novels will endure as long as the language itself' Peter Ackroyd

'When Dickens has once described something you see it for the rest of your life' George Orwell

For more classic fiction, read Red
www.penguinclassics.com/reds

He just wanted a decent book to read ...

Not too much to ask, is it? It was in 1935 when Allen Lane, Managing Director of Bodley Head Publishers, stood on a platform at Exeter railway station looking for something good to read on his journey back to London. His choice was limited to popular magazines and poor-quality paperbacks – the same choice faced every day by the vast majority of readers, few of whom could afford hardbacks. Lane's disappointment and subsequent anger at the range of books generally available led him to found a company – and change the world.

'We believed in the existence in this country of a vast reading public for intelligent books at a low price, and staked everything on it'
Sir Allen Lane, 1902–1970, founder of Penguin Books

The quality paperback had arrived – and not just in bookshops. Lane was adamant that his Penguins should appear in chain stores and tobacconists, and should cost no more than a packet of cigarettes.

Reading habits (and cigarette prices) have changed since 1935, but Penguin still believes in publishing the best books for everybody to enjoy. We still believe that good design costs no more than bad design, and we still believe that quality books published passionately and responsibly make the world a better place.

So wherever you see the little bird – whether it's on a piece of prize-winning literary fiction or a celebrity autobiography, political tour de force or historical masterpiece, a serial-killer thriller, reference book, world classic or a piece of pure escapism – you can bet that it represents the very best that the genre has to offer.

Whatever you like to read – trust Penguin.

Praise for *Sixty Degrees North*:

'It is a brave book in its honesty and self-exposure, I think, and a beautiful book in terms of the subtlety of its thinking and the quality of its descriptive prose, that at times possesses the lucidity of the northern light in which so much of it is set'
Robert MacFarlane

'a subtle, thoughtful study of life on the sixtieth parallel'
Financial Times

'It's a joy to read, its prose as clear as the light on the Greenland ice-cap. In the past year I've read three or four books combining travelogue and memoir in which a writer, unmoored by loss, seeks a resolution of some kind on a journey; this was the best'
Michael Kerr, *Daily Telegraph*

'Malachy Tallack is the real deal, a writer given over to pure curiosity, honest witness and that most precious of gifts, an unself-conscious sense of wonder. *Sixty Degrees North* reveals, not just a vibrant new voice, but a wise, questioning and highly sophisticated talent'
John Burnside

'The high point of the book is the acute and sensitive evocation of the natural world. Tallack's imagery is apposite without becoming self-consciously poetic . . . He does not suffer from naïve romanticism about the north'
Stuart Kelly, *Times Literary Supplement*

'Tallack is one of a burgeoning group of young travel writers who have reinvigorated their increasingly tired genre with elements of psychogeography: the study of how places make us feel . . . Tallack does travelogue well, acutely balancing fact and fancy'
Will Self, *Guardian*

SIXTY DEGREES NORTH

Malachy Tallack has written for the *New Statesman*, the *Guardian*, the *Scottish Review of Books*, *Caught by the River* and many other publications, online and print. He won a New Writers Award from Scottish Book Trust in 2014, and a Robert Louis Stevenson Fellowship in 2015. As a singer-songwriter he has released four albums and an EP, and performed in venues across the UK. He is contributing editor of the online magazine *The Island Review*, and co-editor of *Fair Isle: Through the Seasons*. His next book, *Undiscovered Islands*, will be published by Polygon in 2016. He comes from Shetland and lives in Glasgow.

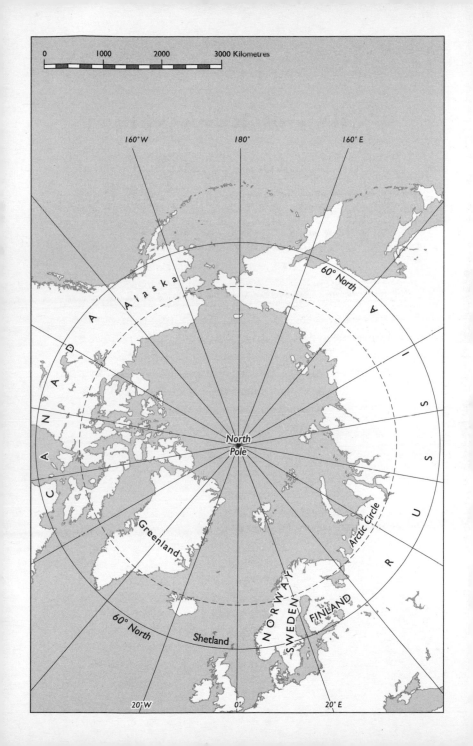

SIXTY DEGREES NORTH

around the world in search of home

Malachy Tallack

First published in 2015 by Polygon. This paperback edition
published in 2016 by Polygon, an imprint of
Birlinn Ltd
West Newington House
10 Newington Road
Edinburgh
EH9 1QS

www.polygonbooks.co.uk

Extracts from *Sixty Degrees North* have previously been published in
Irish Pages, *PN Review* and *Earthlines*

ISBN 978 1 84697 342 0

British Library Cataloguing in Publication Data
A catalogue record for this book is available from the British Library.

Typeset in Sabon at Birlinn

Printed and bound in Great Britain
by Clays Ltd, St Ives PLC

SWORD ARt ONLINE ALternAtive
GUN GALE ONLINE I

CONTENTS

LINK #001: PROLOGUE ①

OOOOO
(WHOOSH)

AAAGH!!

AH!

BIKU
(TWITCH)

TA
(TA

TA

DAMN! THAT'S ANOTHER ONE DOWN!

WATCH OUT! WE'RE DEALING WITH A SLIPPERY ONE!

HFF!

HFF!

WHERE'D SHE GO!?

I'M GONNA FIND THAT SHRIMP!

HUH?

DOKI
(BADUM)

DOKI

GYUUU
(SQUEEZE)

OH GEEZ, THEY'RE GONNA SPOT ME......

THIS WAY?

OH NO!

JARI
(SCRAPE)

AND NOT GONNA LIE, I WAS ENJOYING WATCHING A TINY GIRL SHOOT A BUNCH OF UGLY MEN.

OH, I THOUGHT YOU'D BE ABLE TO HANDLE THEM ALONE.

TAN (CHUP)

PITO-SAAAN! STOP WATCHING AND HELP! WE'RE SUPPOSED TO BE A TEAM!

OH, TRUST ME, I'M PAYING YOU A COMPLIMENT, LLENN-CHAN.

ZURIRI (GRUB)

AND THIS CUTE, TINY LITTLE GIRL IS MY PLAYER AVATAR—

LLENN.

PARA (PLINK)

WELL, THAT'S GREAT.

YOUR OLDER SISTER CAN'T WAIT TO SEE HOW YOU TURN OUT!

I WOULDN'T HAVE PEGGED YOU FOR THE TYPE TO BE ABLE TO SHOOT A MAN IN THE CROTCH IN YOUR FIRST PVP BATTLE.

THIS ECCENTRIC PERSON IS A SENIOR PLAYER I RECENTLY MET...

...PITOHUI-SAN.

STOP TEASING ME! I WAS TRYING MY HARDEST...!

HFF!

HFF!

HFF!

I CAN'T JUST BE EXPECTED TO GET OVER THAT FROM THE GET-GO...

I MEAN, I KNOW THEY'RE JUST AVATARS, BUT THEY'RE PEOPLE, YOU KNOW?

THOSE PK-ING* GEAR THIEVES DESERVE THEIR COMEUPPANCE.

DON'T LET IT BOTHER YOU.

I THOUGHT WE WERE HERE TO HUNT MONSTERS, NOT PLAYERS...

*PK: PLAYER-KILLING. DEFEATING OTHER PLAYERS.

Where'd she go?

I know she went this way!

BUT, IT'S FUNNY, THOUGH... THEY LOST SIGHT OF ME SEVERAL TIMES.

I SEE!

OH, THAT?

THAT CUTE PINK COLOR YOU WEAR BLENDS INTO THE SCENERY. IT'S GOOD CAMOUFLAGE.

AUGUST 2025 (FIVE MONTHS PRIOR)

...BUT IN THE REAL WORLD......

I MIGHT BE TINY AND CUTE IN THIS GAME...

THANK GOD FOR THE WASTELAND.

HEAR, HEAR!

ALL OF MY HARD WORK HAD LEFT ME AS LONELY AS EVER.

SU (SHH)

I DIDN'T END UP MAKING ANY CLOSE FRIENDS LIKE I'D HOPED.

AH HA HA!

......BUT IT WAS AN ESCALATOR SCHOOL, SO THE OTHER GIRLS HAD ALL BEEN TOGETHER FOR YEARS...

WAI (CHATTER)

WAI

HEE HEE!

HEE HEE!

WHEN I'D SEE THE GIRLS FROM THE ATTACHED HIGH SCHOOL...

...IT MADE ME WONDER IF I MIGHT'VE HAD A YOUTH LIKE THEIRS, IF NOT FOR MY SIZE.

EU
(SWISH)
~zo

GU
CLENCH

WHOA...
DID YOU
SEE
HER...?

WHILE
EVERY-
ONE
ELSE
ENJOYED
THEIR
YOUTH...

TA
(STAMP)

ELZA'S
THE ONLY
ONE WHO
MAKES
ME FEEL
BETTER!

PI
(BEEP)

Elza Kanzaki
Ulza and Frozen

...AND
ATE MY
LUNCHES
ALONE...

UGU
CMUNCH)

UGU

...I MADE
SURE TO
ATTEND
ALL OF MY
CLASSES
...

...

AHH...

...WITH AN
EARBUD IN
WHENEVER
I GOT THE
CHANCE.

Hey,
she'll
hear
you!

I
can't
see
the
board
...!

BOSO

BOSO
(WHISPER)

There are plenty of *R games* like that, but the problems they all give you random appearances.

WELL... I WANNA PLAY A GAME THAT LETS ME BE A REALLY CUTE CHARACTER.

ACK!

I've never been prouder!

So— what do you wanna know?

So you've finally seen the light of video games, Kohi!

I HAD ONE GAMER FRIEND BACK IN HOKKAIDO...

*VR GAME: A SENSORY-IMMERSION GAME PLAYED WITHIN A VIRTUAL REALITY (VR) ENVIRONMENT.   SCREEN: MIYU SHINOHARA

So I'd recommend just trying out a bunch of different ones until you get a character you like!

GAME B

CONVERT

GAME A

However, there's also a conversion feature that allows you to take one character with you to other VR games.

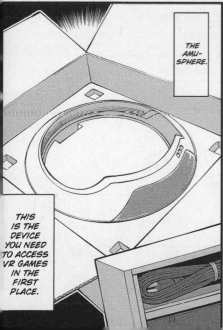

THE AMU-SPHERE.

THIS IS THE DEVICE YOU NEED TO ACCESS VR GAMES IN THE FIRST PLACE.

But to do that...

...you'll need the hardware first.

.COM   YO

TRUCK: SHIPPING

14

TRIED COUPLE OF OTHER TIONS, AS GGESTED, UT NONE OF THEM AVE ME AT I WAS AFTER.

WH-WHY!?

WHY'D I HAVE TO GET A TALL AVATAR!?

S-sorry...

HMPH!

KOTSUN (TUNK)

YOU WOULDN'T GET IT, MIYU.

SFX: TSUN (POKE) TSUN

But the more the AmuSphere's safety mechanisms work, the higher your heart rate goes? That's funny!

篠原美優

I forgot you were worried about your height, Kohi.

LINK START.

MIGHT AS WELL GIVE IT ONE LAST SHOT.

KACHA (CLINK)

GISHI (CREAK)

ALFHEIM ONLINE

SWOR ONLIN

GUN GALE ONLINE

HUH? WAIT, DID I NOT GO THROUGH THE ENTIRE LIST...?

GUN... GALE ONLINE ...?

—THAT...

PETA
(TAP)

FINALLY! I'VE FINALLY FOUND YOU!

FURU
(TREMBLE)

FURU

THAT'S... ME...?

WELCOME TO THE NEW, CUTE, TINY ME!

ooo
(CHEER)

AND THAT'S HOW I FOUND UP IN GGO, THE VR GAME WITH THE AVATAR I ALWAYS WANTED.

FURU

FURU

OOOOH!

FURU

FIRST THREE MONTHS OF THE GAME

I MASTERED THE IN-GAME TUTORIALS...

TAN
TATAN
TAN (TAT)

...KILLED A BUNCH OF MONSTERS...

I'LL USE MY STAT POINT ON... AGILITY!

...AND EARNED EXPERIENCE POINTS AND CREDITS.

PIN! (BEEP)
Level UP

YAY, LEVEL UP!

H' GA H' GA H' GA H' GA H' GA H'² (BLAM)

YOU THINK SHE'S CUTE TOO, RIGHT?

WHOA, SHE'S TINY!

NOW I'VE GOT MONEY TO SPARE, AND I EVEN TURNED MY GEAR PINK!

HEE HEE!

I'VE NEVER SEEN AN AVATAR THAT SMALL.

OOH, I LOOK SO CUTE!

GUNSHOP

I WONDER IF I CAN GET IT IN PINK TO MATCH!

A NEW GUN, HUH...

...AND HAD A VAST COLLECTION OF EXPENSIVE, RARE, AND ODD WEAPONS.

T WAS THINK-ABLE THAT NYONE OULD MASS MANY APONS AYING UALLY.

...WAS THAT SHE USED DIFFERENT GUNS EVERY TIME...

ONE THING I DID LEARN...

YOU CAN ACQUIRE IN-GAME GGO CREDITS AND ITEMS WITH REAL MONEY.

BASICALLY, YOU PAY RATHER THAN USE YOUR TIME.

OH, THESE? REAL MONEY, OF COURSE.

YOU'VE GOT SO MANY GUNS, PITO-SAN. HOW'D YOU GET THEM ALL?

EVENTUALLY, I'M GONNA HAVE MY ENTIRE PRIVATE GUN LOCKER STUFFED WITH EVERY KIND OF GUN.

SURI (RUB)
SURI
SURI

......

SO SHE'S RICH IN REAL LIFE...THAT MAKES ME EVEN MORE CURIOUS ABOUT WHAT SHE DOES.

OH!

...HMM? Y'MEAN IRL?

DO YOU HAVE ANY OTHER INTER-ESTS?

MY FAVORITE SINGER IS ELZA KANZAKI.

I-I LIKE MUSIC.

ASE あせ (SWEAT) ASE あせ

ASIDE FROM THIS GAME...? NOT REALLY.

...... SORRY. I SHOULDN'T HAVE ASKED YOU ABOUT IRL STUFF.

PORI (SCRITCH)

PFFT! I CAN'T EVEN READ MUSIC. I BET I'D SURPRISE YOU IF YOU SAW ME IN REAL LIFE.

REALLY? I GUESS I WOULD'VE THOUGHT YOU'D BE MORE OF A MUSIC FAN.

HEH.

MUSIC HUH? BAREL'* EVER BOTHE* WITH THAT.

WHOA... DID YOU SEE HER ...?

ZUKIN (THROB)

WELL, WE GET ALONG PRETTY WEL* IN HERE. SOMETIMES I FEEL LIKE WE COULD HANG OUT IRL TOO.

BUT... DO YOU HAVE THE GUTS... AND THE DETERMINATION?

BUT I BET... YOU'LL BE SURPRISED WHEN YOU SEE ME TOO, PITO-SAN...

YEAH, I'D... LIKE TO MEET UP TOO...

BUT—

KOKU (NOD)

KOKU.

IF I... BEAT YOU...?

WELL, HOW ABOUT THIS? IF YOU CAN GIVE ME A REAL CHALLENGE AND ACTUALLY WIN SOMEDAY, I'LL MEET YOU OFF-LINE!

NOBODY— AND THAT'S WHAT MAKES THE WAIT FUN.

TRAIN YOURSELF WELL, UNTIL THAT FATEFUL DAY YOU CAN GET THE BEST OF ME WITH YOUR PRECIOUS P-CHAN!

WH- WHO KNOWS WHEN THAT COULD BE!?

TRAIN MY-SELF...

A-ALL RIGHT!

JI (STARE)

YUP, THAT'S WHAT I LIKE TO HEAR.

IN THAT CASE...

BI (WAVE)

JUST YOU WAIT! I'LL BEAT YOU SOME-DAY!

I MEA... YEAH

KIIN (CLING)

...IT'S A PROMISE BETWEEN WOMEN!

SAAA (WHOOSH)

I HOPE THAT DAY COMES...

TH-THAT'S NOT WHAT I MEAN—

STILL HESITANT TO PULL THE TRIGGER ON PEOPLE?

HA HA!

YOU CAN TOTALLY HACK IT. YOU DON'T FIGHT LIKE A ROOKIE AT ALL!

MAYBE I SHOULD TRY THAT MANEUVER MYSELF... BUT I'M TOO BIG FOR IT TO WORK.

...YOU FELT A LITTLE THRILL, DIDN'T YOU? BE HONEST.

BUT...

I COULD SEE IT ON YOUR FACE.

I... DIDN'T SAY...

...RATTLED BY ALL THE CHAOS. IT WASN'T ANYTHING LIKE...

I...

I WAS JUST...

HOW—?

HOW DID I KNOW? I CAN TELL!

SO YOU CAME TO GGO TO BLOW OFF STEAM—NO, TO ESCAPE YOUR TROUBLE.

CHI (CHAK)

GA (BLAM)

IF YOU ASK ME, THERE'S SOMETHING ABOUT THE REAL WORLD THAT'S GOT YOU DOWN, KIDDO.

IT'S WHY I INVITED YOU TO HANG OUT.

WHA...

THAT'S HOW IT WAS FOR ME TOO!

GAKIN (SLIDE)

PARA (PLINK)

PARA

I GET TO COME GUNS BLAZING, AND KILL TONS OF MONSTERS AND PEOPLE.

SO I TEAR IT UP IN HERE INSTEAD.

...THAT GETS ME DOWN OR PISSES ME OFF.

GACHIN (KACHIK)

......THERE'S WAY TOO MUCH STUFF IN THE REAL WORLD...

YOU'LL NEVER GET TO TRY A TEAM BATTLE ROYAL GUNFIGHT IN THE REAL WORLD, RIGHT?

GU (GULP)

WHAT'D I TELL YOU? IT'S NO FUN BEING SO SHACKLED TO REAL LIFE...

...THAT YOU CAN'T GET AWAY FROM IT IN THE VIRTUAL WORLD.

SO LET'S GO WILD! WHADDAYA SAY?

GA BA (SPIN)

...I...

GUGU (GRIP)

......

I WANT...

GAN (BLAMO)

SWORD ART ONLINE ALTERNATIVE

GUN GALE ONLINE

39

DON'T SCREW IT UP THIS TIME!

Y'ALL CAN TAKE THE TATTOOED LADY.

ZA (ISH)

BOSO (MUMBLE)

THE... SHRIMP...

I'LL HANDLE THE SHRIMP.

ZUZU (LOOM)

I WAS FORGETTING THAT, AT THIS MOMENT—

WHY HAVE I BEEN HESITATING?

WHAT? TOO SCARED TO SPEAK UP?

FURU (SHAKE)

FURU

GARI (KRGH)

...YOU MIGHT THINK YOU CAN WIN WITH SPEED...

SAAAA (SWOOSH)

ZA (ZSSH)

...BUT I'VE GOT THIS SHIELD.

I PLAY A STRENGTH AND DURABILITY BUILD.

A FEW BULLETS FROM YOUR PEA-SHOOTER WON'T HURT ME!

BA (BAM)

...OR WILL THAT THING RUN OUT OF AMMO?

OOOO (WHOOSH)

WILL I GIVE UP THE GHOST...

I THINK...

DOKI (BADUM)

DOKI

...HEY, TURTLE...

...I KIND OF ENJOY THIS GAMESMAN-SHIP.

WHICH'LL HAPPEN FIRST?

I JUST HAVE TO MOVE FASTER THAN HE CAN DEFEND...

...I GOT YOU!!

...AND EMPTY MY CLIP FROM HIS BLIND SPOT—

!?

46

48

THIS ISN'T THE PLACE!!

52

SORRY, PAL.

THIS ISN'T ENOUGH FOR ME YET.

I WAS UP ABOVE.

...YOU THINK YOU'VE WON, JUST 'COS YOU GOT RID OF MY GUN?

I DON'T NEED ONE—

55

TOGETHER!!

GAKA
(KRUNCH)

HYU
(SWISH)

GISH
(CREAK)

AH!

FU
(LOOM)

THAT SHRIMP LURED ME INTO—

THAT STRENGTH WILL BE YOUR DOWNFALL.

GI
(STICK)

—DAMN! SLIPPERY, LITTLE...

GET IT ALL OUT.

ALL OF THAT...

ALL OF THIS...

NICE WORK, LLENN-CHAN.

HOW DO YOU FEEL?

MUCH BETTER!!

GU (FWIP)

I'VE MADE UP MY MIND!! I'LL GIVE THE SQUAD JAM A TRY!

THAT'S MORE LIKE IT!!

JANUARY 30, 2026
TWO DAYS BEFORE
THE EVENT

OOOOO
(WHOOSH)

ZAWA

ZAWA
(MURMUR)

ZAWA

ZAWA

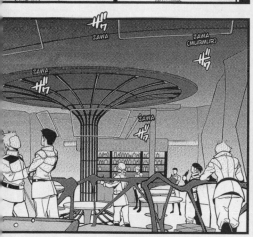

HEYA!

SHU
(SHOOM)

LLENN-
CHAN,
OVER
HERE!

62

WAIT, "PARTNER"? SINGULAR? NOBODY ELSE, JUST ME AND ONE OTHER PERSON?

OH, SORRY. YOUR TEAM PARTNER'S ALMOST HERE.

I THOUGHT THIS WAS A STRATEGY MEETING. WHERE ARE THE OTHER MEMBERS?

THAT'S RIGHT. ONLY ONE PERSON COULD MAKE IT.

BAN WHAM

KYORO (TURN)

KYORO

BUT ISN'T IT SIX TO A TEAM? JUST TWO WILL PUT US AT SUCH A DISADVAN- TAGE...

BUN

BUN (SHAKE)

BUT DON'T WORRY— I ONLY REACHED OUT TO PEOPLE WHOSE SKILLS I KNEW I COULD TRUST.

SHU

THAT'S SO IRRE- SPONSI- BLE...

SORRY FOR BEING LATE.

PLUS, IT'S SKILL THAT DECIDES A BATTLE, NOT NUMBERS!

GU (PUMP)

YEAH, BUT THINK ABOUT HOW COOL IT'LL BE IF YOU WIN AS A DUO!

GO
(RUMBLE)

GO

GO
(GO)

THAT'S YOUR PARTNER. *GOOD* LUCK!

DEFINITELY NOT A GOOD GUY, THOUGH.

HONESTLY, HE'S KIND OF A WEIRDO—AND DEEP DOWN, HE'S PRACTICALLY A CRIMINAL—BUT HE'S NOT A BAD GUY.

FURU
(SHIVER)

FURU

WHOA...

WHAAAT—!?

YOU GUYS ARE GONNA KICK ASS AND TAKE NAMES.

GAKU

GAKU
(RATTLE)

...THIS ONE'S A LITTLE... SCARY...

ゴ GO

ゴ GO (CRUMBLE)

ゾゾゾゾ ZOOOO (SHIVER)

ゴ GO

IT'S NOT THAT I FEEL ESPECIALLY AWKWARD AROUND MEN, BUT...

CHIRA (PEEK)

THERE! INTRO-DUCTIONS ARE OVER.

パン PAN (CLAP)

KOKU (NOD)

コク

...SO I'LL JUST GO OVER THE THINGS RELEVANT TO US NOW.

THE RULES OF THE SQUAD JAM EVENT ARE BASED ON THOSE OF THE SOLO BATTLE ROYAL, THE BULLET OF BULLETS, BUT I'M SURE YOU'VE ALREADY READ THOSE IN THE RULE BOOK...

FIRST, LET'S GO OVER THE RULES OF THE GAME YOU TWO WILL BE PLAYING.

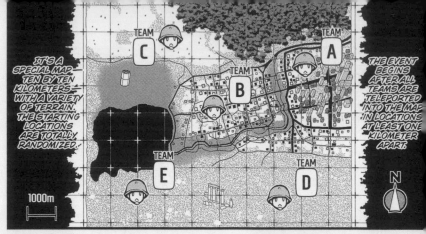

IT'S A SPECIAL MAP. TEN BY TEN KILOMETERS WITH A VARIETY OF TERRAIN. THE STARTING LOCATIONS ARE TOTALLY RANDOMIZED.

THE EVENT BEGINS AFTER ALL TEAMS ARE TELEPORTED INTO THE MAP IN LOCATIONS AT LEAST ONE KILOMETER APART.

1000m

TEAM C

TEAM B

TEAM A

TEAM E

TEAM D

N

ORDINARILY, IN GGO, A DEAD PLAYER CRUMBLES AND VANISHES, BUT IN THIS TOURNAMENT, THE BODY STICKS AROUND WITH A TAG.

DEAD

...THERE ARE DRIVABLE VEHICLES LITTERED AROUND THE MAP.

IN ADDITION TO YOUR OWN GEAR THAT YOU BRING INTO THE GAME...

TEAMS CAN BE MADE UP OF ANYWHERE BETWEEN TWO AND SIX PLAYERS.

MIN

MAX

...SO ONLY THE TEAM LEADERS ARE DISPLAYED, AND NO TEAM NAMES.

IF ALL PLAYERS WERE SHOWN, IT'D BE TOO CHAOTIC ON THE SCREEN...

THERE'S A SATELLITE SCAN EVERY TEN MINUTES, WHICH BRIEFLY DISPLAYS PLAYER LOCATIONS ON YOUR NAV DEVICE.

...IS THE WINNER.

THE LAST TEAM STANDING UNDER THESE CIRCUMSTANCES...

THAT'S LL FOR THE RULES!

PI (BING)

HEH HEH!

AWW...

......

SQUAD LEADER !?

HI

BIKU (JUMP)

...SQUAD LEADER LLENN?

......ANY QUESTIONS UP TO THIS POINT...

...

WHA...?

70

CALL IT A STRATEGY FOR SUCCESS.

AM I JUST A DECOY!?

AWA (FRET)

AWA

IF THE SCAN ONLY SHOWS THE LOCATION OF THE TEAM LEADER...

AH!

M-SAN LOOKS PLENTY TOUGH. WHY ISN'T HE—?

WHY ME!? I CAN'T DO THIS!

GATA (RATTLE)

...ARE YOU SURE YOU CAN'T JOIN IN, PITO-SAN?

GABA (LURCH)

ズルルーー...

ZURURUUU (SLUMP)

YOU'RE KIDDING ME. TWO MEMBERS ON THE TEAM, AND ONE OF THEM IS JUST BAIT...?

DOKIN (BADUM)

...HÜH?

Y-YOU THINK SO?

KIRA

KIRA

KIRA (SPARKLE)

KIRA

I'M PRETTY SURE IF YOU JOIN US, OUR CHANCES OF VICTORY JUMP WAY HIGHER...

GO
(RUMBLE)

GO

GO

GO

HE'S LIKE A BEAR FROM THE ZOO...

I'M SCARED HE'S GONNA EAT ME, HEAD-FIRST!!

ZAWA (SHIVER)

WHOA!

...
UM
...

EX-CUSE
...

GU (CLENCH)

I WANNA PULL OUTTA THE SQUAD JAM AND LOG OFF RIGHT NOW...

LET'S DO THIS.

UM...?

LISTEN...
LET'S T-TRY NOT TO BE TOO NERVOUS, SHALL WE...?

—ER, I MEAN ...

BIKU (FLINCH)

EX-CUSE ME.

AH!

... GOOD POINT.

HEE HEE...

...PITO WILL BEAT ME UP LATER.

IF WE ACT TOO POLITE AND STUFFY.

ジュル (DARA) (DRIP)

DARA

THANKS, LLENN.

I'LL BE MORE CASUAL TOO, THEN.

I'M GLAD HE'S NOT AS SCARY AS HE LOOKS...!

YEAH, SURE.

OH, CAN I JUST CALL YOU THAT? I'M A BIT... UNCOMFORT- ABLE WITH THE WHOLE "-CHAN" THING.

... ACTUALLY, I WAS HOPING...

?

I WAS ASSUMING WE'D DO A LITTLE MONSTER- BATTLING AS A SORT OF MEET AND GREET...

...BUT SHE SURE DIDN'T STICK AROUND VERY LONG...

NOPE.

...BY THE WAY, DID YOU HEAR WHY SHE GOT US TOGETHER TODAY?

—I WANTED TO GO SOMEWHERE IN PARTICULAR.

GOOOO (WHOOOSH)

...PRACTICE GROUNDS?

POKAN (DAZE)

ARE THESE...

po

OH... YEAH, SURE.

HUH!?

LISTEN, I WANT YOU TO TRY THE MANEUVER I MENTIONED. CAN YOU DO THAT NOW?

I DIDN'T REALLY UNDER-STAND AT FIRST...

TEN ROUNDS, SEMIAUTO, AS FAST AS POSSIBLE.

THE OTHER THIRTY, FULL-AUTO.

I TRIE A BUNCH OF STUFF M-SAN TOLD ME TO

THERE' A BARR FORTY METER AHEAD

FACE IT DIRECTLY, STANDING UP, AND FIRE.

WHEN YOUR MAGAZINE'S UNDER EIGHT ROUNDS, EXCHANGE IT.

TOUCH IT, THEN SPRINT BACK.

TWO HUNDRED METERS TO THE RUINED TRUCK. SPRINT FOR IT CARRYING THE P90.

EMPTY YOUR ENTIRE CLIP ON AUTO AS YOU RUN.

IT WAS ONLY PARTWAY THROUGH THAT I UNDERSTOOD HE WAS GAUGING MY ABILITY.

HOW FAR TO THE HOLE BEHIND IT?

HOW MANY METERS TO THAT ROCK WOULD YOU GUESS?

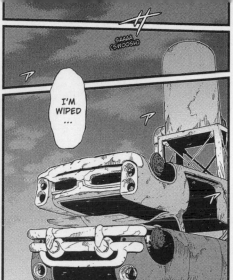

SAAAA
(SWOOSH)

I'M WIPED...

YOU'RE NOT SUPPOSED TO BE ABLE TO GET TIRED IN-GAME, THOUGH...

...ALL RIGHT, I'VE GOT A GOOD PICTURE NOW. THANKS.

YEAH. I FIGURED I SHOULD GET AN IDEA OF WHAT YOU CAN DO BEFORE THE EVENT.

...SO YOU WERE TESTING ME...?

PAAA
(SPARKLE)

...YOU... SHOW POTEN-TIAL.

AND... HOW WAS I?

DOKI
(BADUM)

...I'D SAY...

DOKI

AND IT LOOKS LIKE YOU COMPLEMENT ME DECENTLY ENOUGH.

IS THAT YOUR MAIN WEAPON?

*ENHANCED BATTLE RIFLE

IT'S AN M14 EBR*.

IT'S A POWERED-UP VERSION OF THE OLD M14 BATTLE RIFLE.

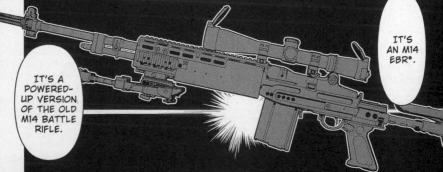

...INDOORS, I USE THIS...

...A GERMAN HECKLER & KOCH HK45.

HYUTA (FWHIP)

BIN (PING?)

VIIN (VIIIN)

...AND THEN FIRE.

TATAN (BLAM)

(AH!)

KO (TOK)

FLIP UP THIS SWITCH AND THE SAFETY ON.

CHI (TIK)

DROP IT LEVEL...

I... I MIGHT...?

DOKI (BADUM)

DOKI

KOKU (NOD)

KOKU

YOU OUGHTA LEARN HOW TO HANDLE THIS, SINCE YOU MIGHT END UP USING IT.

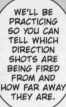

THERE'S MORE?

...WE'LL REPEAT THE PROCESS WITH OBSTACLES, LIKE ROCKS AND CARS, IN THE WAY.

HUH?

ONCE THAT'S OVER.

GAAN (GONG)

OH MAN, THIS IS GONNA BE SUCH A PAIN...

YOU NEED TO KNOW THE DIFFERENCE IN SOUNDS...

NEXT DAY (EVE OF THE EVENT)

NOW I KNOW THINGS NO ORDINARY COLLEGE STUDENT SHOULD EVER NEED TO KNOW.

THE LATTER STUFF HE WAS TEACHING ME WAS GNARLY...

I GUESS THAT WAS KIND OF...AN ENTRANCE TEST?

I DIDN'T THINK IT'D LAST ALL THE WAY TO THE MIDDLE OF THE NIGHT.

YAWN...

I'M HOME...

POFU (FWUMP)

KACHA (CLICK)

MM!

M-SAN SAID I SHOWED PROMISE...

I HOPE I CAN PERFORM ON THE BIG DAY...

BA (FWUP)

GISHI (CREAK)

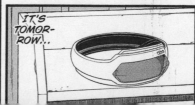

IT'S TOMOR-ROW!...

Elza Kanzaki
A Book At Cafe
00:00 ——— 04:35

bl (BEEP)

THIS IS MY CHANCE TO UNWIND!

—WAIT, WHY'M I WORRYING ABOUT THAT NOW?

AHH...

DOSA (THUMP)

THERE'S NOTHING LIKE ELZA KANZAKI TO CALM ME DOWN......

No luck here either!!

They were all sold out already...! ......How'd you do, Miyu?

YEAH, THE TICKETS ARE IMPOSSIBLE TO GET, BUT...

GORON (ROLL)

TOMORROW'S HER LIVE CONCERT. WISH I COULDA GONE.

...YOU'D THINK THEY COULD BOOK A BIGGER VENUE FOR HER...

······

BA
(WHOOSH)

DANG IT! I'M GONNA WORK OUT MY FRUSTRATION IN THE SQUAD JAM!

KI
(FLASH)

"DEAR ELZA KANZAKI..."

KARI
(SCRITCH)
KARI

BA
(FWAP)

LETTER PAD

HEY, IT'S WORTH A SHOT!

TEE HEE!

I GOT CARRIED AWAY AND WROTE ABOUT MY HEIGHT AND GGO AND STUFF.

STICK TO THE TOPIC.

KARI

I HAVE A COMPLEX ABOUT MY HEIGHT. LISTEN
TO YOUR SONGS WHEN I'M FEELING D
CHEERS ME UP. BUT RECENTLY
A VR GAME I CAN

OOPS.

...SO PLEASE HOLD YOUR CONCERT AT A BIGGER MUSIC HALL—

BUT I LOVE HEARING YOU SING IN THE REAL WORLD, SO I WAS HOPING TO GET TO LISTEN FROM THE VER

KARI

KARI

KAAA (BLUSH)

...

DID IT!

BA

KAREN KOHIRUIMAKI

...WELL, BETTER GET A GOOD NIGHT'S SLEEP FOR THE BIG DAY TOMORROW.

KOTO (CLACK)

B-BUT THEN AGAIN, SHE'S PROBABLY NOT GOING TO READ IT ANYWAY!

...... MAYBE I GOT A BIT TOO PERSONAL IN THERE.

KARI

KARI

AND IF YOU DIE...

...YOU ONLY DIE.

I...I, UH......

....

LINK #004:
PROLOGUE ④

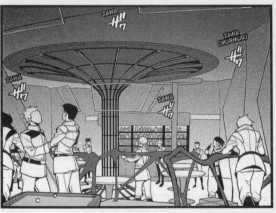

ZAWA

ZAWA
(MURMUR)

ZAWA

ZAWA

BAR

RIGHT ON TIME.

92

"YOU HAVE TO WIN"!

"Y...

GOOD POINT! WE SHOULD LOOK ON THE BRIGHT SIDE.

.......A MATTER OF FACT...

...PITO TOLD ME...

IF YOU GO DOWN AND I'M SURROUNDED, I MIGHT JUST SURRENDER...

...I TOLD HER.

BUT WE'RE ALREADY AT A DISADVANTAGE, JUST BEING A TEAM OF TWO.

I TOLD HER...... WE'D DO THE BEST WE CAN.

YEAH...... THAT SOUNDS LIKE HER...

...I SEE...

AHH...

I BET IF I WIND UP ALONE, I'LL GIVE UP TOO.

WE'RE GONNA GIVE IT OUR BEST SHOT, OF COURSE, BUT A GAME'S A GAME.

...YEAH.

WHAT'S WRONG WITH THAT?

NI (GRIN)

HEH...

GATA (RATTLE)

We will now teleport you to the standby area.

Hey, all you Squad Jam competitors! Thanks for waiting!

BA (JUMP)

...EVEN SO...

GATA

YEAH!

...WE'VE GOTTA GO AS FAR AS WE CAN.

GATA

LET'S HAVE FUN SEEING HOW FAR WE CAN GET WITH JUST THE TWO OF US.

KOKU (NOD)

YOU GOT IT!

KYU!!! (WHISH)

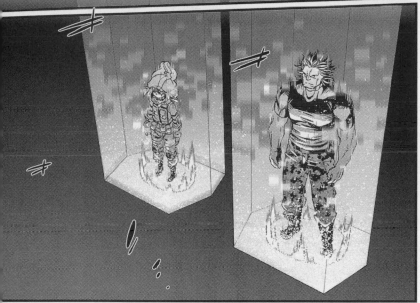

FUDOON
(FWOM)

WHEN THAT COUNTS DOWN TO ZERO, WE'LL GET TELEPORTED TO THE MAP, AND THE BATTLE WILL BEGIN.

ad Jam Begins Soo

Time Remaining: 09:53

0001!

Squad Jam Begins Soon

Prep Time Remaining: 09:55

HUH? WHAT'S THIS?

ROGER THAT!

PIN
(BEEP)

THERE'S NO TIME TO WASTE. LET'S DO A FINAL INSPECTION OF OUR GEAR.

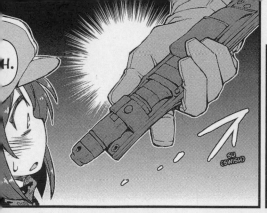

H.

OKAY, ALL READY —

YOU FORGOT ONE THING, LLENN.

I HAVE TO CARRY ONE AFTER ALL...

AW...

...HUH? WHAT'S THIS?

JUST WHAT IT LOOKS LIKE.

oooo (WHOOSH)

I KNOW WHAT A KNIFE IS, SMARTY-PANTS.

I MEAN, WHY ARE YOU GIVING IT TO ME?

I DO, BUT...

...WHY DO I NEED THIS WHEN I HAVE P-CHAN?

ZUI (LIFT)

I'M GONNA TEACH YOU HOW TO USE IT. YOU'VE GOT THE STRENGTH POINTS TO EQUIP THAT, RIGHT?

DARA
(DRIP)

BEST OF ALL, YOU CAN NEUTRALIZE AN ENEMY WITHOUT MAKING A SOUND.

DARA

DARA

UHHH...

HIKU
(TWITCH)

AND GIVEN HOW MANY PEOPLE WILL BE IN THE SQUAD JAM, YOU COULD WIND UP GOING HAND-TO-HAND.

UHH...

IT CAN BE A USEFUL BACKUP WEAPON WHEN YOU RUN OUTTA AMMO.

NOTHING WRONG WIT' LEARNING TO USE A KNIFE.

UH...

...ALL RIGHT, I'VE GOT NO EXCUSE.

GAKU
(SLUMP)

...ESPECIALLY WITH SOMEONE AS AGILE AS YOU.

IT'S OFTEN THE CASE THAT A KNIFE TRUMPS A GUN IN CLOSE-QUARTERS COMBAT...

AFTER A FEW DOZEN MINUTES OF ABSOLUTELY UNBEARABLE DETAILS...

......
ROGER THAT...

GOOD! THEN WE'L START WIT' THE BASIC

THAT'S A LOW-DAMAGE KNIFE, SO DON'T WORRY ABOUT HURTING ME.

OOO (WHOOSH)

......LET'S TEST IT OUT NOW. SEE HOW WELL YOU RETAINED THE DETAILS.

...I HAD TO ACTUALLY PERFORM.

TREAT ME LIKE AN ENEMY. FIGHT FOR REAL.

I WON'T HOLD BACK EITHER.

GU (GULP)

ZU (GGMP)

CHIKI (CHIK)

GUESS I'VE JUST GOT TO RESIGN MYSELF...

HYUTA (THWIP)

LET'S SEE... FIRST THING...

...PULL IT LOOSE BACKHAND WITH THE RIGHT—

IF WE COME FACE-TO-FACE—

MOST FOES WILL BE BIGGER TARGETS THAN MY AVATAR.

RIGHT FOR THE HEAD SHOT!?

RAWA (SHIVER)

BA (WHIP)

CHARGE

TATATAN (RATATAT)

HEY!

HYU (SWISH)

WHOA!

YOU'RE ACTUALLY TRYING TO KILL ME!!

IS THIS REALLY TRAINI—

HYUN

HYU

DA (DASH)

I WON'T HOLD BACK EITHER.

THIS LOOKS LIKE BAD NEWS IF I GET SLOPPY...

...OH.

DOKIN (BADUM)

I'M SUPPOSED TO USE MY SPEED TO CLOSE THE GAP...

HYU (SWISH)

WHEN THIS HAPPENS—

BI (IK)

...AND SLASH THE FEMORAL ARTERY!!

...SLIDE UNDER THE ENEMY'S GROIN, TURN TOWARD EITHER THIGH...

PAN (SLICE)

EVEN IF THEY COLLAPSE, DON'T AIM FOR THEIR CHEST OR STOMACH. ASSUME THEY'RE WEARING DEFENSIVE PLATES THAT'LL BLOCK YOUR BLADE.

!?

BA (FWIP)

UH.

GA (GRAB)

OH NO, I FORGOT ...!

UH-OH—

BIKU (FLINCH)

HYUTA (FWMP)

GU (TUG)

DO
(NHAM)

GON
(VMM)

FU
(TENSE)

THAT MEANS THERE'S ONLY ONE PLACE YOU CAN DO HEAVY DAMAGE WITH A BLADE.

ASIDE FROM THE NECK, YOU CAN GO FOR THE FACE, BUT REMEMBER THAT HUMAN BONES ARE TOUGHER THAN YOU'D THINK.

S-SORRY!

AWA (FRET)

AWA

BA (WHIP)

AH!

FU (SWISH)

NO NEED TO APOLOGIZE.

YOU PASS.

HEH!

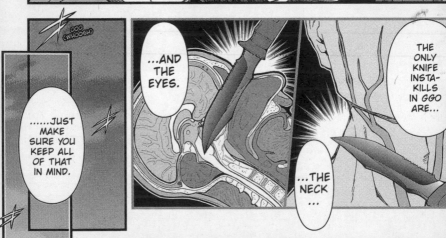

FOO (WHOOSH)

......JUST MAKE SURE YOU KEEP ALL OF THAT IN MIND.

...AND THE EYES.

THE ONLY KNIFE INSTA-KILLS IN *GGO* ARE...

...THE NECK...

I'M SURE I'LL NEVER NEED TO USE IT...

...BUT IT CAN'T HURT TO KEEP IT AROUND FOR NOW... RIGHT?

CHA CCHK

JUST WHO IS M-SAN ANY- WAY...?

SURE.

TH- THANKS ...

I'M JUST PRAYING HE DIDN'T LEARN ALL THIS THROUGH PRACTICAL EXPERIENCE...

We're just about ready.

YEAH.

Looks like the comm works.

Test, test.

KIN (CHING)

GACHIN (KACHIK)

ining: 00:02

Prep Time Remaining: 00:04

:01

HERE GOES!

n Begins Soon

emaining: 00:03

Prep III

...IT'S A FOREST.

GASA
(RUSTLE)

...... YEAH, A FOREST.

YOU CAN'T SNIPE TARGETS BECAUSE THERE'S NO LONG DISTANCE IN THE WOODS.

OH... RIGHT.

...... THIS ISN'T GOOD.

SAAAA (SWOOSH)

I STAND OUT LIKE A SORE THUMB!

AND WORST OF ALL—

AH!

PASHI (SHWAP)

EXACTLY.

GOT IT!!

PUT THAT ON UNTIL WE GET OUT OF THE WOODS.

WE'LL CHECK THE MAP BEFORE WE MOVE.

BA! (FWAP)

THE SCAN PASS THAT LETS US KNOW WHERE THE OTHER TEAMS ARE IS ON A TEN-MINUTE INTERVAL... WE WON'T GET THERE IN TIME FOR THE FIRST ONE, BUT I WANT TO USE THE CITY AS MUCH AS WE CAN.

FIRST, WE EXIT THE WOODS. IT'S NOT A GOOD AREA FOR US.

...OKAY, SO...

UH... ROGER THAT!

HUH?

YOU TAKE THE LEAD, AND I'LL BACK YOU UP IF ANYTHING HAPPENS.

...WE'RE GOING DEAD SOUTH.

I MEAN, I GUESS HE'S RIGHT THAT I OUGHTA BE IN THE LEAD, BUUUT...

"IF ANYTHING HAPPENS"...

JUST GOTTA PRAY WE DON'T RUN INTO ANYONE IN THE FOREST...!

125

SAAAAA
(WHOOSH)

M-
SAN?

...UM,
HELLO?

WE
MADE IT
SAFELY
THROUGH
THE...

WHERE
ARE
YOU?

KURU
(SPIN)

I'm
three
hundred
meters
behind
you.

...SO
I TOOK
SOME
DISTANCE.

Really?
That
far?

THE
FIRST SCAN
IS ABOUT TO
POP. THEY'LL
LEARN YOUR
LOCATION...

THAT MAKES IT SOUND LIKE I'M JUST BAI—

HEY!

If that happens, fire around like crazy and pull back from tree to tree. I'll snipe anyone who comes in after you.

If we're unlucky enough to be near an enemy, they'll come pounce on you.

SO WHAT SHOULD I DO!?

VUVU (VMM)

TIME FOR THE SCAN...

BA (FWIP)

...THAT!?

R...

ROGER...

You just keep an eye around us.

BA

BA

GOTTA CHECK MY HAND-HELD!

I'll confirm the lo-cations of the enemy.

Thirty seconds to scan. Describe as much as you can.

ENEMY SPOTTED!

M... M-SAN!

They're stopping to watch the scan come in. They'll realize where you are.

—OH, THEY ALL STOPPED!

UM, THEY'RE AT LEAST TWO HUNDRED METERS AWAY...I THINK. THEY'RE IN THE CITY AREA, AT LEAST FIVE OF THEM, HIDING IN A RUINED BUILDING...

THE SCAN'S ABOUT TO START. JUST STAY PUT.

...arn, ...ust ...hen I ...otted ...em ...rst!

No point from that range, not with the P90. They'll spot you either way.

GU (SQUEEZE)

WH- WH- WH—?

WHAT SHOULD I DO? F-F-FIRE? DO I OPEN FIRE?

...... GOT IT.

AWW...

CHI

CHI

THERE'S A TEAM RIGHT BETWEEN THE CITY AND THE HIGHWAY, OVER TWO HUNDRED METERS OFF.

CHI

CHI

CHI

HAHH.

......We're all right. No one close enough to start a battle anytime soon.

GAKUN <SLUMP>

<STARE>

...

A-ANYONE ELSE?

That' the grou you spot- ted.

DOKI <BADUM>

DOKI

DOKI

CHI

CHI

THAT'S A RELIE—

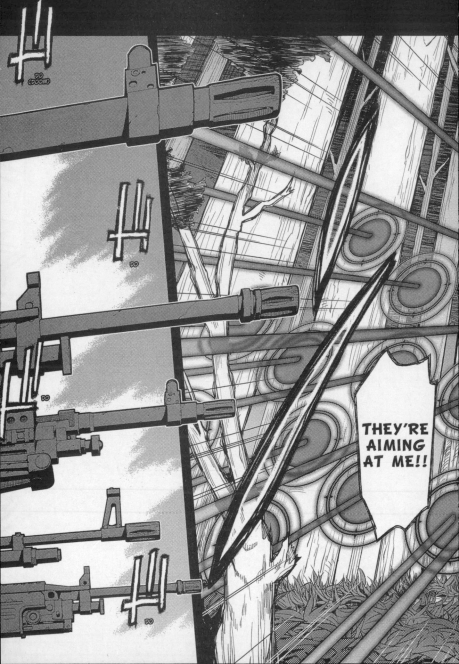

134

138

WHAT'S GOING ON!!?

DEAD

H-HEY, THERE GOES ANOTHER ONE!!

141

...
HMM?

THE SHOOTING... STOPPED? I WONDER WHAT HAPPENED.

SAAAA (SWOOSH)

WHICH MEANS...

...UM...... WHAT, EXACTLY?

OH... YOU'RE RIGHT.

PARA (PLIK)

PARA

You heard the three different shots, right? That saved us.

A team in the city proper got within range of them.

Exactly.

Unknown

They're farther south, in the middle of the city.

I didn't mention it earlier, but the scan showed another team in range, aside from the machine gunners.

I SEE...... SO THEY RUSHED IN TO ATTACK THE GUYS BUSY SHOOTING AT ME...

ZEMAL

LM

142

DID YOU REALIZE THAT WOULD HAPPEN, SO YOU LEFT ME UP THERE AS BAIT?

BA CSWISH

CASA

CASA (RUSTLE)

IN ANY CASE, IT WAS MESSY WORK.

EITHER THE MACHINE GUNNERS GOT SLOPPY AND ASSUMED THE OTHER GUYS WERE TOO FAR AWAY, OR THEY GOT DISTRACTED BY HOW CLOSE YOU WERE.

WHAT KIND OF A PARTNER ARE YOU? I COULD HAVE—

I'LL HEAR OUT YOUR COMPLAINTS WHEN WE'RE SAFE.

ZA (ZSH)

I DID.

HMPH!

WE'LL LIE LOW HERE AND WATCH.

...UM, OKAY...

YOU DON'T HAVE ONE OF THESE, DO YOU? USE IT.

WHOA!

PASHI (FWUP)

...?

AND THREE ARE ALREADY DEAD.

FIVE OF THOSE GUNNERS IN ALL.

YOU COULD TAKE THAT SHOT EASY-PEASY, RIGHT, M-SAN?

THE OTHER TWO ARE SITTING DUCKS!

HERE THEY COME ...

HUH? WHY N—?

NO. WE'RE NOT ATTACKING AT THE MOMENT.

HMM ......

I COULD CHECK THE BUILD-INGS...

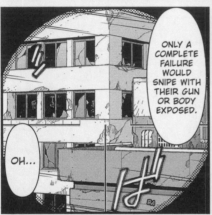

ONLY A COMPLETE FAILURE WOULD SNIPE WITH THEIR GUN OR BODY EXPOSED.

OH...

I DON'T SEE ANY-ONE.

THEY'RE NOT GONNA BE STANDING ANYWHERE YOU'LL BE ABLE TO SPOT.

IT TAKES GUTS TO SPLIT UP A TEAM HEN YOU ONLY HAVE SIX, MAX. ANY TEAM THAT CAN DEPLOY THAT STRATEGY WITHOUT HESITATION...

...IS REALLY TOUGH.

ULP.